THE
THIRD
PILLAR

ALSO BY RAGHURAM RAJAN

I Do What I Do

Fault Lines

Saving Capitalism from the Capitalists
(with Luigi Zingales)

THE

THIRD

PILLAR

HOW MARKETS AND THE STATE
LEAVE THE COMMUNITY BEHIND

RAGHURAM RAJAN

PENGUIN PRESS
New York
2019

PENGUIN PRESS
An imprint of Penguin Random House LLC
penguinrandomhouse.com

Library of Congress Cataloging-in-Publication Data

Names: Rajan, Raghuram, author.
Title: The third pillar : how markets and the state leave the community behind / Raghuram Rajan.
Description: New York : Penguin Press, [2019] | Includes bibliographical references and index.
Identifiers: LCCN 2018054881 (print) | LCCN 2018058588 (ebook) |
ISBN 9780525558323 (ebook) | ISBN 9780525558316 (hardcover)
Subjects: LCSH: Economic development--Social aspects. | Economics--Sociological aspects. |
Capitalism. | Democracy--Economic aspects. | Communities.
Classification: LCC HD75 (ebook) | LCC HD75 .R3435 2019 (print) | DDC 306.3--dc23
LC record available at https://lccn.loc.gov/2018054881

Printed in the United States of America
1   3   5   7   9   10   8   6   4   2

DESIGNED BY MEIGHAN CAVANAUGH

To Radhika

CONTENTS

PART III

RESTORING THE BALANCE

PREFACE

We are surrounded by plenty. Humanity has never been richer as technologies of production have improved steadily over the last two hundred fifty years. It is not just the developed countries that have grown wealthier; billions across the developing world have moved from stressful poverty to a comfortable middle-class existence in the span of a generation. Income is more evenly spread across the world than at any other time in our lives. For the first time in history, we have it in our power to eradicate hunger and starvation everywhere.

Yet even though the world has achieved economic success that would have been unimaginable even a few decades ago, some of the seemingly most privileged workers in developed countries are literally worried to death. Half a million more middle-aged non-Hispanic white American males died between 1999 and 2013 than if their death rates had followed the trend of other ethnic groups.[1] The additional deaths were concentrated among those with a high school degree or less, and largely due to drugs, alcohol, and suicide. To put these deaths in perspective, it is as if ten Vietnam wars were simultaneously taking place, not in some faraway land, but in homes in small-town and rural America. In an era of seeming plenty, a group that once epitomized the American dream seems to have lost hope.

The anxieties of the moderately educated middle-aged white male in the United States are mirrored in other rich developed countries in the West, though perhaps with less tragic effects. The primary source of worry seems to be that moderately educated workers are rapidly losing, or are at risk of losing, good "middle-class" employment, and this has grievous effects on them, their families, and the communities they live in. It is widely understood that job losses stem from both global trade and the technological automation of old jobs. Less well understood is that technological progress has been the more important cause. Nevertheless, as public anxiety turns to anger, radical politicians see more value in attacking imports and immigrants. They propose to protect manufacturing jobs by overturning the liberal rules-based postwar economic order, the system that has facilitated the flow of goods, capital, and people across borders.

There is both promise and peril in our future. The promise comes from new technologies that can help us solve our most worrisome problems like poverty and climate change. Fulfilling it requires keeping borders open so that these innovations can be taken to the most underdeveloped parts of the world, even while attracting people from foreign lands to support aging rich country populations. The peril lies not just in influential communities not being able to adapt and instead impeding progress but also in the kind of society that might emerge if our values and institutions do not change as technology disproportionately empowers and enriches some.

DISRUPTIVE TECHNOLOGICAL CHANGE

Every past technological revolution has been disruptive, prompted a societal reaction, and eventually resulted in societal change that helped us get the best out of the technology. Since the early 1970s, we have experienced the Information and Communications Technology (ICT) revolution. It built on the spread of mass computing made possible by the microprocessor and the personal computer, and now includes technologies ranging from artificial intelligence to quantum computing, touching and improving areas as diverse as international trade and gene therapy. The effects of the ICT revolution have been transmitted across the world by increasingly integrated markets for goods, services, capital, and people. Every country has experienced disruption, punctuated by dramatic episodes like the Global Financial Crisis in 2007–2008 and the accompanying Great Recession. We are now seeing the reaction in populist movements of the extreme Left and Right. What has not happened yet is the necessary societal change, which is why so many despair of the future. We are at a critical moment in human history, when wrong choices could derail human economic progress.

This book is about the three pillars that support society and how we get to the right balance between them so that society prospers. Two of the pillars I focus on are the usual suspects, the state and markets. Many forests have been consumed by books on the relationship between the two, some favoring the state and others markets. It is the neglected third pillar, the community— the social aspects of society—that I want to reintroduce into the debate. When any of the three pillars weakens or strengthens significantly, typically as a result of rapid technological progress or terrible economic adversity like a depression, the balance is upset and society has to find a new equilibrium. The period of transition can be traumatic, but society has succeeded repeatedly in the past. The central question in this book is how we restore the balance between the pillars in the face of the ongoing disruptive technological and social change.

I will argue that many of the economic and political concerns today across the world, including the rise of populist nationalism and radical movements of the Left, can be traced to the diminution of the community. The state and markets have expanded their powers and reach in tandem, and left the community relatively powerless to face the full and uneven brunt of technological change. Importantly, the solutions to many of our problems are also to be found in bringing dysfunctional communities back to health, not in clamping down on markets. This is how we will rebalance the pillars at a level more beneficial to society and preserve the liberal market democracies many of us live in.

DEFINITIONS

To avoid confusion later, let us get over the tedious but necessary issue of definitions quickly. Broadly speaking, *the state* in this book will refer to the political governance structure of a country. In much of this book, it will refer to the federal government. In addition to the executive branch, the state will also include the legislature and the judiciary.

Markets will include all private economic structures facilitating production and exchange in the economy. The term will encompass the entire variety of markets, including the market for goods and services, the market for workers (the labor market), and the market for loans, stocks, and bonds (the capital or financial market). It will also include the main actors from the private sector, such as businesspeople and corporations.

According to the dictionary, a *community* "is a social group of any size whose members reside in a specific locality, share government, and often have a common cultural and historical heritage."[2] This is the definition we will use, with the neighborhood (or the village, municipality, or small town) being the archetypal community in modern times, the manor in medieval times, and the tribe in ancient times. Importantly, we focus on communities whose members live in proximity—as contrasted with virtual communities or national religious denominations. We will view local government, such as the school board, the neighborhood council, or town mayor, as part of the community. A large country has layers of government between the federal government (part of the state) and the local government (part of the community). In general, we will treat these layers as part of the state. Finally, we will use the terms *society, country,* or *nation* interchangeably as the composite of the state, markets, communities, people, territory, and much else that compose political entities like China or the United States.

WHY THE COMMUNITY
STILL MATTERS

Definitions done, let us get to substance. For early humans the tribe was their society—their state, markets, and community rolled into one. It was where all activities were conducted, including the rearing of children, the production and exchange of food and goods, and the succor of the ill and the elderly. The tribal chief or elders laid down the law and enforced it, and commanded the tribe's warriors in defense of their lands. Over time, as we will see in Part I of the book, both markets and the state separated from the community.

Trade with more distant communities through markets allowed everyone to specialize in what they were relatively good at, making everyone more prosperous. The state, aggregating the power and resources of the many communities within it, not only regulated markets but also enforced the law within its political boundaries, while defending the realm against aggressors.

Markets and the state have not only separated themselves from the community in recent times but have also steadily encroached on activities that strengthened bonds within the traditional community. Consider some functions the community no longer performs. In frontier communities, neighbors used to help deliver babies; today most women check into a hospital when they feel the onset of childbirth. They naturally prefer the specialist's expertise much more than they value their neighbor's friendly but amateurish helping hand. On a more mundane level, we used to offer to take our elderly neighbor shopping because she did not have a car. Today, she orders her groceries online. Similarly, the community used to pitch in to rebuild a household's home if it caught fire; today the household collects its fire insurance payment and hires a professional builder. Indeed, given the building codes in most developed countries, it is unlikely that a home reconstructed by neighbors would be legal.

The community still plays a number of important roles in society. It anchors the individual in real human networks and gives them a sense of identity; our presence in the world is verified by our impact on people around us. By allowing us to participate in local governance structures such as parent-teacher associations, school boards, library boards, and neighborhood oversight committees, as well as local mayoral or ward elections, our community gives us a sense of self-determination, a sense of direct control over our lives, even while making local public services work better for us. Importantly, despite the existence of formal structures such as public schooling, a government safety net, and commercial insurance, the goodness of neighbors is still useful in filling in gaps. When a neighboring engineer tutors our son in mathematics in her spare time, or the neighborhood comes together in a recession to collect food and clothing for needy households, the community is helping out where formal structures are inadequate. Given the continuing importance of the community, healthy modern communities try to compensate for the encroachment of markets and the state with other activities that strengthen community ties, such as social gatherings and neighborhood associations.

Economists Raj Chetty and Nathaniel Hendren attempt to quantify the economic impact of growing up in a better community.[3] They examine the incomes of children whose parents moved from one neighborhood into another in the United States when the child was young. Specifically, consider neighborhood *Better* and neighborhood *Worse*. Correcting for parental income, the average incomes of children of longtime residents when they become adults is one percentile higher in the national income distribution in neighborhood Better than it is in neighborhood Worse. Chetty and Hendren find that a child whose parents move from neighborhood Worse to Better will have an adult income that is, on average, 0.04 percentile points higher for every childhood year it spends in Better. In other words, if the child's parents move when it is born and they stay till it is twenty, the child's income as an adult will have made up 80 percent of the difference between the average incomes in the two neighborhoods.

Their study suggests that a child benefits enormously by moving to a community where children are more successful (at least as measured by their future income). Communities matter! Perhaps more than any outside influence other than the parents we are born to, the community we grow up in influences our economic prospects. Importantly, Chetty and Hendren's finding applies for a single child moving—movement is not a recipe for the development of an entire poor community. Instead, the poor community has to find ways to develop in situ, while holding on to its best and brightest. It is a challenge we will address in the book.

There are other virtues to a healthy community. Local community government acts as a shield against the policies of the federal government, thus protecting minorities against a possible tyranny of the majority, and serving as a check on federal power. Sanctuary communities in the United States and Europe have resisted cooperating with national immigration authorities in identifying and deporting undocumented immigrants. Under the previous US presidential administration, communities in the state of Arizona resisted in the opposite direction, ignoring the federal government while implementing stern penalties on undocumented immigration.

Although no country can function if every community picks and chooses the laws they will obey, we will see that some decentralization in legislative powers to the community can be beneficial, especially if there are large differences in opinion between communities.

A critical function the community plays in modern market democracies is to serve as a training ground for aspiring politicians—recall that Barack Obama was a community organizer—with the community itself constituting a ready-made structure for political mobilization. Furthermore, it is community-based movements against corruption and cronyism that time and again prevent the leviathan of the state from getting too comfortable with the behemoth of big business. Indeed, as we will see in the book, healthy communities are essential for sustaining vibrant market democracies. This is perhaps why authoritarian movements like fascism and communism try to replace community consciousness with nationalist or proletarian consciousness.

In sum, the proximate community is still relevant today, even in cosmopolitan cities where ties of kinship and ethnicity are limited, and even in individualistic societies like those of the United States and Western Europe. Once we understand that the community matters, then it becomes clear why it is not enough for a country to experience strong economic growth—the professional economist's favorite measure of economic performance. How that growth is distributed across communities in the country also matters immensely. People who value staying in their community are not very mobile. Since they cannot move to work where growth occurs, they need economic growth in their own community. If we care about the community, we need to care about the geographic distribution of growth.

What then is the source of today's problems? In one word, *imbalance*! When the three pillars of society are appropriately balanced, society has the best chance of providing for the well-being of its people. The modern state provides physical security, as it always has, but also tries to ensure fairness in economic outcomes, which democracy demands. To do this, the state sets limits on the markets while also ensuring they offer people a level playing field. It also has to make sure that most people have the ability to participate on equal terms in the market, and are buffered against its fluctuations. The competitive markets ensure that those who succeed in it are efficient and produce the maximum output with the resources available. The successful have both wealth and some independence from the state, thus they have the ability to check arbitrary actions by the state. Finally, the people in industrial democracies, engaged in their communities and thereby organized socially and politically, maintain the necessary separation between markets and the state. By doing this they enable sufficient political and economic competition that the economy does not descend into cronyism or authoritarianism.

Society suffers when any of the pillars weakens or strengthens overly relative to the others. Too weak the markets and society becomes unproductive, too weak a community and society tends toward crony capitalism, too weak the state and society turns fearful and apathetic. Conversely, too much market and society becomes inequitable, too much community and society becomes static, and too much state and society becomes authoritarian. A balance is essential!

THE EFFECTS OF TRADE AND THE ICT REVOLUTION ON THE COMMUNITY

The pillars are seriously unbalanced today. The direct effects of the ICT revolution through automation, and the indirect but more localized effects through trade competition, have led to large job losses in some communities in developed countries. Typically, these have been middle-income jobs held by the moderately educated. With male workers least able to adjust, families have been tremendously stressed, with an increase in divorces, teenage pregnancies, and single-parent households. In turn, these have led to a deterioration in the environment for children, resulting in poor school performance; high dropout rates, the increased attractiveness of drugs, gangs, and crime; and persistent youth unemployment. Importantly, community decline tends to feed on itself, as still-functional families escape so that their children do not get affected by the unhealthy environment.

In the United States, minority and immigrant communities were hit first by joblessness, which led to their social breakdown in the 1970s and 1980s. In the last two decades, communities in small towns and semirural areas, typically white, have been experiencing a similar decline as large local manufacturers close down. The opioid epidemic is just one symptom of the hopelessness and despair that accompanies the social breakdown of once-healthy communities.

The technological revolution has been disruptive even outside economically distressed communities. It has increased the wage premium for those with better capabilities significantly, with the best employed by high-paying superstar firms that increasingly dominate a number of industries. This has put pressure on upper-middle-class parents to secede from economically mixed communities and move their children to schools in richer, healthier communities, where they will learn better with other well-supported children like themselves. The poorer working class are kept from following by the high cost of housing in the tonier neighborhoods. Their communities deteriorate once again, this time because of the secession of the successful. Technological change has created that nirvana for the upper middle class, a meritocracy based on education and skills. Through the sorting of economic classes and the decline of the mixed community, however, it is also becoming a hereditary one, where only the children of the successful succeed.

The rest are left behind in declining communities, where it is harder for the young to learn what is needed for good jobs. Communities get trapped in vicious cycles where economic decline fuels social decline, which fuels further economic decline . . . The consequences are devastating. Alienated individuals, bereft of the hope that comes from being grounded in a healthy community, become prey to demagogues on both the extreme Right and Left, who cater to their worst prejudices. Populist politicians strike a receptive chord when they blame the upper-middle-class elite and establishment parties.

When the proximate community is dysfunctional, alienated individuals need some other way to channel their need to belong.[4] Populist nationalism offers one such appealing vision of a larger purposeful imagined community— whether it is white majoritarianism in Europe and the United States, the Islamic Turkish nationalism of Turkey's Justice and Development Party, or the Hindu nationalism of India's Rashtriya Swayamsevak Sangh.[5] It is populist in that it blames the corrupt elite for the condition of the people. It is nationalist (more precisely, ethnic nationalist, but I will leave the nitpicking for later) in that it anoints the native-born majority group in the country as the true inheritors of the country's heritage and wealth. Populist nationalists identify minorities and immigrants—the favorites of the elite establishment—as usurpers, and blame foreign countries for keeping the nation down. These fabricated adversaries are necessary to the populist nationalist agenda, for there is often little else to tie the majority group together—it is not really based on any true sense of community for the differences between various subgroups in the majority are usually substantial.

Populist nationalism will undermine the liberal market democratic system that has brought developed countries the prosperity they enjoy. Within countries, it will anoint some as full citizens and true inheritors of the nation's patrimony while the rest are relegated to an unequal, second-class status. It risks closing global markets down just when these countries are aging and need both international demand for their products and young skilled immigrants to fill out their declining workforces. It is dangerous because it offers blame and no real solutions, it needs a constant stream of villains to keep its base energized, and it moves the world closer to conflict rather than cooperation on global problems. While the populist nationalists raise important questions, the world can ill afford their shortsighted solutions.

RESTORING THE COMMUNITY PILLAR TO HEALTH

Schools, the modern doorway to opportunity, are the quintessential community institution. The varying qualities of schools, largely determined by the communities they are situated within, dooms some while elevating others. When the pathway to entering the labor market is not level, and steeply uphill for some, it is no wonder that people feel the system is unfair. They then are open to ideologies that propose abandoning the liberal market system that has served us so well since World War II. The way to address this problem, and many others in our society, is not primarily through the state or through markets. It is by reviving the community and having it fulfill its essential functions, such as schooling, better. Only then do we have a chance of reducing the appeal of radical ideologies.

We will examine ways of doing this, but perhaps the most important is to give the power the state has steadily taken away back to the community. As markets have become global, international bodies, driven by their bureaucrats or the interests of powerful countries, have drawn power from nations into their own hands, ostensibly to make it easier for global markets to function.

The populist nationalists exaggerate the extent to which power has migrated into international bodies, but it is real. More problematic, within a country, the state has usurped many community powers in order to meet international obligations, harmonize regulations across domestic communities, as well as to ensure that the community uses federal funding well. This has further weakened the community. We must reverse this. Unless absolutely essential for good order, power should devolve from international bodies to countries. Furthermore, within countries, power and funding should devolve from the federal level to the communities. Fortunately, the ICT revolution helps in doing this, as we will see. If effected carefully, this decentralization will preserve the benefits of global markets while allowing people more of a sense of self-determination. *Localism*—in the sense of centering more powers, spending, and activities in the community—will be one way we will manage the centrifugal disorienting tendencies of global markets and new technologies.

CIVIC NATIONALISM

Instead of allowing people's natural tribal instincts to be fulfilled through populist nationalism, which combined with national military powers makes for a volatile cocktail, it would be better if they were slaked at the community level. One way to accommodate a variety of communities within a large diverse country is for it to embrace an inclusive *civic* definition of national citizenship—where one is a citizen provided one accepts a set of commonly agreed values, principles, and laws that define the nation. It is the kind of citizenship that Australia, Canada, France, India, or the United States offer. It is the kind of citizenship that the Pakistani-American Muslim, Khizr Khan, whose son died fighting in the United States Army, powerfully reminded the 2016 Democratic National Convention of, when he waved a copy of the United States Constitution. That document defined his citizenship and was the source of his patriotism.

Within that broad inclusive framework, people should have the freedom to congregate in communities with others like themselves. The community, rather than the nation, becomes the vehicle for those who cherish the bonds of ethnicity and want some cultural continuity. Of course, communities should be open so that people can move in and out if they wish. Some will, no doubt, prefer to live in ethnically mixed communities while others will choose to live with people of their own ethnicity. They all should have the freedom to do so. Freedom of association, with active discrimination prohibited by law, has to be the future of large diverse countries. We will eventually learn to cherish the other, but till then let us live peaceably, side by side if not together.

Markets too must become more inclusive. Large corporations dominate too many markets, increasingly fortified by privileged possession of data, ownership of networks, and intellectual property rights. Credentialed licensed professionals dominate too many services, preventing competition from those who do not have the requisite licenses (one reason friendly neighbors cannot help rebuild a house today). In every situation, we must locate barriers to competition and entry and remove them so that opportunity is available to all. Thus, as we strive for an inclusive state and inclusive markets, which embed the empowered community in society and keep it engaged and dynamic, we will achieve an *inclusive localism,* which will be essential to community revival and a rebalancing of the pillars.

Even in such a setting, though, community effort to pull itself up will be critical. Consider the community of Pilsen on the southwest side of Chicago, a few miles from my home. This once terribly damaged community is now turning a corner.

A REAL COMMUNITY PULLING ITSELF UP

Pilsen used to be populated by Eastern European immigrants, working in manufacturing establishments around Chicago. Since the middle of the last century, Hispanic immigrants and African Americans moved in steadily, and the Eastern Europeans moved out.[6] In 2010, Hispanics or Latinos made up 82 percent of the population, and African Americans 3.1 percent. Non-Hispanic whites composed 12.4 percent of the population in 2010, up from 7.9 percent in 2000.

Pilsen is poor, with median household income averaged over 2010–2014 at $35,100, about half that of metropolitan Chicago as a whole. It has an unemployment rate of nearly 30 percent averaged over 2010–2014. Over 35 percent of individuals over twenty-five have not graduated from high school. Only

21.4 percent of individuals over twenty-five have a bachelor's degree, less than half the comparable ratio in the overall US population. Nearly half of renters or homeowners have housing costs that account for more than 30 percent of their income. Keeping people in their homes is essential for community stability, and Pilsen has a hard time of it.

Low education, low incomes, and high unemployment are a recipe for drugs, alcohol, and crime. At its peak in 1979, there were 67.4 murders per 100,000 residents in Pilsen, over double the wider city rate. In comparison, Western Europe averages a murder rate of about 1 per 100,000 per year. The average military death rate for Germany and the Soviet Union during World War II was about 140 per year per 100,000 of population.[7] Pilsen was thus truly a war zone—in 1988, a *Chicago Tribune* reporter counted twenty-one different gangs along a two-mile stretch on the main 18th Street thoroughfare. The 1980s and 1990s were years of horrific gang fights and bloodshed.

Yet Pilsen is a community that is trying to pull itself up. One sign it is succeeding is that the murder rate has been significantly below the overall Chicago rate for a number of years since the early 2000s, exceeding it slightly only every few years. As we will see, communities typically do not pick themselves up spontaneously—leaders emerge to coordinate the revival. Among those driving Pilsen's revival is Raul Raymundo, the CEO of the Resurrection Project, a nongovernmental organization (NGO) whose motto is "Building relationships, creating healthy communities." Raul came to the United States from Mexico as a seven-year-old immigrant, went to Benito Juarez High School in Pilsen, attended college (including some time in graduate school at the University of Chicago), and started helping out in the community. He found his vocation after the murder of a young man just outside his church, when his pastor asked the congregation what the community was going to do about it. Answering the call, Raul and a few others started the Resurrection Project, with $5,000 each from six local churches. When the candidate they found to head the project declined to take the job, Raul stepped in, and he is still there, after twenty-seven years. Today, the Resurrection Project has funneled over $500 million in investment into the community.

As with other revival projects, the community first undertook an inventory of its assets to figure out what it could build around. It had its churches that would provide moral, vocal, and financial support for any revival, it had decent schools, it had a strong Mexican-American community with tightly knit families, and it was in Chicago, a city that goes through ups and downs but is still one of America's great cities.

The first order of action was to make the community more livable, which meant keeping it clean, ridding the streets of crime, and strengthening the schools. Residents were organized to hound the city sanitation department to do their job—clean the streets and collect garbage. People were urged to form block clubs and ad hoc groups against crime. They would walk out of their houses when they saw suspicious activity so as to crowd the criminals out, or jointly call the police so that the criminals would not know who to blame. The community campaigned successfully for a moratorium on city liquor licenses in Pilsen, got some especially problematic bars closed down, and worked with police, churches, and absentee landlords to target and close down known gang houses.[8] Remedial education, after-school extracurricular programs, and job-training programs increased, enabling young people to get more from their schoolwork, and giving them a ladder to jobs. Parents were urged to get involved in the schools, and they did. New school programs started—one example is the Cristo Rey Catholic School, which aims to give its students a quality education like that obtainable at St. Ignatius, one of Chicago's premier Catholic schools, while keeping it affordable. Cristo Rey raised funds from local businesses, in return for which students work one day a week for their sponsoring business. The student attends school the other four days, getting both a good education and work experience each week.

As the community members saw revival efforts paying off, they got more engaged, and virtuous cycles started emerging. As some older gang members turned to legitimate business, their prosperity inspired other gang members to develop skills other than the ability to inflict violence. The proliferation of youth-oriented programs at the schools gave them a way to escape their past. As crime came down, new businesses started opening, including franchises like McDonald's, and they offered low-level entry jobs that drew youth into work. With Chicago becoming more of a hub for the regional distribution of goods, more jobs were created as wholesale warehouses and refrigeration centers opened in Pilsen, drawn by the still-low real estate prices and falling crime.

With the area more livable, the Resurrection Project turned to keeping the poor, some of who have very few assets and very little buffer against a sudden loss of job or illness, in their rented homes. This would stabilize the community. Ironically, it is getting harder as the community strengthens because rents are increasing and buying is becoming costlier. Large banks, of which a growing number have now set up in the community, are not well equipped to understand community practices. This hampers their lending. In Pilsen, a working woman's mother will often cook for her and babysit her children, so the worker's salary goes a much longer way because she does not pay for these services. Similarly, family members may lend each other money, making it possible for someone to keep up loan payments even if their income is volatile. Typically, such practices are hard for a loan officer from a large bank to substantiate or document, which is why he has to go primarily on the explicit record of income.[9] Community-based financial institutions, where decisions are made locally based on the soft information available in the community, understand the worker is more creditworthy than her salary slip might suggest. Being free from the tyranny of requiring hard documentation, they are more willing to lend locally than large banks.

Recognizing the importance of local institutions, in 2013 the Resurrection Project helped rescue a failing community bank, Second Federal. At that time, 29 percent of the bank's mortgages were delinquent, and many local borrowers would have faced eviction if the bank had been closed or sold outside the community. Vacancies would have depressed house prices and brought back crime. Second Federal's delinquencies are now down to 4 percent of its mortgage portfolio, because it worked with its borrowers and nursed the loans back to health. People continue to use its branch as a community center, meeting there to chat with neighbors, or bringing their mail to have it translated by tellers.

The Resurrection Project has itself built affordable housing that it rents to needy families, nudging them to move out when they can afford market rents. One of its developments, Casa Queretaro, looks sleek and welcoming, seeming more luxury housing than affordable—in management's view, there is no reason why so much affordable housing should look run down. The Resurrection Project also tries to increase access to credit locally. Its volunteers work with community members to improve their financial understanding, to get them to build and improve their credit histories by, for example, paying their utility bills regularly and on time.

There is much more to community revival, but the picture should be clear. Pilsen is by no means a rich or prosperous community but it now has hope. It has built on its Mexican connections—it has a National Museum of Mexican Art—though it is proudly American. Cinco de Mayo, a Mexican festival, is celebrated with great gusto, but over two hundred fifty thousand people join the Fourth of July parade in Pilsen. Raul Raymundo's aim is to welcome people of every ethnicity into Pilsen while building on the core stability of the existing community. As he tells people when they buy a house, "You are not buying a piece of property, you are buying a piece of the community."

FINAL PRELIMINARIES

Who am I and why do I write this book? I am a professor at the University of Chicago, and I have spent time as the Chief Economist and head of Research at the International Monetary Fund, where we gave advice to a variety of industrial and developing countries. I also was the Governor of India's central bank, where we undertook reforms to improve India's financial system. I have experience working in both the international financial system and in an emerging market. In my adult life, I have never been more concerned about the direction our leaders are taking us than I am today.

In my book *Fault Lines: How Hidden Fractures Still Threaten the World Economy,* published in 2010, I worried about the consequences of rising inequality, arguing that easy housing credit before the Global Financial Crisis was, in part, a way for politicians to deflect people's attention from their stagnant paychecks. I was concerned that instead of drawing the right lesson from the crisis—that we need to fix the deep fault lines in developed societies and the global order—we would search for scapegoats. I wrote:

"The first victims of a political search for scapegoats are those who are visible, easily demonized, but powerless to defend themselves. The illegal immigrant or the foreign worker do not vote, but they are essential to the economy—the former because they often do jobs no one else will touch in normal times, and the latter because they are the source of the cheap imports that have raised the standard of living for all, but especially those with low incomes. There has to be a better way . . ."[10]

The search for scapegoats is well and truly on. I write this book because I see an increasingly polarized world that risks turning its back on seventy years of widespread peace and prosperity. It threatens to forget what has worked, even while ignoring what needs to change. The Populist nationalists and the radical Left understand the need for reform, but they have no real answers as they resort to the politics of anger and envy. The mainstream establishment parties do not even admit to the need for change. There is much to do, and the challenges are mounting. The state, markets, and the community can be brought into a much better balance. We must start now.

The rest of this book is as follows. I start by describing the third pillar, the community. To some, the community stands for warmth and support. To others, it represents narrow-mindedness and traditionalism. Both descriptions can be true, sometimes simultaneously, and we will see why. The challenge for the modern community is to get more of the good while minimizing the bad. We will see how this can be obtained through the balancing influence of the other two pillars—the state and markets. To continue our exploration, we must understand how these pillars emerged historically. In Part I, I trace how the state and markets in today's advanced countries grew out of the feudal community, taking over some of its activities. I explain how a vibrant market helped create independent sources of power that limited the arbitrary powers of the state. As the state became constitutionally limited, markets got the upper hand, sometimes to the detriment of communities. The extension of suffrage reempowered communities and they used it to press the state to impose regulatory limits on the market. People also demanded reliable social protections that would buffer them against market volatility. All these influences came together in the liberal market democracies, which emerged across the developed world in the early twentieth century. However, market downturns, especially following technological revolutions, were, and are, disruptive. The Great Depression, followed by the Second World War, seemed to sound the death knell of liberal market democracies in much of the world, and the ascent of the state.

In Part II, I describe how the United States shaped the postwar liberal order, and how both the state and markets grew once again. Democracy was given firmer roots. The thirty years of strong postwar growth, however, were followed by years of relative stagnation as developed countries struggled for new ways of reviving growth. In response, the Anglo-American countries empowered the markets at the expense of the state, while continental European reforms favored the superstate and the integrated market. Both sets of reforms came at the expense of the community. These different choices left countries differently positioned for the ICT revolution, the subsequent Global Financial Crisis, and the backlash against the global order. I describe the reasons for the rise of populism and trace related developments in China and India.

I turn to possible solutions in Part III. To strengthen the chances that society will stay liberal and democratic, we need profound changes that rebalance the three pillars in the face of technological change. We need more localism to empower the community while drawing on the state and markets to make society more inclusive.

Finally, some caveats. I intend this book to be comprehensive, but not exhaustive. Therefore, I illustrate the course of history with examples from prominent countries, but it would tax the reader's patience (as well as my editor's) if I substantiated points with the detail that specialists require. This book offers a broad thesis of its own, and draws on much academic work, but it is aimed at a wide audience. I also offer policy proposals, not as the final word but to provoke debate. We face enormous challenges, to which we need not just the right solutions but also ones that inspire us to act. It is worth recalling the words of Chicago architect Daniel Burnham, "Make no little plans; they have no magic to stir men's blood and probably themselves will not be realized."[11] I hope this book stirs your blood.

THE
THIRD
PILLAR

THE THIRD PILLAR

Why do our neighbors matter when we can reach people across the world with a click? What role do proximate communities play today in an advanced country that has both a well-functioning state and vibrant markets? Despite the state and markets having taken up many of the early community's functions, the proximate community still performs important ones. It helps define who we are. It gives us a sense of empowerment, an ability to shape our own futures in the face of global forces. It also offers us help in times of adversity when no one else will. Of course, the community can also be narrow-minded, traditional, and resistant to change. A successful modern community supports its members even while being more open, inclusive, and dynamic. We will see why it is difficult for a community to do all this, but also why it is necessary if the community is to address the problems we face.

THE PROXIMATE COMMUNITY

We are shaped by the people who surround us. Our joys are more pleasurable when they are cherished by our friends, our successes more enjoyable when they are applauded by those whose opinions we care about, our protests are less lonely and our indignation less unsure when shared by our supporters, our hatreds more corrosive when goaded by fellow zealots, our sorrows less burdensome when borne with our family. Moreover, we gauge our actions based on how they affect people near us, on the indentations our actions make on their lives. Without such effects, we would be ephemeral passersby, with little evidence of ever having existed. Each one of us draws from multiple overlapping communities that help define who we are, that give us identity over and above the core we think is uniquely us.

There are varieties of communities, some more tightly bound than others. A community could be a group of people who are linked together by blood (as a family or clan) or who share current or past physical proximity (as people in, or having emigrated from, a village). A community could be those who have a common view on how to live a good life (as in a religious sect), share a common profession (as in the movie industry), or frequent the same website or chat groups (as in my college alumni group, where everyone seems to have a different opinion on everything that they absolutely must express). Each one of us has multiple identities, based on the groups we belong to.[1] Moreover, some of us have virtual identities in addition to real ones.

As communication has improved, and transportations costs have come down, more distant communities have gained importance. For some of us, these communities may be much more important than our neighborhood. Indeed, a central concern in this book is about the passions that are unleashed when an imagined community like the nation fulfills the need for belonging that the neighborhood can no longer meet.

Nevertheless, we will focus on the proximate community for much of the book for a variety of reasons. Through most of history when distances really mattered, it was the only kind of community that had a serious influence on most people's lives. Even today, it is where much economic activity is centered. For most of us, the neighborhood is still what we encounter every day, and what anchors us to the real world. It is where we participate as sociable humans, not as clan members, coreligionists, professionals, or disembodied opinions on the web. It is where we have the best chance of persuading others that our humanity unites us more than our ethnicity, profession, or national origin differentiates us. It certainly is where we debate and persuade as we elect officeholders and participate in the governance of the local public services that affect us. It is where we congregate to start broader political movements. As we will see later in the book, a healthy, engaged, proximate community may therefore be how we manage the tension between the inherited tribalism in all of us and the requirements of a large, diverse nation. Looking to the future, as more production and service jobs are automated, the human need for relationships and the social needs of the neighborhood may well provide many of the jobs of tomorrow.

In closely knit communities, a variety of transactions take place without the use of money or enforceable contracts. One side may get all the benefits in some transactions. Sometimes, the expectation is that the other side will repay the favor, but this may never actually happen. In a normal family, members typically help one another without drawing up papers and making payments. In many societies, friends don't really care who pays the bill at dinner, indeed the ability to not keep count is the mark of true friendship.

Contrast transactions within a community with a typical market transaction. I just bought a bicycle tire tube. I searched for one of adequate quality at a reasonable price through an online platform, paid by credit card, and the tube was delivered within the time promised. Even though this transaction took little time, there is an elaborate explicit understanding or contract behind it. If the tube is not delivered or it proves defective, I have contractual remedies. The transaction is arm's length and one-off. Neither the seller nor I know each other. Each one of us is satisfied we are better off from the transaction even if we never transact again. We do not look for further fulfilment through a continuing relationship.

The more explicit and one-off the transaction, the more unrelated and anonymous the parties to the transaction, and the larger the set of participants who can transact with one another, the more the transaction approaches the ideal of a *market* transaction. The more implicit the terms of the transaction, the more related the parties who transact, the smaller the group that can potentially transact, the less equal the exchange, the broader the range of transactions and the more repetitive transactions are over time between the same parties, the more the transactions approach a relationship. The thicker the web of relationships tying a group of individuals together, the more it is a community. In a sense, the community and the market are two ends of a continuum.

In his magisterial work, *Gemeinschaft und Gesellschaft* ("Community and Society"), nineteenth-century German sociologist Ferdinand Tönnies argued that in a community tied together by strong relationships, individual interests are suppressed in favor of the collective interest whenever these interests diverge. By contrast, in a market transaction, "nobody wants to grant and produce anything for another individual, nor will he be inclined to give ungrudgingly to another individual, if it not be in exchange for a gift or labor equivalent that he considers at least equal to what he has given."[2] In this sense, only individual interests matter, and they have to be met transaction by transaction.

In this chapter, we will examine what makes communities useful.[3] Those hearkening to the past, as in many a fantasy novel, often invoke an idyllic view of the community. Typically, this is a village—an arcadia where simple honest people look out for one another, offering goods and services without demanding prompt or equal compensation. The village community can be warm and supportive. Yet, it can also be small, closed, and intrusive. We will see how a community facilitates economic and social transactions, but we'll also recognize there are limits to community effectiveness, and indeed situations where a community may be harmful to its members' interests. That will be why a community works best as part of the balance.

THE POSITIVE ROLES OF THE COMMUNITY

Evolutionary psychologists argue that we help others who are related to us or look like us because it is genetically hardwired into us—to the extent altruism toward kin is a genetic trait that helped its own survival in the Stone Age, when much of our evolution happened, it helped itself be passed on.[4] Similarly, we may be genetically evolved to help others, provided they reciprocate the favor, and we are programmed to have a strong distaste for freeloaders who do not. Since evolution is slow, we are fully adapted to the challenges of the Stone Age, and we continue to retain such propensities, even if no longer critical for survival. In other words, we are predisposed to be social.

We have built on this predisposition. People have always banded together because a group is better at defense (or attack) than an individual. In modern society, healthy communities continue to police themselves and their surroundings to ensure safety for their members. They do more, though—much more.

They offer their members a sense of identity, a sense of place and belonging that will survive the trials and tribulations of modern life. They do this through stories, customs, rituals, relationships, and joint celebrations or mourning so that when faced with a choice between self-interest and community interest, or between community members and others, members are more inclined to put their own community first. Often, communities inculcate shared values and goals in members, as well as imbue in them a sense of personal utility from various actions that benefit the community.

The community also monitors economic transactions as well as noneconomic "favors" within the community, and it sees that everyone delivers their promised part fairly, if not immediately then over time. It assists those falling behind, as members contribute to those in need. It also aggregates the capabilities of all its members and brings them to bear to enhance collective well-being. Let us examine all these roles in greater detail.

Survival: Training and Socializing the Young

A community needs to train its young to be productive, to take over from current adult members as they age. Equally important, the values of the young members have to be shaped to protect the well-being of the community. Most communities train their young through apprenticeships, where they are taught skills and learn to internalize the norms and values of the community.

Apprenticeship often ends with a rite of passage that signals the coming of age of a youth into adulthood. In a number of tribes such as the Aborigines in Australia or the Papuans of New Guinea, the rites were so physically brutal that those up for initiation occasionally died.[5] Not only did the ordeal prevent those who did not have the requisite tolerance for pain, or desire for greater power and responsibility in the tribe, from achieving full manhood, but those who did survive it also would likely be even more committed to the tribe.

Modern communities like fraternities at colleges, law firms, research universities, or the military have their own rites of passage, differing only in the degree of physical or mental pain from tribal initiation ceremonies.

The community plays a very important role in supporting education, even in modern schooling systems. As Chicago Nobel laureate economist James Heckman emphasizes, a child's attitudes toward learning, as well as her future health, are shaped in the critical preschool years where the family and community matter far more than the formal education system. Moreover, even after children enter the formal schooling system, the community determines whether they make use of it to the fullest extent. Whether children are given the time, encouragement, and the support to do homework depends on the environment at home and the attitude of their friends toward academic effort.

Linkages between the school and the community are also important. Parents will be more eager to monitor and support teaching if they feel they can influence how the school is run—many successful schools draw on parents for school boards, for staffing and supporting extracurricular programs, as well as for providing funds for equipment that is not accounted for in the normal budget. Communities help the young outside schools, whether it is through preschool learning, summer jobs, or watching out for, and counseling, teenagers who might stray. Equally, teachers, coming from the community, can work to build alternative local social supports for students whose families are broken. Schools are also an important focal point for parents to build mutual friendships, as they are drawn together in a common endeavor.

The community shapes the views of its members about one another, so as to encourage mutual support. The elderly are a store of knowledge and have experiences and wisdom that can be very important in guiding the community. Nevertheless, in environments where reproductive capabilities matter enormously or much of the work is physically taxing, the elderly may be a dispensable burden. To give the elderly an incentive to share their wisdom, even while protecting their position, the socialization process often inculcates respect for age. In modern South Indian Brahmin marriages and coming-of-age ceremonies, the elderly have an important position as they guide the young on the specific rituals to be followed. The young signal their acceptance of the natural order by repeatedly prostrating themselves before anyone older, asking for their blessings. Rank or position in the outside world is immaterial in determining who prostrates themselves before whom—all that matters is age. More generally, communities may allocate authority and power in ways that have nothing to do with economic capability, but help keep the community together.

Creating Binding Social Relationships

In close-knit communities, few transactions are explicit exchanges of broadly equal values. A mother nurses her child with no thought of sending a bill for services rendered, while we ply dinner guests with food and wine with no concern of when they will reciprocate. As ties get weaker in the community, more reciprocity is expected, but usually in such a way that the original gesture is never fully reciprocated so as to "close the account."

American anthropologist Laura Bohannan spent years working with the Tiv people of Northern Nigeria. When she arrived to study the community, she was inundated with gifts by the very poor villagers—a common experience for guests in traditional societies. Not wanting to appear rude, she accepted them but was eventually taught the appropriate etiquette by the headman's wife, who told her to "stop wandering aimlessly about the countryside and start calling to return the gifts" she had received. Bohannon concluded:

"What had been given must be returned, and at the appropriate time—in most cases, within two market weeks. For more valuable gifts, like livestock, one should wait until the giver is in sudden need and then offer financial aid. In the absence of banks, large presents of this sort are one way of saving. . . . I couldn't remember [who gave what]; I didn't think anyone could. But they did, and I watched with amazed admiration as Udama [the headman's wife] dispensed handfuls of okra, the odd tenth-penny and other bits in an endless circle of gifts in which no one ever handed over the precise value of the object last received but in which, over months, the total exchange was never more than a penny in anyone's favor."[6]

Gifts among the Tiv, as in most societies, serve to strengthen social bonds. That a gift is not returned in exact and equal measure prevents gift exchange from becoming a market transaction. Indeed, the very point is that nothing is demanded in return by the giver—social ties are built only when the giver seemingly forgets the gift as soon as it is given. Yet someone who only receives and never gives is quickly ostracized, hence the advice to return the gifts. Relationships are built not just by offering gifts but also by offering services. As Bohannan sat with neighbors assisting a woman's childbirth, she reflected:

"I also remembered that my great-grandmother had her first child alone with her husband on the frontier; in her diary, she had longed for another woman then. . . . More generally, though, I could see that where we multiplied specialists and services, these people multiplied personal relationship . . ."

In small communities where there are few specialists to provide services, neighbors fill in the gaps. For example, in Amish communities in rural Pennsylvania, everyone comes together in "barn raisings" to build a barn for someone in the community. It is as much a community celebration as collective work. Such actions broaden the areas of interaction and help deepen relationships within the community. Indeed, every transaction within a community, whether economic or not, is just the most recent link in a set of cross-linked block chains which stretch back into the past, and likely will well into the future.

The ties within a community enable it to act as a support of last resort. When all is lost, we can always return to our family or village, where we will be helped because of who we are rather than what we can pay or what we have accomplished. A study finds that 20 percent of households within a caste group in India in 1999 sent or received transfers of money.[7] The transfers amounted to between 20 and 40 percent of the receiving household's annual income. Each sending household sent between 5 to 7 percent of its annual income, implying a number of them combined to help a household that had major contingencies like illness or marriage. Even with modern sources of social insurance such as unemployment benefits and pensions, the community is critical in filling holes that are left by the formal government and market systems.

Facilitating Transactions

Communities facilitate internal trading by monitoring behavior and ostracizing defaulters, cutting them off from further transactions and community support.[8] Some embed differential treatment of insiders and outsiders into their norms. Anthropologist Douglas Oliver observed that to the Siuai of Solomon Islands, mankind consists of relatives and strangers. "Transactions with relatives ought to be carried out in a spirit devoid of commerciality." With few exceptions, however, "persons who live far away are not relatives and can only be enemies . . . One interacts with them only to buy and sell— utilizing hard bargaining and deceit to make as much profit from such transactions as possible."[9] With such an attitude, it would take a particularly confident outsider to contemplate trading with the Siuai, ensuring outside trades would be few and far between. But that may be the point! Parochial as the attitude may seem, it fortifies the community by strengthening within-community trade and limiting opportunities for members to stray outside.

ENCOURAGING FAVORS AND RESOLVING CONFLICTS

Bonds between members are obviously stronger if they grow up together, undergo common socialization processes and rites of passage, and share common values and traditions. However, bonds can also build between members of a community in a more modern setting where they come together only in adulthood. Indeed, despite having access to a modern legal system, neighbors may rely on community norms to resolve potential conflict because it is cheaper.

Robert Ellikson, a legal scholar at Yale University, studied ranchers in Shasta County in Northern California and found that their community had developed a variety of unwritten norms to deal with various frictions. For example, cattle from one ranch might trespass onto another rancher's land. If that rancher discovered an animal wearing someone else's brand, he would inform the owner. The owner, though, might take weeks to pick up his animal in a collective roundup—it is too costly to go fetch each animal as it strays. In the meantime, the rancher would incur costs of hundreds of dollars for feeding the trespassing cattle. Nevertheless, he typically did not charge the owner for this.

Ellikson conjectures this is because in the thinly populated rural areas of the county, neighbors expect to interact with one another on multiple dimensions such as fence repair, water supply, and staffing the volunteer fire station, and these interactions will extend far into the future. Any "trespass dispute with a neighbor is almost certain to be but one thread in the rich fabric of a continuing relationship." Therefore, most residents expect giving and receiving to balance out in the long run—a shortfall in the trespass account will be offset by a surplus in the fence repair account.

Accounts need not balance over time. When a transfer is necessary to square unbalanced accounts, neighbors in Shasta County prefer using in-kind payments, not money, for the latter is thought "unneighborly": If one's goat eats a neighbor's plants, the neighborly thing to do would be to replant them, not offer money. Indeed, when one of the ranchers paid to settle a trespass dispute, others rebuked him for setting an unfortunate precedent.[10] The point is that neighbors prefer to keep an ongoing cooperative relationship rather than end it through "cold hard cash," which can signal an arm's-length dealing and poison the atmosphere. It is the web of credit and debit accounts within Shasta County ranchers, settled with favors rather than with money so that no one quite knows what the balance is, that seems to tie the community together.

In every such community, there will be potential deviants, who are happy to take but will not give. Ellikson describes a rising set of penalties for defaulters, starting with adverse gossip within the close community. A besmirched reputation is enough to stop the flow of favors, so most ranchers are very careful not just about adhering to the norms but about being *seen* to be adhering to the norms. If the deviant does not really care about his good name, aggrieved ranchers may take sterner action like killing the trespassing animals after giving the owner due warning, or reporting the owner to county authorities. While disputes are resolved under the shadow of the law, legal remedies are rarely invoked, and even then, typically against outsiders. As one rancher put it, "Being good neighbors means no lawsuits."[11] More generally, as we will see, communities can be diminished by the intrusion of the state, and it is not surprising that Shasta County tries to avoid relying on it.

THE VALUE OF COMMUNITY

It is easy to see why the community is so appealing. Apart from contributing to our sense of who we are, a richer range of transactions can be undertaken within the community than would be possible if everything had to be contractual and strictly enforced by the law. The record of what one does for the community continues to be visible in the community, and it does not vanish into an anonymous marketplace. This leads to greater pride, ownership, and responsibility. The community comes together to raise its young and to support its weak, elderly, and unlucky. Because of its proximity, and the degree of information it receives, the community can tailor help to the specific needs of the situation. It also recognizes freeloaders far better than any distant government could and can shut down their benefits. As a result, given any quantity of available resources, it can offer a far-higher level of benefits to the truly needy. Communities therefore aid the individual, preventing them from drifting—untaught, unaided, and unanchored—in life.

The work of economic theorists like Oliver Hart, who won the Nobel Prize in Economics in 2016, offers a related explanation for the economic value of communities. The real world is plagued by the problem of incomplete contracts. We cannot fully anticipate what will happen in the future, and even if we can, we do not have the ability to prove who did what, and when, to the satisfaction of a court of law. We cannot thus write the full range of arm's-length contracts that would be necessary to deal with all the problems that might arise in real life. For instance, to deal with the problem of stray cattle with explicit arm's-length contracts, every rancher would have to contract with every other rancher on what ought to be done if his cattle strays, as well as on the necessary payments for services rendered. With little ability to verify when the cattle wondered off the ranch, or what the quality of their treatment was in the hands of the rancher who found them, lawsuits could proliferate. The system of implicit community responsibility and enforcement might be far more effective in protecting cattle and minimizing transactions costs than using explicit contracts and the legal system. Communities thus can be more than the sum of individuals who compose them.

Finally, an important modern function of communities is to give the individual in large countries some political influence over the way they are governed, and thus a sense of control over their lives, as well as a sense of public responsibility. Well-structured countries decentralize a lot of decisions to local community government. To the extent that individuals can organize collective political action within the community more easily, it affords them a vehicle to affect issues on a national stage. The community then magnifies the power of the individual. We will return to the political role of the community later in the book.

DYSFUNCTIONAL COMMUNITIES

We have seen what functional communities do. Consider now a classic picture of a dysfunctional community and what it does not do. Dysfunctional communities in developed countries can be virtual war zones, with widespread drug addiction, crime, failing schools, and broken families. Who would expect significant public engagement if even leaving home is dangerous? This is why the Pilsen community we discussed in the Preface set about tackling crime as the first step in community revival. However, dysfunctional communities are present in even fairly safe areas around the world.

In the mid-1950s, social anthropologist Edward Banfield spent nearly a year studying a poor village in Southern Italy, to which he gave a fictitious name, Montegrano. The extent of underdevelopment of the village can be gauged by the fact that many of the inhabitants were illiterate and did not have toilets with running water. The village remained underdeveloped even in an Italy that was then undergoing a miraculous economic transformation, in part, as Banfield argues, because of "the inability of the villagers to act together for their common good."[12] Anyone who has been to dysfunctional communities around the world will recognize some of Montegrano in those communities.

The main occupation in Montegrano was agriculture, but with limited untilled land and small land holdings, it was unlikely that peasant families would prosper by staying in agriculture. Even so, the main path of upward mobility for children, education, was largely blocked. Only five grades of school were taught in the village, the schools were poorly equipped, teachers poorly paid, and attendance, both by students and teachers, was irregular. Moreover, "After finishing the fifth grade some students can barely read or write or do simple sums . . . According to a Montegrano school official, one-third of the [school] graduates are illiterate several years after graduation."[13] Many children did not attend schools regularly, and some farm people sent their children to school willingly only so long as they were too young to work in the fields.

An engineer from Northern Italy, who was shocked at the lack of professionalism among teachers in Montegrano, perhaps best captured what was wrong: He noted that during the summer vacation, a teacher from more prosperous Northern Italy might hold informal classes, take children for walks into the country and explain a bit about nature, or even go on picnics. In contrast, teachers in Montegrano spent their summers "loafing in the *piazza*," and did not speak to their students when they saw them. The teachers simply did not care if their students learned anything.[14]

Apathy was evident elsewhere too. There were no organized voluntary charities in the village. An order of nuns from outside the village maintained an orphanage for little girls in a crumbling monastery, but even though girls from local families were at the orphanage, "none of the many half-employed stone masons has ever given a day's work to its repair."[15] There was not enough food for the children, "but no peasant or land proprietor ha[d] ever given a young pig to the orphanage."[16]

The nearest hospital was five hours away by car, and few villagers could afford the trip. There was no organized effort to bring a hospital nearby, despite villagers complaining for years about the lack of access to medical facilities. Stopgap measures to improve access to education and health care, such as rescheduling public bus timings to transport village children to schools elsewhere, or funding an ambulance to carry emergency cases from the area to the hospital, were simply not considered.

A functional community would have put pressure on the local government to improve public services, failing which volunteers would have gathered to undertake the task. While Montegrano had an elected mayor and council, decisions "even to buy an ashtray" were taken by the prefect, a member of the civil service sitting in Potenza, the nearest large town.[17] Similarly, the director of schools reported directly to Potenza, public works were not under the purview of local government, and the police were under the Ministry of Justice in Rome. Too few important decisions were taken locally, a problem we will discuss later in the book, but even so, villagers did not even try to influence them.

The problem in Montegrano, as Banfield argues, was the extreme distrust between villagers, their worry about losing relative social position if they helped someone else improve their lot, and their corrosive envy of those who did succeed. Given this attitude, anyone who undertook a public-spirited action felt they incurred the full costs of acting, would probably receive only a small part of the public benefits, and would feel diminished by the public benefits that went to others. As one teacher explained, not only was there little public spirit, but many people positively wanted to prevent others from getting ahead.[18] Such public apathy explains why voluntary efforts to supply public services—for example, masons repairing the monastery—simply did not emerge.

There are a variety of reasons why these attitudes exist in communities. When economic opportunity is very limited, economic activity might be seen as zero-sum—your gain comes at the expense of mine. The problem is exacerbated when families are at risk of slipping in social status, from the barely self-sufficient but still respectable to the "deplorable," who are dependent on others for subsistence. With few savings and little wealth, many peasants were just one hailstorm or one pig's unfortunate death away from a winter of deprivation or worse. While families were willing to help one another tide over temporary misfortune, more general public spirit required a degree of comfort with their economic situation that they simply did not have. Given the difficulty of staying afloat economically, villagers' focus was on providing for their immediate family rather than maintaining a broader public spirit.

This inward focus may actually do public harm. A common example of what Banfield calls "amoral familism" is visible in many developing countries, where people keep their houses spotlessly clean, but unceremoniously dump the garbage collected inside on the street outside. The ultimately self-defeating effects of having unclean and unhygienic public spaces surrounding clean homes can only be explained by extreme public apathy, a fundamental characteristic of dysfunctional communities.

The state, despite being recognizably apathetic, distant, and nonfunctional itself, nevertheless dampened initiative in Montegrano. The faint hope that the government will dig a latrine, pave a road, or discipline school teachers can prevent the local population from organizing to do so. In frontier towns in the United States, the community raised a barn or built a road itself, knowing there was no one else who would do it. In dysfunctional communities where the government is closer, the misplaced expectation that the ghost of the inefficient government will eventually appear and do the job crowds out what little private initiative there is.

WHEN DO COMMUNITIES WORK AND WHEN DO THEY NOT?

Communities can be fragile even without becoming dysfunctional. They tend to work best when they are small and have little competition. Community relationships are built when members have limited choices, both at a point in time and over time. Relationships, and thus communities, become more fragile when the available set of choices expands, as when communities grow or when the outside market starts offering more opportunities to community members. Communities can also distort decisions, reducing the incentives for individuals to move, change, or adapt. While this may be the right individual choice, when many members make such choices it can drag down a community.

Too Many Alternatives

Mitchell Petersen of Northwestern University and I were interested in uncovering the effects of the greater availability of potential financial partners on the strength of relationships.[19] We examined the relationships between small firms and their banks. Small firms typically find it hard to get finance, and young small firms especially so. Most economic theories would suggest that in areas with greater bank competition, young small firms would be better off.

Interestingly, we did not find this. Instead, in areas in the United States served by fewer banks, and hence with a less competitive banking market, we found small young firms got more bank loans, and at lower interest rates than similar small young firms in areas with many more banks. Importantly, they also seemed to pay back for this help. As the young firms aged, the interest rate they paid on their borrowings moved up faster in areas with few banks, with older firms paying more in such areas than in areas with more competitive banks.

Why were banks more willing to help out young firms in areas where firms had less choice of banking partners? The answer seemed to be that they knew they could build stronger relationships. As in the community relationships described above, a banking relationship is based on give and take over time. Lending to untried young firms is costly because even a small loan requires a fair amount of due diligence by the banker, and the size of the loan does not allow the bank to recoup the cost of the effort invested quickly. Moreover, many small firms fail, adding further to the bank's costs as such loans have to be written off. A bank therefore takes a chance on an untried young firm only if it is reasonably confident the firm will survive, grow, and give it more profitable business in the future.

In areas with many banks, a successful firm could always renege on its implicit promise to the bank that helped it early on, by replacing it with a new banking partner at better terms. In areas with few other banks, however, the successful firm would likely stay with its original banker because of the lack of choice, and thus would compensate the bank with additional profitable business for the risk the bank took when the firm was young. A bank in such an area, being more confident in the (forced) durability of the relationship, would then be more eager to support young firms.

Thus, relationships seem to be stronger when the members of the community have fewer alternatives, for it gives the members confidence that they will stay mutually committed. An interesting corollary is that communities within a larger economy that are partially ostracized by others may flourish because members build stronger ties within the community. For instance, a disproportionate number of entrepreneurs during England's Industrial Revolution were nonconformists such as Unitarians and Quakers, who were excluded from civil or military office and from Oxford or Cambridge University.[20] The silver lining may have been that, given their exclusion from the larger community, nonconformists trusted one another more to continue maintaining business ties, with marriages eventually cementing the community links that provided initial business finance and business partners. Not only was entrepreneurship one of the few attractive career outlets that was not proscribed to capable Quaker youth, many a budding entrepreneur got help from others in the community as he started out.

In sum, in a small community, not only am I assured that those I help will stay committed to me, but I also know if I don't help someone in deep trouble, my community may shrink and leave me worse off. In a small community, therefore, everyone has a stake in everyone else's well-being. We are spoiled for choice as the community grows, which could hurt the community.[21]

Relationships also work better if partners interact over multiple activities—if one's neighbor is not just a source of the odd gardening tool but also helps deliver our child, we are likely to have stronger bonds. However, this requires the community not to have specialists, else most of us would prefer our child be delivered by a professional midwife or gynecologist. There is no point specializing as a midwife if one is to serve a community with only a handful of women of childbearing age, but it makes more sense if there are hundreds—as Adam Smith famously wrote, "the division of labor is limited by the extent of the market." As the community grows larger, therefore, we can call the professional midwife when a child is being born and the professional fire service when a cat is stuck up a tree, instead of our neighbor. Members have more choice, and the quality of goods and services they have access to increases, but the breadth of interactions that take place between members narrows. This social distancing or alienation once again diminishes the strength of relationships and the value of community.

Members could try to preserve a sense of community as it grows larger and more anonymous, urging everyone to take into account community benefits in deciding whether to transact locally or in the larger marketplace. They then run into the free-rider problem. We may all benefit from having a local bookstore, where we can browse through books before buying, and meet for coffee or for book events. It may well be that the associated benefits of building community through purchases from the local bookstore outweigh the lower price from ordering more cheaply online. However, if everyone else does their purchasing locally, the bookstore survives, leaving me free to cheat and patronize the cheaper online bookseller. The anonymity of a larger community will make individual transactions harder to police. When everyone acts in a rational self-interested way, the neighborhood bookstore closes down, to the detriment of all.

Too Little Incentive to Change

We have just seen that self-interested people do not take into account the loss of benefits to community health when they transact outside the community. Equally problematic is when they rely overly on community support when they make individual decisions, staying too long within the community when the outside makes more sense. One situation where such incentives may be at work is when an important source of livelihood in the community is threatened by technological change or trade. A well-documented tragedy of the Industrial Revolution in England is the fate of the handloom weavers.[22]

The automation of spinning toward the end of the eighteenth century meant that there was much more yarn available to be woven. Automated power looms were only slowly being introduced, so there was strong demand for the labor of handloom weavers to weave the now abundantly available yarn into cloth. Unfortunately, the writing was on the wall—these jobs would be automated also. Indeed, because it was costly to let expensive power looms lie idle, the handloom weavers were already the first to be deprived of work when business slowed. Nevertheless, even as wages in handloom weaving fell as automation and the entry of workers created a labor surplus, the numbers joining the handloom weaving sector continued to increase. Eventually many ended up unemployed and destitute. Why did so many workers continue to stay in, or join, an industry that was so clearly doomed?

We will see such behavior again in modern United States. The explanation cannot be disassociated from community. Handloom weaving meant following the traditional family occupation, staying at home in the village with family and community close by, and enjoying all the benefits of community support. Changing jobs would mean moving to a dirty slum in a town and working in a hot, noisy factory. For the individual household that moved, this would have also meant foregoing the support the community could offer, and essentially tearing up all the implicit claims they had on it. Staying, even if the likelihood of job loss was high, was made less unpleasant by the prospect of community support.

As the entire handloom weaving industry collapsed, though, the weaver communities were severely weakened and unable to provide the support that was expected of them. Destitute unemployed weavers were forced to petition for public support from the government, which never came—in fact, the Poor Act in England was reformed in 1832 to tighten the conditions of eligibility for public relief.[23] While it would not be fair to place the entire burden of this tragedy on the community, it is reasonable to conclude that the presence of the community can distort the decisions of its individual members. When trade and technological change affect many members of the community, their suboptimal individual decisions can end up dragging the community down with them as they place too much of a burden on it.

THE COSTS OF
INSULAR COMMUNITIES

Communities through history have understood how detrimental the free and unconstrained choices of their members can be to community survival. For much of history, this did not matter because people had few alternatives, and change was slow. At times of great change, however, communities have had to react. Some of their actions may have made the communities much less useful in promoting social well-being.

Take, for example, the problem of excess outside choice that we discussed earlier. Most obviously, communities can prohibit or restrict contacts between their members and the outside, especially if such contacts can infuse new and uncomfortable ideas or make members more economically independent of the community. As we will see in the next chapter, feudalism was an example of enforced community, and was perpetuated by severe restrictions on what people could do.

Such restrictions are not imposed solely to protect the community, they also protect the powerful in the community against challenge and the community from desirable change. Ellen Barry of the *New York Times* followed the travails of a group of women from the Nats community in Meerut, a few miles from New Delhi.[24] During the wedding season, the community men worked as musicians in wedding bands, but begging was the traditional off-season occupation for the community. As India started exporting buffalo meat in large quantities, some women started to work in a nearby meat-processing factory, and earned considerably more than their husbands. With the women contributing to family finances, and reducing the extortionate stranglehold of moneylenders, the male elders of the caste, some of whom not coincidentally were moneylenders, struck back. They decreed that the women should stop work, ostensibly so that they would not be exposed to the sexual advances of outside men.

The real reason, Barry surmised, was that the women's earnings had begun to undermine the existing order. When some of the women refused to obey the decree, they were ostracized by the community. Of course, when community members want to break free, ostracism may have little punitive effect, so it was followed by violence. The women were forced to appeal to the police and the judiciary to protect them, as well as to ensure their constitutional right to work. In older India, neither would the job opportunity have arisen nor would the legal system be open to helping them. Markets and the state do open up the community, reducing the extent to which it can become oppressive.

In addition to remaining small to build relationships, the community may also need to remain small if it is to share information effectively.[25] Apart from the costs of foregone growth, information sharing has its downsides. The community can be very intrusive and cloying, poking its nose in members' private affairs. Gossip can be helpful in straightening out aberrant behavior, but it can also be mean, hurtful, and intolerant of deviance from age-old traditions. Transparency can highlight budding problems, but those in the community fishbowl, naked to the view of all, may be civil in public while hiding seething resentment. By comparison, the anonymity of the city can be liberating, even though it distances us from social relationships.

The pressure in some communities to stay small and only transact internally can also come at some cost to the broader system. Medieval Chinese master craftsmen typically found apprentices within the family or the close-knit clan. In contrast, the guild system in Europe allowed masters to take on apprentices from almost anywhere, and apprentices, on becoming masters, similarly could move to their hometowns to set up their workshops. According to economic historians de la Croix, Doepke, and Mokyr, a consequence of the looser guild structure in Europe was that technical knowledge was shared widely, improved upon, and shared again.[26] In contrast, it remained relatively stagnant when confined within the clan in China. They argue that this can explain the vast improvements in Europe between 1500 and 1750 in a variety of technical areas, such as watchmaking, relative to China. It is a lesson that we will take to modern times when we examine firms and patent rights later in the book.

Communities may also try and hold together by overemphasizing traditions as the source of the community's strengths. In doing so, the community risks making members suspicious of the choices presented by the modern world, allowing them to become trapped by the past. This is particularly problematic in matters of science. Economic historian Joel Mokyr argues that a major spur to the scientific discoveries in the seventeenth century was the realization that Aristotle's scientific observations were often wrong.[27] Equally energizing for scientific progress was the comfort that contemporary scientists like Galileo, Newton, and Leibnitz had extended the boundaries of knowledge far beyond what was contained in the ancient texts, and there was nothing extraordinary or eternal about the classics. This led scholars to challenge old knowledge in every area, breaking from their earlier conformism. In contrast, centers of Islamic learning, perhaps to promote the commonality and thus cohesiveness of historic Islamic thought in a rapidly expanding and disparate community, turned their gaze backward. Islamic scholars, whose predecessors had kept scientific knowledge alive and expanding during Europe's Dark Ages, started studying older Islamic texts to uncover their eternal verities, and contributed little to the progress of science from the thirteenth century onward.

CONCLUSION

Although communities can be supportive, they are effective in special circumstances. Either community members are socialized to be concerned about the greater utility of the community and its members relative to their own—typically true of groups that grow up together or are ethnically homogenous—or the community needs some surplus value (what economists term "rents") embedded in relationships for members to find cooperation worthwhile. As we saw with banking relationships, arguably the most important problem the community faces is the centrifugal pull of the outside on community members—the competition that emanates from the outside world erodes rents within the community. Ideally, the community would offset that centrifugal pull by the centripetal attraction of the warmth of its relationships and the noncontractual support it provides. Indeed, the point of inclusive localism, as we will see, is to create enough benefits through proximity that the community can afford to be inclusive. Nevertheless, the human desire to protect its valuable relationships and to create new ones by limiting competition and the pull of the outside, will be a recurrent theme throughout the book.

PART I

HOW THE PILLARS EMERGED

There are ninety and nine who live and die
In want and hunger and cold
That one may live in luxury
And be wrapped in a silken fold
The ninety and nine in hovels bare
The one in a palace with riches rare…
And the one owns cities, and houses and lands,
And the ninety nine have empty hands.

Published in the *Farmers' Alliance*, July 31, 1889, at the time of the Populist revolt in the United States

I n the Introduction, we explored some of the benefits of the community, the third pillar in our narrative, and also saw some of its downsides. In the next four chapters, we go back in history to trace how the three pillars we see today emerged from the original single pillar, the community. We will see the functions of each pillar and the interrelationships between them when society was, arguably, simpler. This will help us understand our current challenges as we recognize in today's problems echoes from history. Also, we will see that pillars waxed and waned in strength through history, creating disequilibria. Society eventually adapted to restore balance. As we face another period of disequilibrium today, history should give us some confidence that we will find answers.

We start in Chapter 1 with the archetypal medieval community, the European feudal manor. The most valuable asset at that time, land, was rarely sold, since it was tied to a family or clan rather than an individual, and land rights were based on customs that involved feudal rights and obligations rather than explicit ownership. Goods were largely exchanged within the manor. The lord of the manor governed the community, adjudicating disputes and meting out justice. Thus, for all practical purposes, the community also contained the other two pillars. We use the quintessential market transaction, debt, as a focal point, and trace how both the state and markets separated from the feudal community over time. We will also follow changing public and scholarly attitudes towards business and markets, and see they have not been static. Instead, they often mirrored the economic and political necessities of the time, as they do today.

With the rise of the nation state, the state pillar was in ascendance. We turn in Chapter 2 to the emerging nation-state in England, and see how competitive markets helped England solve a fundamental conundrum—how the state can obtain a monopoly of military power within the country, and yet give up its powers to act arbitrarily and outside the law. This is essential for markets to be confident that private property is protected. We will see the importance of an efficient commercially-minded gentry as well as independent businesspersons in aggregating power through Parliament and imposing constitutional checks on the monarchy. Once the state was constitutionally limited, the way was open for truly competitive markets—individuals no longer needed the anti-competitive feudal structures such as guilds that also served to protect them against the state. At the same time, both widely-held private property as well as competitive markets were necessary to create an independent private sector that could protect property and constrain the state. In sum, the constitutionally limited state freed markets and free markets limited the state.

Once the markets were free of the fear of expropriation by the state, they flourished. As we will see in Chapter 3, the market pillar was dominant as countries experienced the First Industrial Revolution but often to the detriment of the community. The fight for broader suffrage was, in many ways, a fight by the community for more democratic power, this time to protect labor, not just physical property. The empowered community then, through movements like those of the Populists and the Progressives in the United States around the turn of the nineteenth century, played its role in restoring the balance by pressing the state to keep markets competitive and opportunity alive for the many.

The democratic community may not always want markets. In Chapter 4, we will outline three situations when the community does not push for competitive markets—when market players or practices are deemed illegitimate and the state seems a better alternative, when the state is weak and the community is easily bribed to stay apathetic, and when neither the state nor the community offer people the capabilities and the support they need to participate in volatile, changing markets. For people to desire markets, an effective state together with an engaged community have to create mechanisms that will provide people the capabilities and support that will allow them to benefit from markets. We will see how the balance came together in the liberal market democracies that emerged across the developed world by the early twentieth century. We will cover a thousand years of the evolution of the pillars in four chapters—a little too fast for the historians, but just right for our purpose, which is to give a sense of what problems they solved.

History's lessons are important. They will give us a sense of why each pillar matters and how the pillars fit together to produce the liberal market economy. Patterns of their interaction reproduce, not exactly but recognizably. Nevertheless, readers who want to jump ahead to recent times might skim through Part I and go to Part II, where we move quickly through the post World War II–era to explain the genesis of today's problems. They could then come back to Part I for a historical perspective.

1

TOLERATING AVARICE

In this chapter, we will see how the markets and the state separated from the medieval manor community and became powerful pillars in their own right. We will follow these developments through the use of the quintessential market contract: debt. The Catholic Church will play a cameo role in this story, initially filling the vacuum left by the absence of a strong state, then competing with the state to both protect and exploit people. Crucially, though, for our narrative, the Church managed to stand up to the state, armed only with the power of religion. It established the idea that there was a higher legitimacy that constrained state actions, over and above temporal power. As we will see, this was an important step toward a constitutionally limited state, which in turn was necessary for markets to have full play.

THE DEBT CONTRACT

Unlike the favors we have been discussing between members of a community, a loan contract is an explicit commitment by a borrower to repay the loaned amount with interest at a prespecified time, failing which the lender will be able to use the force of the law to recover the value lent. Typically, she will do so by seizing pledged collateral. If the security offered by the borrower is valuable—such as a farmer borrowing against his land—the lender need not know very much about the borrower or monitor his activity closely. By making terms explicit, the debt contract frees the lender from dependence on the whims or fortunes of the borrower. No longer is it the borrower's choice whether to repay and when to do so—he must pay on the contract's maturity or face the stipulated penalties, which in some societies were as harsh as slavery or death. Since the debt contract is written down, it is not dependent on the frailty of human or community memory. Favors can be forgotten—debt cannot.

Debt is thus an arm's-length exchange of money for interest, untrammeled by the need to maintain social ties. This can draw in lenders from outside the community. In fact, such lenders may be the best at getting repaid because they will not sympathize with a borrower who has fallen on hard times, unlike a lender from within the community. Shylock, who hated Antonio, Shakespeare's merchant of Venice, was, in a sense, the ideal lender, since he was perfectly willing to take his pound of Antonio's flesh if Antonio did not repay the debt. Because Antonio then had every incentive to repay, Shylock was willing to lend.

These attributes of debt—that it is explicit, often secured by collateral, and impersonal—seem to favor the lender. They also make it much easier, though, for a potential borrower to get a loan at a low interest rate in competitive environments—somewhat paradoxically, the harsher the debt contract and the more it seems weighted in favor of the lender, the greater and broader the borrower's access to finance. If, in contrast, sympathetic courts were to suspend the lender's power to recover whenever the borrower was in difficulty, lenders would not be eager to lend to anyone who was even moderately risky, and lending would dry up. The few loans that would still be made to risky borrowers would be at sky-high interest rates. So it is from the very harshness of the debt contract, and the lender's ability and willingness to enforce it, that the borrower gets easy access to funds. None of this is to say that borrowing is appropriate for everyone who wants money, or that debt forgiveness is bad, only that the debt contract is fit for its purpose.

In the relationships we have discussed so far, one member of the community does a favor to another without the expectation she will be repaid in full measure. In the typical debt contract, the terms including the interest rate are calculated so that both sides are satisfied if the contract is adhered to, even if they never see each other again. A relationship leaves possibilities open-ended; the debt contract calculates them to closure. A relationship requires parties to have some empathy for each other or some sense they are part of a larger, longer-term whole; the debt contract is entirely self-contained. It is in these senses that the debt contract represents the quintessential individualistic arm's-length market transaction.

Despite the usefulness of debt, lending for interest, otherwise known as usury, has been proscribed by many religions and cultures. Usury laws capping interest rates prevent the equalization of benefits to both borrower and lender. The lender gets less than what he might obtain in a free market. Why did such laws emerge?

THE PROHIBITION ON USURY

Societies have often prohibited lending at more than a specified moderate rate of interest. The *Arthashastra,* attributed to Indian Emperor Chandragupta Maurya's adviser, Kautilya, and written around 300 BCE, has detailed prescriptions on the maximum rate of interest that can be charged for different kinds of loans. The ceiling was 1 1/4 percent per month or 15 percent per year for ordinary loans to people, intended to finance consumption or emergency needs.[1] It went up to 5 percent per month for ordinary commercial loans, 10 percent per month for riskier commercial transactions that involved travel through forests, and 20 percent per month for trade by sea. The only exception to these limits was in regions where the king was unable to guarantee security, where judges were asked to take into account customary practices among debtors and creditors. Thus, ancient India recognized a distinction between consumption loans and loans taken to fund profitable commerce, with lower ceilings on interest charged on the former. It also saw the need for the lender to receive a higher interest rate when the commercial enterprise was riskier.

The Old Testament was much less tolerant of usury. For instance, according to Exodus 22:25, "If thou lend money to any of my people that is poor that dwelleth with thee: thou shalt not be hard upon them as an extortioner, nor oppress them with usuries." Elsewhere in the Old Testament, though, there is an exception—strangers. In Deuteronomy 23:19–20: "Thou shalt not lend upon usury to thy brother; usury of money, usury of victuals, usury of anything that is lent upon usury. Unto a stranger thou mayest lend upon usury; but unto thy brother thou shalt not lend upon usury."

Is the payment of interest unjustified compensation? After all, the lender has to postpone her own use of the money—think of all those middle-aged people investing money in a debt mutual fund for their old age, which the fund then lends to firms. Postponed gratification, as well as the loss of convenience in not having the money at hand for emergencies, requires some compensation. So too does any cost of preparing the loan document, checking the borrower's credentials, and administering the loan. The lender also takes the risk the borrower may not repay, or may repay only partially, despite all the safeguards built into debt. So she also needs compensation for the risk of default. Finally, the lender's use for money, as well as her ability to buy goods with it when she gets repaid, may be very different from today. This is another risk she bears.

The economically defensible interest rate therefore includes the time value for money plus transactions costs for making the loan plus the compensation to the lender for the risks she takes. The final piece that is tacked on is the lender's profit, based on how pressing the borrower's need is and what the alternative sources of loans are. So why would the ancient Hebrews prevent lenders from getting what modern economists think is their legitimate due? The answer relates to three factors: the size of the community, the condition of the borrower, and the extent of competition between potential lenders.

THE RATIONALE FOR PROSCRIBING USURY

In biblical times in Palestine, tribes were small, people poor, and the occasional borrower needed money typically to buy food or shelter for survival. The prohibition on usury within the community essentially meant the members of the community insured one another against adversity. If one tribesman's goats died accidentally, he could go to others who were not similarly afflicted for help while he rebuilt his herd, promising to repay the favor when his luck improved.

A prohibition on taking interest would have a number of beneficial effects here. When people are living close to the edge, they are willing to promise anything for their family's survival. If the community is poor and only a few have resources to spare at any given time, those few would then have tremendous bargaining power over the needy. If there were no prohibition on charging exorbitant interest, a temporary setback to some members of the tribe could lead them to become permanently indebted and thus enslaved to other luckier members. Over time, the enslaved would have little reason to work, the tribe would become even more impoverished, and conflict would increase.

In contrast, though, if the charging of interest were limited or even prohibited, the better-off members would have little profitable use for surplus resources. They would be forced to help out proximate neighbors or kin with interest-free loans, thus accumulating favors they could draw on when they themselves were hit with adversity. Those on the verge of starvation would have much more use for the shekel saved in interest than the well-fed lender.[2] Moreover, in a small tribe, helping close tribe members survive would also be a matter of self-interest. These would be the people one would trade and work with over time. The bonds of friendship aside, if one's trusted associates perished in hard times, one would have to build relationships with unfamiliar others, a potentially costly endeavor. Given the tribesmen's choice between freely given mutual help and debt bondage, with uncertainty about who would come out as master and who would be enslaved, perhaps it is not surprising that they might have chosen to prohibit the latter. In a sense, therefore, the prohibition on usury created a rent, or surplus—the interest that could not be charged—that would be shared within the community to strengthen bonds.

Of course, a lender could get around the usury prohibition by disguising interest; for instance, a lender could finance the unlucky tribesman's purchase of additional goats but demand milk every day in lieu of interest. This is where religion came in. Knowing that God saw what the tribal authorities might overlook, in an age when the fate of the soul was more important than earthly existence, the fear of retribution in afterlife played an effective role in ensuring the usury prohibition was respected in letter and spirit.

The prohibition on charging interest thus helped strengthen communal bonds and mutual support in small poor communities where anyone could be hit by adversity, and the identities of those in need fluctuated almost randomly over time. To be your brother's keeper, to practice a kind of communism, made sense.

The prohibition was also a form of early consumer protection vis-à-vis outside lenders. With the poor borrower not knowing how to read, having a very rudimentary understanding of interest, and also often being in a position of deep distress, the possibility that dispassionate lenders from outside the community could take advantage of him was substantial. Better, socially conscious thinkers would have argued, to force the community to take responsibility for the poor than to deliver them into the clutches of the moneylender. Indeed, all these reasons also played out in the Church's attack on usury in Europe in the Middle Ages.

FEUDALISM AND THE CHURCH'S ATTACK ON USURY

In Europe, from the early Middle Ages till about the eleventh century CE, the Church frowned upon the charging of interest on loans but did not prosecute moneylending as a sin.[3] However, from about the middle of the eleventh century, the Church moved aggressively to curb usury, regarding any interest as a sin, prohibited by the Bible. The usurer had to repay all interest received during his life in full before he could aspire for salvation. The attempts to suppress usury reached their apex in the Church Councils of Lyon in 1274 and Vienna in 1312. The punishment for moneylenders included not only refusal of confession, absolution, or burial in hallowed ground—terrible penalties in those times of deep faith—but also excommunication of rulers or magistrates of states that permitted usury. The economic historian Richard Tawney writes about "innumerable fables of the usurer who was prematurely carried to hell, or whose money turned to withered leaves in his strong box or who . . . on entering a church to be married, was crushed by a stone figure falling from a porch, which proved by the grace of God, to be a carving of another usurer and his money-bags being carried off by the devil . . ."[4]

What accounted for the Church's greater zeal in enforcing the ban on usury from the eleventh century onward? And why did it become far less passionate about rooting out the usurer from the late fourteenth century onward? An understanding of these shifts will give us a better sense of why attitudes toward markets change. First, though, we need to understand the quintessential community in those times in Europe: the feudal manor.

THE FEUDAL COMMUNITY

Under feudalism, everyone except the king held his share of land in trust from his overlord. Because land, the principal source of value, was not freely saleable, it was allocated to trusted supporters. In return for the use of the land and the overlord's protection, the vassal swore fealty to the overlord and paid him in kind. If the vassal was capable of fighting, payment was through military service; if he was a peasant, payment was through produce from the land or labor. In a sense, feudal obligations and relationships arose from the land and the produce it generated, neither of which could be marketed.

Feudalism in Europe reached its zenith as the Muslim expansion from the seventh century onward shut off Europe's access to traditional overseas markets. The proliferation of little principalities as well as banditry reduced the size of markets and increased the cost of transporting goods for trade.[5] With little to buy, market transactions and the use of money diminished, and feudal relationships proliferated.

The feudal manor was thus a closed, hierarchical community, producing much of what it consumed. The peasant's land holdings were typically in the form of strips in two or three large open fields, intermingled with those of his neighbors. Each peasant followed the same rotation of crops as the others, and had free access to common pastures and woods where each peasant had grazing rights for a certain number of cattle, sheep, or pigs, as well as the right to collect firewood. All this required a fair amount of coordination and give-and-take (the strips were not separated by fences and the commons were open to all in the manor), which required building consensus in the community.

Each peasant had enough to ensure a subsistence existence. There was little incentive to produce more, since there was not much of a market to sell the surplus in.[6] Because the peasant was tied to the land, though, the feudal community was stable, albeit poor. As one historian noted, "Most men have never seen more than a hundred separate individuals in the course of their whole lives, where most households live by tilling their great-grandfather's fields with their great-grandfather's plough."[7]

THE COMMERCIAL REVOLUTION

The nonmonetary feudal economy did relatively well when there were few trading opportunities. Over time, though, Europe learned to trade with, and through, the Muslim lands. Moreover, demand for agricultural products from the growing towns, as well as travel routes that were safer from brigands, helped the revival of trade and commerce. Feudal lords now not only had the opportunity to convert the manor's produce into money, the money could buy an increasing variety of goods. The growing attraction of producing for, and consuming from, the market did not sit well with traditional feudal practice.

For key to the feudal system was that the individual did not own the land outright; instead, the peasant managed it while he was able-bodied and passed the management on to his kin when he could no longer manage.[8] Everyone in the family had customary rights to the land, which made those rights difficult to sell or turn over. In turn, this ensured that a long-lived community built around that land, but productivity was generally low, since a farmer's kin were not necessarily good farmers. In fact, the absence of a market protected the peasant—his low productivity hurt his household's production, but did not jeopardize his right to farm land.

As feudal lords became more attracted to monetary income, and as land became easier to sell, this changed. In order to enhance production, the feudal lord had to be able to transfer land to more productive tenants or owners. In England, soon after the turn of the millennium, the courts started overlooking the customary rights of kin, making freehold land easier to bequeath or sell.[9] Even tenancy that was tied in with feudal obligations, known as copyhold tenancy, became better defined and easier to transfer over time.[10] Scholars argue over whether there was a dramatic change in the legal treatment of property, or whether England was intrinsically more favorable to sales. Whatever the reason, the interests of the Church also lay in freeing property from customary entanglements. If the rights of inheritance, for example, narrowed to direct relatives rather than residing with all kin, land would be easier to bequeath to third parties or to sell. And a primary beneficiary of bequests to third parties was the Church. An elderly childless widow or widower could easily be persuaded that their route to salvation lay in willing the bulk of their property to the Church. Even if they were not persuadable, often the only one who could write down a will or hear last orders was the not entirely disinterested parish priest.[11]

The net effect of a freer land market was that less-productive peasants had an incentive to sell or were strong-armed into doing so, often to larger landowners who had surplus cash, and who could farm the combined land more profitably. Land holdings became more concentrated in fewer hands but agriculture also became more productive. Unfortunately, a number of peasants were forced into marginal holdings or entirely out of the manorial community as they sold, or were evicted from, the land that tied them to it. At the bottom, holdings became smaller as the size of the peasant family grew. As the small peasant's holdings were subdivided and average incomes fell, a growing number of second and third sons had to fend for themselves outside the feudal manor. The expansion of the market, as is sometimes its wont, resulted in growing inequality.

These were therefore extremely difficult times for many European peasants, especially those who no longer had the protection of the manorial community. Average incomes were not only barely above the level needed for subsistence but also were highly variable over time.[12] The failure of a harvest or the death of livestock were not infrequent events. One estimate suggests that even the relatively wealthy English peasant could expect to face serious calamity every thirteen years.[13] Some work did open up outside farming, especially in the growing towns where merchants and artisans prospered, but it was rarely enough.

Despite their low and highly variable incomes, death by starvation was surprisingly rare among the peasantry. The reason was simple: Informal community support within the manor for those who still belonged to one, and formal charitable institutions run by the Church, such as almshouses, leper houses, pilgrim centers, educational institutions, and monastic hospitals, for those outside the manor, constituted a social safety net. Harder times for the poor explain why the Church became more aggressive in its fight against usury.[14]

Usury prohibitions limited the profits that anyone with excess wealth could make by lending to those in difficulty. At the same time, a lender faced a loss of social status and even excommunication if he was condemned as a usurer. Perhaps the businessman was willing to take this risk when young. As he grew older and came closer to the feared inevitable meeting with his Maker, the graphic pictures painted by the clergy of the torments that awaited him in hell were an increasing source of worry. The prohibition on usury thus helped channel the wealth of the rich away from making usurious consumption loans and toward helping poorer unfortunates. Such help could be given informally, or formally through charitable donations to the Church. As in the Hebrew tribes, the prohibition on usury suppressed the market in favor of the community. Thus as the commercialization of agriculture created greater numbers of the poor, the Church took their side by restricting the debt market.

The Church's actions were also not unrelated to the political battles it was fighting at that time with the secular authorities. The reforms initiated by Pope Gregory VII in 1075—the so-called Papal Revolution—attempted to separate the Church from the feudal hierarchy, especially the domination of the Holy Roman Emperor.[15] The details of the conflict, which culminated in the victory of the Church, need not concern us but some aspects are important. In order to attract support for their cause, Church scholars systematized and rationalized the Church's vast legal traditions. A comprehensive body of canon law emerged, which could now guide ecclesiastical courts, and which helped reaffirm that all Catholic authorities, including the powerful emperor, were constrained by a higher, principle-based, law. Furthermore, in response to competition from the now-more-reliable ecclesiastical courts governed by canon law, feudal rulers developed their own legal system.

Both the Church and the ruler competed to offer better justice to attract plaintiffs into their courts. Since the poor and the powerless benefited disproportionately from the law, courts consequently became more sympathetic to their problems. Better-enforced usury prohibitions became one element of that competition.

The Church's actions thus had mixed effects on the poor peasant. The Church may have helped make property more alienable in order to expand its own wealth.[16] Easier alienability allowed feudal lords to move unproductive peasants off their land, rendering them destitute. However, the Church was probably also motivated by the welfare of these very same peasants and concerned about the stability of the community when it banned usury and exploitative market transactions. And it did use some of the wealth it accumulated to provide charity to the destitute.

THE INTELLECTUAL SUPPORT FOR THE BAN ON USURY

The Church could appeal to a long line of thinkers, past and present, for support for the ban on usury. The Greek philosopher Aristotle, who was being rediscovered in this period, was firmly against interest on loans. He saw the production of goods to satisfy physical wants such as food and clothing as useful economic activity. Farming, the raising of livestock, and manufacturing were all productive. In contrast, trade, which simply exchanged goods for one another; hire, which lent out goods for money; and usury, which lent out money for money, produced nothing that satisfied physical wants. Of the three, "The most hated sort, and with the greatest reason, is usury, which makes a gain out of money itself, and not from its natural use of it. For money was intended to be used in exchange, but not to increase at interest."[17]

St. Augustine, a guiding light of the early Church, similarly warned about the three sins of fallen men: the lust for power, sexual lust, and the lust for money. Of these, he was most ambivalent about the lust for power, which if accompanied by a sense of civic duty and honor, could protect the community against external attack.[18] He also discussed in his startlingly frank *Confessions* how his private desires such as sex—as a young man, he was sexually active, and later, he lived with a mistress who bore him a son—came in the way of his relationship with God. Here too he seemed to be ambiguous, if not understanding. About the lust for money, though, he was clear in his condemnation.

Drawing on such sources, Church scholars in the Middle Ages concluded that trade or enterprise was necessary but perilous to the soul. The businessman could always be tempted to hanker after excess profit by charging more than the just price—the price that provided adequate income for the seller to maintain his station in life. This constituted avarice, a deadly sin. Working hard to enhance profits was clearly not in accordance with medieval thinking. Worse still was finance, which "if not immoral, was at best sordid, at worst disreputable."[19] These strongly Aristotelian attitudes, which still dominate many societies today, reflected a suspicion of the middleman. They were thought to make money not by adding intrinsic value to the traded item, but by moving goods or money to areas of shortage, or even, many believed, by creating the shortage in the first place.

WHY THE CHURCH BECAME MORE TOLERANT OF USURY

Important developments eventually moderated Church hostility toward business and finance in Europe. The Black Death, a plague more deadly than any before in Europe's recorded history, did much to shake the distribution of income and social structures. There were now relatively fewer poor to protect. Moreover, commercial activity also picked up; the development of new military technologies led to larger states, and therefore larger, safer, internal markets. There was consequently more opportunity to trade. Lending to businesses to finance trade increased. With the state also demanding loans to finance its larger spending, lending did not seem so exploitative—it was no longer primarily consumption loans to the poor untutored peasant but rather loans to financially sophisticated borrowers (as the modern parlance goes). Furthermore, it was less important for the Church to protect the borrower as more of the wealthy competed to lend. Also, the Church itself became an important usurer as it lent out the enormous wealth it had accumulated following the Papal Revolution.

Eventually, the Church's wealth made it a target for the state. As critics attacked the Church during the Protestant Reformation, monarchs seized an opportunity to cut the Church down to size, and it was rarely a factor in governance again.

THE BLACK DEATH

In October 1347, twelve Genoese trading ships docked at the Sicilian port of Messina after a long journey through the Black Sea. Many of the sailors on board were dead, covered with black boils that gave the illness its name, the Black Death. The Sicilian authorities ordered the "death ships" out of the harbor, but it was too late. Over the next five years, and over the course of subsequent recurrences, the bubonic plague pandemic would wipe out an estimated third of Europe's population.

The humanitarian catastrophe had a thin silver lining. The lucky peasantry that survived the Black Death now could farm much larger land holdings, could concentrate on better land, and were thus significantly richer. For instance, in 1341 in the English village of Stoughton, 52 percent of landholdings were eleven acres or less. By 1477, only 16 percent were that size, with 58 percent of holdings larger than thirty acres.[20] With many in the community becoming more prosperous, life became less precarious, and the need for emergency consumption loans and Church charity diminished.

The poor were still around, albeit fewer in number. Fortunately, with more people possessing surplus resources, competition to lend to those in adversity increased. With vast tracts of now-untilled land as well as commercial opportunities in towns beckoning the poor, the extremes in bargaining power that might have led to debt bondage no longer prevailed. Indeed, across much of Western Europe, the Black Death precipitated the end of serfdom.[21] Greater prosperity and competition to lend that prosperity now diminished the old rationales for prohibiting usury.

As we will see throughout the book, natural or economic catastrophes and technological progress are the big drivers of societal change. After the Black Death, technological progress took over. Francis Bacon, the seventeenth-century courtier and philosopher, saw gunpowder, printing, and the compass as the three greatest inventions known to man.[22] Their arrival in the West played a part in the expansion of markets, and the further weakening of the feudal community as well as the Catholic Church. They also heralded the rise of the nation-state, a key player in our narrative.

CANNONS AND
INTERNAL COMMERCE

In feudal Europe around the turn of the first millennium, all that it seemed to take to create a self-sufficient political entity—it would be too much to call this a state—were fortified walls and a retinue of armed men. Indeed, often the first use of the independent taxation authority a town received was to build a strong wall—a policy that still appeals to some of our politicians.[23] In the fourteenth century, by some counts there were over one thousand separate political entities in Europe.[24] Each entity levied its own duties, taxes, and tolls, especially on goods crossing its borders, which increased the cost of transporting goods over long distances. These were just the legal impediments to commercial traffic; entrepreneurial lords could indulge in their own banditry, while sea captains could engage in piracy. If you drive alongside the Rhine near Frankfurt today, you will see the castles of the original robber barons at regular intervals, though today they only relieve tourists of their money, and in a far more civilized way than in the past. All these impediments ensured that the size of the market any producer could safely and profitably access was quite small—often only within the borders of the little political entity he resided in.

The cannon changed everything. The Chinese invented gunpowder, but it was the Europeans who fully discovered and developed its destructive potential. At the battle of Crecy in 1346, English bowmen used small bombards, which, primed with gunpowder, shot little iron balls to frighten enemy horses.[25] A hundred years later, massive siege cannons could demolish even the strongest fortifications. Techniques of fortifying changed in response, so the net effect of the cannon was to increase both the cost of attack and of defense.

Military techniques also changed. Cannonballs and musket fire could slaughter charging armored knights on horseback. However, muskets took time to reload, which meant an experienced musketeer even in the beginning

of the seventeenth century could shoot a round only once every two minutes.[26] Against a cavalry charge, this meant essentially only one shot between
the enemy coming into range and the commencement of hand-to-hand combat. The tactical solution was to have musketeers drawn up in long parallel
lines, with the first line firing then stepping behind the second to reload, and
so on, so that near-continuous volleys of fire could be directed at the enemy.
To be effective, the army needed many more recruits with substantial drilling
and discipline, which meant a large standing army.[27] The size of armies of
some states increased tenfold between 1500 and 1700.[28]

To afford both cannonry and an army, any political entity required a larger
catchment area, both to find peasant recruits and to find taxes to pay their
bills. Little political entities no longer had the population nor could afford the
minimum necessary expenditure. The average size of the state increased as
entrepreneurial rulers started integrating smaller entities in the fifteenth
century, and by the end of the century, the number of entities had halved to
around five hundred. By 1900, these were down to twenty-five or so.[29]

The expansion in the size of the political state also meant an expansion in
the size of its domestic market. Monarchs increasingly obtained monopoly
control over violence within their country by controlling the powerful landed
magnates, a subject we will explore in greater detail in the next chapter. They
also suppressed the entrepreneurial robber barons and pirates, making trade
routes safe.

This meant that producers could sell in the entire national market. Moreover, in the thirteenth and fourteenth centuries, aids to navigation like the
dry compass and the astrolabe, coupled with new technologies in ships such
as multiple masts with lateen sails and the sternpost-mounted rudder, which
improved ship maneuverability and stability, meant ships no longer had to
hug the coast, and could venture much farther out at lower risk. This expanded trade, and thus added to the size of the accessible market. With larger
available markets, producers could specialize, as well as raise the scale of
their production, thus reducing unit costs of production. As the prices at
which they were willing to sell fell, demand for goods increased.

In sum, political consolidation led to economic integration. When combined with maritime technological innovation that allowed trade with more
distant land, producers could now exploit economies of scale. European pro-

duction of crafts and manufactured goods, centered in towns and cities, expanded. And as markets delivered all manner of goods, the manor too specialized, with some focusing on cash crops like grapes, transformed into wine, instead of the earlier emphasis on necessities like cereals—for cereals could now be bought with the money obtained from selling wine.[30]

The increase in production and trade played an important role in weakening the case against usury. A master craftsman or merchant wanting to borrow to finance an expansion in his business or trade was not in the sympathetic position of an illiterate peasant living at the margin of starvation. As the community turned from consumption loans to small production or trade loans, public attitudes toward usury became more favorable. After all, it seemed only fair that those who sought commercial loans to make profits should pay a share of their profit out as interest.

THE POWERFUL INTERESTS

Moreover, the monarch was now an interested party. With the increase in the expense of fighting wars, he needed additional sources of revenue. The merchants, artisans, and moneylenders in the growing towns could be taxed, but yet more tax revenue could be obtained if they were freed somewhat from Church regulations concerning the just price at which transactions could be done or the interest that could be charged, and allowed to make larger taxable profits.

Furthermore, when rulers still needed funds after squeezing all they could out of the taxpayer, debasing the currency, and seizing the estates of weak lords, they had to make their way to the moneylender. There was always a danger that the king could turn on his lenders, labeling them usurers and refusing to repay. The few who did lend did so at high rates. They kept the impecunious monarch on a tight leash so that if he defaulted, he risked shutting off further recourse to loans, which might especially weaken his ability to fight off his enemies. So monarchs repaid enough to keep the loan spigot open, and were inclined to look for ways to permit such lending.

There was also a mighty potential lender: the Church itself. It had become rich, in part because of the way it had shaped rules governing usury and inheritance. Church treasuries were full of reliquaries, candlesticks, and vessels made of precious metals, which not only increased the grandeur of Church services, but also could easily be melted down, coined, and loaned. The French historian Henri Pirenne asserts that "the Church was the indispensable moneylender of the period."[31]

With both monarchs and the Church administration inclined to allow some borrowing and lending, ways had to be found. Many in the Church were not comfortable with violating what they believed was a Scriptural ban. Financial innovation helped satisfy those in the Church looking for a fig leaf that the letter of the interest prohibition was not breached. For example, bills of exchange allowed a borrower to pay interest to a lender provided the borrowing was done in one currency and repayment in the other. The interest payment was hidden in the rate at which one currency was exchanged for the other, but could also be justified as a compensation for the exchange rate risk the lender bore.[32]

Similarly, the Church, following Roman law, allowed a penalty imposed for late payment, *poena detentori*. It was then a simple matter to lend with a fixed date for repayment and an implicit agreement that the borrower would not repay by that day. When he paid a few days later, a penalty was tacked on, which surprisingly approximated the market interest that ordinarily would have been charged by less conscientious lenders! When there is a will, the market finds a way around impediments; financial innovation helped finesse the Scriptures, much as it helps aggressive financiers avoid regulations today.

THE STATE MOVES AGAINST THE CHURCH

Not only was the Catholic Church inclined to turn a blind eye to some types of lending, it was becoming weaker politically once again. Its pronouncements, including on usury, began to carry less weight. The Church's wealth made it an attractive target for monarchs. They preferred their subjects' wealth to stay within their control rather than be transferred into the hands of a distant, and possibly antagonistic, Rome.[33]

Much as social media today has allowed politicians to reach people directly, bypassing the filters of the mainstream press, Gutenberg's movable-type printing press allowed critics of the Church, abetted by the local prince, to gain direct access to the masses. The reduced cost of printing pamphlets, as well as the spread of literacy, especially among the growing business community, ensured that the Church could be challenged and the arguments would reach many more people than in the past. Indeed, conservatives at that time warned that "printed books and broadsheets would undermine religious authority, demean the work of scholars and scribes, and spread sedition and debauchery."[34] They were right! For instance, over three hundred thousand copies of Martin Luther's theses against the Catholic Church were circulated between 1517 and 1520, something that would not have been possible without the press.[35]

Additional pressure for reform came from secular law and secular courts that increasingly competed with the Church to try usury cases. Over time, though, as commercial and state activity necessitated the charging of interest, secular courts became willing to enforce loan contracts, especially when interest rates were moderate. French and English monarchs adopted the legal fiction that their moneylenders, both lay and clergy, were to be considered Jews for legal purposes, and came under secular law courts.[36] Judges, however, needed more than workarounds. Scholarly arguments were made to support the practical judgments of secular courts. As monarchs grew more powerful and independent of the Church, this meant more protection to usury.

As selective violations of usury prohibitions, such as royal or commercial borrowing as well as Church lending, increased, usury prohibitions became ever more difficult to justify as a purely religious matter. As the historian Richard Tawney has argued, the religious arguments for the prohibition on usury, by their very nature as moral arguments, had to apply universally, even though they were meant primarily for consumption loans to the poor. With the emerging range of new, seemingly defensible, reasons for lending at interest, the Church faced questions about how general the religious arguments really were.[37]

THE CHURCH REFORMS ITS ATTITUDES TOWARD BUSINESS AND INTEREST

As the Reformation swept across Europe, scholars proposed new doctrines to rationalize the expanding markets and growing prosperity, as well as the needs of the emerging powerful monarchs. Perhaps the most important of these from a commercial perspective was the sixteenth-century French theologian and pastor John Calvin, who fled Catholic France for the Swiss city of Geneva, where he became extremely influential. Indeed, in *The Protestant Ethic and the Spirit of Capitalism,* the German social historian Max Weber attributed the rise of the archetypal capitalist to the teachings of John Calvin.

In Weber's view, the true capitalist is not the flamboyant gambler who risks all or the unscrupulous speculator who wheedles his way to riches, but the temperate, reliable, hardworking businessman, "with strictly bourgeois opinions and principles."[38] The essence of modern capitalism is the steady accumulation of wealth, not because of the pleasures it can buy or the material needs it can satisfy, but for its own sake. Indeed, far from unbridled greed and debauchery, rational capitalism combines a single-minded focus on accumulation with a frugal lifestyle. What Calvin did for capitalism, according to Weber, was to provide it a moral legitimacy in a world where avarice was a sin.

Calvin emphasized the notion of calling, or predestination—that God has chosen some to be saved from damnation, and that their moral obligation is to do their duty in the world. Rather than abandoning the world, as was the Catholic monastic ideal, one had to embrace it. The practicing Calvinist had to have faith that he was one of the chosen, and had to demonstrate this faith through worldly activity. Business success was a sign of being one of the elect. Therefore, the accumulation of wealth was no longer to be condemned as avarice, but instead celebrated. Indeed, it was condemned only if wealth was spent on luxuries and high living—not only did conspicuous consumption reduce the savings necessary for investment, but it was also a waste of time, detracting from man's true calling. The Calvinist vision of capitalist society was austere—and Geneva under the Calvinists was a harsh dull place—but it gave the single-minded entrepreneur a moral compass and justification that he did not have before. Various Protestant sects influenced by Calvinism then spread to Scotland, the Netherlands, and England, and thence to New England in the United States.

Calvin's views on usury were consistent with his arguments about business. He maintained that the arguments against usury in the Old Testament were so that "mutual and brotherly affection should prevail among the Israelites," so that they could trade conveniently among one another without conflict.[39] It was an argument for a different age and different community circumstances, and could not be deemed universal—even in the Old Testament, usury had been permitted to strangers. Therefore, usury was permissible "if it is not injurious to one's brother."

Taking on Aristotle, Calvin asserted that money was barren only if unused. If used productively—invested in land or trade—the borrower is not defrauded when he pays a portion of his profits for the use of money. Thus all interest need not be condemned for otherwise "we would impose tighter fetters on the conscience than God himself."[40] Nor, Calvin argued, do the Scriptures prohibit a reasonable charge for money. Observing that the Hebrew word for interest, *neshek,* meant "to bite," Calvin argued that the Bible prohibits only "biting" interest, which oppresses the poor.[41]

So while Calvin's theology sanctified the pursuit of wealth and removed the associated taint of avarice, it also created a space for saving and lending at moderate interest rates. Such a positive interest rate was necessary to give the accumulative capitalist the incentive to be ascetic in his spending and save. It was also a pragmatic recognition that the needs of capitalistic business differed from those of the penurious household. While urging continued protections for the poor, Calvin opened the way for ordinary business lending.

Weber argues that Calvin also paved the way for the rise of capitalism. Instead, Calvinism may simply have been a rationalization and legitimization of emerging business practices rather than the wellspring for capitalism. Nevertheless, by transforming business from a furtive activity done in dark corners hidden from religious authorities to one that was publicly praiseworthy and indeed a route to salvation, Calvinism did much to encourage the further growth of business. Calvin may have imbued the bourgeoisie of Western Europe in the sixteenth century with a sense of being chosen and predestined, much as Marx anointed the proletariat of the nineteenth century.[42]

In sum, from about the middle of the fourteenth century, the Church's attitude toward usury softened, probably as much by necessity as by conviction.[43] Usurers were allowed to be buried once again in church graveyards, and various kinds of contracts involving interest were declared non-usurious, with only excessive interest being deemed sinful. While the Church's views of business were not irrelevant after the Reformation, its influence certainly diminished greatly.

Moreover, religion was no longer a significant unifying national force in the emerging Western European nation-states—some nations had both sizable Catholic and Protestant populations, while nations with predominantly Catholic populations needed an identity that differentiated them from coreligionists elsewhere. As we will see in the next chapter, a new form of devotion, nationalism, started edging out religious zeal across Europe. It too would affect attitudes toward business and finance, as well as the community.

CONCLUSION

Around the end of the first millennium in the Common Era, commerce and finance started stirring once again in Europe. As monetary transactions started undermining the stability of the feudal community, the community via the Church struck back and imposed severe limitations on the behavior permitted in finance and goods markets. Over time, and as both the unifying power of the monarch and the size of the market grew, some of the restrictions on business and finance started impinging on economic activity as well as on the monarch's finances. The antibusiness scholarly ideology protecting the feudal community and constraining the market gave way to a more tolerant view, which gave individuals greater freedom to transact—the dominant scholarly view changed with public need, as it invariably does, even though theoretical reasoning is not supposed to have such flexibility! Trade, land sales, and debt weakened reciprocal feudal obligations and replaced them with market transactions. The state and the market grew together, even as the feudal community weakened.

The Church's power also declined, leaving the nation-state in ascendancy.

However, its period of power had served a purpose—to push the state, at least in some parts of Western Europe, to acknowledge the possibility of a higher law, and to prod it into developing a more rational legal system. Two struggles now became more salient. One was the struggle for supremacy within a country as the king attempted to subdue the few powerful landed magnates who had the ability to match the king's military spending. An equally fierce struggle was between the emerging nation-states in Europe, as each tried to establish its dominance over others. These two struggles were the crucibles in which the constitutionally limited state and modern markets were forged.[44]

2

THE RISE OF THE STRONG
BUT LIMITED STATE

I n the last chapter, we saw how new military technologies such as siege cannons developed to overcome traditional fortifications and unify territories. No longer could every town or manor stand up to the king's men simply because it had strong walls. (I will use "king," since they were mostly kings, with due apologies to queens like Mary Tudor and Elizabeth I.) The emerging nation-state's military power was too much for the traditional feudal community and broke its protections down. The centralizing of governance powers had begun, though limited by the difficulty of governance at a distance in times when the fastest means of communication was through bonfires or via riders on horseback.

The nation-state still had to accomplish at least three tasks before it came to even remotely resemble today's strong state. The first was for the king to obtain a monopoly of military power within his territory so that it was a unified whole with a common market. To do this, he had to suppress the large magnates—the domestic dukes and princes—who had the lands and revenues to rival his military power. We will see that this took different forms, but in England, it was achieved through direct confiscation as well as, interestingly, through competition in markets.

The second task was to create an identity that would replace religion—since religion did not distinguish one nation-state from another in Europe.

That identity had to give people a sense of larger purpose. Increasingly, an identity that suited many requirements, including the king's need to lead a unified country, was identification with the nation.

Even after unifying the land under his power, the king faced external threats. Some European country was always trying to establish supremacy—first Spain, then France, and in modern times, Germany and Russia. Any European country risked subjugation if it was not militarily powerful. As his feudal vassals' obligations to supply arms and men waned with the demise of feudalism, the king needed money to maintain a strong military to defend the country against these external threats. Much of the subsequent development of the state can be seen as a consequence of steps taken to enhance its ability to raise revenues—the third task.

The nation-state that emerged had somewhat contradictory powers. It was strong in its ability to defend itself against external enemies and defeat internal threats to the state, yet it was compelled to respect the private property rights of its citizens. The constitutionally limited state was an important milestone in the path towards free markets. The security of private property did away with the need for private players to protect themselves through anti-competitive medieval business associations, such as guilds. It allowed them to compete as individuals. Greater competition raised efficiency and output, increasing the economic power of the nation-state that could foster it. The markets pillar and the state pillar now fortified each other.

Since different nation-states went through these developments in different ways, and my intent is to illustrate, not be exhaustive, I will focus on the path England followed, primarily because it was the first large nation-state with a constitutionally limited government. The process of stabilizing governance in the English nation-state took the Crown over two hundred years, spanned the reigns of two houses—the Tudors and the Stuarts—and involved substantial amounts of chance. Even though England's path to constitutionally limited government and freer markets was unplanned and idiosyncratic, through war it imposed competitive pressures on other European countries to change if they wanted to survive. Eventually, many reached the same endpoint, albeit in their own ways.

THE DECLINE OF THE MAGNATES

As we have seen, the new military technologies required scale. At the outset of nation building, the monarch was not personally much wealthier than the most powerful of the landed aristocracy. He needed to build his own power as well as reduce theirs. In the process of eliminating the threat of the high aristocracy, the English king unleashed market forces that would help create entities that would eventually curtail his own freedom of action. Interestingly, as the king lost the ability to act willfully and outside the law, as his identity was submerged in the broader apparatus of the state, the state's access to financing from its citizens increased. It could now expand in ways, such as maintaining a large army, which would earlier have raised public apprehension about the monarch's intentions. Somewhat paradoxically, the limited state became strong and improved its capabilities even while bolstering the confidence of the citizenry in the security of their property. Let us see how this happened.[1]

Henry VII, the first Tudor monarch, was the last king of England to win his crown on the battlefield in 1485. There were others who had some right to the throne, so Henry's claim to be monarch other than by "right of conquest" was questionable, at best. From the outset, therefore, the Tudors had to dominate other aristocrats through sheer power. This was not a simple or quick task, and spanned the reigns of successive monarchs.

The monarch's problem was complicated in two different ways. First, the landed aristocracy had built militias out of their armed servants, and could also summon their vassals and tenants to fight for them. Even as Henry VII passed a series of Acts asserting that the prime loyalty of every subject was first to the Crown and only then to his lord, feudal tradition militated otherwise.[2] The monarch only had control over a small militia, and was otherwise reliant on conscription. This meant that in any emergency requiring a prompt response, such as an internal rebellion by one of the lords, he needed the help of the other lords to defeat it. Second, the king did not have a large bureaucracy to collect taxes. He depended on the high lords to collect and pass taxes on to the royal treasury. With the king so dependent on the aristocrats, he simply could not take them all on at the same time.

Time and infertility were on the king's side. He had no need to create powerful new aristocrats, and indeed no dukes were created by the Tudors.[3] Furthermore, because some lords did not have male children, which was not an infrequent occurrence, existing houses came to an end. Through such means, Henry VII doubled his revenues from Crown lands.[4] Individual rebellious lords could also be picked off, convicted of treason, and executed, as was the duke of Buckingham by Henry's son, Henry VIII, and their lands seized by the Crown. Nevertheless, what really clipped the wings of the landed aristocracy was more indirect and perhaps unintended—the dissolution of monasteries and the great price inflation of the sixteenth century.

THE DISSOLUTION OF THE MONASTERIES AND THE RISE OF THE GENTRY

The Tudors were hungry for land, and looked for easy targets. After Henry VIII broke with the Pope over his marriage to Anne Boleyn, he turned his attention to the Church's wealth in its various monasteries, which had grown substantially since the Gregorian reforms. Monastery property had two attractions. First, it was unprotected by armed men, unlike the land of the magnates. Many monasteries had also grown complacent and neglected their duties toward the needy. As a result, they enjoyed only modest public support. Second, and perhaps more important, monastery land was poorly managed, which attracted the attention of the capable, who felt they could do a better job using the latest methods of agricultural management.[5] So when Henry VIII seized monastery property, giving abbots and abbesses the choice between being accused of treason, convicted, and put to death cruelly (they needed to be convicted because only the property of traitors went legally to the Crown), or ceding property "voluntarily" to the Crown, most made the obvious choice, and few among the public protested.

The seized property was soon sold, as the king needed funds to fight wars. Those who bought the land were primarily local moderately wealthy land owners—the local gentry. These were typically minor nobility, who did not have the vast land holdings the aristocracy had, but owned more land than well-to-do peasants. The landed high aristocracy were only a few dozen, while the gentry numbered in the thousands. The gentry had made their money managing their own properties well. They could bring their expertise to the new properties, especially because they knew local conditions and were closer to the land than the landed magnates. Since land ownership was the route to social status in those times, successful wealthy town-dwellers such as merchants and lawyers also bought land so that they could rise to the status of country gentlemen.

These men improved the management of the land they bought; including bringing unused land into cultivation; ending unproductive traditional techniques such as leaving one out of two fields fallow instead of one out of three; and appropriating customary-use common areas by enclosing them, and shifting them into more lucrative sheep rearing. Rather than continue with the feudal practice of demanding unpaid labor from tenants, which was anyway grudgingly given, these "new" men instead hired labor directly for commercial wages. They raised rents on existing tenants commensurate with the commutation of labor obligations and the increased incomes from the more productive land. Not all were successful in making a go of land management, but the unsuccessful sold out to others who were more expert. At any rate, land management improved substantially, increasing agricultural output. Some economic historians argue that England's prosperity in Elizabethan times was in substantial part due to higher national income growth resulting from the seized lands.[6]

Importantly, the successful country gentlemen, both old and new, went on to acquire more land. Some of the richer gentry came to own as much as the poorer aristocrats. Furthermore, because many of the high lords were not particularly good managers—after all, they and their ancestors had established their prowess on the battlefield, not in estate management—the incomes of the richer gentry far exceeded that of the poorer aristocracy. For crops that had a national market, the more efficient cheaper production from the gentry lowered prices and thus aristocratic incomes. The old guard was at risk of being blown away by the gales of competition.

The aristocracy, who no longer could distinguish themselves easily from lesser mortals based on land ownership or income, found new grounds for differentiation. What distinguished them from the nouveau-riche Calvinist gentry was their lavish entertainment and the liberal hospitality they showered on guests who passed their social threshold, their free-spending enjoyment of fashion, art, and architecture, and their sympathetic treatment of unproductive customary tenants paying low rents. These were exactly the wrong elements to distinguish themselves by as prices started rising.

THE GREAT INFLATION

The gold and silver flowing into Europe in the sixteenth century from its colonies in Africa and Asia first, then the Americas, raised prices of goods, as the growth in their production did not keep pace with the growth of coined precious metal. For the aristocracy, the tremendous increase in spending that was necessary to keep up their lifestyle and their army of retainers collided with the stagnant tenant rents that noblesse oblige demanded of them. Something had to give. For those who could not bring themselves to manage their lands commercially, it meant land sales and further decline—until some social-climbing wealthy merchant or member of the gentry could be persuaded to underwrite the aristocratic expenditure in return for a status-enhancing marriage alliance. For those who wanted to maintain their distance from the arrivistes, there was no alternative to moving to new techniques of agricultural production, raising rents on tenants who could cope, and terminating the tenancy of those who could not, for more capable ones who could.

The demands of the market—the competition from the gentry accentuated by the great inflation—thus killed the capacity of the aristocratic lord to look out for his tenant and see him through difficulty, the essence of the feudal obligation. At the same time, it also killed any loyalty the tenant might have had to his lord.[7] Transactions were now on strictly commercial terms—the market, by competing away the rents on aristocratic estates, once again had eroded community ties. No longer would tenants flock to their lord's banner in times of military need. For the monarch, this was a distinct relief, since his army was based far more on recruits drafted for a wage than on loyal feudal retainers.[8]

The king also undermined the landed aristocracy in matters of local governance. As the gentry grew more prominent, the monarchy appointed them as justices of peace to judge small claims and local cases, as sheriffs, and as tax and military draft commissioners. These positions were unpaid, but offered their occupants prestige and local influence. And they became essential to administering local justice as well as collecting taxes and administering services for the poor. As one historian put it, "the gentry were essential to the power of the king, but he was not essential to theirs."[9]

THE POWER OF THE GENTRY

All this meant that even though the aristocracy had been undermined, as had the Church before it, the monarchy did not have absolute power; a new power, the gentry, now stood in the way. The king was vastly more powerful than any single member of the gentry, but he could not treat them like Henry VIII treated the monasteries. Unlike the poorly managed monastery land, the gentry used their superior knowledge of farming and the locality to manage their land productively. There were no unrealized bonanzas that could be obtained through expropriation.[10] It made far more sense for the king to tax the gentry regularly than to expropriate some of them and risk upsetting an entire class. Ironically, one of the most infamous violations of property rights in history, the expropriation of the monasteries, had strengthened property rights by moving land into the most productive hands. With the markets having done much of the work, courts and their judgments soon established property rights over land more firmly, eliminating the last vestiges of feudal constraints on property ownership and transfers, while protecting contractual ownership and tenancy rights.[11]

The gentry also dominated the House of Commons in Parliament, an institution whose purpose we will describe shortly. It offered them a venue to coordinate their actions if they perceived any threat from the monarch such as moves toward expropriation or levying additional unapproved taxes. With their limited individual influence, they preferred an arm's-length rule by law that would protect all of them. They were collectively wealthy—a peer ruefully noted in 1628 that the House of Commons could buy up the Lords thrice over—so together, they could influence the nature of those laws.[12] And they were closer to their tenants than the great lords were, and thus could command more of the much-diminished sense of loyalty in their locality than either the great lord or the king. The gentry, not the landed magnates, thus became the primary source of possible opposition to the Stuart kings.

As an aside, the belief that widely distributed property leads to better security of property and stronger constraints on the state has a long tradition. Some societies set maximum limits on the amount of land anyone could own so that it would be distributed widely. The Roman Republic had an agrarian law that limited how much land any one person could own, which of course was breached as it progressed toward empire. In his treatise, *Oceana,* James Harrington, a writer in seventeenth-century England, argued that ownership of property was the source of all power, and the group that had the most property dominated government.[13] Influenced by Harrington, Jefferson's draft constitution for Virginia, written in 1776, required that each adult have fifty acres of land. The minimum limit would ensure that the owner would be reasonably prosperous and independent—if not quite a member of the gentry.[14] Yet we have seen, it is not just how land is distributed, the efficiency of owners also makes a difference—the inefficient monasteries were not powerful while the gentry were. The vibrant land market had the dual effect of moving land into the hands of the efficient and, through their competition, eliminating the last vestiges of the feudal community such as the loyal but inefficient hereditary tenancy. Such arrangements were sustainable only when competition was muted.

THE TOWNS, GUILDS, AND MONOPOLIES . . .

Even as they were suppressing the landed magnates domestically, monarchs continued to face external threats, which was the source of their perennial problem, their need for funds. The competition with other European nations for political supremacy was bloody and never-ending. Whenever any state became strong enough to potentially acquire an enduring advantage, the other states banded together to defeat its quest for domination and achieve a new balance of power.[15] Yet dreams of supremacy never faded.

Any money the monarch could access to fund his military machine, whether through borrowing or tax revenues, ultimately was supported by economic production. So competition between states for supremacy, in the long run, would favor states that had stronger economies with which to sustain their war machines. Every country faced steady pressure from the outside to beef up its economic capabilities, else risk subjugation.

It was not just enough to produce more—the monarch had to be able to collect his share in taxes. The more he threatened to take in taxes, and the more unpredictable his behavior in doing so, the less his people would want to invest in, or put effort into, income-generating economic activity. Instead, they would focus on hiding their income and wealth. The monarch needed a mechanism to signal that he would tax reasonably, even in times of war when he might be tempted to levy huge taxes or expropriate property in order to preserve his reign. So the king had to create institutions that would limit his own ability to be arbitrary, thus convincing people that their taxes would not be used to extort yet more from them. The Church was one such institution, but as discussed in the last chapter, its power was fading. In most European countries, monarchs therefore committed to levy new taxes or raise old ones only if approved by the representatives of the rich and propertied who, in England for instance, were seated in Parliament (and the Estates General in France and the Riksdag in Sweden). Given the difficulty of getting anyone to approve higher taxes on themselves, monarchs tried to find ways to not put the question to the representative bodies if they could find other ways of gathering revenues.

The obvious alternative was to do cozy deals with the businessmen in the towns, which the emerging absolute monarchs of sixteenth- and seventeenth-century Europe proceeded to do. Europe's first stab at a regime more tolerant of business resulted in a pro-business but not pro-enterprise economy. Government and business formed a closed community—or what would be called crony capitalism today. The towns were certainly not free markets.

Taxing Towns

As agriculture became more commercialized and prosperous, it could provide more taxable income. There were limits, though, on how much the powerful landed could be taxed—in France they were not, and in England, landowners colluded to pass laws in Parliament to avoid taxes.[16] Moreover, the king needed every last bit of revenue for the new forms of mass warfare because, as Louis XIV declared, "after all it is the last Louis d'or which must win."[17] So the king looked to the towns and ports, where excise duties could be levied on goods like beer and bricks and customs duties could be charged on imports. In England, for instance, over two-thirds of government revenue from taxation came from Customs and Excise in the early eighteenth century.[18]

In order to tax urban production, the monarch had to deal with town bodies like the guilds that had formed for different trades and crafts, as well as the emerging monopoly merchant companies. In the same way as the manorial community protected the peasant against the uncertainties of life lived at the economic margin, the guild in a town protected its members from competition, both from others within the guild and from outsiders. It fixed membership fees; hours of work; the prices the master craftsmen could charge, and the wages they could offer; the terms, number, and fees for apprenticeships; and it negotiated on behalf of its members with the monarch or with town leaders for restrictions to be placed on outside competitors. If the response from the authorities was inadequate, the guild was not above taking the law into its own hands. Some organized armed expeditions of their members to search out and destroy any competitor that tried to do business in the territory they had earmarked for themselves.

The guild was effectively a cartel trying to ensure all its members got a decent living in an environment of weak economic growth, but also seeing to it that none was so energetic or entrepreneurial so as to put the others at a disadvantage. Like the manor, it aggregated the power of its members, a necessity in times when the law was weak, and might often right. It was also a social organization like the medieval manor, providing economic support to those in need and encouraging interactions between its members. A somewhat disapproving description of members of the merchant guild of the Dutch city of Tiel dating from 1024 comments that members "begin their drinking bouts at the crack of dawn, and the one who tells dirty jokes with the loudest voice, and raises laughter and induces the vulgar folk to drink, gains high praise among them."[19] Like the manor, it ensured stability and comradery, at the cost of innovation and efficiency.

The Alliance of Town and Crown

The interests of the towns were initially opposed to those of the landed nobility. For the peasant working in the lord's fields, the town represented new opportunities. The efforts of towns to attract additional labor set them in opposition to the lords, who resented the attractive pull of the town on their field workers. Furthermore, while towns wanted cheap food for themselves and their workers, and thus preferred low tariffs on food imports (and high tariffs on manufactured goods), the landed nobility who produced food and consumed manufactured goods preferred the opposite. Also, the increasingly wealthy merchants and financiers were a challenge to the social status of the landed nobility.

The alliance of the town and Crown was more than just a matter of befriending the enemy of the enemy. Each offered something important to the other. For the merchant or the craftsman, the king offered protection, not just from physical attack or intrusion from manorial or canon law, but also from competition—he endorsed the anticompetitive guild and its practices through a royal charter. The resulting monopoly profits were the rents that are so necessary to sustain relationships. It kept the guild members united, creating a tight-knit association that was a powerful defense against other predatory powers of the time. The guild shared some of those profits with the king through periodic fees or loans, thus fulfilling its side of the Faustian bargain.[20]

Why Monopolies?

Why could the king not tax his people directly, instead of leaving them to the tender mercies of the monopolist guilds? As we have seen, taxation required authorization by Parliament. Instead, the king could offer royal charters directly, thus bypassing Parliament. Royally licensed monopolies were less clearly offensive to the people, since high monopoly prices were an implicit concealed tax. So long as they were on a relatively few items, they would be borne with only a little grumbling.

Equally important, the nation-states in their early incarnations had weak bureaucracies and therefore limited abilities to collect taxes, tolls, or custom duties. The king benefited far more by investing scarce revenue in an army of soldiers than in an army of tax collectors. Therefore, the guilds and the merchant companies essentially served as the king's tax collectors, estimating and collecting what was owed from their members. They often paid directly to the treasury upfront for the monopoly privilege, which reduced the king's need to borrow or rely on a costly corrupt bureaucracy to collect taxes.[21] Moreover, monopoly profits came into the guild's coffers as repayment for the advances it had made the king, so it did not have to stand in line outside the treasury for an uncertain repayment, unlike ordinary creditors. Finally, because the privileges came directly from the king for the most part (only some were authorized by Parliament), the guilds and monopolist companies became his loyal supporters, if nothing else because their continued fortunes depended on his survival. Every side benefited except the consumer who paid the higher cartelized prices!

The monopoly charter was not a secure form of property right. It was an easily transferred charter, not fortified by the competence of the holder—indeed, the longer the monopoly was held, the more inefficient the holder would get, and the easier it would be to expropriate, as was the case with the monastery land. What kept the monarch from large-scale taking-back-and-reselling of monopolies was probably concerns about the risk of angering a large group of merchants or craftsmen in the guilds or companies, as well as the loss of reputation and the damage it would do to the sale price of future monopolies. These were fragile supports on which to build large-scale investments, and typically such businesses invested little.

. . . AND MERCANTILISM

The alliance of town and Crown was not without other vulnerabilities. Foreign producers could compete with domestic ones and push prices down. Monarchs, however, had a very short-term view of economic might, perhaps influenced by the multiple reign-ending military threats they faced. They essentially believed that economic prowess depended on what was produced in the country in the short run, and thus sought to discourage imports and encourage exports—a practice which was called *mercantilism*. It was thought this would create more domestic jobs and income, exactly the argument that today's populist politicians put forward. A collateral benefit would be that as a country sold more abroad than it imported, it would accumulate gold and silver, allowing it to reduce its dependence on foreign loans. So over and above the domestic restraints on competition, nations imposed tariffs on imports, and encouraged exports by offering subsidies. Not only did all this subject domestic consumers to yet higher prices, it gave domestic producers yet another layer of protection from the need to compete and innovate. Indeed, that was the purpose of mercantilism—to favor domestic producers over consumers.

Mercantilism, as we have seen with the recent export-led growth of Asian economies, can be helpful in the initial stage of a country's growth, provided other countries do not join in. If, however, other countries practice a tit-for-tat mercantilism, it impoverishes everyone. Moreover, as economic philosopher David Hume argued, if a country did prove successful in exporting more than it imported through mercantilist policies, the resulting inflow of gold and silver would eventually raise domestic wages, rendering its producers uncompetitive.[22] Furthermore, mercantilism, appealing as it was to producer interests in the short run, created distortions over the long run. It led to inefficient production methods and investment in the wrong industries. It raised prices of goods domestically, and hurt consumers who consequently had to consume less. It prevented the imports of capital equipment that could help make industry more competitive (in some industries, then as now, countries also forbade the export of capital equipment or knowhow or even travel by expert workers for fear of giving up their competitive edge). Finally, it made producers yet more dependent on the sovereign for protection, preventing them from emerging as an independent power.

Clever monarchs repeatedly emphasized national identity as an alternative to religious, regional, feudal, or community loyalties. This made mercantilism easier for the public to swallow. Nationalism helped justify higher prices, for they were the cost of keeping jobs at home, thus making the nation stronger. For example, the preamble to the Book of Rates in 1610 (which set trade tariffs in England) appealed to this sentiment, stating that importing unfinished raw materials from other countries was better for "the people of our kingdom might thereby be set on work." Other finished goods imports were frivolous and not "for the necessary use of our subjects or any ways for enriching our kingdom." If it was desirable to prefer "our own people to strangers," it was better to set tariffs on such imports "than that the people of our own kingdom should not be set on work or the country impoverished by the importation of unprofitable or unnecessary merchandises."[23] There is probably no pithier statement of mercantilist nationalism—import less, consume less, produce more!

Nationalism attempted to bring the country together under one monarch. The advantage, then as now, is that it provided a potent force to motivate citizens to support a national program, usually war, as the power of religion to motivate waned. It also allowed the monarch to break down internal barriers—instead of town-based guilds with small local markets, the monarch encouraged nationwide guilds. The disadvantage, then as now, is that it could be misused to persuade people to support unnecessary wars or policies like mercantilism that served narrow interests, and were against the collective good.

Fortunately for England, it was hard to suppress competition and the market indefinitely. As with the feudal manor, market forces started eroding some of these cozy restrictive arrangements.[24] Skilled craftsmen who were unwilling to put up with the guild's anticompetitive rules moved to suburban and rural areas, outside the guild's reach.[25] Adam Smith wrote, "If you would have your work tolerably executed, it must be done in the suburbs where the workmen, having no exclusive privileges, have nothing but their character to depend upon, and you must then smuggle it into the town as well as you can."[26]

Competition from foreign producers was also a constraint on how restrictive local guilds or monopoly companies could be. In countries with long coastlines close to major towns such as England or the Netherlands, ships could bring goods quickly in bulk. If there was a sufficient gap between foreign and domestic prices, either because the guild set prices high or because it produced too little given unexpected demand, imports would flood in. The guild could collude with the mercantilist government to impose high tariffs, but with governments having limited resources with which to police borders, smuggling went on all the time to thwart such intent.[27] Most entities therefore had to be somewhat competitive, and could not become overly dependent on the state for protection and profits. Along with its independent gentry, therefore, England had a number of independent merchants and craft-masters, even amidst the monarchy-sanctioned monopolies.

In the next section, we will see how the monarchy became constitutionally limited and more able to borrow directly from citizens, but once it achieved this, it had no real need to continue to privilege certain businesses, especially as it also built out a reliable revenue service to collect its taxes. Conversely, with the government more predictable and solvent, business did not need the extra protection of organizations like guilds or merchant companies. Guilds became largely toothless in the two most constitutionally limited and market-oriented European states, England and Holland, by the end of the seventeenth century. They morphed into brotherhoods and friendship societies, characterized by annual dinners full of pomp and show and plenty of alcohol, but with little actual business.[28]

SUSTAINABLE FINANCING FOR THE STATE

Let us return to the problem of state revenues. Ideally, the state's *freedom* to act would be limited to legitimate actions, not arbitrary or despotic ones, but it should have the *capability* to act firmly and quickly to deal with the nation's domestic or external problems when needed. Herein lay the catch. If the king had a powerful standing army and a professional revenue service that collected substantial taxes, that is he had the capability to act, he also typically obtained the freedom to commit any act—hence the absolute monarchy of Louis XIV in France, for example. An alternative was to have a king with very modest government capability, for example one with a small army and no revenue service, as in England under the Stuarts. However, even though the weak monarchy's capabilities were constrained by the need to raise money to fund any new action, it had not given up its freedom to act. As a result, it tussled constantly with Parliament. England needed firm prespecified boundaries on what the monarch could do so that he could be freed to roam within them.

The gentry and the increasingly independent merchants and moneylenders were a potential bulwark against the king, a force that could place these boundaries. The king had to unite the forces against him, though, for them to have enough influence. This the Stuarts unwittingly managed to do.

The Stuarts' Errors

The Stuarts' need for funds led them to antagonize the propertied, both land-owners as well as businessmen. James I started selling knighthoods, a prac-tice continued by his son, Charles I. When the going rate for a title declined because so many were sold, they sold higher titles and even peerages. Not only was the old aristocracy aggrieved because their status had been diluted as they were joined by the newly wealthy, even the latter were angry because the titles they had paid so much for were devalued through overissue. Busi-nessmen were angry because customs duties were raised frequently without notice or Parliamentary approval, and when no other sources of revenue could be found, loans were extracted forcibly from the wealthy, offering little prospect of repayment. There were other irritations, but having united pow-erful elements of the landed interests and rich businessmen against them, was it any surprise that the English Civil War between the Royalist support-ers of the Stuarts and the Parliamentarians ended in the victory of the latter and the beheading of Charles I in 1649? Parliament and the forces it repre-sented, when provoked, was stronger than the king.

The Stuarts got another chance. After the death of the parliamentary leader, Oliver Cromwell, the Stuarts were restored to the throne. However, what Talleyrand said of the Bourbons was true of the Stuarts too: "They had learned nothing and forgotten nothing." The Stuarts tried to weaken Parlia-ment once again. Matters came to a head during the reign of James II, who was suspected of having Catholic sympathies. Catholicism was associated with an absolute despotic monarchy, as exemplified by Louis XIV. [29] With the economy buoyant and customs revenues pouring in, James did not need Par-liament to vote on new taxes to fund his small standing army. He increased Parliament's sense of alarm by recruiting Catholic officers into the army, and expanding it.[30] Parliament was further weakened because the king could dis-solve it at his whim, and he did so repeatedly until he got one that was coop-erative.

In his attempt to restore the dominance of the monarchy, as well as possibly Catholicism, James went too far and united the opposition. When James's Catholic wife gave birth to a son who would be a Catholic successor to the throne, both the party of the landed interests, the Conservatives, and the party of the moneyed commercial interests, the Whigs, invited William of Orange and his wife Mary to take the throne of England, setting off what would be termed the Glorious Revolution of 1688.

THE DECLARATION OF RIGHTS

James fled England. Given a second chance to restrain the monarchy with a shorter leash, Parliament was determined not to err again. An elected Convention, which later became the new Parliament, presented to William and Mary a Declaration of Rights, which listed the legal rights of the subjects that James had violated, and that the monarchy now was expected to uphold. The supremacy of Parliament over the king was established de jure, and the sovereign was now the "king in Parliament," not the king alone.[31] The monarch could no longer call or disband Parliament at whim, the monarchy's independent sources of revenue were curtailed, and all taxes had to be approved by Parliament, which could monitor spending and veto it if necessary. Similarly, the monarch's ability to override courts was substantially weakened, and judges were made independent by taking away the king's power to remove them. They were liable to removal only through conviction or by vote of both Houses of Parliament.

By curtailing the arbitrary powers of the sovereign, Parliament essentially allowed the monarch to become more trustworthy. He could be permitted to acquire more capabilities without raising concerns that he would convert them into unfettered power over citizens. For instance, the government built a dedicated reliable service to collect excise taxes. Between 1690 and 1782, the number of full-time government employees in this function rose from 1211 to 4908, an over-fourfold increase.[32] Similarly, standing military forces, especially the navy, were augmented substantially. England became a leading European power.

Of particular importance, the government's access to borrowing, especially long-term funds, increased. This did not happen overnight, and England had its share of luck in its early borrowing years as we will see, but the government's ability to raise financing cheaply, quickly, and easily from its increasingly wealthy citizens became key to England's subsequent military prowess. For instance, because of its better ability to finance goods purchases for its ships by issuing naval bills, the English fleet could stay on the seas for a period of six months without returning to shore. This was far more than the few weeks that were possible when its finances were weaker.[33] The fleet was now more effective, for instance in enforcing economic blockades of enemies. Money had indeed become the sinews of power.

Constraints and Capabilities

The Glorious Revolution changed nothing for England overnight. Indeed, the initial loans that were available to the new government were still short-term, and the first attempt at issuing long-term debt in 1693 ended in abject failure, raising just over one tenth of the desired amount.[34] Subsequent attempts were more successful but the greatest share of early borrowing was not from the public but from government debt issued to an entirely more traditional source, three monopoly joint-stock companies, the East India Company, the Bank of England, and the South Sea Company.

The Revolution's effects did manifest themselves over time. The Crown's borrowing was no longer on the personal account of the monarch, but was the responsibility of a permanent sovereign entity, the state. Future governments would continue to bear responsibility for repayment so debt could be issued for a longer term and repayment smoothed out. With improved and more professional dedicated tax administration, tax revenues were more predictable. So debt could be assigned specific streams of revenues. Lenders had more confidence in such "funded" debt for they knew that the tax revenues that were earmarked could not be diverted elsewhere without the Parliament's notice.

These "tripwires" were backed by an elaborate mechanism of monitoring. Many of those with savings to invest, as well as the stockholders in the three joint-stock companies, came from the landowning or business class, with a presence or influence in Parliament. So investors in government debt, through Parliamentary reports and committees, had information about government finances, and could vote to curtail or repurpose government spending if it impaired the chances of them recovering their investments. Property rights were protected by political power.

Government debt became traded in the market over time, so investors who might need money quickly could still invest in long-term government debt and sell it in the market if they had a need for funds—their loans were now liquid. Also, if they became worried about government finances, they were not locked in, and other, more optimistic, or more influential (over government) investors could buy. The availability of a liquid resale market for long-term government paper thus increased demand for it, and broke the need for investors to be tied for the long term to the government.

Even the three monopoly companies were not inconsequential in the development of the government debt market. The East India Company built a colonial empire in the East that was an important contributor to England's fortunes. The Bank of England, with its monopoly over banking services, could issue stock easily, and the proceeds were invested in long-term government debt. It also proved reliable in funding the government's short-term needs, which enhanced the public's perception that the government would not run short of funds. Greater surety about the availability of funds to the government enhanced the public's confidence that long-term government debt would be a safe investment. Over time, the Bank of England lost its banking monopoly, but it became England's central bank and retained a monopoly over money creation.

And finally, the South Sea Company, which was granted the dubious monopoly of trading with the South Seas (where there was little trade), helped in putting government finances on a sustainable track in a very fortuitous way.[35] The initial issuances of government debt after the Glorious Revolution were in the form of very high interest annuities that could not be redeemed by the government. The South Sea Company offered a deal to the government: It would buy the annuities from current holders and turn them over to the government in return for lower-interest government paper (and monopoly privileges). It offered its annuity holders the choice of its own stock or cash in exchange. In the meantime, both the government and company directors talked up the prospects of the South Sea Company into a full-blown stock bubble. Drawn into the frenzy, annuity holders converted to company stock at inflated prices expecting it to go up further still. Fully 85 percent of the government's high-interest debt was converted into low-interest debt. The erstwhile comfortable annuity holders were devastated when the stock price crashed. England's government finances benefited, stabilized in its early years by the South Sea Bubble.

More generally, all these developments meant that the high-cost short-term borrowing or bills that the government issued to fund emergencies like wars could be converted to lower-cost long-term borrowing once the war was over. Repayment would then be stretched out to smooth the burden on the taxpayer. The government's increased capacity to borrow during those emergencies meant there was little likelihood it would invoke the specter of national emergency to expropriate money from the wealthy through extortionate taxes or forced loans. For wealthy landowners and businessmen, healthy government finances meant greater predictability about continued moderate taxation. This gave them the confidence to make larger fixed investments in canals, roads, and eventually railroads that paved England's path to wealth, and indeed the Industrial Revolution.

Sounder government finances also meant the government no longer had to do special deals with a few favored individuals or companies to raise money. It could set itself more at arm's length, more bureaucratic in the sense of working according to a set of transparent rules, and thus create a level playing field for all its citizens. This also meant the possibility of a less-constrained, freer, and more arm's-length market. And the drumbeat for that, as we will see in the next chapter, started increasing.

WHAT DID THE GLORIOUS REVOLUTION DO?

As economic historians Douglass North and Barry Weingast argue, the Glorious Revolution tethered the monarchy more effectively through Parliamentary and judicial oversight so that its freedom to go in inappropriate directions was more limited.[36] What was not spelled out in any detail is what would happen if the tether was cut—for example, if some monarch turned his standing army against Parliament in violation of the unwritten constitution. This is where the previous history was relevant. Parliament had demonstrated through the Civil War, and by deposing James II in the Glorious Revolution, its ability to come together to defend its rights. Its power to have its way when provoked is what gave teeth to the Declaration of Rights and subsequent reforms.[37]

This point sometimes gets lost in the debate about the role of institutions in development. There is a strong correlation between the existence of "good" institutions in a country and its economic growth and prosperity, so much so that one of the more influential recent papers on the subject is titled triumphantly, "Institutions Rule."[38] While institutions matter, they rest on a bedrock of an underlying distribution of power among the constituencies in a country, which may have its sources largely elsewhere. For instance, the independent power of the gentry came from their commercial aptitude, their wealth, and their closeness to their tenants, who looked to them for sound management and good livelihoods. Unlike the landed magnates, no member of the gentry was extremely powerful on their own, hence they needed transparent rules and law to protect them, as well as a body like the House of Commons to help them coordinate their actions. At the same time, their numbers meant they could not be expropriated with the stroke of a pen or collectively accused of treason. The mistake when institutions function well is to believe that they would function similarly well elsewhere, ignoring the possibly different underlying distribution of power. The United States Constitution, when adopted by Liberia, turned out to be just a piece of paper, with none of the effective checks and balances that fill the Federalist Papers and characterize how the United States works.[39]

While we know a fair amount about the kinds of institutions that exist in advanced states, there has been far less study of how to create the right distribution of power. Simply distributing property does not help, because what is given can be taken back. As we will see again and again in this book, the existence of vibrant competitive markets that allow productive and independent owners to emerge is a large part of the answer—markets help constrain the state and protect property as part of the balance. As our discussion of England's emergence as a constitutionally limited state suggests, getting the right distribution of power also involves much luck. Perhaps this is why nation-building exercises in Libya and Afghanistan have largely proved failures so far.

OTHER COUNTRIES

The transformation from feudal vassal to commercial tenant, and the resulting shift in power from the landed magnate to the more numerous and dispersed gentry, did not take place everywhere, and rarely in the same way. Nevertheless, while every modern liberal democracy had its own idiosyncratic path toward constitutionally limited government, there were generalizable elements from England's experience. The key development, as argued in this chapter, was the transfer of large unproductive land holdings from the monasteries and aristocrats into the hands of the more commercially minded gentry. In the process of dispersing economic and political power away from the church and the aristocracy, a new independent constituency arose that benefited from a more open rule-based system.

In the United States in the early nineteenth century, settlers poured into the newly surveyed and auctioned lands in the West. Land was widely owned, and those who could not make a go of it sold quickly to those who could, so it was also productively held. The exception was the South, where both corruption and climate conspired to create large, concentrated plantations run on the backs of slave labor.[40] Studies show wider distribution of land, especially when also efficient, helped improve local governance. Rodney Ramcharan of the University of Southern California finds that US counties where there were large farms and concentrated land holdings (because of the kind of crops favored by rainfall patterns) tended to have less spending on education, a key measure of the democratic responsiveness of the government to public need.[41] In a joint study with him, we found that such counties had far fewer banks per capita in the early twentieth century, a measure of broad-based economic opportunity.[42] We traced such differences to the nature of governance in those areas. Therefore, even within a developed large country not so long ago, land distribution affected local governance, and thence economic opportunities.

As economic historians Stanley Engerman and Kenneth Sokoloff have argued, there is a more general pattern here. For example, countries in Latin America that started out with more plantation-based agriculture, and thus large concentrated land holdings, tend to have less broad-based political and social institutions today.[43] The lesson is not simply that land holdings concentrated among the few are bad for democracy—a point made forcibly by political sociologist Barrington Moore—but that substantial wealth held by a few with close ties to government reduces the possibility of the state working for the many. Such lessons apply even today. It is one reason we should be concerned about the rise of megacorporations dependent on intellectual property, as I will argue later in the book.

Market forces also do not always work to weaken the politically powerful, especially if they have alternative outs. The precise circumstances matter. As Barrington Moore argues, the boom in prices as well as the expanding market for grain exports in the sixteenth century in northeast Germany had the effect of strengthening, not weakening, the power of the landed nobility.[44] With labor scarce, the landed nobility could have moved to paying peasants market wages, and commuting feudal obligations. Instead, by common arrangement, they increased the labor obligations of the peasants, eliminated their ability to sell or bequeath property, and reduced their ability to marry, or even move, off the manorial estate.

What was different in northeast Germany (and Eastern Europe more generally) from England was that the peasant did not have much market choice himself. Central authority was weak and there were no royal courts that might have protected his rights against the nobility. Moreover, even though it was a common feudal practice that a serf who escaped the manor and lived in a town for a year and one day became free, towns had declined in size and prosperity in northeast Germany, and there were not enough of them to hide him or give him a livelihood, unlike in more urbanized England. In Poland, the land market was suppressed because of laws that prevented ownership from passing outside nobility.[45] As a result, rich businessmen, lawyers, and merchants could not buy land, put it to more efficient use, and put pressure on feudal arrangements. With few checks on the power of the landed nobility, market pressures increased peasant oppression and feudal obligations rather than diminishing them. Even today, perhaps because it stayed feudal much longer, much of northeast Germany is less prosperous than southern Germany.

CONCLUSION

The absolute monarchy symbolized by the Tudors and attempted by the Stuarts gave way to a state that obtained more capabilities after giving up its power to be arbitrary. Such a state enjoyed broader legitimacy among the propertied because of the widespread belief that it would continue to adhere to a social contract with its wealthier citizens and investors. This also assured it of access to finance from the wealthy. With the confidence that it had few domestic challenges to its legitimacy, and that it could borrow the money to meet external challenges when that necessity arose, the state did not need to favor a select few. It could operate at greater arm's length from the market. Cronyism steadily gave way to a more open business environment, which in turn created many more competitive independent entities that could check state power.

As England became militarily powerful on the basis of its strong state finances, and economically powerful based on its competitive markets (which positioned it well for the Industrial Revolution), other European countries took note. They did not want to lose out in the great European quest for supremacy. It would be too much to claim there was only one way to a constitutionally limited state. The United States, despite inheriting a very English governance ethos and becoming an independent republic, went through a civil war to suppress its own Southern landed interests.[46] France went through a bloody revolution, followed by war and empire before it eventually became a constitutional republic (barring a few short relapses). Germany went through unification, empire, war, democracy, fascism, and war again before it too became a constitutional republic. As we will see, the United States played an enormous role in post–Second World War Western Europe in ensuring that countries continued to see value in both a democratic limited state and in markets. Nevertheless, many Western European countries needed only a nudge postwar, because the underlying distribution of political power and the existence of structures promoting competitive markets made them fertile ground for creating a constitutionally limited state.

The recognition of private property in land, and the emergence of a market for produce and land, also hurt many as the feudal community was destroyed. While independent private property owners could coordinate through Parliament or Congress to influence the state, the peasant and increasingly the worker in manufacturing establishments, dislodged from their traditional communities, had no explicit rights and no say in their own governance. In the next chapter, we will track the final steps toward liberal democracy as industrialization picked up. The demand for a voice came especially from workers in the growing cities, whose squalid filthy communities needed public services. Having obtained democracy, as we will see in the next chapter, communities organized to get the political establishment to pay attention to their demands, especially that unbridled crony capitalism be controlled. The third pillar grew in strength once again.

3

FREEING THE MARKET ...
THEN DEFENDING IT

As the state eliminated military challenges within its territory, and as parliamentary bodies came to be dominated by propertied individuals, the wealthy no longer felt their lives or property were under constant threat. Parliament would limit the government to legitimate activities. With the state constitutionally limited, trade- or community-based organizations that would provide members physical security and protect their business were no longer required. Nor were restraints on competition that made these organizations possible. Economic philosophers could now preach the virtue of free and unfettered markets, while political philosophers could extoll the benefits of individual liberty and minimal government, even while both sets of thinkers took the safety of life and wealth for granted. In the eighteenth and nineteenth centuries, markets were on the ascendance.

Laissez-faire, first propounded by French philosophers known as the Physiocrats, sought to take the emerging relationship between the state and markets to its logical conclusion: The state should leave business alone to do what it must, letting the full forces of market competition play out. The philosophers did not explain what they would advocate if market participants tried to subvert market competition with the aid of the state—a development that Adam Smith worried about—or shut it down themselves by cartelizing the market. Nevertheless, as a blunt theoretical argument with which to

bludgeon the remaining anticompetitive vestiges of both feudalism and mercantilism, laissez-faire was successful.

Yet, even as the votaries of the market celebrated, opposition was building.
Not everyone benefited from the commercialization of agriculture, even in
England. There were losers other than the high aristocracy, most importantly
those who benefited from the old manor community. The worst affected were
older peasants, whose tenancy was terminated as their fields were given over
to more productive uses or users, but who could not migrate to the towns unlike the young. Peasants also saw their customary right to graze animals,
hunt for game, or pick firewood in the commons disappear without compensation, as the common grounds were legally enclosed and appropriated by the
politically powerful landed. As a popular ditty went:

> *The law locks up the man or woman*
> *Who steals the goose from off the common*
> *But leaves the greater villain loose*
> *Who steals the common from the goose.*[1]

The commercialization of agriculture broke up many a traditional English
village community, resulting in masses of unemployed peasants who migrated to the towns in search of work. This was Marx's "reserve army" of the
unemployed, which fed the Industrial Revolution.

The jobs in the hellish factories that mushroomed in the growing towns
were hard and dangerous. They did put food on the table but too many children
worked long hours, simply because they were more nimble than adults, and
parents did not know where to leave them while they worked. Families had few
alternatives since work back in the village had disappeared. Worse than the factory jobs were the appalling, polluted, overcrowded, and unsanitary urban
ghettos where the workers lived. Few employers were enlightened enough to do
anything about these living conditions. With everyone subsisting at the margin, there was little sense of community, let alone community support in these
anonymous, unfamiliar industrial towns. Every worker feared the job losses
from the emerging business cycles and financial booms and busts, which could
quickly convert a barely tolerable existence into utter destitution.

Parliaments, as we have seen, arose to protect the wealth of the propertied against the state. To ensure the right members were elected, legislatures also instituted a property qualification for voting. Constituencies were small and easily influenced while the middle class, labor class, and the poor were disenfranchised. With no political representation, and limited competitive pressure on employers to treat workers better (given that so many were looking for work), workers had little hope from the system for either an improvement in the workplace or in living conditions.

The workers, and urban dwellers more generally, needed representation if matters were to change. Their push for democratic voice had varying degrees of success over the course of the nineteenth century, but male workers obtained the vote in most countries in North America and Western Europe by the beginning of the twentieth century, for reasons we will detail. The expansion of the vote typically resulted in the authorities putting greater emphasis on public goods like sanitation, schooling, and safety nets. It did not lead to the newly enfranchised expropriating the wealth of the rich, as was much feared. The broader realization was that the democratically empowered community was not against markets or private property, it was perfectly happy to respect them when there was a sense that respecting these rights broadly benefited the community. Indeed, to the extent that the earlier balance between the constitutionally limited state and markets was based on the efficient holding of property, it was a distribution that the democratically empowered community could also respect.

With the expansion of the vote, the broader electorate's views on the state, the markets, and the relationship between them had the potential to matter. As we will see, democratic community-based movements like Populism and Progressivism in the United States toward the turn of the nineteenth century helped avert the cartelization of markets and the closing of opportunities for the small businessperson. With the democratic community's prodding, the state's role expanded, with new functions like antitrust and product safety regulation keeping the markets competitive and orderly, and friendlier to small entrepreneurs as well as consumers. Democracy became the mechanism through which the organized and vigilant community could influence the state and shape markets—parliaments started their transformation from solely protecting the property of the few to creating and preserving opportunity for the many. Let us now elaborate.

FREEING THE MARKETS

In his book *An Inquiry into the Nature and Causes of the Wealth of Nations*, published in 1776, Adam Smith argued that by producing for the market and maximizing his own profits, the manufacturer maximized the size of the public pie, and thus the wealth of the nation. Smith thus made the case for allowing the invisible hand of the competitive market, working through self-interest, to drive economic prosperity. The real damage was not caused by avarice or even the self-indulgence of the rich, it emanated from restraints on competition and the resulting distorted prices and quantities.

Seen in this light, Adam Smith was pro-market, not pro-business. Indeed, he was no fan of the businessmen of his time because of their cartelizing tendencies. In arguing against guilds and monopoly corporations, he wrote, "People of the same trade seldom meet together, even for merriment and diversion, but the conversation ends in a conspiracy against the public, or in some contrivance to raise prices."[2] About businessmen's suggestions for regulation, he emphasized that these should be "carefully examined, not only with the most scrupulous, but with the most suspicious attention. It comes from an order of men, whose interest is never exactly the same with that of the public, who have generally an interest to deceive and even oppress the public, and who accordingly have, upon many occasions, both deceived and oppressed it."[3] Smith was no starry-eyed forerunner of Ayn Rand, convinced of the heroism of the business class. Instead, he pushed for eliminating anti-competitive privileges, such as those enjoyed by the monopolist corporations of his time.[4]

He was equally scathing about mercantilism. He dismissed the notion that an accumulation of gold would make a country more powerful and able to wage war—for a country like Great Britain, any feasible accumulation of gold would be too small given the huge costs of war. What was needed to sustain a long war was greater domestic productive capacity. To give domestic producers a monopoly by levying high import tariffs or prohibiting imports was therefore either "useless or . . . hurtful." If the local product could be made and sold as cheaply as the foreign product, the prohibition was useless for domestic production would be competitive on its own. If local production was not competitive, the tariff was harmful for it raised domestic prices of the product, and diverted precious domestic productive capacity toward its making. Smith wrote:

"It is the maxim of every prudent master of a family, never to attempt to make at home what it will cost him more to make than to buy. The tailor does not attempt to make his own shoes, but buys them of the shoemaker. The shoemaker does not attempt to make his own clothes, but employs a tailor . . . What is prudence in the conduct of every private family, can scarce be folly in that of a great kingdom. If a foreign country can supply us with a commodity cheaper than we ourselves can make it, better buy it of them with some part of the produce of our own industry, employed in a way in which we have some advantage."[5]

Therefore, Smith pushed hard for freeing the domestic market from the hold of guilds and monopolists, while bringing down the barriers to foreign trade erected by the mercantilists. In the spirit of laissez-faire, Smith thought little of a government that tried to direct production or investment by the businessman from afar, for "every individual, it is evident, can in his local situation judge much better than any statesman or lawgiver can do for him." Indeed, Smith believed the government had only three essential duties: "First, the duty of protecting the society from . . . invasion of other independent societies; secondly, the duty of protecting, as far as possible, every member of the society from the injustice or oppression of every other member of it, . . . and, thirdly, the duty of erecting and maintaining certain public works, and certain public institutions, which it can never be for the interest of any individual, or small number of individuals to erect and maintain."[6]

A PHILOSOPHY FOR THE MARKET

It was a short step from Adam Smith's work to the manifesto for individualism and the free market, *On Liberty,* written by British economist John Stuart Mill. It was published in 1859, soon after the death of his wife Harriet, whom he acknowledged had influenced the work greatly.[7] Mill defended individual thinking and speech against the tyranny of the majority. He argued that the views of the community tended to be the views of the powerful or the majority, and there were good reasons to subject that view to challenge, including the obvious possibility that the majority view could turn out to be wrong.

Mill saw all individual actions as permissible that did not hurt the interests of others. Apart from this, he saw an individual's duty to society as sharing in "the labors and sacrifices incurred for defending the society and its members from injury and molestation." Society had no call on the individual beyond this. He argued he was not advocating selfish indifference to the community, but voluntary engagement. Not only would an individual's engagement on his own terms improve social enterprise, he believed "the free development of individuality is one of the leading essentials of well-being." Individuality should be valued in its own right and not just as a means to a societal end.

Mill thus sought to restore free will's role in the vibrancy and variety of human existence that Calvin had rejected. Calvinism emphasized obedience—"You have no choice; thus you must do, and not otherwise: 'whatever is not a duty, is a sin.' Human nature being radically corrupt, there is no redemption for anyone until human nature is killed within him." Instead, Mill argued that "Pagan self-assertion" is as much an element of human worth as "Christian self-denial," that it is "not by wearing down into uniformity all that is individual in themselves, but by cultivating it, and calling it forth, within the limits imposed by the rights and interests of others, that human beings become a noble and beautiful object of contemplation," and "in proportion to the development of individuality, each person becomes more valuable to himself, and therefore capable of being more valuable to others." He declared that "genius can only breathe freely in an atmosphere of freedom," for "the general tendency of things throughout the world is to render mediocrity the ascendant power among mankind."

Mill's was thus an attack on the stultifying effects of the community, the "despotism of custom." He viewed the freedom of trade, contracts, and markets as consistent with his beliefs on liberty. This also meant limits on the state, for "where everything is done through the bureaucracy, nothing to which the bureaucracy is really adverse can be done at all." Instead, the state should be an "active circulator and diffusor, of the experience resulting from many trials . . . [enabling] each experimentalist to benefit by the experiments of others; instead of tolerating no experiments but its own."

The state and the market had grown together from the crumbling edifice of feudalism. The constitutional limitations on the state that we traced in the last chapter did not shrink the state. Instead it helped the state build out its military and fiscal capabilities as it gained access to finance. Once the state had created a framework to ensure security and protect property rights, the proponents of laissez-faire started questioning how much more it should do. Smith and Mill were not rabidly antigovernment. Smith, for example, accepted a role for the state in education, as well as other services that would not be privately provided. For these reasons, he argued that the state in a civilized country would be larger than in a barbaric one.[8] Yet these nuances were ignored, as were his asides on the perfidy of businessmen if they were entrusted with their own regulation. Instead, public debate became focused on steadily eliminating any restraints on business practice, as well as any protections to labor.

Perhaps more than anyone else, the Reverend Thomas Robert Malthus epitomized the heartless side of liberalism, when taken to its extreme. In the various editions of his *Essay on the Principles of Population* published in 1798, he emphasized the tendency of man to reproduce faster than food supply. Man could restrain himself through self-imposed checks like delayed marriage or sexual abstinence, but Malthus did not believe these would work. Instead, disease, war, and famine would be the natural checks on mankind's lack of self-control. No wonder historian Thomas Carlyle termed economics "the dismal science"! Malthus was wrong. Humans do not have an uncontrollable urge to reproduce. Indeed, prosperity has been a powerful contraceptive, with people becoming less willing to have children, even as they can afford more of them. Fertility rates for women are now below population replacement rates, not just in rich countries but in a number of emerging markets. Nevertheless, his views offered those who opposed even humanitarian government aid a theoretical rationale. Any relief schemes for the unemployed or the poor only encouraged them to reproduce more, and thwarted natural checks and balances. The indigent should be left free to starve, for only through a market-induced cull would succeeding generations have a better life.

Even if such callous theorizing was never actually translated into action, it did help harden policies toward the poor and the destitute. As the eminent historian and sociologist Karl Polanyi pointed out, the Poor Law in England, which mandated parish support for the indigent, was made harsher in 1834, especially for able-bodied males. This was just as difficult economic times and the new machines of the Industrial Revolution were putting thousands out of work.[9] Some tried to put a better light on these policies, arguing they placed the community back in charge of any voluntary support, others claimed rich farmers were misusing Poor Law subsidies. There was some truth to these explanations. It was also true that Parliament was dominated by the propertied well-to-do, who had been complaining about the high taxes they had to pay before the Poor Law was reformed. Clearly, they were also voting for their pecuniary interests.

With the demise of feudal institutions, the powerful no longer had an obligation to the weak in the community, while market fluctuations and automation left workers, especially those who had left their traditional communities, utterly exposed. Something between the extreme individualism of unregulated markets and the enforced collectivism of an authoritarian, overweening state had to be rebuilt on the ashes of feudalism. Before getting to that, though, what did a market freed from all restraint look like?

THE UNBRIDLED MARKET

Initially, it resembled the perfect competition of textbooks, with producers competing with one another to give the consumer the best deal, but this did not last. For as Adam Smith recognized, competition drove down profits, making any producer's life greatly uncertain. The inexorable political tendency of a free, unfettered, unregulated market was for the producers, after experiencing the rigors of competition, to attempt cartelization.

John D. Rockefeller, the richest man in the world in his time, made his money in rock oil or petroleum, in the early days of the industry when oil's primary uses were for fueling lamps and lubricating steam engines. Rockefeller was not attracted to the risky business of prospecting for oil. Not only was unscientific drilling more likely to unearth dry wells than oil, excess production whenever oil was found in a locality could bankrupt producers as prices plunged.[10] Rockefeller wanted a more stable business, and he found it in oil refining in Cleveland, the urban portal to Oil Creek, Pennsylvania, where oil had been discovered first. As Rockefeller worked to make his refinery the lowest-cost producer—at one point reducing the number of drops of solder on the tin cans used to carry kerosene from forty to thirty-nine after checking that any further reduction would cause the can to leak—he managed to drive out the truly incompetent and gained market share.[11] Yet many, having sunk money in their investments, and having debts to pay, refused to quit, and kept the price of refined products low—so long as the price was a little more than their incremental cost of refining, the zombie producers staggered on. At one point in the 1870s, refining capacity was three times greater than demand.[12]

Rockefeller wanted to bring order to refining, and his first target was the twenty-six remaining independent Cleveland refiners. In 1872, as Ron Chernow details in his biography of Rockefeller, Rockefeller struck a deal with the railroads serving Cleveland, whereby Rockefeller and his cartel would get discounts (from the posted transport price) for the crude and refined oil they shipped. More egregious, the railways agreed to pay the cartel for every barrel shipped by the competing independent non-cartel refiners. Effectively, this meant the railways would face a higher cost to transport non-cartel products, and thus would have to charge the cartel's competitors more.[13] In addition, the cartel was to get full information about the oil shipped by competitors. In exchange, the three participating railroads each got a fixed share of the oil that the cartel shipped, and fixed transport fees, thereby eliminating the cutthroat competition they otherwise engaged in. The arrangement would bring stability to their revenues. Rockefeller's keen business sense helped him recognize that both refiners and railroads might want to cartelize, and the combination would be deadly to those not in the cartel.

With no alternative methods of transport, the angry oil drillers along Oil Creek decided to boycott the cartel and sell only to local independent refiners. Protesters attacked the railroads, emptied oil cars and spilled their contents on the ground, and ripped up tracks. Even as the industry was in turmoil, though, Rockefeller bought up twenty-two of his twenty-six Cleveland competitors. As an owner recounted, "There was a pressure brought . . . that if we did not sell out we should be crushed out . . . It was said they had a contract with the railroads by which they could run us into the ground if they pleased."[14]

In the face of prolonged public protests, legislators eventually withdrew the charter for the shell company at the center of Rockefeller's cartel, while Congress started investigations. The railroads, who were much more dependent on government favor and public opinion for their activities, backed down, and instituted uniform rates for all shippers once again. In the meantime, Rockefeller had created a refining monopoly in Cleveland, as well as a strategy that would serve him well going forward—cost efficiency was good, but monopoly on top of it was even better. Five years after what became known as the Cleveland Massacre, Rockefeller's company, Standard Oil, controlled 90 percent of oil refined in the United States. There were about a hundred struggling small independent refiners still in existence at that time in the United States, which allowed Rockefeller to maintain the pretense of competition in the refining industry.

In Rockefeller's mind, he had only helped his inefficient competitors end their misery by taking them over—in many cases, he closed their plants.[15] The surviving refiners would enjoy greater economies of scale and more stable prices, their workers would be more secure in their jobs, and customers would benefit in the long run. This argument for cooperation among producers—coordinated by Rockefeller—instead of competition, while not entirely implausible, was entirely self-serving. Competition was the only guarantee in a free market that a producer would be solicitous to customers, whether through innovation, better customer service, or low prices. Faced with a refiner monopoly, customers were dependent on Rockefeller's benevolence. How much could it be trusted?

Rockefeller was a superbly efficient businessman in the Calvinist mode; he saw his work as his calling. His confidence in his own capabilities blinded him to alternative paths. He saw unfettered competition as greed, causing unnecessary booms and busts, and impoverishing the entire industry. What he tried to restore were cooperative structures such as trusts, pools, and monopolies that brought order to markets—and he had no hesitation in bribing entire legislatures or misleading public hearings with fake testimonials to get his way.[16] Manipulating government was just another means to business success. Many successful businessmen of the time thought similarly—Rockefeller was just more successful at executing plans. Many at the receiving end saw the kind of order he brought, which was spreading to a number of industries in the United States such as railroads and steel, as monopoly capitalism, perhaps the worst form of calculated greed. For essentially, the capitalists at the center of these cartels insisted that they, not the free market, knew what was best for the public.

The free market was not perfect. Bouts of euphoria, fueled by easy money, undoubtedly led to overexpansion and industry hangovers. However, eliminating these wasteful and volatile episodes would also eliminate the innovation, dynamism, and creative destruction of the free market. What the cartels called waste was in fact the constant experimentation fostered by the market, energized by competition. In a sense, the magnates of the late-nineteenth-century Gilded Age in the United States wanted to restore the aristocracy, where they decided what was best for the public, but without the explicit responsibilities of the feudal manor.

In many ways, Rockefeller's personal life was exemplary. He lived in the Gilded Age but was not of it. In the latter part of his life, he did take public responsibility seriously, figuring out how to spend his enormous fortune on the well-being of society. Among the extraordinarily successful institutions he founded are the University of Chicago, where I teach. His dismal view of competition had less resonance with Adam Smith, though, than with another insightful economist, Karl Marx.

THE MARXIST RESPONSE

The Industrial Revolution that started in Britain in the late eighteenth century created tremendous new possibilities as well as widespread despair. I have already referred to workers displaced by new machines like the power loom. In addition, though, the promise of new technologies, as well as new lands, especially in the Americas, made accessible by railways and the steamship, prompted waves of euphoria fueled by finance. The business cycle, with its production booms and busts, emerged in many industrializing countries, as did the financial cycle, with sustained booms in lending and euphoric rises in land and stock prices, followed by crashes. In the United States, there were serious financial panics about once every twenty years between 1819 and the start of the Great Depression in 1929. Among these were the Long Depression, a series of global downturns between 1873 and 1896, bookended by financial crises. The seventy years or so of relative financial calm between the bank failures of the Great Depression and the Global Financial Crisis in 2007–2008 were an aberration, not the norm.

Barring a few at the top of the societal pyramid, people in preindustrial times had experienced collective poverty. While industrialization, transmitted through the competitive market, lifted average living standards steadily over generations, what was also new was great dispersion in incomes across society at any particular point in time, and great volatility over time. The market offered bountiful rewards and merciless punishment, which was both its greatest economic strength and its greatest political weakness. Economic security, not physical security, was now the primary public concern in industrializing countries.

Karl Marx was wrong in some ways, especially in his economic theories, but he was one of the greatest social thinkers of modern times. He recognized that society adapts to, and is therefore shaped, by the underlying production technologies of the time. "The hand mill gives you society with the feudal lord; the steam mill society with the industrial capitalist," he wrote.[17] Subsistence agriculture bred feudal arrangements, while industrialization and machines facilitated capitalistic corporations run by the emerging bourgeoisie. The technology of production did not fully determine the nature of society, of course, but Marx was right in that it was influential.

Unlike Rockefeller, who wanted capital to be left alone to create its monopolies, or utopian socialists like Robert Owen who, touched by the plight of the worker, called for a responsible, sharing, capitalism, Marx and his long time coauthor, Frederick Engels, were convinced that capitalism itself was fundamentally flawed and would collapse because of its own contradictions. Moreover, instead of appealing to the social conscience of the elite, Marx wanted to eliminate them. He believed that it was both morally right and economically beneficial for property to be commonly owned. Marxists did not look for crumbs off the capitalist's table, they wanted the whole table itself to belong to those they thought were its rightful owners, the community of workers.

In their view, the industrialist exploited the worker through his ownership of the fixed plant and equipment of the factory, its capital, which was also why capitalism contained the seeds of its eventual downfall. Marx believed labor was the source of all value, and the only reason the industrialist made a profit was because the industrialist's ownership of the means of production gave him bargaining power over workers. Any worker could go off on her own and become self-employed, but without the machines she would be unproductive. The industrialist would pay her a better wage than the self-employment alternative, but less than the value she produced for him. The difference between the value she produced working for the industrialist and her wage was the surplus value accruing to the industrialist, the source of his profits.

The more unemployed workers there were—the so-called reserve army, set adrift as enclosures rendered agricultural labor redundant and better machines rendered industrial workers redundant—the lower would be the employed worker's alternative options, her bargaining power, and hence her wage. The industrialist's profits would rise. By emphasizing labor as the only source of value, Marx was wrong, but not out of line with economic thinkers of his time. This theorizing also meant that all profits ought morally to belong to labor, and the profits accruing to the industrialist were mere exploitation, made possible by his property rights over capital.

But Marx went further to say that the capitalist structure of ownership was economically unsound, and the world should change for this reason only, even if it was not convinced by the moral argument. Essentially, competition would force the profit accumulated by the industrialist to be reinvested in yet more productive machines, forcing more workers out of the labor force, pushing wages further down. Crises, where product prices collapsed and industrial losses exploded, could arise for a variety of reasons. Along the lines of Rockefeller's thinking, it could stem from the myopic greed or irrational exuberance of industrialists, pushing to get a greater share of the market, and ending up overinvesting and overproducing. It could arise when overindebted industrialists, pressed by bankers to repay, dumped their excess inventory and machines on the market. Most important, it could arise because the true source of industrial profits was appropriating the surplus value of labor. As the quantity of labor fell relative to accumulated capital machinery, Marx believed it was inevitable that the rate of profit would also fall, and hence the susceptibility of the system to accidents and crises would rise. A more modern version would be that as labor's wages were squeezed, the ability of workers as consumers to buy what was produced would fall, leading to overproduction and crises.[18]

When crisis hit, the Rockefellers of the industrial world would buy up failing competitors, close them down and fire their workers, and eventually restore equilibrium between supply and demand, but with much distress for all. The collapse of capitalism was not inevitable—it might be stuck in perpetual torment. As the Russian revolutionary Leon Trotsky wrote, "capitalism does live by crises and booms, just as a human being lives by inhaling and exhaling. First there is a boom in industry, then a stoppage, next a crisis, followed by a stoppage in the crisis, then an improvement, another boom, another stoppage, and so on. . . . The fact that capitalism continues to oscillate cyclically . . . merely signifies that capitalism is not yet dead, that we are not dealing with a corpse. So long as capitalism is not overthrown by proletarian revolution, it will continue to live in cycles, swinging up and down. Crises and booms were inherent in capitalism at its very birth; they will accompany it to its grave."[19]

The Marxist solution to the problem—ending competition—resembled Rockefeller's, except Marxists wanted to replace the monopolist capitalist with the dictatorship of the proletariat. Since they argued capital was essentially accumulated profit extracted by squeezing labor (or amassed from other dishonorable activities buried in a typical family enterprise's past like smuggling, bootlegging, usury, war profiteering and outright theft), the capitalist should be expropriated. All property would be held by the state in the name of the working proletariat, and a centralized bureaucracy would make production decisions. As Frederick Engels wrote, "If the producers as such knew how much the consumers required, if they were to organize production, if they were to share it out amongst themselves, then the fluctuations of competition and its tendency to crisis would be impossible."[20]

Therefore, instead of the benevolent Rockefeller directing production and prices, it would be the benevolent revolutionary turned bureaucrat. Once again, what would prevent the benevolent from becoming self-interested? No amount of idealistic Marxist literature prevented the chosen elite, the *nomenklatura,* a superclass that had access to the best shops and the choicest luxuries, from emerging in every Marxist country, even as the fundamental inefficiencies of centralized monopolistic production slowed growth. Without competition to show up inefficiencies and penalize the merely greedy, and without the decentralized decision making that Adam Smith and later Friedrich Hayek thought was essential to make best use of local information, centralized monopolies eventually ended up as a sclerotic mess, as exemplified by the former Soviet Union.

In a sense, though, revolutionary Marxism had the potential to be much worse than monopoly capitalism, for it eliminated political competition explicitly, concentrating political power and economic decision making in the same hands. Anarchists like Mikhail Bakunin fought against the centralized state implied by Marxism, and argued for decentralized self-governing structures, only to see their influence in radical Left circles diminish. The communists, like Rockefeller, wanted to retain all the power to decide for themselves.

Fortunately, neither Rockefeller's nor Marx's vision was realized in the industrializing West. Democracy preserved market competition, and market competition preserved democracy. That is what we will examine in the remainder of this chapter, and in the next one, focusing on the special role played by the community.

EXTENDING THE FRANCHISE

Early in their industrialization, most market economies concentrated economic and political power in the same hands—even in the middle of the nineteenth century, British cabinets were dominated by the landed peerage. However, as the dissatisfaction of the working classes mounted, the elite recognized that while their explicit responsibility for the rest had evaporated with the end of feudalism, some accountability had to be restored for the nation as a whole to function with more cohesion. The centralized government of the nation-state had stripped the community of some of the powers to determine local policies, even while the Industrial Revolution and the changing market brought many new pressures that the community needed addressing. Those lower down on the economic pyramid demanded a political say— else their plight would simply be dismissed, as it always has been, as the unpleasant but unavoidable consequences of progress. Undoubtedly, if the state was weak and ineffective, a coup or revolution from below was always a possibility. If it was stronger, though, the underprivileged had to stay broadly within the system to change it. In nascent democracies, this meant pushing for broader enfranchisement.

In feudal England, the right to vote was reserved for male "freeholders," that is, those who had independent ownership of land.[21] Ostensibly, these would have a long-term interest in the well-being of the community.[22] More plausibly, property holders believed that by keeping the vote restricted to people like themselves, they would protect their property from the poor. They would also prevent the state from expropriating their wealth to finance imprudent spending. Indeed, despite a war of independence against the British in which Americans from all economic strata participated, the newly independent colonies of the United States typically restricted the right to vote to those men with property, with only Pennsylvania and South Carolina going further to allow all men who paid taxes to vote. In all these would-be states, women and slaves were excluded.

Over time, the vote was extended. None of the states that joined the Union after the original thirteen had property requirements restricting voting eligibility. Even the majority of the original thirteen colonies that entered the Union eliminated the property requirement by the middle of the nineteenth century, with the battle over economic-based restrictions on franchise waged seriously only in the older states like Massachusetts, New York, and Virginia, where land or wealth inequality was more pronounced, and populations more diverse.[23] Even in venerable old England, suffrage steadily expanded during the nineteenth century as property requirements for eligibility were whittled down, in 1832 to include the middle class, in 1867 the urban worker, and in 1884 rural workers.[24]

The expansion of the suffrage was typically followed, both in the United States and the United Kingdom, by an increase in local public spending: on local schools open to all, on health care and public heath necessities like sewerage systems and public toilets in urban areas, and on local support systems for the indigent and elderly.[25] Thus community powers and activity centering on local spending strengthened as the voting franchise broadened.

The expansion of the suffrage was rarely linear. For instance, in the United

States, at the same time as economic-based restrictions on voting eligibility were abandoned under the populist president Andrew Jackson, groups that were deemed unsuitable for participation in community decisions, such as blacks, women, Native Americans, the mentally incompetent, criminals, and the newly resident, were explicitly excluded.[26] Indeed, on the eve of the Civil War, only the five New England states where blacks were few, and New York, which had a $250 property requirement applied only to blacks, still allowed blacks to vote. When Southern blacks obtained the right to vote after the Civil War, they started being excluded again through a variety of targeted measures such as literacy and residency tests.

Latin America also followed a similar pattern, starting with strict property requirements, followed by an extension of the franchise as pressure on landowners came from other citizens of European descent, and eventually a replacement of economic restrictions with literacy tests so as to specifically exclude workers and the poor, especially Native Americans. By the end of the nineteenth century, suffrage was still far from universal in much of Western Europe and North America, with women and minorities generally excluded (New Zealand was the first modern country to let women vote in 1893). However, there had been a substantial expansion in the electoral franchise to nearly all white men, a significant broadening of the franchise since the minuscule electorates at the beginning of the century. Why did this happen?

WHY WAS THE FRANCHISE EXTENDED?

As markets became more integrated, both nationally and internationally, economic adversity from far away could affect a community, and disproportionately the less well-to-do. In the same way that a free market decentralized economic decision making, a more democratic structure would allow many more voices to be heard, allow the local community to influence their representatives and the federal government, and allow people to feel more in control of their destinies. Political empowerment could compensate, in a small way, for the lack of economic empowerment.

Why did legislators, whose allegiance was to those who already had the vote, extend the franchise? After all, few who have power want to share it. We can dismiss the possibility that the legislators suddenly absorbed the spirit of the Enlightenment, believing that in the interests of fairness, suffrage should become universal, and in the interests of legitimacy, every one among the ruled should have a voice in government. While the rallying cry of the American Revolution was "no taxation without representation," it said nothing about the representation of those who did not pay taxes. In fact, the franchise was typically extended in steps, not in one go (as might have been the case if legislators became suddenly enlightened). Therefore, we have to look elsewhere for explanations.

FEAR

Economist Daron Acemoglu and political scientist James Robinson argue that an important reason for the elite to extend the franchise was perhaps the fear that if it were not extended, the unwashed masses might revolt.[27] The French Revolution was a warning to those in power that if they were not careful, many of their heads could end up mounted on pikes. And yet the Revolution could also be read as a cautionary tale of what could happen if revolutionaries were given a role in government. The archconservative Edmund Burke warned "the occupation of a hair-dresser . . . cannot be a matter of honor to any person . . . Such descriptions of men ought not to suffer oppression from the state, but the state suffers oppression if such as they . . . are permitted to rule. In this you think you are combating prejudice, but you are at war with nature."[28] This then was the dilemma that tormented the guardians of political power: Should the masses be kept outside the gate, with the hope that the gate would withstand their anger, or should they be let inside with the hope that they would be tamed?

Widespread economic adversity did certainly precipitate violent political agitation for greater inclusion. For instance, after the failure of the harvests of 1829 and 1830 in England, agricultural laborers burned the fields of the gentry under the orders of a mysterious Captain Swing and destroyed threshing machines.[29] Some argue that this led to the first voting Reform Act of 1832. Yet the state repressed the agitation fiercely, with over two thousand people arrested, five hundred transported to Australia, six hundred imprisoned, and nineteen executed. Moreover, the Reform Act gave the vote to those with property having a rental equivalent of 10 pounds a year, a sum far outside the reach of the laborer. It was widely alleged that the elite were buying off the middle class. At any rate, the newly enfranchised certainly were not in the crowd with pitchforks.

Strong incumbent governments might well resist acquiescing to the expansion of the franchise at the point of a gun; this could enhance the prestige and following of the opposing radical leadership, as well as lead to significant changes in the nature of government and of property rights as the followers of the radicals voted them into power. That is often why the threat of violence was, and is, met with savage police and judicial repression, as was the case again in Britain in 1839 when the pro-vote militant Chartist movement gathered revolutionary steam. The Chartist movement failed, in part because as Lord Russell—a Whig leader who favored expanding the suffrage—indicated, to give in to a demand backed by the threat of force would undermine the authority of the state.[30]

Nonviolent agitations for voting rights have indeed been successful. Those in power find sustained civilized protests—sometimes through economic channels like national strikes—unpleasant, morally deflating, and economically costly. Such protests also typically mean no dramatic change in the fundamental nature of the government and property rights when the demands are acceded to. While greater enfranchisement has typically been followed by greater spending on public services, it has not been followed immediately by drastic "soak the rich" policies, suggesting it stems from a compromise between those in power and the moderates among the protesters.[31]

Put differently, the violent excluded have seized power and fundamentally changed the nature of government, as in the American, French, or Russian revolutions. They have also been crushed, as in England. However, their movements may have shaken those in authority enough that it allowed their calmer cousins to negotiate their own participation in democratic governance, as in the expansion of the electorate in England. Fear played a role but did not always empower the violent.

NECESSITY

In some countries, those in power were convinced to share it because of sheer economic necessity. As economic historians Stanley Engerman and Ken Sokoloff argue, in frontier areas of the United States, land was plentiful, the existing population was few in number, and there was a great need to attract more settlers.[32] Perhaps this was why none of the states that entered the Union after the initial thirteen had a property requirement for voters—would-be settlers usually came without property. Moreover, as states competed for people, even the original thirteen were forced to weaken their voting requirements so as to not lose people.

If attracting people was so important, though, why did states continue to exclude women and minorities? One can only speculate here. Perhaps states felt that going against the prejudices of the time would attract fewer, not more of the favored settler, white men. Perhaps they thought women would follow with their husbands or fathers and few single women would migrate anyway. Perhaps they did not believe there were sufficient free blacks to attract. Nevertheless, even though the extension of the franchise was far from universal, and did not seem to rise above the prejudices of the time, the founders of new states were willing to extend the franchise, even without an agitation by the excluded.

In contrast, in countries which were already well populated, where property inequality within the population was more significant, and the inequality aligned with racial or ethnic divisions, as in the plantation economies of Latin America, the right to vote was kept far more exclusive and for far longer. For instance, the literacy requirement in the Peruvian constitution was maintained till 1979. Exclusion may have served a dual purpose here. On the one hand, it prevented a rise in public spending, which would have to be funded by a tax on the privileged property owners. On the other, it kept a large part of the population uneducated (because of the absence, or poor quality, of public schools), which meant they would provide a docile labor force for the plantations and other menial jobs, even while they were kept from ever acquiring the learning to pass literacy tests and get the vote.[33] Universal suffrage made a much later appearance in these countries, and the delay was not without costs.

For a variety of reasons, therefore, the propertied extended the franchise, especially when they felt the extension would not jeopardize, and might even reinforce, their property rights. Democracy then offered a way for communities to express themselves on the national stage, to feed policies like worker rights and worker safety up rather than to accept top-down commands from the state. In fact, as we will now see, it was essential if market competition were to survive.

POWER AND PERMANENCE

Power prefers permanence. Unregulated markets tend toward concentration as the successful try and entrench themselves by pulling up behind them the ladder of competition that they themselves climbed. Equally, the politically powerful are tempted to suppress any competitive threat to their future posed by democracy. James Madison was persuaded that democracy would work in the United States because in a large country with many different competing political interests, it would be hard for any specific interest to dominate.[34] Yet interests can coalesce.

It is when the behemoth of monopoly enterprise consorts with the leviathan of the authoritarian state that both are likely to achieve permanence. History is strewn with examples of these collusive arrangements, some of which we have already encountered. Communism brought all business enterprise under government planning and control, with the state dominated by the Communist Party, the self-appointed representatives of the proletariat. Business and the state were united under the proletarians. Fascism was different only in the language of the dominant group and its stated aims, which was national supremacy instead of the communist paradise of the universal brotherhood of workers. In practice, fascism too involved permanent party dominance of the state, and state control of industry. Today, we have milder versions of these totalitarian regimes, with state-controlled capitalism in countries like China and Russia, and authoritarian capitalism in Turkey.

While the nomenclatures vary, at the heart of such regimes is a pact between the cartelized market and the state, leaving little room for economic or political competition, or the community. Such arrangements are examples of what political economists Douglass North, John Wallis, and Barry Weingast call *limited-access* societies.[35] In contrast, the liberal market democracies in developed countries are what they call *open-access* societies, combining free and open markets with vibrant democratic control over the government. Implicit in the work of a number of political scientists is the belief that open-access societies are the desirable pinnacle of social development, and they will not regress back to limited-access societies because of the strong institutions that protect them. They are probably right in believing that open-access societies are the best we can do for now, but they are mistaken in thinking that open-access societies cannot regress. To prevent regression, it is critical that the balance be maintained. As we will see now, communities of citizens, expressing their interests through democracy, played an important role in the United States in preventing a corrupt compact between the state and the markets.

HOW THE UNITED STATES PRESERVED A COMPETITIVE MARKET

In a recent study, Harvard economists Edward Glaeser and Claudia Goldin graphed the relative frequency of the appearance of the words "fraud" and "corruption" in the *New York Times* relative to the word "political" over time.[36] They find a steady decline from the time of the notoriously corrupt Ulysses Grant presidency in the 1870s (not coincidentally, about the time of Rockefeller's Cleveland Massacre) till about the time of the Nixon presidency in the early 1970s. They conclude that political corruption declined steadily in the United States, especially between the late 1870s and 1920s.

Two great democratic reform movements date from around this time, first the Populists from the 1870s till the mid-1890s, then the Progressives from the mid-1890s till the end of World War I. The first movement was born out of adversity and anger, and the second was a middle-class movement, which flourished largely in a time of prosperity. As they fought against the privileged, and for the ordinary unconnected individual, these movements introduced a measure of restraint on political corruption and the associated creeping monopolization of American business. Both movements sought to constrain the unfettered market in order to make it work for the forgotten common man. While neither was entirely successful in its aims, together they provided a needed course correction for the United States.

The Sources of Corruption

Political corruption was an issue from early on in US history. Most accusations centered on the close ties between big business and politicians.[37] For example, legislatures could grant monopoly charters of incorporation to banks but also to infrastructure like pipelines and canals. Particularly problematic were the railways, which used their influence over legislatures to secure land grants, tax exemptions, municipal and state subsidies, and public loans. Historian John Hicks, in his classic, *The Populist Revolt,* asserts that entire legislatures and governments were bought by the railways, sometimes by the simple expedient of giving everyone who might be remotely useful a free and unlimited railway pass.[38]

With high levels of corruption as the nineteenth century came to an end, the United States was in danger of turning into a plutocracy where large trusts and corporations like Standard Oil, United States Steel Corporation, or Consolidated Tobacco, coordinated by financiers like John Pierpont Morgan, controlled large swaths of the corporate landscape as well as government policy. The two successive reform movements helped arrest and reverse the drift toward crony capitalism.[39]

The Populists

In the United States, populism, then and now, is typically a movement that emphasizes the purity of the common people and their simple values, the self-interested, corrupt, and undemocratic behavior of the elite, and the need for the people to organize against the elite to effect change. In the last quarter of the nineteenth century, the Populist movement arose out of the discontentment of indebted small farmers. Farmers had been lured West by the expansion of railroads and the steady eviction of the Native Americans. As land became increasingly settled, unoccupied land was hard to find, and land prices went up.[40] Unlike their predecessors who arrived when the West had not yet been settled, the new settlers took on significant amounts of debt as they purchased land. If harvests failed, they could not simply up stakes and move to new lands—there were no good lands left that were cheap. Moreover, they had the millstone of unpaid debt tying them to their farms.

When, in 1879, the United States returned to the gold standard, the debt the farmers owed was fixed to the steady dollar price of gold. The prices for their produce continued falling, though, in what is known as the Great Deflation between the 1870s and 1890s. The deflation was caused, in part, by the limited availability of gold, which caused everything else to fall in price relative to it (and the dollar). In the words of Populist leader William Jennings Bryan, with fixed payments on debt and falling revenues, farmers had been crucified by the Eastern financial establishment "on a cross of gold."

The situation of farmers worsened as droughts devastated the Great Plains in the late 1880s. Some returned to the East from whence they had come— one returning wagon bore the sign, "In God we trusted, in Kansas we busted."[41] Many tried to make a go of it, though, some because they had no alternative—they had given up their horses and wagons as collateral for loans and could not move, even if they wanted to. In addition to their concerns about financial injustice, the farmers had grievances: against monopolist railroads that had sold them overpriced land in the first place, and now arbitrarily increased freight rates for transporting their produce; against the elevator operators who charged them exorbitant rates for storing grain, as well as against Eastern manufacturers who lobbied for protective import tariffs that increased farmer input costs, even while resisting tariffs for farm produce.

The farmers tried to make common cause with others who were aggrieved. The Populist platform of 1892 emphasized this broader coalition: "We meet in the midst of a nation brought to the verge of moral, political, and material ruin. Corruption dominates the ballot-box, the Legislatures, the Congress, and touches even the ermine of the bench . . . The newspapers are largely subsidized or muzzled, public opinion silenced, business prostrated, homes covered with mortgages, labor impoverished, and the land concentrating in the hands of the capitalists. The urban workmen are denied the right to organize for self-protection, imported pauperized labor beats down their wages . . .

The fruits of the toil of millions are boldly stolen to build up colossal fortunes for a few . . . and the possessors of these, in turn, despise the Republic . . ."[42]

The Populists wanted silver to be added to scarce gold in the monetary base so that farm produce prices would increase and farmer indebtedness (in terms of produce) would fall. They sought a program that would allow farmers to borrow money from the federal government to store their crops until prices rose enough for them to be profitable. And they wanted debt relief. In fact, the Populists were really asking for a safety net to replace the natural safety net that the wide-open frontier had provided earlier settlers. In addition, the Populists wanted to reduce the concentration of economic power through antitrust laws (they wanted to nationalize the railways) and a graduated income tax, and bring more political power to the people by making the ballot secret and giving them the right to elect senators directly.

The movement largely ended soon after the 1896 presidential election. It probably petered out because growing farm prosperity from the mid-1890s on, coupled with inflation of farm produce prices as gold was found in Alaska, the Yukon, and South Africa, rendered farm debts more manageable. A bankruptcy code enacted in 1898 further relieved those who could not pay. The Populists were also not entirely ineffective in obtaining legislative responses to other grievances. Congress set up the Interstate Commerce Commission in 1887 to regulate railway freight rates, and passed the Sherman Antitrust Act in 1890 to prevent the creation of large monopoly trusts. While recent academic studies question the effectiveness of these legislative acts, they were symbolic blows for the principle that the market could not be left unfettered.[43] Finally, the Populists did secure the secret ballot and direct elections of senators.

More broadly, Populism was a cry from people who wanted more from their democracy, and whose geographically dispersed communities were brought together by widespread economic distress. The more universal themes of the Populist movement—that the market has to be saved from the anticompetitive actions of its strongest participants and that the federal government has some responsibility for public welfare—continue to resurface even today.

THE PROGRESSIVES

As the Populist movement petered out with rising prosperity, the Progressive movement gained strength. In contrast to the Populist farmers, the Progressives, many of whom came from solid middle-class urban backgrounds, were not so concerned about their own capacity to survive economically. Their worries had more to do with the shrinkage in economic opportunity for the small businessman as giant trusts colluded with corrupt politicians to dominate certain industries. They also were perturbed about relative decline. Growing inflation—which they believed was accelerated by monopoly prices—and the stupendous fortunes being accumulated by the rich, diminished their own comfortable positions by comparison. Paralleling today's middle-class concerns about the "top one percent" earners, they were appalled by the incomes and uninhibited behavior of the rich "upper ten," even as they feared the threats to their own way of life in cities that were exploding in size and diversity. They worried about the safety of the workplace, the quality of the food they ate, the temptations men faced from alcohol, prostitution, and gambling as they ventured out of the home, the second-class citizenship of women, and the quality of the education their children received. They were perturbed by growing class conflict such as the bloody Pullman Strike of 1894 and the United Metal Workers strike of 1902. They did not want to overthrow the system, they simply wanted to reform it to reflect middle-class values.

The Progressives believed a level playing field created by transparent, well-enforced regulations would restore broad-based economic freedom. They also wanted these freedoms to be tempered by responsibility toward the family and the broader community. Such changes in human behavior could be effected gradually, through education and socialization, but that would take time. In the short run, therefore, the Progressives pushed for greater government involvement, as well as the professionalization of functions like teaching and medicine to force the change in behavior. Unfortunately, the federal and state governments were rarely content to stay confined to the precise areas identified by the Progressives, and usually the government bureaucracy, as well as the professional organizations such as teacher associations assumed much more power. In turn, this tended to usurp power from the communities, reducing local control as well as the customization of policies to local needs, leaving citizens less engaged. We will examine some of this in the next chapter.

Opposition to the Progressive program mounted after the end of World War I, when people, having just emerged from a bloody war, became tired of Progressive sermonizing and government-imposed constraints on their behavior, such as Prohibition. Jazz and the Roaring Twenties were certainly not part of the Progressive agenda, and effectively marked the end of the movement.

The Progressives nevertheless had an important, lasting, influence. They emphasized three ways short of socialism that big business could be contained, thus preserving competition in the market. The first was through antitrust legislation and judicial enforcement. The second was through regulation. The third was through taxation. All three are still with us.

The most important was antitrust or competition law, which prohibited collusive practices in industry as well as the formation or continuation of corporate structures that might substantially reduce competition. In the choice between protecting property rights and preserving competition, antitrust law came down firmly on the side of competition.

One of the biggest initial targets was Rockefeller's Standard Oil. Between 1902 and 1904, Ida Tarbell, the daughter of one of the oil producers who had been squeezed by Rockefeller in Oil Creek, wrote nineteen articles in *McClure's Magazine* exposing "The History of the Standard Oil Company." Tarbell, a dedicated investigator who pierced through the mass of seemingly impenetrable corporate structures and deals, detailed how Standard Oil had achieved its dominance. Even though "there was not a lazy bone in the organization, not an incompetent hand, not a stupid head," she concluded, "They had never played fair, and that ruined their greatness for me."[44] In 1906, responding in part to the public furor stemming from Tarbell's articles, the federal government filed a suit under the Sherman Antitrust Act to dissolve Standard Oil, and in 1911 the Supreme Court finally upheld a verdict demanding its breakup.[45] In 1914, the Clayton Act further clarified and barred anticompetitive practices and the Federal Trade Commission was set up to enforce antitrust legislation.

An alternative to breaking up a monopoly, especially if it was in an industry that was more productively serviced by a single company (also termed a "natural monopoly") was to regulate it. Regulation also made sense when the consumer could not discern product quality up front or had to rely on promises of responsible corporate behavior such as adequate after-sale service.

Once again, the "muckraking" press played a role in energizing public opinion. Upton Sinclair's *The Jungle,* published in serial form in 1905, was primarily about the exploitative conditions faced by immigrant factory workers in the United States, but public attention focused on the filthy, unhygienic practices the book detailed in the meatpacking industry. Perhaps most frightening and revolting was his account of workers accidentally falling into great lard vats and their bodies being ground up along with other animal parts into "Durham's Pure Leaf Lard," which was then sold for public consumption. Once again, public outrage prompted an inquiry, which substantiated many of Sinclair's allegations about unsanitary and unsafe conditions in the meatpacking industry (though not the one about workers being ground up). In 1906, Congress passed the Meat Inspection Act as well as the Pure Food and Drug Act, which established the department that was later renamed the Food and Drug Administration in 1930.

Perhaps the most important regulatory agency of our time was set up in the Progressive era, somewhat ironically, because of the public-spirited actions of private individuals. In 1907, the failure of the Knickerbocker Trust Company set off a panic, which was arrested only when J. P. Morgan (and John D. Rockefeller) invested money along with other New York bankers to support the financial system. Conscious that the nation's financial system had become overly dependent on one banker, and aware of the potential for abuse, Congress passed the Federal Reserve Act of 1913. It brought the monetary system of the United States under the aegis of the Federal Reserve Board. The Populist anger with large Eastern banks was, however, only fully propitiated in 1933, with the passage of the Glass-Steagall Act, breaking up the large banks and forcing them to divest their investment banking arms.

The third element of the package to contain big business was taxation. This was perhaps the least-important piece, for there was really no desire to tax big business out of existence—after all, scale might be a source of efficiency and could reduce costs of production. Instead, following increasing public concern about large inherited fortunes and conspicuous consumption, taxation emerged as a tool to limit excessive concentration of business ownership, especially in the hands of individual inheritors. In the 1890s, fifteen states instituted taxes on large inheritances; more than forty states had inheritance taxes in place by the 1910s.[46]

Each of these ways of containing big business has limitations. As Adam Smith recognized, regulatory bodies often become subservient to the powerful among the regulated—in which case, paradoxically, regulations become a tool with which to protect the powerful and stifle competition. Once again, democratic vigilance can prevent an excessively cozy relationship between the regulator and the regulated—the balance is critical. Both the Populist and Progressive movements managed to push through important reforms that prevented large corporations and trusts from shutting off business opportunity or abusing the public. They set limits to laissez-faire, and far from killing the market, preserved competition and thus its vibrancy.

CONCLUSION

As the state became constitutionally limited through Parliament, which was dominated by the propertied interests, these interests no longer needed feudal protections against it. Free of the fear of expropriation by the state, the markets flourished, but sometimes to the detriment of the community. The fight for suffrage was, in many ways, a fight by the community for some of its lost power. As it regained power, the community helped restore the balance.

This was necessary because, in the absence of any restraints, the new robber barons who emerged from the initial frenzy of market competition preferred to secure their positions by eliminating competition. The tendency toward monopolies that was so apparent in feudal times emerged once again, this time blessed by a corruptible government. The balance was in jeopardy. Fortunately, important elements of the public, coordinated by parties, associations, and a competitive press, pressed democratically for transparency and reform.

Politically engaged largely self-governing communities were a natural unit of organization, and facilitated organized protest. Common economic causes could then bring them together in a movement across the United States, as with the Populists and Progressives. The sense that the system had worked earlier gave the movements confidence that they could reform it and therefore did not need a revolution. Chance also helped. The tragic assassination of the pro-business president William McKinley and his replacement by a reform-oriented Theodore Roosevelt conspired to empower the anti-monopoly movement in a timely way.[47] These democratic movements pushed back against the system's natural drift toward cronyism.

In the next chapter, we will see that the reverse is also true. By creating a healthy competitive private sector, competitive markets also help keep the state's authoritarian tendencies in check, and democracy vibrant. Thus, markets and democracy could be mutually supportive. I emphasize "could" because there are circumstances where the voting public is apathetic to public policy, and others where it might actively turn against private wealth and competitive markets. This is why democratic protest works best when it is timely, before people believe the system is beyond reform.

4

THE COMMUNITY IN
THE BALANCE

In a modern country, there are very few powerful actors that are independent of the government. Some elements of the state such as the judiciary or the central bank can be structured to be quasi-independent, but since their members are appointed by the government, a government with sufficiently long tenure can mold these institutions into its way of thinking. The power of promotion is another powerful tool. Within every state organization, no matter how seemingly independent, there are a spectrum of views. By promoting sympathizers over opponents, the organization's views can be aligned with the government, more so if opponents understand that to sympathize is the only way up. A determined party in power can shape many of the organs of the state toward its own preferences, given enough time.

An independent private sector is therefore important in a democracy, for it lies outside the state apparatus and embodies tremendous potential power. It is an essential source of funding, both for the parties in government and the political opposition as well as for nongovernmental organizations. Its intent may not solely be to lobby for regulations that enhance its profits, it may also be more public spirited—we will discuss later in the book whose views it might represent. The private sector also provides platforms for, and sometimes orchestrates, public opinion. Recall it was the muckraking press that was instrumental in breaking up Standard Oil as well as bringing regulation to the meatpacking industry. The *Washington Post*, a family-owned newspaper, effectively led the investigation that resulted in President Nixon's resignation after the Watergate break-in. The private sector can also take positions with its business activities that have a political or social slant, and attempt to nudge reforms.

The private sector cannot be independent when it is largely reliant on the state for profits—when the state controls entry through regulations or licensing; elevates industry profits through protectionist tariffs; directs substantial military or government advertising contracts to favored firms; or turns a selective and convenient blind eye to the takeovers and predatory practices that lead to monopolization of industry. It might seem that a private sector that is cozily in bed with the state has the upper hand. After all, it controls the purse that pays the governing party's bills. However, the owners of the largest enterprises are rarely secure in such a society, for they become dependent on the state. Much like Rockefeller, the monopolist may initially be efficient and capable of withstanding competition. Over time, though, without competition to keep them on their toes, monopolies or oligopolies typically become lazy and inefficient. Unable to compete any longer, they now fear competition from imports or new domestic challengers, and become dependent on government protection for their survival. The state thus steadily gains power over the private sector. Dependency breeds further dependency.

Therefore, the main source of private sector independence in a country, and thus also property rights protection, is the private sector's productive efficiency, which comes only through constant competition. A second source, though, is numbers. When a few giant firms dominate the private sector in a country, it is easier for the state to enter into cozy arrangements with them all, especially when each one dominates a specific sector. When activity is dispersed among many firms, their interests are often opposed, and it is harder for the state to capture them all. Those left out have strong incentives to expose the unfair arrangements entered into by those on the inside. Dispersed rather than concentrated production is thus an additional source of independence. This certainly is the lesson that emerges from the power of the gentry in Stuart England.

The danger when the private sector is entangled with the state in a crony capitalist society is that the state can rapidly turn authoritarian. An opportunist demagogue, elected on a platform of rooting out corruption, no longer needs to solicit contributions from business in return for erecting protective regulations and barriers—she can demand tribute just to keep the existing protections and to not expose the cozy past deals to the public. For it is easy for the state to turn public opinion against private business when business is both monopolistic and inefficient. People see the swamps in the capital city filled with lobbyists and reeking of cloyingly sweet deals, even while they experience the high prices and bad service directly. They are primed to believe the worst of business.

More worrying, she can use her anti-corruption campaign to demand fealty from the wealthiest in the economy. Fights against corruption led from the top are rarely attempts to reform the entire system. Instead, because almost everyone is usually implicated in shady deals, the leader intends the campaign to send a message. Periodically one of the wealthy, usually the least pliant, will be crushed publicly, both to satisfy voters that the anti-corruption campaign is alive and to provide a cautionary example to the wealthy about the dangers of stepping out of line. The public applauds the strong leader's action, not seeing that in praising the act, they help her reinforce the message to anyone else who might think of rebelling. The public, however, rarely has the means to distinguish systemic fights against corruption from targeted moves against the ruling establishment's political enemies until too late. Crony capitalism does not always stay benignly corrupt—it risks turning authoritarian.

In contrast, a transparent competitive market system produces winners who have important characteristics that allow them to be a check on the government. They are efficient, so they are not dependent on continuing help from the government to make money. They thus have the confidence to be independent from it. They are usually many and varied, so it is hard for the government to do side deals with all of them. The state cannot coerce each one quietly, and any attempt by the state to strong-arm a number of them publicly will inspire the collective resistance of many others. The government can tax their efficient production and therefore the people benefit from their ownership—replacing the efficient with the inefficient comes at a significant cost in reduced output and reduced taxes, as the government of Zimbabwe discovered when it expropriated experienced white farmers and replaced them with politically connected greenhorns. Moreover, the people are more likely to be sympathetic to the property rights of the efficient if their position is arrived at through fair competition (not the case, though, with white farm ownership in Zimbabwe, which often stemmed from the previous expropriation of African lands). Competitiveness in markets engenders private-sector independence from the state, offers vibrancy to democracy, and, in turn, draws support from the community. Vibrant markets and engaged democracies are mutually reinforcing.

We ended the last chapter describing two democratic movements in the United States that contained the overly strong markets pillar and its corrupt collusion with the state, and created a balance, even if temporarily. In this chapter, we will start by describing three situations when the community does not push for competitive markets—when market players or practices are deemed illegitimate and the strong state offers an alternative, when the state is weak and the community is bribed easily to stay apathetic, and when neither the state nor the community offer people the capabilities and the support they need to participate in volatile, changing markets. That will take us to how mechanisms to provide people capabilities and support evolved, and complete our discussion of the elements of the balance needed to sustain a liberal market democracy.

THE PERCEIVED LEGITIMACY OF MARKET PLAYERS

Property rights in a democracy are a social construct. While we have seen they are reinforced by the economic efficiency of the property holder as well as the collective power of similar property holders, in a democracy they also depend on public approval for enforcement.

PROPERTY AS THEFT

The more that the rich are seen as idle or crooked—as having simply inherited or, worse, gained their wealth through cozy government contracts, monopolies, or theft—the less voters care when the state turns on the rich. In Russia today, for example, property rights of the fabulously wealthy are not seen by the voting public as legitimate because so many of the very rich acquired their wealth through dubious means. They grew rich because they managed the system, not because they managed their businesses well.

Many of today's Russian oligarchs got their lucky break when the cash-strapped Yeltsin government effectively auctioned off prized state-owned enterprises at bargain-basement prices. A few connected insiders, such as Mikhail Khodorkovsky, who bought a 78 percent share in oil company Yukos worth about $5 billion for only $310 million, became fabulously wealthy.[1] That he had never seen an oil field before winning the bid suggests that he was not necessarily the most efficient owner.[2]

The public was enraged, but could do little about it. Yet the dubious circumstances of the acquisition also meant property rights were insecure. Indeed, with many of Russia's largest companies being commodity extractors, it did not take management genius to run them profitably, which meant ownership could always be seized easily by the state and transferred. It was only when some oligarchs like Khodorkovsky developed political interests and decided to take on the government that they realized how weak their property rights, without public support, really were. Khodorkovsky was imprisoned and Yukos was seized by the government. The outside world seemed to be sympathetic to his cause, but many Russians believed he had gotten his just deserts. Few protested on his behalf, and the oligarchs, having received the message, swung into line behind the increasingly authoritarian government. Invariably, the behemoth that thinks it can control the leviathan gets swallowed by it.

Sweet Deals

Even if the people do not question the provenance of the private sector's property, they might not have much faith in a private sector that is tied by the umbilical cord of sweet deals to the state. This could leave them open to a demagogue who promises to drain the swamp and bend the private sector to the will of the state.

In Germany, the links between the state and industry emerged under the

Iron Chancellor, Otto Von Bismarck, in the last few decades of the nineteenth century. Bismarck wanted to insert a wedge between industrialists and land-owners, so as to prevent a concerted move by the propertied, supported by the citizenry, to limit the state.[3] He co-opted industry by nationalizing industries like the railroads, by erecting tariff barriers to foreign manufacturers, and by allocating lucrative contracts for military supplies to favored industrialists. As Germany militarized under Bismarck, continuing into the First World War, there were few checks on the imperial government.

In the interwar period, the close ties between government and industry reemerged. In his study of the rise of Nazis in Germany, Columbia political scientist Franz Neumann observed that Germany never experienced an anti-monopoly movement against trusts and cartels like the Populist and Progressive movements in the United States. The Marxist labor unions in Germany acquiesced to the growing concentration of industry because they were persuaded of the wastefulness of competition and the inevitability of monopoly in the final stages of capitalism.[4] Unlike the Progressives, the German middle class did not also protest, perhaps because they had been ejected from the ranks of the confidently comfortable by the 1923 hyperinflation that robbed them of their savings.[5] They certainly were open to the kind of strong government that the Nazis promised. In this vein, a study by political economists Satyanath, Voigtländer, and Voth suggests that people in communities in interwar Germany that had stronger community engagement, as evidenced by the greater presence of local clubs and associations, were more likely to join the Nazi Party and help its electoral success.[6] They were especially supportive in regions with greater instability of the state government, suggesting a desire for a strong hand there. Communities may not always make the right choice, especially when the pillars are imbalanced!

The concentration of business thus proceeded unchecked. Concentrated business, mindful of its own dependence on government and aware of the many subsidies it enjoyed, especially as the world moved into depression in the early 1930s, did not oppose the authoritarian controls imposed by the Nazis.

CRONY DEMOCRACIES
AND CAPTURED POLITIES

Apart from the misguided conviction that change is in the right direction, communities may be bystanders because of apathy. If state capacity is weak, the people may not see any value to pressing for reforms. Instead, they may not care, as in the Italian village of Montegrano that we encountered in the Introduction, or opt for patronage, thus turning a blind eye to cronyism. The latter situation, prevalent in many developing countries around the world, is one reason we see *illiberal democracies,* a felicitous term used by Fareed Zakaria.[7]

A member of parliament (MP) in India represents a parliamentary constituency of over ten million people.[8] Do his constituents worry about the government's economic performance, its reform plans, or its social agenda? Except for the rare occasion when they are influenced by a popular national wave, for the most part most voters do not really care about public policy. What they want is help with their daily lives, help with filling the holes that a stretched state with limited capacity cannot address.

Therefore, for example, they want him to procure a birth certificate for their child, who was delivered in their shack in a village far away from any medical clinic. The birth certificate is essential for the child to be admitted to the free government school, and no government officer will provide it without suitable gratification, because he has no official document to rely on. The poor do not have the money to bribe so they plead for a call from the MP's office, which will set the wheels of bureaucracy rolling. Once the child is in the local school, the child becomes the MP's responsibility. When she graduates from high school, the MP has to find a college that will admit the student if her grades are modest, and when she gets a degree, he has to persuade some government office to give her a respectable secure job. And when she gets married, he will be invited to the wedding and be expected to give a suitable gift.

In a society where the typical government civil servant is neither civil nor a servant to the poor, the MP is the intermediary who will help them navigate the treacherous world. While the poor do not have the money to "purchase" public services that are their right, they have a vote that the politician wants.

The politician does what he can to make life a little more tolerable for his poor constituents—a land right enforced here, subsidized medical services honored there. For this, he gets the gratitude of his voters, and more important, their vote. Tied to their MP via patronage, they do not really care about how the MP will vote on the bigger issues of the day, whether he supports tax-evading liquor barons, illegal miners, or industrial polluters, so long as these do not intrude directly on their already-hard lives.

Far from rewarding honesty, the system favors the corrupt politician because he is not just richer but, being adept at the game of favors, is better at making the wheels of the bureaucracy creak in favor of his constituents. Such a system is self-sustaining. An idealist who is unwilling to work the system can promise to reform it, but the voters know there is little one person can do. Moreover, who will provide the patronage, the jobs and the wedding gifts, while the idealist is fighting the system? So why not stay with the known fixer even if it means the idealist is defeated? Thus the circle is complete. The poor and the underprivileged need the politician to help them get jobs and public services. The crooked politician needs the businessman to provide the funds that allow him to supply patronage to the poor and fight elections. The corrupt businessman needs the crooked politician to get monopoly rights, public resources, and contracts cheaply. The politician needs the votes of the poor and the underprivileged. Every constituency is tied to the other in a cycle of dependence.

Furthermore, there is little incentive for anyone to improve public administration and public services, because it is by filling the gaps left by the incompetent public administration that the corrupt politician maintains his vital role. Indeed, he is responsible for some of the incompetence of the administration, since it is he who overfills its positions with unqualified but loyal supporters.

More generally, when the state has limited capacity to meet the genuine needs of the people, democracies could turn into machines doling out patronage rather than checks on corruption.[9] One clear counter to apathy is local political engagement, which helps communities come together in broad-based movements, as in the United States. The reintroduction of elected village councils (panchayats) in India in the early 1990s helped energize public political engagement. There is more room today, as a result, for those who want to challenge the system. A second counter to apathy is better public services, which reduces the need for patronage. India is making progress, albeit slowly, here.

Let us turn now to yet another reason people in communities withdraw their support for markets: when most people feel markets are unfair and thus have no desire to protect them. This is perhaps most dangerous for a functioning market democracy, and it typically occurs when jobs are uncertain in the face of large-scale economic adversity or technology-induced change, and the community and state offer little support.

WHEN COMMUNITIES LOSE FAITH IN MARKETS

What does it mean for a market system to be fair? The libertarian philosopher would say that so long as none of the trading choices of market participants are constrained in any way, any outcome they achieve from a set of trades they willingly enter into should be seen as fair. It does not matter if some prosper while others are ruined; what matters is that all transactions are between consenting parties.[10] The Marxist would argue that everything starts from the initial endowment of property or capabilities that people have, and if that is unequal, then everything from then on is unfair. Indeed, because property has often been accumulated in the distant past through theft, conquest, or exploitation, all subsequent property rights are also dubious even in the libertarian light.[11] The followers of philosopher John Rawls might hold that a system that theoretically maximizes the well-being of the worst-off in society, other things equal, is what we would think most just if none of us knew whom we might end up as.[12]

The voting public obviously has a more intuitive and less theoretical sense of fairness. What might be its minimum common demands from an economic system? Importantly, the individual cares about how she is treated by the system. Did she get a chance to get the capabilities that would give her a reasonable chance of success? Does the system give her second chances if she made mistakes with early choices? Is she fairly well protected against the vicissitudes of fortune, against the loss of a job, against illness or disability, and against the misfortune of not having saved enough for old age? The individual also cares about how others are treated, with the degree of care depending on their social proximity, the unfortunate's own efforts to resolve their problems, as well as their degree of misfortune. In assessing whether the market is fair, therefore, individuals primarily examine its operations on both themselves and their community.

Technological Change and Public Anxiety

Most anti-market movements start or gain steam in economic or financial downturns, where the productive efficiency of markets is particularly hard to see, while the damage they do is clear. Nevertheless, we do not see every downturn producing strong anti-market forces. Many voters will stay the course so long as they have some hope they will participate in the recovery, especially if they have some support from the community or the state until it materializes. So long as the perturbations in the environment are small, a liberal market democracy is naturally self-correcting. Its strength is to react and adapt to small pressures. It can even react to large shocks to the environment such as war or natural disasters so long as it is clear they are temporary.

Problems arise when there are large permanent changes in the environment—changes such as the advent of new technologies. In such an environment, people need help to adapt their capabilities, even as they need significant support to cushion the blows to their existing economic activities. When a section of the public is so bereft of the capabilities the market requires of them, such as the handloom workers during the Industrial Revolution, and sees no assistance forthcoming to help them face the long run, their despair combines with their fear to create widespread anti-market revulsion. The market is no longer seen as fair because it excludes many who want to participate and does not help those who simply cannot.

Since the invention of the steam engine, there have been a number of episodes of massive technological change, when vast sections of the population of developed countries have had to upgrade their skills and move to new unfamiliar industries or geographic locales. Economic historians differ on which episodes they think important, but many would agree on three. The First Industrial Revolution, starting with the invention of the steam engine and followed by the development of railroads and steamships, played out between 1775 and 1875 approximately. The Second Industrial Revolution started with the near-simultaneous invention of the internal combustion engine, wireless transmission, and the use of electricity for light and power.[13] These permeated in various ways into the global economy between 1875 and 1970. We are now in the midst of the Third Industrial Revolution, starting with computers in the 1950s and 1960s (the revolutions overlap). Some term the invention of the microprocessor in the early 1970s, continuing with the development of the internet and its applications in the 1990s, and now extending into the use of artificial intelligence, robotics, and big data, as well as their extension into nanotechnology, developments in medicine, and the production, storage, and use of energy as the Fourth Industrial Revolution.[14] As indicated in the Introduction, we will refer to the gamut of recent technological changes as the Information and Communications Technology (ICT) Revolution to avoid confusion in numbering.

Technological revolutions rarely occur suddenly or linearly. It takes time for business to learn the practical uses of scientific discoveries, and to embed them in new products and services. It takes time for people to envisage what is possible with the novel output from business, and to find uses that go beyond what the inventors contemplated. Thomas Edison did not intend the phonograph for playing music; he thought of it as a device for businessmen to dictate letters for their secretaries to type.[15] It also takes time for business and its workers to change their production methods and their own skills so as to take full advantage of the new technologies and the uses that have been uncovered, and yet more time for adoption to move from the early knowledgeable risk-takers to the larger population. Technology rolls out slowly, and in fits and starts, with many mini-revolutions.

By the time the new technology has rolled out fully, though, it ends up affecting every facet of society. For example, the electrification of the home during the Second Industrial Revolution, with electric lighting followed by the washing machine, the steam iron, the refrigerator, and the dishwasher, greatly simplified household chores. Women, and it was only women then, could consequently contemplate working outside the house, even while having a family. Arguably, then, the Second Industrial Revolution helped increase female participation in the labor force outside the house, but few foresaw such an important change with its attendant social implications when the home was first electrified.

The typically long lag between when society anticipates disruption and when the fruits of the technology are finally reaped is beneficial for it gives society time to adjust. It can also be a time of great worker anxiety as uncertainty hangs over which jobs will be needed. Financial markets also try to anticipate, and often overextrapolate, the speed and direction of beneficial change, with attendant booms . . . and busts (when they are proven wrong), further complicating the process of societal adjustment.

TECHNOLOGICAL CHANGE AND FINANCIAL CRISIS

Episodes of innovation have often been punctuated by financial crises and severe economic downturns. The Panic of 1873 in the United States followed speculation in railway stocks, the Crash of 1929 followed a boom in industrial stocks, including utilities, and the Dot-Com Bust in 2000–2001 can be traced to the euphoria surrounding advances in internet technology and commerce. Such a combination of technological innovation followed by financial crisis has been regular enough that economic historian Carlotta Perez argues the two are related—the tendency of financial markets to become overoptimistic about the possibilities for new technologies invariably leads to a financial frenzy followed by a crash, way before the technology delivers on its promise.[16] Eventually the new technology does deliver stronger productivity, growth, and well-being if the market system survives, but this invariably means that society has to deal with the public's fears about the future at a time when the market system does not seem to be working, and when countries have limited resources to help people cope or adjust. The market system, and indeed democracy itself, is extremely vulnerable at such times.

Such times can impel economic and social reform and necessary change, as we saw with the American reform movements around the turn of the nineteenth century. Adversity can also give rise to demagogues who can get the votes to do irremediable long-term damage. The electorate may discover too late that they prefer measured reform to ignorant revolution. Indeed, Greek historian Polybius believed that democracies inevitably succumbed to demagogues.[17]

What Kinds of Support Do Communities Need?

New technologies typically required workers to have new capabilities. So communities needed to provide their members a pathway to acquiring these capabilities, or obtain state help to do so. The technology-induced global economic downturns that periodically hit communities prompted two other demands. One was for financial support as the integrated market unleashed mass economic distress that was hard for any individual community to cope with. Communities often appealed for help from the state. While the state typically responded with ad hoc efforts to address crises, over time it created formal safety nets to assuage its anxious population.

The second demand came to the fore during the Great Depression, a calamity that hit just as the fruits of the Second Industrial Revolution were ripening. The destruction of any savings invested in risky assets, the deep and sustained unemployment across every sector of the economy except the state, the belief that corporate titans and bankers had been engaged in excessive speculation, all brought calls to curb competition and markets. Public sentiment across the industrial world during the Depression now turned to supporting cartels as a way to preserve employment. Let us examine all these issues, focusing first on education and capability building, then on support to the economically distressed, and finally on the curbs on competition.

BUILDING CAPABILITIES

Arguably, the United States has been predisposed to markets because its people, by and large, have had the capabilities to participate in them. For much of American history, people have obtained the high-quality schooling they needed, largely at public expense.

The Community and the Common School

The central purpose of early schools in Massachusetts in the seventeenth century was to teach children to read the Bible, so it was natural that schools supplemented family and community practice. With the American Revolution came additional rationales for schooling—identifying and preparing the talented to govern the new republic as well as improving the ability of the general populace to participate in democratic discourse. Thomas Jefferson pushed the Second Continental Congress in 1787 to take steps toward public funding of schools. It passed the Northwest Ordinance, calling for the sale of federal lands to support education, stating, "Religion, morality, and knowledge being necessary to good government and the happiness of mankind, schools and the means of education shall forever be encouraged."[18] Under the Ordinance, new towns would be laid out over thirty-six square miles, of which one square mile would be sold to finance the schooling of children.[19]

The traditional one-room schools in older, existing towns in the early republic were largely community funded. These common schools, "common" because they bound the community together and taught common skills like reading, writing, basic mathematics and computation, and sometimes history and geography, typically did not separate students into grades. All students were taught in one big room. Households subscribed to the initial capital fund of the school, with wealthier households subscribing more. School teachers were hired annually, with the expenses of the school year (the school teacher's wages, his board, books, and the wood for heating the school) and the length of the school year (sometimes as short as the four or five winter months) determined at the beginning of the year. These expenses were apportioned across the community, and certain members were entrusted with collecting the apportioned amounts either in cash or in kind—many poorer members paid with firewood or helped board the teacher.[20] Poor children could attend for free, but were often stigmatized with the label "charity cases."[21]

With the school situated within the community, and the schoolmaster (and occasionally, schoolmistress) contracted annually, the community had enormous control over what was taught. Because communities had different degrees of engagement, there was considerable variability across common schools in the length of the school year, the subjects taught and the depth of knowledge imparted, the provision of supplies like books and firewood, the enthusiasm and diligence of the schoolmaster, and his basic training for the job. In the early years of the republic, when schools, especially in rural areas, were not really necessary for economic livelihoods, such variability did not

THE COMMUNITY IN THE BALANCE

matter much. What mattered was that the school drew the community together in a common endeavor, offered a meeting place for community members, and allowed them to exercise democratic oversight over what their children learned, even as the children grew up together. The little red schoolhouse has an enduring place in the mythology of the early US republic as a coming together of voluntary initiative and group responsibility.

As manufacturing started picking up with the Industrial Revolution traversing the Atlantic Ocean, and as agriculture became more scientific and commercial, education could usefully be more oriented toward preparing children for jobs. Reformers like Horace Mann, the secretary of the Massachusetts State Board of Education from 1837 to 1848, saw the need to improve the quality of schooling to meet these needs. They sought to professionalize teaching by instituting teacher training programs, examinations, and certificates. Professionalization would enhance the status of the teacher, thus attracting more talented people into teaching. Reformers also sought to bring some uniformity to the student experience by setting a minimum length to the school year.

These reformers were not just motivated by the growing economic needs of the nation, they also saw the school as essential to welding the nation's people together, to inculcating lessons in good citizenry and sound republican values in the young. To combat what they saw as religious sectarianism and intolerance, especially with the growing immigration of the Irish, they sought to separate the schools from the churches. They also wanted every child in school, so they worked hard to ensure that schools were funded by local taxes, and not by fees. To persuade the rich to pay the property taxes that would be required, they emphasized that education was a public responsibility, which would improve the productivity of workers and help bridge the gap between the wealthy and the working classes. Mann argued that as the "balance wheels" of society, schools would reduce social tensions.

For much of its early existence, therefore, the United States had a schooling system that was locally funded and locally controlled, free to all, nonsectarian, and increasingly professional. Schools opened the door widely to opportunity. And there were many schools. Between 1800 and 1915, hundreds of thousands of common schools were set up and controlled by communities.[22]

By 1860, the average years of schooling across the population in the United States was far in advance of any other industrializing country in the world, and it would stay so for nearly a century.[23]

TECHNOLOGICAL PROGRESS
AND SCHOOL CONSOLIDATION

The common school answered the needs of the early- to mid-nineteenth century United States. However, with the onset of the Second Industrial Revolution in the last quarter of the nineteenth century, many more jobs emerged in new, more technically demanding industries like chemicals or iron and steel. Department stores such as Marshall Fields or Wanamaker looked for educated women to help their customers. Small firms searched for bookkeepers and managers as banks demanded transparency and professionalization in the firms they financed. Banks and insurance companies also needed vast numbers of clerical staff to manage their own exploding paperwork. The demand for better-educated workers increased, as did the demand for well-qualified teachers to impart that education. The high-wage premium for the better educated made many more students and their parents look beyond the common school. The stage was set for the second big wave in US education, the public high school movement.

At that time, it was not obvious that education beyond the common school ought to be free. After all, arguably, the public benefits of a literate and civilized citizenry could be had in the late nineteenth century with the six to eight years that students spent in the common school. Nevertheless, the small emerging middle class saw tremendous personal benefits in a free high school. They emphasized it would be open to all, satisfying the widespread desire for upward social mobility into well-paying jobs. In practice, though, in the late nineteenth century, a high school primarily catered to the much smaller group that could afford to keep their children studying and not working. For this reason, the high school certificate in those years attested as much to the holder's middle-class status as it did to her educational attainments.

Despite the narrowness of the population segments that had use for it, the high school was made free for all by the Michigan Supreme Court in

Kalamazoo (1874), which ruled that local funds could be used to support high schools. It believed no one ought to be deprived of a broad liberal education, and therefore high schools should not be foreclosed to anyone who could not afford it—they should be free.[24]

Someone had to pay the taxes that supported the schools. An early argument to persuade the propertied to pay was that property prices would be enhanced if the property owner could advertise "free transportation to a good graded school." Another persuasive argument was that even those who had no children must necessarily rely in their old age on someone in the community who had studied in the public schools, so their "only safeguard lies in giving the best advantages possible to all."[25]

The free public high school offered students a general education—the United States has typically resisted streaming students into vocational training early—so that graduates had the flexibility of joining any industry, where they would get specific training. The rising tide of immigration in the latter half of the nineteenth century also helped to push native-born children into high school. Immigrants had substantial work experience in "older" trades such as baking, cabinetmaking, or blacksmithing.[26] The high school turned from being an escape for the few to being an economic passport for the many, enabling them to bypass the sectors crowded by experienced immigrants, and to obtain jobs in sunrise white-collar industries, technology-intensive manufacturing, or in the emerging construction sector.

In short, in the same way as the common school seemed to be the minimum aspirational level for American society in the early nineteenth century, the high school became the minimum from the beginning of the twentieth century. Free and open access unlocked the doors to opportunity to many. Around the end of the nineteenth century, the median American had only a common school education; by the early 1940s, the median American had a high school education.[27]

THE WEAKENING OF LOCAL COMMUNITY CONTROL

The expanding market and its demands hit at community control. Small communities had the resources to fund and staff the common school. The high school was a different matter. In order to teach the wide variety of subjects in the depth and width required, the high school needed many teachers, an administrative staff, large buildings, a library, scientific laboratories, a gymnasium, and so on. With the large minimum scale required to provide education of the requisite quality, any new high school had to draw a large number of students to be economically viable.

This had a number of implications. First, communities, especially the smaller and the more remote rural ones, often had to come together to found high schools. This immediately meant a weakening in each community's sense of ownership and responsibility for the school. Second, the greater complexity and professionalization of high school administration created the possibility that parental control might not be adequate to the task of monitoring the school, which gave education professionals an excuse to distance parents from school governance whenever possible. Third, the greater resources needed by even rudimentary high schools, coupled with the historic emphasis on local funding, meant that high school quality depended to a much greater extent on local wealth. Students in different areas had vastly different life opportunities because the quality of high schools varied so much. Poorer and rural communities were obviously worse off.

These differences in access to education exhibited themselves in different ways. For instance, in the enormous induction into the military in World War I, rural American youth were found to be far less prepared than urban youth for a modern army, primarily because of poor health stemming from inadequate diets as well as their shocking levels of illiteracy and innumeracy.[28] The rising inequality in the provision of education was a red flag for Progressives in the early twentieth century. Something had to be done, and the response was greater state government intervention in schooling and in its funding.

Even as state governments provided more funding to help school districts that were too poor to afford quality schools, departments of education sprang up in state capitals, insisting on school consolidation to reduce costs, and setting minimum requirements for school size, teacher qualifications, and curriculum. Of the over two hundred thousand one-room schools in 1915, only twelve hundred were open in 1975.[29]

Progressives were not just concerned about the inequality in funding but about educational outcomes in general. Reformers like John Dewey, who founded the University of Chicago's Laboratory School, believed that with industrialization and the growing divide between labor and capital, as well as the increasing ethnic and religious fragmentation of American society, the social distance between groups would tend to increase. The primary school brought together students from diverse backgrounds, while the high school drew students from a still larger geographic area. A rounded school education would give students the experience of interacting with a more diverse population, draw them into civic participation, and inculcate a more democratic attitude toward debating differences. Progressives therefore saw in the school a lever with which to change society, to get students to go beyond the parochialism introduced by their own narrow communities.

Some went further and thought parental control was really parental interference, and therefore not part of the solution. As Woodrow Wilson, who was president of Princeton University before he became president of the United States, stated while speaking of his students, "Our problem is not merely to help the students to adjust themselves to world life. Our problem is to make them as unlike their fathers as we can."[30] Such attitudes could not help but diffuse through the professional educational bureaucracy. As parent-staffed school boards competed with professional state government superintendents of education for influence over the school, local control diminished further. The gap in views between parents and the professional bureaucracy widened.

Even while schools lost local involvement and support, the efforts to make school quality more uniform through centralized funding fell significantly short. State government aid in Massachusetts was supposed to be distributed based on an equalizing formula that gave more to poor districts than rich districts. Even as late as the 1960s, a study found that the correlation between state support and local need was so slight that the state government could have done as well if it had "distributed its largesse in a completely random fashion, as by the State Treasurer throwing checks from an airplane."[31]

Schooling in France

What did other countries do? An especially different approach was that of France, which underwent its own revolution in 1789 soon after the American

Revolution. Instead of revolting against foreign domination, the French revolted against their nobility and the clergy. So right from the outset, widespread public education was seen as a way to reduce the advantages of the privileged. Furthermore, since the clergy could shape young minds against the revolution, and inculcate narrow religious factionalism rather than a broader national spirit, the state thought it important to get the clergy out of education. Also, because France was soon surrounded by enemies who wanted to restore the monarchy, the schools became seen as an important instrument to create national unity.

The French education system, as envisioned by Napoleon, would train students to be loyal to the state. The state would have a monopoly over instruction, there would be an administrative hierarchy supervising schools, and there would be a sequence of central exams intended to sort students into schools, from the most technically demanding downward. At lower levels, all state schools would resemble one another so that everyone got an equal chance. It was as different from the decentralized American schooling system as one could get in that it was state-funded, centrally designed and managed, and ostensibly equitable. Its uniformity made it rigid, though, and the hierarchy was unforgiving of students who tripped up in their studies and did not pass central exams.

In the early 1880s, the Third Republic passed laws that made public education free, compulsory between the ages of six and twelve, and secular. Most teachers and university professors became civil servants, and the state's control over examinations meant that even when it relented to allow private participation in education, the private schools had to mirror public education. Today, in any given grade in schools across France, the curriculum is the same. Nevertheless, the French too have not achieved their goal of uniform access to school education. As is common in centralized systems, the teachers who are assigned to schools in the most difficult neighborhoods are often the ones who have the least power to wangle preferred assignments from the bureaucratic establishment. They are typically the most junior and least experienced. The quality of such schools is lower—in large part because of differences in early childhood learning among the student body and in community support—increasing the desire of any good teacher who is assigned to them to escape as soon as possible.

So while the school system in the United States evolved from one that was totally decentralized, and had substantial community involvement in design, to one that has significantly more central direction in parts than at the outset, the French system has had central control for the last two hundred years. The advantage of a decentralized system is the community can shape it toward its needs; the advantage of a centralized system is that it offers more uniform instruction across the populace. Each system has its problems and fails to prepare people in a variety of communities for the market. As we will see in later chapters, the demands of the market for higher levels of education have increased once again in the twenty-first century, exacerbating these problems.

COMMUNITY AND STATE BUFFERS AGAINST MARKET VOLATILITY

We have been discussing what might be deemed pre-market support, that is, help in preparing the individual to enter the market as a worker or a producer. Let us now turn to what could be labeled post-market support—help to those who are hit by adverse economic conditions, or who, because of disability, misfortune, aging, or technological change, are incapable of earning a living. In a sense, both pre-market support and post-market support could be thought of as substitutes. The more people have the capabilities to participate in and benefit from the market, the less need there is of a safety net, and vice versa. Indeed, the historical US embrace of markets despite the holes in its safety net, may well be due in large measure to its high-quality and widely accessible schooling system. Today, its schooling system is no longer adequate, hence more weight falls on post-market support, which the United States is ill structured to provide, for reasons we will come to shortly.

Worker lives in the early years of industrialization were very difficult. They were, on average, much poorer than today. Wages were barely enough to put food on the table and secure shelter for the family in a noxious urban slum, let alone build a buffer of savings. Indeed, informal workers in many developing countries face similar conditions today; sickness means a loss of pay and skipped meals; and the death of the main wage earner may leave the family destitute, with few alternatives to begging or prostitution. With many workers living at the margin, a safety net is needed in such circumstances at the best of times, let alone in periods of mass economic dislocation.

WHO SHOULD HELP? WHEN? AND HOW?

When are we, as individuals, most impelled to help the unfortunate? We are more predisposed to help when the needy are socially or physically close, so that we can put a familiar human face to them. Moreover, as we discussed earlier, helping someone nearby strengthens the social contract, so that they too are willing to help when we are in need. Moreover, pure self-interest comes into play, for if we help them, they are less likely to riot in the street or burn down our property.

We are also more likely to help when someone looks like us, motivated by two powerful sources of empathy—our genes pushing for their own survival and the notion that "there but for the Grace of God go I." Conversely, population diversity has been an important barrier to mutual assistance. Even today, studies find that countries with high levels of ethnic or linguistic diversity among their people tend to have significantly lower levels of redistribution by the government as a share of GDP.[32] In other words, countries with very different communities opt to live with greater inequality and insecurity.

These are reasons why assistance has historically been provided within the community. Physically proximate communities consist, typically, of homogenous groups of people, with similar ethnicity, language, religion, and class. It is easier to build group solidarity and empathy within such groups. This makes them the appropriate units through which to provide a safety net for their members.

There is another reason for community-based assistance. It is straightforward to identify some who cannot help themselves, such as the very old, the infirm, the mentally unstable, the visually disabled, and children. Such human conditions are hard, or very costly, to simulate. In contrast, the worry with any assistance to able-bodied adults has always been that it might go to "undeserving" malingerers rather than the truly needy. In addition, unconditional assistance might deter the assisted from ever working, and incentivize low-paid workers to drop out and join them, leading to a growing mass of able but lazy loafers sponging on those who labor honestly. The modern embodiment of these fears is the apocryphal welfare queen, who takes advantage of every form of public assistance even while driving in her limousine to buy intoxicants. It is hard to know how quantitatively important freeloading has been, but it is an argument that has always been used against assistance. Given the public's concerns, the advantage of funneling assistance through the community is that it may be best informed to weed out potential malingerers.

As economic volatility increased, British and American parishes or counties set up poorhouses and workhouses. These frightening establishments, aptly described by Charles Dickens, made inhabitants live and work in terrible conditions, so that only the truly incapable or desperate would opt for such assistance. At the same time, where it was clear that the supplicant was not a malingerer, communities also offered *outdoor relief,* a term for sums of money or supplies given directly to the poor household in situ, out of the door of the poorhouse. Outdoor relief was often cheaper and much more humane, and did not dislocate or break up poor families. The community had the information to ensure outdoor relief was not misused. For instance, county supervisors in the United States argued they were not unduly harsh in their decisions on whom to send to the poorhouse, because any time someone "deserving," such as a poor widow with many children, or an injured family man unable to work, came for assistance, their neighbors rallied behind them and pushed for outdoor relief.[33] Essentially, support for relief was crowdsourced.

COMMUNITY ENGAGEMENT AND THE ELBERFELD SYSTEM

Germany was a leader in community provision of assistance in the industrializing world. Its Elberfeld system, adopted in a number of cities, recognized that poverty was a changeable condition, and drew the community into managing it. In the mid-nineteenth century, 10–20 percent of Elberfeld's population received poor relief regularly, which was proving to be beyond the city's capacity to sustain.[34] A group of the city's businessmen devised the eponymous system to bring spending under control, and to ensure that poverty did not become a permanent condition.

The city was divided into districts and further into quarters. A guardian of the poor was appointed for each quarter, and was expected to reside in it. People petitioned for assistance to their quarter's guardian, who then took the case up to a district-level meeting of all guardians. Guardians could approve emergency assistance individually, but only to tide the petitioner over till the next district meeting.

The purpose of assistance was to get the poor back into work, hence applicants had to satisfy guardians that they were looking for work. However, assistance could be given for a variety of reasons, such as old age, illness, or large numbers of children, rather than just joblessness. Moreover, relief was provided as a top-up, after other sources of support, such as personal assets or family, had been exhausted. What made the system different from more modern government welfare departments was the enthusiastic and voluntary involvement of the community. The city's industrialists and bankers occupied the highest policymaking positions in the system, while merchants, master craftsmen, and middle-class homeowners were recruited to be district guardians. Decisions were decentralized to the district-level guardians' meeting, which ensured local responsibility and accountability.

To serve as a guardian was part honor, part obligation. In theory, those who refused to serve could be penalized with higher taxes, but since the effort the role required was demanding, the authorities looked for enthusiastic volunteers rather than reluctant draftees. Each guardian's caseload was kept low, which gave them time to engage intensively.[35] The guardian made periodic visits to the homes of relief recipients, trying to verify their true conditions even while giving them advice and opening doors to emerging opportunities. All this was supposed to be done by the guardian with "energetic love and the spirit of personal sacrifice."

To the modern-day reader, the guardian's role might seem paternalistic and intrusive—indeed, guardians were impolitely referred to as *Pottkieker,* or cooking-pot snoopers. There was a fundamental contradiction to these visitations—which were emulated by voluntary charitable organizations in the United States in the late nineteenth century and many welfare systems today—the ultimate aim was to render the recipient independent of the system, but the path there demanded unconditional obedience to the guardian and her suggestions. Nevertheless, the guardian was from the local community and brought community knowledge and social networks to bear in trying to improve the lot of the poor. Moreover, because the task was done with enthusiasm by volunteers, who were unlike the jaded overloaded professional caseworkers of most social welfare systems today, it was both inexpensive and had a greater chance of success. Indeed, in the decade following the implementation of the system, the share of the city's population receiving public assistance fell to approximately 2 percent, and because the poor were thought to be adequately taken care of, almsgiving and begging reportedly disappeared.[36] No wonder the Elberfeld system was adopted by 170 of the 200 or so major cities in Germany.[37]

As goods markets and the market for labor grew to span many communities within a country, such community-based solutions came under pressure. One problem had to do with those who moved from one community to another in search of work. Internal migration picked up as nation-states emerged and security improved, and as opportunities sprang up in distant parts of the country. Who was responsible for supporting the destitute migrant—the migrant-receiving community or the migrant-sending community? Even today, the European Union struggles with this question.

A second problem was that the size of economic shocks transmitted through manufacturing and finance across the increasingly integrated world economy continued to increase. Such large shocks could overwhelm entire groups of communities, leaving few in a position to hold out a helping hand to the fallen.

THE STATE AS BACKSTOP TO THE COMMUNITY IN RELIEF EFFORTS

The resolution to both these problems was to involve the state. For internal migrants, the state could set rules that would specify who would pay support, and who would fund any gaps. When it came to dealing with prolonged and widespread economic downturns, the state had an advantage over communities in that it had deeper pockets; it could spread the costs of support across all communities in the land, and even to future generations of citizens via public borrowing. Moreover, in times of widespread unemployment, there was little need to distinguish between the truly needy and the habitual malingerer, since the vast majority of those requesting assistance were obviously the former. The community's local knowledge, at least at such times, was not required to channel assistance.

As with schools, once the state answered the call for help, it tended to nationalize the process and take it over entirely. This was not entirely without reason. As soon as the state became a backstop to communities, it had to worry that communities might neglect any preparation of their own, and rely much more frequently on the state. Much as a prudent government helps people hit by devastating floods fix their houses, but then requires them to sign up and pay for government-provided flood insurance so that they bear some cost of staying in flood-prone areas, the state felt that once it had intervened, it had to formalize the system and make it explicit. Across developed countries, the state implemented a variety of social support programs starting in the last quarter of the nineteenth century, often with public contributions.

The first industrializing country to adopt state-sponsored social insurance was imperial Germany under its chancellor, Otto Von Bismarck. Early in its industrialization, Germany already had a number of worker insurance plans run by municipalities. The global depression that started in 1873 overwhelmed municipalities with the number who needed help. Beggars and tramps (essentially the unemployed) flooded the streets of every city.

Bismarck had an important political aim—to neutralize the growing allure of socialist parties that appealed to disgruntled workers and that wanted to start a revolution from below. He sought to undercut the socialists by offering workers a "gift" from the imperial government, a revolution from above, even while banning socialist political activity in 1878. He wanted workers to see the imperial government as their best chance for improved welfare. Unfortunately for Bismarck, the German Reichstag refused to raise the taxes that his proposals would entail, so he had to give up the idea of fully funded government programs.[38]

Instead, Germany passed three sets of laws in the 1880s, essentially making membership in insurance pools compulsory for specified worker groups, and adding employer taxes to the pool. The three risks insured were sickness, industrial accidents, and disability and old-age pensions for those who survived beyond seventy.[39]

The British Liberal government between 1906 and 1911 took the next big leap in state involvement with the passage of a number of important bills including old-age pensions (1908), the Labor Exchanges Act (1909), the Trade Boards Act (1909), which set minimum wages in a number of industries, and the Development and Road Improvement Funds Act (1909), which opened the way for public road works in times of mass unemployment. These efforts culminated with the enactment of unemployment and health insurance in 1911. The German and British reforms were indeed major steps in the creation of reliable nationwide safety nets that would buffer workers against market volatility, but they did diminish the role of the community once again.

Safety Nets in the United States before the Great Depression

As we saw earlier, the United States had systems of local poor relief, with the shadow of the poorhouse intended to keep the able-bodied from shirking. In the late nineteenth century, these were supplemented by a variety of private charitable organizations, voluntary workingmen's insurance plans, "friendly" societies, as well as insurance companies. This safety net proved grossly inadequate when the Depression of 1893 hit the United States hard, with nationwide unemployment estimated at between 17 to 19 percent. Cities were especially badly hit—New York experienced unemployment of around 35 percent.[40] With traditional modes of relief overwhelmed, municipalities turned to public works.

Despite the enormous financial burden on municipalities at this time, the United States did not put in place a nationwide social safety net for its citizens. Even as the world entered depression again in 1929, the United States was the only major developed country without a system of government-supported social security. Compulsory insurance plans as in Britain or Germany were deemed "un-American," and there was little appetite for taxpayer funding. Part of the reason may have been traditional American resistance to the state's expansion, though too much can be made of this. Union Army veterans and their families got access to medical facilities from the Civil War onward. Disability pensions that had been given to wounded Union soldiers were extended to virtually every Union veteran in the 1890s, and became an important source of old-age support.[41] The Progressives also managed to push workmen accident compensation plans through a number of states in the 1910s, paid for by employers, with state-level or private insurance plans available to small employers who feared being bankrupted by accident claims. It is therefore hard to attribute American resistance to the notion that government safety nets were "un-American."

One reason for American reluctance to follow the Europeans was probably the sense that national programs in a large country like the United States would probably be unwieldy and unresponsive to local conditions. In addition, a wide variety of private organizations were engaged in providing health or insurance services, and were opposed to widespread government involvement, which might undercut their business.[42]

Perhaps the most important impediment, however, was the diversity of the American population, especially in cities. In 1910, approximately ten million foreign-born immigrants and twelve million of their locally born children lived in American cities. In most large cities, the children of immigrants outnumbered the children of the native-born. Furthermore, blacks had been migrating away from farms, first into the Southern cities, and then into the Northern cities.[43] Unlike Europe, therefore, the United States, especially in the hard-hit cities in the 1890s, was not an ethnically homogenous population. Empathy, the psychological basis of the safety net, was much harder to generate under these circumstances, and it was far easier for native-born whites to believe that immigrants or minorities were unlikely to have a strong work ethic, and would likely become welfare cheats.

THE GREAT DEPRESSION AND THE SOCIAL SECURITY ACT OF 1935

Then came the Great Depression. At its deepest, the Great Depression was worse than the Depression of 1893. It was also longer-lasting. Right from his acceptance speech at the Democratic Convention in 1932, Franklin Roosevelt laid the grounds for his New Deal program, stating:[44]

"What do the people of America want more than anything else? To my mind, they want two things: work, with all the moral and spiritual values that go with it; and with work, a reasonable measure of security—security for themselves and for their wives and children . . . I say that while primary responsibility for relief rests with localities now, as ever, yet the Federal Government has always had and still has a continuing responsibility for the broader public welfare. It will soon fulfill that responsibility . . . Throughout the Nation, men and women . . . look to us . . . for more equitable opportunity to share in the distribution of national wealth . . . I pledge you, I pledge myself, to a *New Deal* for the American people."

The New Deal had three main objectives—relief (of the destitute unemployed and poor), recovery (of the economy from the Depression), and reform (so that these conditions were not repeated). The administration tried to accomplish these goals through a variety of programs and legislative efforts—at some level, it appeared that the government was willing to try anything, for nothing seemed to be working. Indeed, it was only with the ramping up of production for war in 1939 and 1940 that the United States really exited the Depression. Nevertheless, government action had some effects. Enormous public works, such as the construction of the Lincoln Tunnel and what came to be known as LaGuardia Airport, gave relief through paid employment and helped prevent an even greater collapse in activity. Financial sector reforms such as the Banking Act and the Securities Act, both enacted in 1933, brought stability to financial markets.

Perhaps the centerpiece reform was the Social Security Act of 1935. It established a system of contributory retirement pensions called Social Security, created state-level unemployment insurance plans, and established welfare benefits through the states for poor children in families without a father and for the indigent elderly.

What prompted Roosevelt to propose the program, and what led to its passing? It is important to recognize that the Social Security Act was not part of the initial flurry of plans to facilitate relief or recovery, but was, as is evident from Roosevelt's speech at the Democratic Convention, part of his longer-term reform agenda. Roosevelt was well aware of the historical role of communities in providing support, but believed that these were no longer up to the task. In a message to Congress on June 8, 1934, laying the grounds for social security, he recognized that "security was attained in the earlier days through the interdependence of members of families upon each other and of the families within a small community upon each other. The complexities of great communities and of organized industry make less real these simple means of security. Therefore, we are compelled to employ the active interest of the Nation as a whole through government in order to encourage a greater security for each individual who composes it."[45]

As to which level of government would be involved, Roosevelt was clear that "social insurance should be national in scope," although the states should "meet at least a large portion of the cost of management, leaving to the Federal Government the responsibility of investing, maintaining and safeguarding the funds constituting the necessary insurance reserves."

Roosevelt's insistence that social security be funded through individual payments and payroll taxes—essentially new taxes in the midst of a depression, which could further depress activity—suggested he did not want the pension or unemployment insurance to be a gift from the state but a property right. As he said later, "We put those payroll contributions there so as to give the contributors a legal, moral, and political right to collect their pensions and unemployment benefits. With those taxes in there, no damn politician can ever scrap my social security program."[46]

Roosevelt, therefore, was determined. Why did the political establishment go along then, but not earlier in the 1890s? For one, the latent populism in the United States was being kindled to life again by the terrible economic conditions in the 1930s. The charismatic and somewhat authoritarian Governor Huey Long of Louisiana, who inveighed against privilege, wealth, and Wall Street while extolling the virtues of the forgotten common man, unveiled his "Share Our Wealth Society" plan in 1934. This proposed to confiscate large fortunes, raise income taxes significantly on the rich, and pay the collected sums as a lump sum to every American family, giving each $5,000, enough to buy a home, a car, and a radio (all the better to hear his very popular broadcasts with). In addition, each family would have a guaranteed minimum annual income of $2,500. The math was suspect—the plan was simply infeasible because of the enormous spending that it entailed and could not be financed even with the radical measures he proposed—but the politics were just right.

Roosevelt and the Democrats feared that Long would get enough votes if he stood for election in 1936 to spoil Roosevelt's chances and throw the election to the Republicans.[47] America's deep sense of democratic egalitarianism, expressed through populism, once again was clashing with its fundamental desire to reward success. Roosevelt understood that he occupied the middle ground, between the apparent insouciance of the previous Republican administration and the radicalism of the emerging alternatives. In pushing social security, he exploited fears of what might happen if Congress did not act to appease the radicals.

Moreover, some of the earlier institutional opponents of social security, such as the insurance companies, were also recipients of government aid during the Depression in the 1930s. It was hard for them to call social security "un-American" as they had in the past, when they themselves were feeding at the government trough. By contrast, universal health care did not become part of the social security safety net, in part because of the continued opposition of doctors in the American Medical Association. Doctors, unlike insurance companies, were not dependent on a government bailout.[48]

Perhaps most important, though, population diversity and fears of the undeserving poor, which were significant issues in the Populist and Progressive era, were less of an issue with the Social Security Act. For one, the draconian Immigration Act of 1924, building on a previous act passed in 1917, had limited immigration significantly, and then too, primarily to Western Europeans. It banned Asian immigration entirely. A decade after its passage and enforcement, the native-born public's earlier concern that safety net benefits would go to "undeserving" immigrants was therefore more muted.

As for African Americans, the single largest domestic nonwhite group, the Social Security Act specifically left out agricultural and domestic workers, thus ensuring two-thirds of employed blacks had no part in unemployment or old-age insurance. Moreover, the operation of the schemes, and the design of some, were left to the states, with the full knowledge that Southern states wanted the freedom to discriminate.[49] Indeed, in a recent study of welfare payments by states in the United States, Harvard economists Alberto Alesina and Edward Glaeser conclude that "states with a larger number of blacks are much less generous [with welfare payments] than states with fewer African-Americans."[50]

In sum, both circumstances and design allowed the Social Security Act to assuage the voting public's concerns about the "undeserving" poor that had thwarted such programs in the past. The United States now had a government-facilitated plan of social insurance, but it was a safety net with significant holes. Health care was not covered, nor was a large part of the historically disadvantaged black population. The first has not been remedied fully to date, and it took the Civil Rights movement in the 1960s to force the United States to act on the latter.

THE CURBS ON COMPETITION

Before we end this chapter, it is important to point to a third consequence of the Great Depression. It was an economic cataclysm worse than anything the citizens of developed countries had experienced before. Captains of industry and finance were pilloried as rogues, while the best economic minds could do little to restore prosperity. Many societies blamed corrupt capitalism for the prolonged downturn, and turned to fascism or socialism instead. Even in the United States, the supposed bastion of free enterprise, there was a broad groundswell of opinion that market competition was to blame, and that capitalism would be more stable if it were muzzled.

Across the market economies, competition was constrained, if not stifled, with official support during the Depression. In the United States, states passed "fair trade" legislation that set floors for retail prices, protecting small-town manufacturers and retailers from competition from big business. Custom tariffs went up to curb imports, including the infamous Smoot Hawley Act passed by the US Congress in 1930, which prompted tit-for-tat tariffs across the developed world. Capital controls limited cross-border investment flows, while industry-wide or even economy-wide agreements between firms, and between firms and labor such as the Saltsjöbaden Agreement in Sweden in 1938, sought to sacrifice competition for stability. Governments effectively suspended antitrust. In country after country, the private sector was significantly more heavily regulated, while many industries were nationalized. These efforts to curb competition did not restore growth. Ultimately, it was World War II, with its enormous demand for the machinery of war, that pulled economies out of the Depression. The centralized management of war production, however, further limited competition. In some of the victorious countries, public faith in government solutions increased further.

CONCLUSION

What makes people both able and willing to organize politically? An effective state, which people can rely on for public services, and a well-administered safety net that people have paid for and are thus entitled to, have the collateral effect of freeing them from requiring political patronage of the kind we saw in India. They are able to engage politically. The decentralization of powers and activities to communities draws them into actual political engagement. The community then serves as a base to mobilize protest.

The engaged community, acting as a watchdog, can push politically to reduce cronyism and preserve competition in markets. In turn, as we emphasized in this chapter, competitive markets forge a confident and efficient private sector, which can stand independently of the state and check it when it tends toward authoritarianism. In these ways, the pillars reinforce or check each other.

By the end of the Second World War, though, the state had taken on more and more, while markets and the community did less and less. The changes were neither linear nor continuous, but over time, they were significant. The initial functions the state took on, such as regulation, were necessary to make the market work better in the public interest. The accent was typically on increasing competition and opportunity, reforms that public movements pushed for. However, the public attitude toward competition reversed during the Great Depression. Consequently, the state started favoring cartelization, and also entered a number of activities that were previously undertaken by private business. The state now encroached on markets.

The state was a helpful support to the community, as we have seen in this chapter, but it also started displacing it. Government bureaucracy followed through the door opened by assistance to the community, if nothing else to monitor the usage of public funds. The bureaucratic temptation to build professional empires often reduced local control, crowded out community engagement, and weakened the community as a key pillar of democratic vigilance. Inevitably, government programs also interfered with intra-community relationship building. Milton and Rose Friedman's critique of social security was precisely that in the past, ". . . children helped their parents out of love or duty. They now contribute to the support of someone else's parents out of compulsion or fear. The earlier transfers strengthened the bonds of the family; the compulsory transfers weakens them."[51] Indeed, James Poterba finds the elderly in the United States have been less supportive of education for the young in recent times than before the institutionalization of social security, especially in diverse communities.[52]

One purpose of our historical excursion was to trace the development of the three pillars, from the chrysalis of the tribal or feudal community into their contemporary avatars. As the world emerged from World War II, the modern shapes of the three pillars were recognizable. Among the pillars, the state was in ascendance. We will now turn to the postwar era, to see how today's imbalances developed.

PART II

IMBALANCE

Things fall apart; the centre cannot hold;
Mere anarchy is loosed upon the world,
The blood-dimmed tide is loosed, and everywhere
The ceremony of innocence is drowned;
The best lack all conviction, while the worst
Are full of passionate intensity.

From W. B. Yeats, "The Second Coming," 1919

The world economy was in a mess after World War II. Much of Europe and Japan was in ruins, most economies were geared towards war production, and the state had expanded to crowd out markets. The democratic Allies had defeated the Axis powers in the war, but which way countries would turn politically was still uncertain. The United States was pivotal in tilting the world towards democracy, both with the rules-based global order it created, which steadily opened up trade, as well as with its generous funding of development. Pax Americana was founded on the belief that the United States benefited from the prosperity of other democracies, and it worked. Growth in developed countries was spectacular in the three decades after the war. This strengthened democracies but also led them to further expand the state as they made handsome promises of health care and social security to their people based on the rosy view that strong economic growth would continue well into the future.

Then in the early 1970s economic growth slowed significantly. The state had to give room back to markets if economies were to get to even moderate levels of growth. Across the developed world, the emphasis in the 1980s shifted to deregulation and reductions in barriers to trade and capital flows.

Even as markets regained ascendance, the disruptive effects of the ICT Revolution started being felt. Even though its impact on productivity has been limited thus far, its impact on jobs, both through automation and through trade, as well as its impact on incomes, have been sizeable. The consequences have been very different across communities within large countries, with some communities experiencing significant economic distress and social breakdown and others unimaginable prosperity. The skewness in incomes in developed countries has been exacerbated by incumbents protecting themselves from competition in a variety of ways.

We will examine the roots of popular resentment in developed countries today. Especially concerning is the breakdown of the economically mixed community as the well-to-do move into localities with others from their own income class, which leaves poorer classes stuck in communities with lower quality public services like schools. The reason for such residential sorting is that parents want the best learning environment for their children, given the technology-induced premium accorded to capabilities. In turn, residential sorting ensures that the emerging technology-induced meritocracy becomes a hereditary one. Popular resentment, already at a high pitch after the Global Financial Crisis, has boiled over with Obamacare in the United States and the immigration crisis in Europe. Society has become imbalanced once again, and radicals of all kinds are pushing for change.

Before moving to reform proposals in Part III, we will turn to the two largest emerging markets, China and India. After outlining the reasons for their extraordinary growth, we will see that each one has a different kind of imbalance to deal with. China has a strong state, dominated by the Communist Party. Can China's increasingly sophisticated and complex markets grow while the state continues to be under Party control? For democratic India, the challenge is to make the state more effective, while placing stronger constitutional limits on it. This requires a more independent private sector. As these countries, especially China, play a greater role in global governance, the future is worrying. Populist nationalism in the developed countries will strengthen incipient nationalism in the emerging markets, and make divisive conflict at the international level more likely. This is yet more reason why reforms are urgent.

5

———

THE PRESSURE
TO PROMISE

Competition and markets became terms of abuse in many countries during the Great Depression. The state grew at the expense of markets and the community, and continued growing during the subsequent world war as it organized the war effort. After the defeat of fascism in World War II, various varieties of socialism or communism seemed the natural alternative to capitalism in much of the world, even if not directly imposed by China or the Soviet Union on client states. Postwar Italy and Greece had strong communist parties, and the French Communist Party participated in postwar French cabinets.

Politically, therefore, the market system had to offer an attractive alternative to socialism. After all, the Soviet Union was the development success in the 1940s and 1950s (as China is the success today), having moved from a peasant economy to challenging the United States for world leadership in one generation. As the Second World War ended, the United States, victorious and confident, rebuilt the postwar international system. It created the necessary institutions to manage global trade, investment, and capital flows, and made loans and grants where needed to help countries recover or develop. The United States set in motion the forces that would encourage the formation of liberal market democracies around the world.

Nevertheless, with deep and widespread skepticism about competition dominating public sentiment even in the United States, the revival of the developed economies entailed a significant state presence in the markets. Nationalized firms accounted for a sizeable share of key industries in many countries, a number of prices and interest rates were regulated or fixed, and many market activities were limited or banned. Government-supported cartels permeated the private sector, and industry-wide wage agreements were rife. The visible hand of the state or state-like agencies was everywhere, including in international trade; the International Monetary Fund (IMF) monitored a system where countries had fixed exchange rates, which could be adjusted only after discussion with the IMF; and the General Agreement on Tariffs and Trade (GATT) tried to push all countries toward tariff reduction.

There was also widespread public revulsion with the divisive politics of the 1930s, especially in Western Europe. The establishment parties remembered that they had been outflanked by the radicals even while they were engaged in fighting one another. Perhaps further held together by a fear of the communists, especially with the Soviet Union's reach extending beyond the Iron Curtain into various communist organizations across Western Europe, mainstream parties did their best to accommodate one another and build consensus.

It worked miraculously! The developed world reached levels of prosperity that could not have been imagined in dark days of the Great Depression. Few, however, realized during these decades of high growth that their economy's spectacular performance owed in substantial part to a one-time repair of the damage done by depression and war, as well as a reaping of the remaining fruits of the Second Industrial Revolution. Interestingly, the socialist countries behind the Iron Curtain also grew reasonably, suggesting that command economies could flourish when growth was a matter of catching up with the leaders of the developed world. Communism's lure dimmed, though, as Soviet incursions into Hungary in 1956 and into Czechoslovakia in 1968 suggested that there was no real room for dissent in the Soviet empire, and as growing cynicism about the appropriation of benefits by the favored few in communist economies dampened worker incentives to work hard.

All was not well, though, even in developed countries. In the years of strong growth, the impulse to reward populations for the enormous hardships they had suffered led democratic governments to make promises of social benefits that relied heavily on continued strong economic growth. Government spending expanded enormously in the 1960s. A number of countries also got used to a steady stream of immigrant workers, with immigrants having second-class status and bearing the brunt of job losses in the mild postwar downturns. In the meantime, the inefficiencies stemming from state intervention and private-sector cartelization were masked by the continuing productivity benefits as the Second Industrial Revolution spread to the corners of every country. When these benefits came to an end toward the end of the 1960s, growth slowed considerably in the 1970s, inflation picked up, and resource-strapped governments had to look for new ways of energizing growth.

With the zeal of the long-suppressed and the ignored, the proponents of the market blamed state overreach for the growth slowdown, and pushed back against the state everywhere. The pendulum of public sentiment swung against the state again. The new consensus in developed democracies was to bring down inflation, to liberalize in order to remove the competitive barriers erected during the Depression, to deregulate to give business a freer hand, and to integrate economies further, including allowing freer movement of capital and people. Interestingly, the more individualistic Anglo-American economies emphasized deregulation while the more collectivist continental European economies emphasized integration to revive competition.

Growth picked up in developed democracies from the mid-1980s, though not to the previous heights. This growth, combined with greater openness, created markets for developing country exports, allowing a number to climb out of poverty. Left behind was the communist world, unable to liberalize or innovate to grow further without undermining their defining characteristic— state domination of the economy. Communist governments could manage large state-driven defense or space projects, but were not very good at consumer-oriented innovation. The competitive pressure capitalist innovation and efficiency placed on them proved intolerable. The Soviet empire broke up, with many of its successor countries discarding socialism. China never actually abandoned socialism but, economically, "socialism with Chinese characteristics" seemed a euphemism for managed competition, with privileges carved out for the state sector.

Even as some in the West celebrated the victory of liberal market democracy, the old fault lines started to become exposed. Growth was still insufficient to redeem the social promises that had been made, and government debt grew relentlessly. Furthermore, the early effects of the ICT revolution were exacerbating all kinds of inequality, without contributing significantly to growth. The pressure for workers to acquire new capabilities increased, even as immigration increased the diversity of the workforce, and a stronger embrace of civil rights for all made it impossible for developed societies to neglect anyone. Worried about fiscal sustainability, countries rolled back the welfare state, with its emphasis on post-market support. However, they did not redirect state spending sufficiently into enhancing pre-market worker capabilities. Social attitudes had swung all the way from assuming the state could do no wrong to believing it could get nothing right.

This chapter explains the postwar antecedents of the problems developed countries are experiencing today, which we will detail in the next chapter. It is also important to recognize the tremendous benefits of the postwar rules-based international order, the widespread trust in policy makers, and the political compact between establishment parties, all of which are under threat today. We will also see that public policy has impact with long lags, and tends to persist into futures its makers never envisaged, something we must always remind ourselves of.

THE POSTWAR MIRACLE

In the three decades or so after World War II, the developed world experienced the strongest growth it has ever seen. It was perhaps not so surprising that the United States, which emerged from World War II as the most powerful economic and military power on the planet, would grow strongly. However, Japanese growth was spectacular, as was Western Europe's, even though many of their cities had been bombed into rubble and significant portions of the population faced hunger, homelessness, and unemployment as the war ended.

Many parts of Europe were genuinely underdeveloped as the war ended. Countries like Spain and Portugal were poor even though the war had largely passed them by—one person in two in Spain and Portugal was in agriculture, while 40 percent of the Italian labor force was thus employed. In the late 1940s, the average age of machinery in France, one of the more advanced European economies, was twenty years old, compared to an average age of five years old in the United States. French farm productivity was one-third of the farm productivity in the United States.[1] It was not that the United States itself was uniformly developed. In 1940, only one-sixth of rural farms in the southern United States had electric lights, while over 80 percent still used kerosene or gasoline for lighting. Indeed, fewer than 60 percent of households in the United States had an exclusive indoor flush toilet or a bathing facility at that time; the rest had to do with outdoor privies or shared facilities.[2]

The postwar resurgence was driven by five elements: reconstruction, the resumption of trade, technological upgradation and the movement of workers away from agriculture, greater education and labor-force participation, and the broad political consensus for growth.[3] The immediate task of repairing the destruction caused by war was a source of employment for the semi-skilled in the workforce, and it generated household income that would fuel demand for other goods and services. Reconstruction needed funds, and strapped postwar European governments could tax their populations only so much. This is where American liberality under the Marshall Plan for aid to Europe, announced in 1948, helped tremendously.

The amount was not the most important aspect, though it was substantial and generous—a grant of about two percent of recipient country GDP between 1948 and 1951, or about $115 billion in today's money at a time when the United States was much less rich. What made the difference was the timing, the nature, and the manner in which it was delivered.[4] Europe needed capital goods and machinery, as well as raw materials like cotton, which only the United States could supply at that time. Few European importers had dollars. The Marshall Plan addressed this directly. Importers could order goods from US producers, the US government would pay the American producer directly out of Plan funds, and the European importer would pay its government. In short, the Plan addressed a dollar shortage, even while cleverly giving American politicians and labor a reason to support the plan; it would mean more US jobs.

Moreover, the funds were grants, which meant that the European government could use the "counterparty" funds paid into its coffers to finance domestic infrastructure spending without worrying about paying it back. Finally, the United States encouraged Europeans to discuss among themselves how best to use the funds, thus attempting to instill more economic cooperation among erstwhile enemies. For instance, with everyone looking for dollars, there was a fear that European countries would not import from one another, so as to preserve scarce foreign exchange. To avoid this mutually harmful path, they set up the European Payments Union in 1949, whereby countries agreed to offset claims against all others in the Union, with dollars used only to pay the net remaining claim.

Some of the early postwar structures, both within Germany and across Europe, had the explicit aim of addressing the fear that a resurgent Germany might go to war again. General Lucius Clay, the American military governor of defeated Germany, summarized American goals for the postwar German order as the four Ds: denazification, demilitarization, democratization, and decartelization. He could have added a fifth, decentralization.[5] In addition to breaking the power of the strongest corporations, the postwar administration did not want an overly strong center. The West German national government ceded a variety of powers to the subnational units, the *Länders,* with a powerful independent Federal Constitutional Court overseeing relations between the various units.

At the same time, pan-European structures sought to tie Germany economically to its traditional rival, France. Perhaps the most important new structure was the European Coal and Steel Community launched in 1951. Steel was critical to manufacturing, and for armaments. French Lorraine had massive reserves of ore, while the best coking coal was in the Ruhr Valley in Germany. Both sides had begun past wars trying to seize the other side's resources. The Coal and Steel Community was an attempt to address the issue by creating a supranational authority that would oversee a single market for coal and steel. It worked well enough that the six initial participants, Belgium, France, Italy, Luxembourg, the Netherlands, and West Germany, signed the Treaty of Rome in 1958, establishing the European Economic Community (EEC) and moving toward a common European market in goods and services.

Even outside the EEC, global trade grew as new multilateral organizations like the General Agreement on Trade and Tariffs pushed for lower import tariffs across the world. The IMF helped by monitoring exchange rates so that no country attempted to get an undue advantage from the increased openness by depreciating its exchange rate and exporting more, the "beggar-thy-neighbor" strategy that was much feared during the Great Depression. In addition, if a country started running excessively large trade deficits, the IMF offered it foreign currency loans to give it time to adjust its balances, so that it would not have to curtail its citizens' consumption abruptly. The World Bank initially helped the reconstruction effort in Europe. It shifted focus when Marshall Plan funds started pouring into Europe, to fund infrastructure in other, less-developed, parts of the world.

There was a fundamental change in assumptions underlying this new postwar rules-based order. Countries were no longer on their own bottom, alone unless they were lucky enough to have powerful friends. Implicitly, the new order asked countries to abandon the prewar zero-sum model, where one country's growth diminished the power and security of others. Instead, it urged countries not to be suspicious of one another's growth but to recognize they had a stake in it. Every country's growth and development was seen via increased trade and investment as beneficial to all, especially as the rules constrained selfish behavior or coercive threats by the economically powerful. The system assumed responsibility to help every country in need, provided they signed on to behaving reasonably and following the rules of the system.

American idealism was reflected in the largely democratic governance structures that the United States worked into many of the new multilateral institutions. Moreover, the new international order was rules-based. This meant that even the weakest country had some rights and protections and even the most powerful country, the United States, was theoretically subject to the rules—though practically it could find some outs. The postwar system could only have been set up by a country supremely confident of its capabilities, motivated by a genuine appreciation of the collective potential and possibilities if countries came together. The United States was that country. The reality of the postwar system fell short of its aspirations, but its aspirations were truly inspirational.

Western Europe, the first beneficiary of this new order, became much more productive. Output grew not just from new investment in machinery, but also from the increased use of motor vehicles and the spread of electrification, the resumption of the interrupted rollout of the Second Industrial Revolution. These developments created a variety of virtuous circles.

For instance, as farmers started using tractors, labor left agriculture and moved to work in new factories (that were being set up to utilize the cheap labor), and to live in the growing cities. Manufacturing required more educated workers, and average education attainments improved substantially across Western Europe. An increasing number of graduates filled the huge demand for skilled workers in the industrializing economies. Growing worker incomes then led to greater demand for consumer goods, completing the virtuous circle. As one example of the tremendous growth in manufacturing, in 1951 Italian factories made just 18,500 refrigerators, two decades later they were producing over five million a year.[6] The explosion in supply was absorbed by a matching increase in demand. In 1957, fewer than 2 percent of Italian households had a fridge, in large part because few owned cars with which to shop in sufficiently large quantities to stock fridges. Indeed, Italy had just 7 cars per thousand people in the early 1950s.[7] Today, such a low level of car ownership would rank it at 172 out of 191 countries, putting Italy at a similar level to poor developing countries like Gambia and Niger.[8] By 1970, however, Italian car ownership had increased by more than thirty times that, which would put Italy at the same level as Thailand today.[9] With widespread car ownership came fridges. By 1974, 94 percent of Italian households owned refrigerators, the highest ownership in Europe.

Western European income growth was truly spectacular. Real income per person grew by an average of 6 percent every year between 1946 and 1975 in Germany, by 5.6 percent in Italy, by 4.2 percent in France, and by 2 percent in the United Kingdom. Growth rates seem less impressive in France and the United Kingdom, but that is because their postwar income was not so depressed as that of the defeated powers. By 1975, income per head in these four countries ranged from a low of $10,619 (in 1990 dollars) in Italy to a high of $12,957 in France. By comparison, US per capita income in 1975 was $16,284. Therefore, Western Europe had reached about three-quarters of US income levels from about a third of its level when the war ended. In addition, the postwar baby boom added to its population and to overall economic growth, with the French population growing by nearly 30 percent between 1946 and the late 1960s.[10] No wonder French writer Jean Forastie, writing in 1979 about the postwar transformation of France, titled his book *Les trente glorieuses, ou, La revolution invisible de 1946 a 1975* (*The Glorious Thirty: Or, the Invisible Revolution between 1946 and 1975*). The Germans were no less ebullient about their *Wirtschaftswunder* ("economic miracle").

How did Western Europe know what to do to grow? Western Europe was exceptional but not unique. Japan too experienced a growth miracle as, to a lesser extent, did some of the countries of Eastern Europe. In a sense, growth for all these countries was largely a matter of catch-up, following the tracks of the United States. Specifically, economic growth first comes from putting more people and equipment to work in the most productive sectors (so, for instance, much of the growth of developing countries comes as people leave agriculture for more productive jobs in manufacturing and services). Once resources are allocated to the right sectors, though, and each worker there has sufficient capital equipment and knows the latest techniques of production, more productivity can come only from inventing new useful products or yet better techniques of production.

For much of the first three postwar decades, Europe was putting people to work outside agriculture, equipping them with the right machinery and skills, and imitating and improving on US technologies and production methods developed in the Second Industrial Revolution. Not only did these follower countries have a long way to go to catch up with where the United States already was, the United States was gradually expanding the technological possibility frontier further, with new discoveries and techniques extending the scope and benefits of the fundamental discoveries earlier in the century. As a result, per capita US income growth was a steady 2 percent over those three decades, much the same as its growth since 1870. Despite spectacular growth, and even though Western Europe narrowed the gap significantly, it had not fully caught up even by the early 1970s.

It is one thing to know what to do politically, it is an entirely different matter to do it. That leads us to perhaps the most important element responsible for the three decades of strong postwar growth—consensus politics. Perhaps Western European politicians remembered all too well the prewar bickering that led to unpreparedness among the Allied powers and the fascist takeover in the Axis powers. Perhaps they feared meddling by the Soviet

Union through its local proxies if they gave it a chance. Perhaps they were sufficiently chastened by the terrible war and the subsequent deprivation to try and work together. Or . . . perhaps growth created enough spoils that they were happy sharing it without bringing it to a halt by being greedy. And Western Europe was full of arrangements whereby spoils such as influence over media and the right to appoint supporters to government jobs were shared among the large political parties. So long as grease did not get excessive, it lubricated the paths to political consensus.

Policy was left to the technocrats, like Ludwig Erhard, who led Germany's postwar reforms, or Jean Monnet, the French champion of an integrated Europe, and given that there were few questions about the broad directions, they were left alone as growth continued. The steady opening up to external trade, for example, would have been difficult if politicians were willing to be disruptive in an environment where the public was still wary of competition. As it was, few objected, and growing trade lifted all countries. The willingness to trust technocrats allowed them to build a system that was beneficial for all countries, and therefore beneficial for each country. Growth would have been much more difficult if each policy had to meet today's test of being clearly and immediately beneficial for a country.

THE GATHERING PROBLEMS

Across the developed world, there was a sense that states had finally learned how to tame markets and use their powers effectively. During the thirty heady postwar years, downturns were shallow. Economists believed their Keynesian stabilization policies were effective in smoothing demand and reducing the depth of the recessions; when the economy weakened, the central bank cut interest rates, and the government spent more, and these policies were reversed when the economy strengthened once again. How much the underlying strong intrinsic growth potential of the economy contributed to the effectiveness of Keynesian policies was not something policy makers dwelled on. Instead, they extrapolated strong growth, with minor dips, well into the future. And so they became more expansive on the promises they made, as well as the people they drew in to their countries.

PROMISES MADE . . .

War is perhaps the most extreme exertion of collective national will, and when waged by democracies, it requires tremendous shared sacrifice. In most twentieth-century wars, young working-class men bore the brunt of the war effort, many not returning from the fighting, while others returned physically disabled or mentally scarred. The Second World War did not even spare those who stayed at home. Ordinary civilians, even in countries like the United Kingdom that escaped occupation or a ground war, had experienced severe food rationing, bombing, and fear of invasion, even while they were exhorted to work hard for the war effort. As people came together to fight for the nation, there was a sense that the nation owed something to them and their communities. Therefore, as growth stayed strong and sustained in the postwar years, developed countries loosened their purse strings and promised to share the fruits of growth more widely.

Perhaps the quickest to do so was the United Kingdom. Despite the reforms of the Liberal government in 1908–1911 that we listed in the last chapter, the United Kingdom still had a patchwork of social insurance programs that did not amount to a comprehensive safety net. In the darkest days of the Second World War, economist William Beveridge was asked to chair a committee with the somewhat tedious task of examining the existing safety net and seeing how benefits could be better coordinated—perhaps more as a make-work assignment that would keep the radical economist at a safe distance from immediate policy.[11] His report in 1942 was, however, an instant bestseller, extraordinary for a work that contained 461 numbered paragraphs and appendices filled with detailed calculations. Final sales figures were over half a million, including fifty thousand in the United States. A cheap edition was even printed and circulated to troops at the front, explaining what they were fighting for.

Beveridge proposed a single system of insurance against the important risks faced by a working-class family: childbirth, sickness, disability, unemployment, and old age. He outlined a contributory system where every working person paid into the system at the same rate, and anyone hit by one of these risks was helped with the same subsistence level of assistance. The idea was one contributory rate for one level of benefit for everyone, without any

screens, such as whether the individual earned too much. Beveridge emphasized the principle that everyone would contribute, though employers and
the state would also chip in. His aim was not to redistribute income between
classes, though some redistribution was unavoidable, but to move an individual's income "between times of earning and not earning, and between
times of heavy family responsibility and of light or no family responsibility."[12]

The mandated contributions ensured that people would treat the safety
net as their property right, much as Roosevelt wanted Americans to view
social security in the United States. The setting of benefits at a subsistence
level ensured that they did not deter anyone from arranging for additional
personal buffers such as private insurance, or become so comfortable that a
worker would not seek employment when adversity abated. In addition, the
Beveridge Report recommended child allowances to alleviate the burden on
young families at their point of maximum need, free universal health insurance, as well as government responsibility for delivering full employment.

Even though there were critics—some Conservatives saw Beveridge as
"a sinister old man who wants to give away a great deal of other people's
money"—the Report captured the prevailing sense of national unity and
egalitarianism in a nation under attack.[13] If the nation had to come together,
from the richest to the poorest, to defeat the Axis powers, it was incumbent
on the rich to not let those of more modest means drown when normal life
resumed. In the national election after the war, both Conservatives and Labor
promised to implement the Beveridge Report, and the victorious Labor Party
did implement much of it. Indeed, in 2012, the National Health Service,
which delivers free universal health care in the United Kingdom, was fea-
tured in the opening ceremonies of the London Olympic Games as "the institution which more than any other unites the nation."

Much of continental Europe also strengthened its safety nets in the years
of plenty. For example, the West German Social Security Reform Act of 1957
assured workers of a very generous pension that was tied to their wage on
retirement, and further adjusted with the cost of living. The United States
was initially the exception among developed countries. It did do its bit for
returning military personnel with the GI Bill in 1944, which paid tuition and
living expenses for them to attend high school or college, and ensured they
got a low-interest mortgage or a loan to start a business. And it did raise

marginal tax rates on the wealthy to 94 percent in 1944, arguably as their payment for the war effort.[14] However, it did not go further in strengthening the safety net immediately after the war, despite being the richest country in the world.

What still held the United States back was its minorities. When World War II ended, it was hard for American society to sustain claims of white superiority when the nation had just sacrificed hundreds of thousands of lives combating Nazi and Japanese totalitarianism and their claims of racial superiority. The bells celebrating the victory of the forces of democracy and freedom rang hollow when set against the reality of the black experience—where African American military policemen posted in the southern United States could not enter restaurants in which their German prisoners were being served meals.[15]

Even though poverty rates among African Americans were higher than the average population, they certainly did not constitute the majority of the poor. Nevertheless, any measure to help the poor had to pass muster with Southern politicians, some of whom would have preferred the measures to bypass blacks. Indeed, even though African American servicemen were not excluded from getting benefits under the GI Bill, their actual access to its benefits, especially in the South, was much more limited.

In 1963, from the steps of the Lincoln Memorial, Dr. Martin Luther King Jr. urged Americans to honor the promissory note the founding fathers had given that "all men—yes, black men as well as white men—would be guaranteed the unalienable rights of life, liberty, and the pursuit of happiness." When he declared, "We refuse to believe that the bank of justice is bankrupt. We refuse to believe that there are insufficient funds in the great vaults of opportunity of this nation. So we've come to cash this check, a check that will give us upon demand the riches of freedom and the security of justice," he was speaking both figuratively and literally.[16] The Civil Rights movement undoubtedly pricked the nation's conscience, and, when coupled with the public's generosity buoyed by rising incomes, helped overcome America's traditional reluctance to expand the safety net.

President Lyndon Johnson, who had lived among, and worked with, the poor during his youth and through the Depression years, provided persuasive leadership. The political attractiveness of targeting the votes of blacks who had migrated from southern agricultural jobs for the industrial jobs in northern cities gave politicians the incentive to follow.[17] Congress enacted a radical set of government- and community-based programs intended to wage war on poverty and make the United States into Johnson's Great Society. Funding was increased significantly for welfare, especially for the indigent elderly, for health care (including Medicare for the elderly and Medicaid for the poor), and for education—the Elementary and Secondary Education Act of 1965 was reauthorized by President Bush as the No Child Left Behind Act of 2001, and by President Obama as the Every Student Succeeds Act in 2015.

Importantly, poor communities got direct support from the federal government with a stipulation that it entail "maximum feasible participation" of the local community in decision making, in part so that southern state governments, unsympathetic to African American communities, would not divert support. Poverty levels did come down in the 1960s. As related in a searing critique by Daniel Moynihan in his book *Maximum Feasible Misunderstanding*, though, many of the programs were poorly coordinated and poorly structured. Perhaps there was a fundamental inconsistency in the state taking up the role of strengthening community. Moreover, it was not clear whether the objective of community engagement was to organize a new power structure for the community, confront the existing power structure, or extend or assist the existing power structure.[18] At any rate, the programs did not sit well with existing structures and interests, and did not draw in those in the community with sensible ideas of how to raise economic opportunity.

Traditional political leadership, intent on protecting its turf, pushed back on community involvement, while neighborhood activists fought any structure that was not their own. Almost inevitably, the War on Poverty became more top-down than bottom-up, and failed to sustain enthusiasm even among initial supporters like Dr. King, who wanted more comprehensive, coordinated action. As the Vietnam War consumed President Johnson's political energies, some of the innovative spending was repurposed to support the war effort. As northern blacks became confirmed Democratic voters and not voters in play, political support disintegrated, and the innovative decentralized aspects of the program atrophied.[19] What remained was the increased federal and state spending on social security, health care, and education. US social spending never approached European levels, but the thirty glorious postwar years had seen the spigots opened in the United States as well.

IMMIGRATION

The postwar baby boom would eventually create a larger labor force, but in the meantime, strong growth created many new jobs. As citizens moved up into better-paying jobs, countries needed workers for the jobs they vacated. West Germany, even after absorbing the migrants fleeing East Germany, had yet more jobs to fill, and in the 1960s signed agreements with Greece, Morocco, Portugal, Spain, Tunisia, Turkey, and Yugoslavia whereby they would send "guest" workers to West Germany, on condition they would eventually return. In 1973, foreign workers were one-eighth of the labor force in Germany. France was not far behind, with 2.3 million foreign workers, or 11 percent of the labor force. Many of these were employed for childcare, as cooks, and as custodians.[20] England drew immigrants from the Caribbean and South Asia, including those expelled by Idi Amin from East Africa.

Europe wanted to treat these immigrants as temporary, and many did not enjoy the same workforce protections as citizens. In downturns, these were the workers who were first to be laid off. Employers had little incentive to invest in them or promote them, while countries did not believe they had to work on integrating them. The immigrants themselves, thankful for jobs that payed significantly more than at home, were docile and submitted to a separate and unequal existence, on the outskirts of the cities whose essential services they helped run. Many stayed on, though, and their children were no longer willing to accept a second-class existence. Population homogeneity, which contributed so much to the ease with which European countries had adopted generous social policies, diminished—in many cases, immigrants looked and spoke very differently from the native population. Even at this early stage, politicians, such as Enoch Powell in the United Kingdom, started speaking up (in 1968) about the "sense of being a persecuted minority which is growing among ordinary English people," and warned about "the River Tiber foaming with much blood" as immigrants organized.[21] He was alarmist no doubt, but his speech was of a tradition that resurges periodically.

The United States too amended its immigration laws, which had been reformed in 1924 to both restrict immigration and give preference to Western Europeans. In keeping with the prevailing sentiment against racism, the Hart-Celler Act of 1965 eliminated national origin, race, or ancestry as a basis for immigration, and stopped privileging immigration from Western Europe over other countries. It gave priority to relatives of citizens, as also those with especially needed skills. After its steady decline from about 15 percent of the population in 1910, the immigrant share of the population in the United States hit a trough in 1970 of around 5 percent, after which the numbers started climbing steadily once again with the new, more tolerant, environment.

In tracing problems back to that era, one should not overlook the benefits of the spectacular postwar growth, and the resumption of trade: The incipient authoritarian tendencies of developed countries, manifest in the interwar period, were quelled. Democracy was placed on firmer foundations with strong economic growth, and as pre- and post-market supports built trust in the policies of moderate centrist parties. More developing countries were drawn into the path of liberalism. The treatment of minorities and immigrants improved. The world was, by and large, at peace.

AND THEN GROWTH STOPPED . . .

Unfortunately, as the 1960s ended, and just as governments had promised their citizens a substantial share of the high anticipated future growth, growth suddenly proved much harder to generate. There were plenty of proximate causes: rising inflation in the United States as spending on the Vietnam quagmire added to the new social spending promised in the War on Poverty; the subsequent breakdown of the Bretton Woods system of fixed exchange rates as the United States abandoned the international convertibility of the dollar into gold; the tripling of oil prices as OPEC tested its powers after the Yom Kippur war broke out . . . But perhaps the most obvious reason was that the gains from the Second Industrial Revolution had largely played out.

This would not have mattered earlier in Europe and Japan when they were in catch-up mode. As Europe and Japan got closer to the known frontier of innovation and productive efficiency in the early 1970s, though, they had to shift from imitating ideas and best practices elsewhere to innovating on their own. With the frontier expanding more slowly, their growth also slowed.

Most economists envisage growth for economies at the frontier as periods of path-breaking innovation (when the key innovations of the technological revolution emerge) followed by steady development and implementation until most of the gains from that innovation have been reaped. Tyler Cowen of George Mason University and Robert Gordon of Northwestern University argue that most of the possibilities of the Second Industrial Revolution had been exhausted by the end of the 1960s.[22] For instance, the big innovation that made commercial air travel more attractive than travel by ocean liner was reasonably safe and fast jet planes with pressurized air cabins. During my lifetime, commercial planes have gotten a lot safer and the rides relatively cheaper. Flights are easier to book, less noisy and much more comfortable (the older reader might remember bumpier rides and air sickness), despite the more cramped seating. However, the technology of travel has not fundamentally changed.

Emphasizing this point, Gordon points out that growth in output per hour worked in the United States was at its highest at 2.8 percent in the period 1920 to 1970. This is when the main innovations of the Second Industrial Revolution were being developed and used across the country.[23] After that, though, growth dropped to only 1.6 percent between 1970 and 2014.

An aside may be useful here. We are in the midst of the ICT revolution, when the media breathlessly reports the latest advances in artificial intelligence or in immunotherapy, and yet growth in output per hour over the last few decades has been "only" 1.6 percent per year. How can we call this a revolution, and yet also claim growth is low? To set this in context, note that between 1870 and 1920, a period that included life-changing innovations like the internal combustion engine, the airplane, and electric lighting, growth in output per hour was similar at 1.8 percent. The reality is that growth at the frontier is hard—for much of history, countries grew at a fraction of a percentage point a year, if at all. So 1.6 percent annually is not trivial. Moreover, innovation translates into actual growth after long and unpredictable lags, for it takes time for society to envisage and build systems that can use the innovations productively. For instance, as historian Paul David pointed out, electric power displaced steam power in factories only when factories were rebuilt to use multiple small motors rather than one single large engine.[24] Finally, technological change may have substantial impact in some areas and not in others at any point in time, keeping the overall growth rate moderate even while changing our lives—for instance, I rarely visit a bank or a department store any more as I transact online, while students still go to school every day and sit in classrooms listening to teachers, as they have for centuries.

Growth also slowed because the growth in working population fell. Overall economic growth is, approximately, the sum of the growth in output per person working and the growth in number of people working. While the postwar growth in developed country populations was strong initially because of the baby boom, female fertility rates fell dramatically. The birth rate in West Germany fell from 17.3 per thousand population in 1960 to about 10 in the mid-1970s, and stayed at that level. The falls in Italy and Spain were, if anything, more dramatic.[25] While female participation in the labor force increased for a while and compensated for the overall fall in population growth, it too plateaued by the early years of this century.

As a result of slowing growth in output per hour and the slowing growth of the labor force, US economic growth has been slowing steadily since the 1960s, from an average annual growth rate of 4.5 percent in the 1960s, to about 3 percent in the next three decades, to about 2 percent in this century. While there has been a lot of debate about whether we are underplaying innovation and productivity by under-measuring growth—we don't fully capture the quality of new cars or the safety of air travel, and we don't put a monetary value on many of the services the internet provides us for free—the emerging consensus is that these effects are too small to account for the drop in productivity growth, and that the decline is real.[26] Of course, nothing indicates it could not pick up again, and techno-optimists believe we will eventually see the fruits of the ICT revolution reflected in greater productivity growth, though probably not at postwar rates.

BALLOONING GOVERNMENT DEFICITS

The promises made to the public on health care and pensions in the sixties, which were premised on continuing strong productivity growth and strong population growth, had to confront the reality in the 1970s that growth in both was likely to be much slower. Fewer babies also meant more rapid population aging, and an increasing share of the population of the elderly, whose pensions and health care would have to be paid by a shrinking number of younger people in the workforce—unless the country chose to allow more immigration. Moreover, as the underlying growth potential of economies slowed, recessions were no longer shallow, so outlays on unemployment insurance and poor relief also increased. It was now clear that governments had overpromised in the years of strong growth.

Government spending as a share of GDP ballooned. For a while, central banks accommodated that spending with expansionary monetary policy because they worried about slowing growth. In contrast to the Keynesian prediction, easy monetary policy no longer induced growth. Instead, economies suffered both stagnant growth and high inflation—quickly termed stagflation. The reason was simple. Keynesian stimulus worked well when the problem was insufficient demand—cutting interest rates would make people spend more thus restoring growth. In the early 1970s, though, the problem was supply—the lack of competition was beginning to tell. In the immediate postwar decades, the reallocation of labor to more productive sectors, coupled with greater capital investment and more effective production techniques, had allowed supply to keep pace with strong demand. Now, inefficient management practices and overstaffing began to limit what could be supplied at a price people would pay. More demand stimulus under such conditions would just result in more inflation, not more growth.

The misery index, the sum of the annual inflation rate and the unemployment rate, climbed across the developed world. It reached its highest level in the postwar United States under President Jimmy Carter. Taming inflation was now a political imperative. Carter appointed Paul Volcker as chairman of the Federal Reserve, and Volcker embarked on a no-holds-barred fight against inflation, raising the federal funds interest rate to 19.1 percent in 1981, a level that had not been seen postwar (or since). That did the job, though the United States suffered a double-dip recession. As the United States brought inflation under control, central banks across the world made low and stable inflation their primary objective.

Inflation fell but states, beset by low tax revenues and high spending on unemployment and attendant benefits, found it hard to bring down their deficit spending. In the United States, initiatives to "starve the [government] beast" and bring down taxes contributed to yet higher deficits. Public debt as a share of GDP in developed countries climbed steadily beginning in the late 1970s—primarily because jolts of higher inflation were no longer available to reduce its real value. In the United States, for example, postwar government debt as a fraction of GDP hit a trough in 1981 and has climbed since (the only exception being the late 1990s when high economic growth and fiscal surpluses brought debt down temporarily). Across the developed world, states realized they had to find new ways of reenergizing growth because productivity growth from technological change was no longer readily available. They turned for help to the markets.

THE SEARCH FOR GREATER EFFICIENCY

The postwar consensus was that the state had an important role to play in the market, if not in actually producing goods and services, certainly in regulating them and restraining excessive competition. Too little competition was not deemed a problem. The only deviation from this consensus was that impediments to trade were collectively self-defeating, so customs and tariff barriers were reduced steadily after the war. Now, states reexamined the anticompetitive consensus, as the public grew impatient with rising inflation and unemployment. The votaries for the market, such as the University of Chicago's Friedrich Hayek and Milton Friedman, who had been ignored during the period of state ascendancy, now found a wider audience, including among influential politicians. The growing realization that all manner of cozy oligopolies had taken hold of the productive sector, and that greater competition could be a source of productive efficiency as well as growth, spurred reforms.

These included deregulating industries, privatizing public-sector firms, reducing the extent to which workers were protected from layoffs by law, eliminating restrictions on securities issuance and pricing in financial markets, as well as on competition between banks, brokers, and other financial institutions, and further reducing barriers to trade and capital flows. Interestingly, as industries in one country got more competitive, the effects flowed through trade, and increasingly capital flows, to spur reform and competition in other countries.

Consider some examples. Within industry, all manner of regulations restrained price competition. Since being set up in 1938, the US Civil Aeronautics Board assumed powers to award routes to carriers, to regulate the entry of new carriers, and to approve fares. In exercising these powers, it typically favored incumbents. Ticket prices were high, service was good, and pay as well as travel perks were excellent for those who could get jobs in airlines. Airline pilots and air stewards led a glamorous and much-envied existence.

Airline deregulation in 1978, driven by economist Alfred Kahn under the Carter administration, changed all this. Prices of tickets fell steadily, airports became more congested as air travel was no longer a preserve of the elite, service quality fell as airlines cut out the frills and focused on getting people from point to point on time, and airline worker benefits were cut steadily as new airlines entered and challenged existing ones. As measured by growth in travel, and the reduction in prices to the consumer, deregulation was a tremendous success. It certainly has democratized air travel. Of course, one can also complain about surly airline staff, narrow seats, and the tendency of airlines to contemplate charging for everything including bags, meals, and (fortunately not yet implemented) visits to the restroom. In a sense, airlines are only responding to what the market wants, and those who want (slightly) better service only have to pay for it. The terms of engagement have, however, also changed for airline staff, something we will return to in the next chapter.

The United States, first during Jimmy Carter's presidency, then under President Ronald Reagan, deregulated a number of other industries such as electric power, trucking, and finance. Both Ronald Reagan and Prime Minister Margaret Thatcher in the United Kingdom gained substantial public support by facing down powerful unions. In 1981, Reagan fired over eleven thousand striking unionized government air-traffic controllers, and banned them from federal service for life. Thatcher went against unionized public-sector coal miners, who were protesting the closure of collieries. The self-defeating yearlong strike that started in 1984 broke the back of the poorly led union, and freed the government to close coal mines. It eventually privatized a much-diminished coal sector. The Thatcher government also put a large number of public-sector firms like British Telecom and British Airways up for sale. In a further attempt to spread private ownership, Thatcher reserved some of the shares sold in privatized firms for the small shareholder, while she also sold off much of the public housing stock to current occupants, and then more broadly.

Paradoxically, for someone who spoke about returning power to the people, Thatcher centralized government, taking away both the funding and powers from local government through the 1986 Local Government Act.[27] Thatcher did not believe in the value of community, preferring individuals and families to navigate the world alone. She had a vision of an individualistic market economy, shepherded by a strong but limited state, with no real place for social structures, the community, that might balance the two. She pushed toward this goal whenever opportunities arose. As she put it to the doubters in her party, "You turn if you want. The lady's not for turning."

Across developed countries, states liberalized not just the industrial sector but also financial markets. As with airline deregulation, competition among financial institutions and on market exchanges reduced the public's costs and improved its access to financial services. It also led to narrower margins and lower intrinsic profitability for financial-sector firms, greater volatility in financial markets, and greater pressure to innovate and take risks. The right state response to such pressures would have been for better, more thoughtful regulation. There was, unfortunately, no room for nuance.

The Conservative and Libertarian academics and intellectuals who had been preaching in the wilderness since the Depression did not expect to ever have the ear of policy makers. Now that they had it, they did not want to let it stray. Their reaction to the postwar state overreach was often ideological, and sometimes untainted by the realities of the world. The market had to be given full and unfettered reign, and liberated from the shackles that had been imposed on it, they asserted. Only then would it achieve its full potential and the strong economic growth that everyone desired. Regulation was unwarranted, they claimed, because competition would punish the incompetent, as well as the excessive risk-takers. Indeed, if given a chance, they stressed, incumbents would influence regulators in ways to restrict competition.

There was some truth to all this. Equally, though, the complete absence of regulatory oversight could lead to cartelization or excessive risk-taking, both diseases that the unfettered market is prone to. The public debate needed balance, but the decades of past state overreach had fostered a strong, hitherto silent, opposition. The regulatory pendulum was swinging back, and it gained momentum as the initial liberalization proved successful. The pervasive sentiment on regulation among the liberalizing governments was "less is more."

FULL SPEED AHEAD ON INTEGRATION IN EUROPE

Unlike the United States and the United Kingdom, continental Europe did not react to the slowdown in the 1970s with a wholesale move toward deregulation and liberalization. While market "fundamentalism" along with individualism were seen as Anglo-American fetishes that were not conducive to civilized conduct or social harmony, European politicians were also reluctant to confront the electorate after thirty glorious years of growth with the reality that they had promised too much.

The kinds of protections that Europe had built for incumbent workers were also not conducive to social harmony. So long as immigrants from Southern Europe and Turkey bore the brunt of job losses in business cycle downturns, Western European workers could have it all. As growth slowed significantly in the 1970s, however, unemployment mounted even among the native born. *Eurosclerosis* was the term German economist Herbert Giersch used to describe Europe's slow growth and high unemployment, brought about by the postwar accumulation of regulations and social protections. While the incumbent "insider" workers who had jobs were well protected, the unlucky few who lost their jobs or the youth who entered the labor market were shut out.

So continental Europe faced pressures to change. It now received a push. The deregulation of financial markets did much to spread further market reforms, from the Anglo-American economies, across the developed world. As capital started moving rapidly across borders and became hard for any single state to control, it limited the extent to which individual states could buck the liberalizing trend. For instance, François Mitterrand was elected president of France in 1981 on a traditional Socialist platform of raising wages, lowering working hours and the retirement age, adding a fifth week of holiday, and, most important, nationalizing banks, financial houses, and the largest industrial corporations.[28] These measures were, in part, meant to reassure Mitterrand's coalition partners, the Communists. They were certainly not calculated to improve business confidence. As French growth slowed further, unemployment increased, and fears of larger fiscal deficits (in part to pay for the nationalizations) and additional taxation to bring them down took hold of markets. Capital started fleeing the country. The franc was devalued multiple times in the European exchange rate system.

France had to choose between continuing with its statist policies, clamping down on cross-border flows, and withdrawing from closer economic ties with its European neighbors, or doing a volte-face. The ever-pragmatic Mitterrand chose the latter, freezing wages, cutting public spending and raising taxes, and thus stabilizing the inflation rate and the exchange rate. He used the crisis to end his cohabitation with the Communists in 1984, and shifted toward market-friendly policies.

The European integration project was running out of steam in the mid-1980s, and Mitterand's government now transferred its energies to reviving it. Three important impediments to a unified European market were a plethora of rules and regulations that differed across countries, impediments to the movement of firms and labor across countries, and currency fluctuation. In a series of negotiated agreements, starting with the Single European Act in 1986, the Maastricht Treaty in 1991, and the Treaty of Amsterdam in 1997, much of Europe agreed to merge into a Union which would implement the four freedoms—the freedom of movement of goods, services, people, and capital across the borders of the signatories. They agreed to a common European citizenship, over and above national citizenship. In addition, a subset of the countries decided to adopt a common currency, the euro. The hope was that as barriers came down between countries, new sources of growth would emerge that would relieve the politicians of hard decisions. Moreover, as cross-border competition picked up, countries would reform, but they hoped in a more gentle way.

CURRENCY INTEGRATION

The most important step toward integration in continental Europe was the movement toward a single currency. Historically, France and the other "southern" countries like Italy and Spain were politically more willing to accommodate worker wage demands and less quick to tighten budgetary deficits than Germany, which still remembered the hyperinflation in 1923. As a result, these countries had a higher propensity for inflation. In addition, the independent German Bundesbank enforced tight monetary policies that kept inflation in Germany much lower than in France and Southern Europe. As wages in domestic currency rose faster in France and Southern Europe compared to Germany, they needed a steady depreciation of their exchange rate in order to retain competitiveness. Corporations disliked having to manage the resulting exchange rate volatility—it was costly to hedge exchange risk, and unhedged contracts could become unprofitable overnight. Therefore, after the breakdown of the Bretton Woods system of fixed exchange rates, a number of countries in Europe tried to tie their currencies to the deutsche mark under the European Exchange Rate Mechanism (ERM), hoping to inherit Germany's low inflation and low interest rates, even while reducing currency volatility with respect to their most important trading partners.

Unless they implemented Germany's conservative fiscal and wage policies, though, countries were likely to have to adjust their exchange rates periodically, even under the ERM—as France did in the early 1980s. Rather than quit, France and Southern Europe decided to double up. In a classic example of the triumph of hope over experience, France persuaded Germany to adopt a common currency, the euro, as the price for accepting German reunification. A common currency required similar national policies on government budget deficits and on wages. Governments were, in effect, promising to be less sympathetic to union wage demands. Similarly, a sovereign government that agreed to rules on its ability to spend more, or tax less, was giving up some ability to respond to the democratic demands of the people. Nevertheless, in the Stability and Growth Pact in 1997, European Union countries agreed to common rules on the size of the deficits they could run (3 percent) as well as the stock of debt they could issue (60 percent), beyond which they had to implement corrective measures.

THE PROBLEMS EMERGE

In their rush to integrate, leaders were all too willing to suspend disbelief about one another's behavior. The Stability and Growth Pact was intended to make sure that no country became a charge on the others by overspending and running large fiscal deficits. The pact, however, imposed little fiscal discipline when truly needed. Some countries like Greece hid the true extent of their deficits before they entered. Moreover, there were sixty-eight violations of the terms of the pact before the Global Financial Crisis without any action being taken against the violators.[29] Large countries like France, and yes, even Germany, ignored the rules imposed by the Stability and Growth Pact when it impinged on their policies. Without discipline on wages or fiscal deficits, the countries in the euro area had very different levels of inflation. The overspending southern periphery, not surprisingly, had higher inflation. Nevertheless, all countries had similar interest rates since they had one common central bank, and no one believed any country would default. Greek government bond rates approached German government bond rates. As we will see, differing inflation and common interest rates was a recipe for disaster because it made borrowing seem very cheap in the high-inflation periphery.

Another source of potential friction was the free movement of people within the Union. With widely differing social protections, countries worried that those with stronger social protections would attract the needy from elsewhere. The Union simply did not have the mutual empathy to absorb such flows. It was not that the leaders were unaware of the consequences of their push to integration. Yet they seemed to be confident they had the solutions.

For instance, to facilitate trade and investment, leaders agreed to the harmonization of rules and regulations. The agreements could be intrusive and impinge on national sovereignty. Therefore, the Union agreed to the principle of *subsidiarity*—in which, except for matters that fell within its explicit jurisdiction, the Union would not attempt to override national, regional, or local policies unless its intervention was deemed more effective. At best, this was vague, for how would effectiveness be determined?

At the same time, national policies were undercut in two immediate ways. First, the Union agreed that a country could not ban an imported product that conformed to quality and safety standards in the member country in which it was produced. For example, Germany could no longer keep out Belgian beer because it violated the Bavarian purity law of 1516 banning additives.[30] Second, in order to expedite policy agreement as the membership of the Union expanded (and to prevent small countries from blackmailing the Union for extra funds, as had been the practice for some), the Union did away with vetoes for each country for many policies and went to majority rule. Countries now had to implement commonly agreed Union policies, even if they were against it. All this introduced a new form of inequality and resentment in the Union. Essentially, small countries had given up some of their sovereignty to the Union bureaucracy and to the powerful large countries that could influence Union policy.

In summary, then, Europe bet more on integration, on a supranational Union with a common integrated market to deal with slowing growth. While the European Union harmonized rules and regulations, national governments still took major decisions. Europe was trying to have it both ways— enjoy a seamless common economy while retaining some degree of national political autonomy. It did not work well.

THE LOSS OF SOVEREIGNTY

European integration was fundamentally a political project, driven by leaders who initially wanted to entangle Germany economically so that it could prosper without becoming a threat once more. Germany was happy to go along, with Europe becoming the vehicle for the national ambitions it could not express, and its financial contributions the price of atonement. Over time, as the war became more distant in memory, a new rationale became more prominent: Integration in Europe could be a way of generating stronger growth without taking hard decisions, and might even generate enough growth to allow Europe to fulfil the promises made in the years of plenty. Intra-European immigration could supplement aging populations, and avoid the need for culturally very different immigrants. Moreover, to the extent that reforms were pushed by the bureaucrats of the European Union, they could also be a convenient scapegoat for unpopular decisions. "Brussels made us do it" became a convenient mantra for pusillanimous politicians. As economic integration progressed, yet another rationale came to the forefront. Integration allowed the Union's leaders to be taken seriously by the United States and China in a way that no country leader on their own could hope to be. European integration was, in sum, a top-down project of the elites.

The problem was that no one asked their people how much more Europe they wanted, and how much sovereignty they were willing to give up—so long as the economic benefits added up, leaders took assent largely for granted. The process of integration was, therefore, profoundly undemocratic. As the then prime minister of Luxembourg, and currently the president of the European Commission, Jean-Claude Juncker, put it, "We decide on something, leave it lying around and wait and see what happens. If no one kicks up a fuss, because people don't know what has been decided, we continue step by step until there is no turning back."[31] As integration moved forward, few among the public knew what they had signed up to. Indeed, sometimes leaders themselves did not know, since in the interest of quick integration, the terms of agreements were often left deliberately vague.

Ultimately, though, integration succeeds only when there is deep social empathy between people. The leaders and top bureaucrats, for the most part, understood one another well, and were even friends, after countless meetings in Brussels, Frankfurt, or Paris. As poorer countries with different historical experience and cultural attitudes came into the Union, the ties between ordinary people of different nationalities became more tenuous. At any rate, it was not clear that people across Europe felt that they were in anything more than a common, barrier-free single market. Instead of emphasizing markets, as did the United States and the United Kingdom, Europe had emphasized a European superstate. Neither solution quite worked, as we will see, because both neglected the community.

CONCLUSION

The postwar consensus in favor of the state and against the market worked for a while. The market expanded through trade, but it was heavily regulated. Growth was strong, not because the market was hog-tied but because of other factors that came to an end by the early 1970s. The years of strong growth entrenched democracy in the developed economies. These countries also made two important sets of commitments that will continue to reverberate into the future. They made substantial promises of social security to their populations. Many also expanded immigration, and over time, emphasized their respect for the civil rights of both their minority and immigrant populations. These were commitments made by prosperous confident societies based on projections of continuing strong growth.

When growth stalled, the prevailing consensus shifted across the developed world, from anti-market to anti-state. In Anglo-American countries where there was always a latent individualism, the intellectual and political pushback against the expansionary state was particularly strong. In some countries like the United Kingdom, it included reducing the role of the community. Politicians campaigned to take away powers that they believed had been usurped by the state, but let them lapse instead of allocating them elsewhere.

As markets were liberalized across the world, and capital flowed more easily across borders, even countries that were not ideologically predisposed to markets had to worry as much about market reactions to their government's policies as they did to voter reactions. Even as markets placed limits on government policy, some governments also tied themselves to supranational arrangements like the European Union or the single euro currency, which placed further limitations on the sovereign or local capacity to act.

Thus as the ICT revolution started affecting jobs, trade, and through trade, jobs again, neither the debt-strapped, overcommitted, and much maligned state nor the disempowered community were in a strong position to respond to the needs of the people. Moreover, in good times the states had set in place immigration policies that were changing the very composition of the communities, without a strong sense that the necessary empathy to hold them together would be in place when times changed. But the times were changing. Technological progress spread rapidly through globally integrated markets, with few borders to slow them down. The people in some developed countries were largely left to respond on their own. The able adapted quickly and well, making matters much more difficult for the rest. These were left in increasingly dysfunctional communities, with growing resentment against the system that had been imposed on them.

THE ICT REVOLUTION
COMETH

An alien who visited Earth in the mid-1980s and came back today would see one clear difference—far more people in public spaces ignore the world around them and stare at a small rectangular device, which she would later learn is called a "smartphone." Soon, the smartphone may be replaced by a device implanted in our body that connects with our mind and provides instant access to both computing power and enormous databases. Computer-enhanced humans are no longer the realm of science fiction. The ICT revolution has fundamentally changed what we spend time on, how we interact with one another, what work we do and where we do it, and even how people commit crime. Most importantly, it has upset the balance between the three pillars once again.

As we will see, the ICT revolution has not just followed the course of previous revolutions by displacing jobs through automation, it has also made it possible to produce anywhere and sell anywhere to a greater degree than ever before. By unifying markets further, it has increased the degree of cross-border competition, first in manufacturing and now in services. Successful producers have been able to grow much larger by producing where it is most efficient. This has created spectacular winners, but also many losers.

The technology-assisted market has had widely varying effects across productive sectors in a country. Some of the effects stem naturally from technological change, some from the reaction of people and firms to it. Indisputably, it has raised the premium on human capabilities. As a result, some well-educated communities in big cities have prospered, while communities with moderately (typically high school) educated workers in semirural areas dominated by manufacturing often have not. More generally, as with past technological revolutions, the need for people to adapt has come rapidly, before the benefits have spread widely. Indeed, the communities that are required to adapt the most, as always, are the communities that have been experiencing the greatest adversity, and have the least resources to cope.

The anti-state ideology that gained momentum from the late 1970s has not been inconsequential. While the withdrawal of the state induced more competition in markets that were deregulated, it also allowed the acquisition of rents by the few and the relative shrinkage of opportunity for the many. Technology-induced inequality and human-induced inequality have built on each other.

The shift in attitudes was best epitomized in a new paradigm to guide corporate behavior, the principle of shareholder value maximization, which focused the corporation's energy on enhancing value for a narrow class of investors. While, by and large, this has moved corporations toward greater efficiency and away from vague notions of doing social good, it has also undermined their public support by legitimizing actions the community believes are grossly unfair. Corporations have compounded their political vulnerability by attempting to enhance profits, not just by building a better mousetrap, but by influencing rules and regulations in their favor. As a result, not only is the private sector more dependent today on state benevolence to sustain such anti-competitive barriers, which make it a less effective counter to state power, it is also less likely to enjoy broad public support if the state moves against it because it is seen as part of the crony swamp.

Another important consequence of the ICT revolution is that by enhancing the wage premium that go to those with strong capabilities, it has strained community cohesion. To build the capabilities in their children that the market demands, people who have the incomes and the choice are tempted to move out of mixed or declining communities into communities of people like themselves. This is a phenomenon that can be seen in the United States, but it is also happening elsewhere. While the truly rich have always lived apart, the upper middle class has also been pushed to secede into their own enclaves.

Even as job opportunities become more unequal, economic diversity within communities has fallen while diversity between communities has increased. This sorting of human capital across communities has increased the inequality in access to the capabilities necessary to compete in the market.

Inequality, not just in economic outcomes but in opportunities, has therefore become an enormous problem. In the United States it shows up between residents of big cities or rich suburbs and small, economically devastated rural towns, between workers in big young successful service firms and small older struggling manufacturing ones, and between the top earners and the rest. The roots of this inequality lie not only in technological change, but also in the failure of the community and the state to balance and modulate markets.

These inequalities are also present, if not to the same degree, in continental Europe. Moreover, the path of integration that continental Europe has chosen has highlighted new inequalities: between the protected jobs of the older generation and the poorly paying jobs available to the youth or immigrants, between the political power of the large European countries and the weakness of the smaller ones, as well as between the economic well-being of disciplined Northern Europe and the relative backwardness of the unreformed southern periphery. Through integration, all these inequalities have come into the European fold.

In this chapter, we will focus specifically on how the ICT revolution has affected markets, especially job markets, incomes, and trade between countries. We will examine how the various interests in the economy have reacted to the increased competition. In the next chapter, we will turn to how this has affected communities.

THE EFFECTS OF THE ICT REVOLUTION ON JOBS

The ICT revolution has had a direct effect on jobs by eliminating certain categories of jobs, while enhancing the importance and reach of other kinds of jobs. It also has had an indirect effect via trade, allowing certain tasks to be outsourced, while increasing the insourcing of other tasks.

The Direct Effects on Jobs

As a number of researchers have pointed out, in recent years new technologies have eliminated jobs that involved well-specified routines or simple, predictable tasks.[1] For example, the Amazon Go store (opened first in Seattle) tries to create a shopping experience with no lines and no checkout counters.[2] As you walk in, you use the app on your phone to register your presence, pick up what you need, and walk out. Later, your Amazon account is billed. Computer vision and machine-learning algorithms, similar to the ones used in driverless cars, help identify what you pick up and tote up your bill. Not only does this do away with checkout clerks, the underlying software has also reduced the need for someone to monitor stock levels, order new inventory, or reconcile the store's books at the end of the day. The automated system does it all.

Of course, it has not done away entirely with the need for humans. There are still shop assistants to help guide people to where they might find products they are looking for, to stock shelves as they run out, and to prepare some of the fresh meals that Amazon sells. The point is that humans have moved to handling exceptions, and to intermediating as experts between ordinary people and the system. So long as stores structure all this well, they improve the overall buying experience, even while cutting down on costs.

Routine jobs have been automated out of existence for decades now, regardless of whether the jobs required skills or not. Banks had hundreds of thousands of cashiers taking in and paying out cash, as well as counting it at the end of the day—a routine job that required integrity but no higher skills other than basic numeracy. The job paid decent wages in order to attract honest people, and keep them that way. Automatic teller machines (ATMs) and cash-counting machines displaced them, and now electronic payment systems like Alipay or Apple Pay, which bypass cash entirely, are rendering physical cash and the security apparatus that services it, redundant. Sweden has many bank branches that now refuse to take cash. Churches flash their bank account numbers on a screen so that parishioners can contribute their weekly offering using their cellphone.[3] No doubt payments will get easier still in years to come. Yet, if anything, employment in banking has gone up as more, cheaper, bank branches are opened, and tellers morph into relationship managers advising retail customers on their loan options and their investment portfolios.[4] According to the Bureau of Labor Statistics in the United States, jobs in commercial banking and related areas have gone up from 2.4 million in 1990 to 2.7 million in 2017 despite widespread automation, and an intervening banking crisis.

New jobs are being created even as old jobs are lost. Consider, for example, skilled tax accountants, whose specialty was to know every arcane element of the tax code. Such jobs have also been displaced, in this case by tax software available for a few dollars. Interestingly, this leaves the highly trained tax lawyer, whose work is to erect customized international tax shelters for her high-net-worth clients, unscathed. Her work is not routine, since each shelter has to be crafted for the client's specific situation, where her knowledge of the tax code, prior cases, as well as her creativity are essential. The ICT revolution helps her do her job—she can access prior cases or the relevant tax code much more easily—but it has not displaced her, at least not yet. Indeed, because she can create shelters faster using more readily accessible information, and because she becomes known internationally, both the supply of her services as well as the demand for them increase, enhancing her income significantly.

Importantly, tax software also creates new jobs for people with moderate skills. A high school graduate with some training and familiarity with computers, employed by a tax preparation agency, can assist ordinary people with their taxes—people who do not want to spend the time doing it on their own, or are unfamiliar with computers. Earlier, they could not afford an accountant. Now, they can afford the assistant.

Let us focus on this last example more carefully. Historically, the complaint about machines and automation was that they rendered the craftsman redundant. For example, it is well known that Henry Ford added tremendously to his workers' productivity by manufacturing cars in a moving assembly line. The assembly line broke car assembly into multiple sequential tasks, allowing each worker to specialize in only one of many tasks. Equally important, and less well known, is that Ford insisted parts be honed to high tolerances so that they were interchangeable, that each part did not have to be specially machined to fit the car. Interchangeability, coupled with the breaking down of tasks, allowed Ford to dispense with craftsmen and hire modestly skilled workers for his assembly lines, thus creating the mass-market car. We see similar de-skilling with tax software, with the middle-class tax accountant replaced by a lower-paid computer-literate assistant with only a few weeks' training. The assistant, aided by software, is probably more competent than most accountants, but less creative. Most people don't want their tax accounting to be creative. De-skilling makes ordinary craftsmen or accountants largely redundant, but making the car or tax service cheaper increases demand and may increase jobs overall.

We often think about technological change assuming the aggregate amount of work is fixed, and therefore what is displaced by automation will increase unemployment. Economists sometimes refer to this as "the lump of labor" fallacy—that there is only so much work to go around. To the extent that progress makes products cheaper, there could be more demand for them, and the overall quantum of human work can even increase. The new work will, however, be different.

Of course, this means some kinds of workers will no longer be needed, at least in their old jobs—the afore-mentioned accountant, for example. Even so, as routine work gets automated, there is more demand for skilled people who can handle the nonroutine exception that is thrown up.[5] In Ford's time, mechanics who truly understood cars could set up repair shops, where they diagnosed and fixed the unique problems that each mass-produced Model T developed through wear and tear. Similarly, the accountant who can go beyond the routine can find employment at the tax-preparation agency or the tax-software firm to handle special-situation queries—for an additional fee. Since such accountants don't really do routine work anymore, they need more capabilities and enthusiasm than the ordinary accountant, but may be better rewarded for it.

Thus the direct effect of technological change, at least for the foreseeable future, may not be so much on the aggregate quantum of human work—unemployment in most developed countries is at historical lows at the time of writing—but its redistribution. The rich skilled tax lawyer earns significantly more, and has more work than she can handle; the middle-class tax accountant is typically worse off; and there are entry-level jobs for the computer-literate assistant, without much hope for additional skilling or career progression embedded in it.

The data certainly are consistent with an increase in the number of jobs at both ends of the skill spectrum, and a decline in the middle. Both better-paid managerial, professional, and technical jobs and lower-paid service jobs have increased significantly in the United States as a share of jobs in the last three decades, even while middle-wage jobs have fallen.[6] This polarization of jobs, with low-pay/low-skill occupations and high-pay/high-skill occupations gaining at the expense of jobs in the middle is not just a US phenomenon. Studies find that in fifteen of sixteen European countries for which data are available, high-paying occupations expanded relative to middle-wage occu-pations in the 1990s and 2000s, and in all sixteen countries, low-paying oc-cupations expanded relative to middle-wage occupations.[7]

THE INDIRECT EFFECTS OF TECHNOLOGY ON JOBS THROUGH TRADE

In the last chapter, we discussed how trade grew substantially after World War II. Apart from falling tariff barriers to trade, there are really two impor-tant factors that determine whether goods produced in one part of the world can be sold in another. The most obvious is transportation costs. Less obvious but equally germane, as we will discuss shortly, are communica-tions costs.

An important contributor to lowering transportation costs was a seem-ingly innocuous innovation, the standardized container. An American trucking entrepreneur, Malcolm McLean, sent fifty-eight containers in 1956 on a converted tanker from Port Newark to Houston, Texas. His idea was to save on the time to load and unload ships, and to streamline the process by which goods were then transported by train or truck to their destination.[8] As his idea caught on, containers became standardized in size, and cranes, con-tainer ships, storage facilities, and railcars were purpose-built to handle them. Not only did the container allow cargo to be packed only once at the sender's end and unpacked only once at the destination, it increased the amount of goods a dock worker could load in an hour by almost twenty times.[9] It allowed ships to reduce their idle time in port significantly. Impor-tantly, because cargo was sealed, it reduced pilferage by dock workers and thus the cost of insurance—which fell to a sixth of its earlier level.[10] A study of trade between developed countries estimates that containers raised the amount of trade between countries in the industries that were amenable to containerization by about twelve times over a period of fifteen years, far more than can be accounted for by all the tariff cutting.[11] While emerging markets were late to the game, many started building specialized container infrastructure from the 1980s onward, which reduced their cost of sending goods to developed countries tremendously.

When communication costs also fell, production and trade were transformed. Traditionally, trade consisted of making the entire product—say, a motorcycle—and then shipping it to the destination where it would be sold to a consumer. The country exporting the good had to be able to do it all, right from research and design to manufacturing, and even after, sales service. Multinational firms did open factories in other countries, but largely to supply local demand. As communication costs came down, though, firms started asking whether it made sense to do everything in-house and domestically. Why not break up the production chain and undertake each segment in the country where costs of production were lowest? After all, the cost of transportation was already low, so moving the intermediate product back and forth was not very costly. By tracking the production of each segment carefully using the latest computer and communication technologies, and intervening early when there were signs of trouble, firms could make sure there was no danger of stock outs and production disruptions. Indeed, if communication channels were seamless, a firm could have a trusted supplier take over a segment of the value chain. Given the low cost of moderately skilled labor in emerging markets, manufacturing segments of the value chain were typically outsourced.

Apple, for example, has produced internationally from its early days, but had a manufacturing presence in the United States until 2004, when it closed its last US manufacturing facility. It then proceeded to exit manufacturing entirely. Apple is one of the most profitable companies in the world despite manufacturing virtually nothing. The reason for its success, quite simply, is that it holds on to everything outside manufacturing, including research and development, design, content (including its profitable iTunes store and the apps that are made for its products), marketing, and finance. Let me repeat an oft-cited example here, oft-cited because it makes the point so clearly: The

Apple iPhone XS Max costs Apple about $390 to make, and is sold to retail buyers for $1,250, a price that is more than three times its manufacturing costs.[12] Most of the final manufacturing is done in China by firms like Foxconn, but much of the profit is retained by Apple as compensation for the intellectual property and software platform it has created. More generally, even as they outsource the low-value-added manufacturing segments of the production chain, developed countries retain the high-value-added and profitable premanufacturing segments like R&D and the equally profitable postmanufacturing segments like marketing and finance.[13]

Such a division of labor is not unattractive to emerging markets that are trying to move up the complexity chain to build more technology-intensive products. Since the early 1990s, the possibility of participating in global supply chains has convinced a number of these countries to lower their tariffs, improve their business environment, sign treaties protecting foreign investment, and enhance their protection of intellectual property. This has eased the way for more segments of the value chain to be moved to emerging markets.

Even while developed-country firms are outsourcing manufacturing to the emerging markets, emerging-market firms have been relying on developed-country firms for R&D and design. Many manufacturers of generic drugs in the emerging markets reverse engineer drugs that go off patent after they are initially made by developed-country firms. Indeed, the Indian pharmaceutical firm Cipla developed an anti-HIV three-drug cocktail, which it offered to poor African countries and AIDS groups at a dollar a day in 2001, which was one-thirtieth of its then price.[14] Pharmaceutical firms around the world were forced to lower prices, and AIDS treatment has become affordable everywhere. Having built their business imitating, emerging-market firms in China and India are now contributing to original drug research.

Who wins and who loses in this process? Highly educated and creative designers, scientists, and engineers, as well as advertising and marketing mavens now have a world market. Initially, this has favored the highly educated and skilled in developed countries, much as has technological development. As emerging markets train their own people well (with students often finishing with an advanced degree from a developed country), capabilities are migrating to the rest of the world. The highly educated and skilled everywhere now compete for business from global supply chains. In some countries, their wage differential relative to others, while high, is plateauing or even falling.[15] The losers are clearer: the moderately educated workers in developed countries. When the supply chain was entirely in the developed country, they benefited from the competitive edge that developed-country design or R&D gave them. Their jobs were safe, protected by the indivisibility of the production process, which allowed them to bargain for higher pay, lower and more predictable work hours, and more safeguards at work. As the production process fragments, though, they have been exposed to the full force of competition from cheaper, more flexible, but equally competent labor elsewhere. Of course, consumers everywhere, like the AIDS patients who now have access to cheap drugs, benefit from more competitive and efficient production.

As communications and information technology improves, more and more service value chains will be subject to the same competitive scrutiny as manufacturing value chains. Providers will reexamine what can be outsourced and what ought to be retained. As economist Alan Blinder has argued, all impersonal services that can be delivered electronically at a distance, with little or no degradation in quality, are potentially vulnerable.[16] What will be harder to replace are human creativity, customization, and human empathy.

Job Losses Due to Trade and the Effects on the Community

Let us look at job losses in a developed country, specifically the United States, more carefully. Job losses can be a sign of a dynamic free enterprise economy, not necessarily evidence of an economy in decline. Around 40 percent of all US workers were in agriculture at the beginning of the twentieth century, while only 2 percent were thus occupied at the end of the century, but the 2 percent produced significantly more than did the earlier 40 percent. Similarly, with all the talk of the United States losing competitiveness, few realize that employment in US manufacturing peaked in 1944 at 39 percent of the labor force and has been on a steady decline since then to 8.5 percent of the labor force in 2017 (this probably overstates the decline since aspects of manufacturing ranging from product design to factory cleaning are now done by specialized outside firms and relabeled manufacturing-related services). Nevertheless, the share of real US GDP coming from manufacturing has not fallen in the last fifty years.

This means that manufacturing activity has not migrated away from the United States, at least not in the aggregate, but it has become more productive and high tech. Certainly, smokestack industries like iron and steel have moved to developing countries like China, as has furniture making, but in their place the United States has cleaner factories in more technologically advanced fields such as aircraft or communications equipment. However, fewer workers are classified as being strictly in manufacturing—5.8 million fewer from 1999 to 2011 alone. Those who remain are typically more skilled or qualified workers, because more of the output now comes from technologically advanced sectors.[17]

How many of these job losses come from increased imports, especially from China, which increased its share of world manufacturing value added from 4.1 percent in 1991 to 24 percent in 2012? A recent study by economists Daron Acemoglu, David Autor, David Dorn, Gordon Hanson, and Brendan Price estimates that the direct effects of Chinese imports on job losses—such as a furniture factory closing down in North Carolina because the firm now imports from China—is only about 10 percent of US manufacturing job losses over the period 1999 to 2011, which spans China's great export boom.[18] When the losses in output of US firms that buy from, or sell to, the now-closed factory are added in, imports from China can account for about 18 percent of job losses in manufacturing. While estimates of the sources of job losses are by their very nature imprecise, the evidence suggests that increases in productivity through automation and computerization, which account for the majority of the remaining job losses, have been the larger source of job losses. So why is there so much more public anxiety about trade?

The job losses due to trade have been more centered in low-tech manufacturing with well-paying unionized jobs. Such establishments have typically been located near smaller towns, such as the US Steel plant in Granite City, Illinois, and rural areas in the interior of countries, where the cost of living and thus of labor has been low, and regulation light. These establishments have dominated the local community, providing the incomes that keep the local hairdressers, laundries, and shops in business. If unable to keep up with competition from imports, the establishments close down local operations, and may move machinery to a country where labor is cheaper. Since manufacturers in an industry cluster together, they are likely to decide to lay off workers or close down at similar times, compounding the magnitude and impact of the job losses. Of the 1,250 workers represented by the steel workers union in Granite City, only 375 were working at the end of 2016.[19] As described by Amy Goldstein in her book *Janesville,* which follows the Janesville community after General Motors closed a large plant there, the effects on the community can be devastating.

In contrast, the job losses due to greater automation and computerization have been spread across manufacturing and services, and typically have hit firms that are more likely to be located near urban areas. Moreover, instead of the whole factory or office closing, a few workers doing routine jobs that can be automated are let go periodically. The remaining workers doing nonroutine work continue to be employed, and typically now are more productive. Higher productivity allows their employer to lower prices, sell more, and hire more workers in nonroutine jobs to meet the increased demand. The demand of all these workers for local goods and services such as haircuts and dry cleaning increases, creating new local service jobs that offset the lost jobs.

Indeed, a study that separately examines the effects of trade competition and technological progress in the United States finds stark differences in their effects on jobs in the local community.[20] Over the period 1990 to 2007, manufacturing-dependent communities that are hit by trade competition see a significant fall in employment across all jobs—routine and nonroutine, skilled and non-skilled. They also experienced an increase in the share of local unemployed, and an increase in working-age workers who leave the labor force permanently. In contrast, manufacturing-based communities that are most prone to automation saw little overall job losses in the local labor market over the period.

This does not mean there were no effects on jobs due to automation. As one might expect, the study finds automation reduced the number of jobs in routine activities like production, assembly, clerical and administrative support. However, the study finds the loss of routine jobs was offset by an increase in nonroutine skilled jobs such as management, professional services, and technical personnel, as well as an increase in nonroutine jobs for the moderately skilled, such as automobile repair and hairdressing.

Given the twin threats of automation and trade, laid-off workers have two clear options. One is to go back to college to acquire or refresh their managerial, professional, or technical capabilities. This requires investment of time and money, but pays off eventually in higher salaries and greater job security. The second is to move down the pay scale to service jobs like that of a security guard, waiter, or a driver that require fewer educational credentials but are immune for the time being to automation.

In cities, automation has forced many moderately educated manufacturing or service workers into minimum-wage service jobs such as that of a "fulfillment" associate, pulling products off shelves to make up online orders in a large warehouse, while a digital assistant whispers instructions in an ear. The fall from comfortable middle-class unionized jobs into the struggle to make ends meet is extremely painful, but at least there are jobs.

Moderately educated workers whose firms close because of trade competition typically have few palatable alternatives. With few new jobs near the small towns or semirural areas where these firms are located, and most such jobs to be found in firms in the same industry beset by the same competitive woes, workers have bleak prospects if they stay put. Nevertheless, a US study tracking the careers of these workers finds that while better-educated management workers move quickly elsewhere to jobs in new industries, many of the moderately educated seem to have clung on to nearby, and progressively less-well-paid, manufacturing jobs as long as they could.[21] When these were no longer available, many quit the labor force altogether, to go on Social Security disability insurance and Medicaid—the only supports available to working-age workers who no longer feel they can find work.[22]

Why does the moderately skilled manufacturing worker hit by trade competition not retrain to get a better-paid skilled job or take a low-paid manual-service job, just as those hit by automation do? For the worker affected by trade, both choices typically require a physical move away from the community, for the local economy is usually devastated. Retraining is not easy, especially for manufacturing workers who went to work after high school many years ago, and who really have not used computers at work or at home.[23]

Moreover, a job as a medical technician requires a few years' training, significant expenditure on courses, and no income in the meantime. The US government's Trade Adjustment Assistance program, the primary program for workers affected by trade competition, meets only a fraction of the likely expenditures, and has onerous qualification requirements. For males, a job as a nurse also requires an acceptance that old stereotypes—for example, that nursing is for women—no longer apply.

A well-paying job at the end of this odyssey is not assured. Many workers would deem such investment both costly and risky. Easier perhaps would be to move to take a service job that does not require additional training in a flourishing city. Here too, as we will see shortly, options are narrower because of occupational licensing. Moreover, after paying the higher rents in a strange costly city, there is little left over to support a family. For many, perhaps it is easiest to stay put and hope past jobs return, even while the local economy and the community decline further—after all, there are still friends and family. The behavior of these workers is not dissimilar to that of the handloom workers during the Industrial Revolution who kept entering the industry even as its impending demise was clear. It may not change unless the community or the state come up with more viable options.

THE EFFECTS OF TECHNOLOGY AND TRADE ON INCOMES

Let us now turn to incomes. If technology and trade affect the nature and number of jobs, they must also affect wages and incomes. A wage is a price for labor services, so it will be affected not just by the jobs available (crudely speaking, demand) but also by the available applicants for those jobs (the supply). There are two important patterns in the data. First, there has been an increase in incomes of the college educated (those with an undergraduate degree or higher) relative to the moderately educated (those with a high school diploma). Second, incomes for the very top earners (say the top 1 percent of incomes) have been running away from the incomes for the rest.

THE STAGNANT MEDIAN WAGE DEBATE

A number of studies have documented rising income differentials since the late 1970s in the United States between workers at the ninetieth percentile of the income distribution (typically college educated) and workers at the fiftieth percentile of the income distribution (typically only high school educated). This has two aspects to it. First, except for a brief period of growth between 1996 and 2004, the real hourly wage in the United States (the money wage deflated by the Consumer Price Index [CPI]) for the worker in the middle of the wage distribution has stagnated, so that in 2014, it was about the same as in 1980.[24] These facts are not disputed, but they need not mean that the worker in the middle is no better off. For one, the worker takes home the median wage after taxes are subtracted and government transfers are added. Taxes at the middle have fallen and transfers have increased since the late 1970s so worker income, after tax and transfers, has grown. Second, actual inflation experienced by households has been lower than the CPI, which means real wages have grown more. Finally, Americans have smaller families, with many living alone, so there are fewer people dependent on any single income. Correcting for these factors, the Congressional Budget Office concludes that median household incomes have increased by about 50 percent since the late 1970s.[25] This is not spectacular over a period of about forty years, but it is much better than stagnation.

Less disputed is that the wage premium for those who have been to college has increased steadily since 1980. The wages of the college educated have been running away from the wages of the merely high school educated, though even for the college educated the job market has moderated in recent years.[26] Across the world, the highly educated earn a premium over the moderately educated, who in turn earn more than the uneducated. On average, across the Organization for Economic Co-operation and Development (OECD—informally, the club of rich countries) in 2015, those who had not completed high school earned only 79 percent of the wages earned by high school graduates, those with bachelor's degrees earned 46 percent more, while those with master's degrees earned 98 percent more.[27] The educated are also much more likely to be part of the labor force—either working, or actively looking for work—and also less likely to be unemployed.

In the United States, the premium on education is higher than the OECD averages. The few who have not completed high school earned only 68 percent of the wages earned by high school graduates, those with bachelor's degrees earned 66 percent more, while those with master's degrees earned 132 percent more. The average wage premium for the educated does not mean that everyone with an undergraduate or graduate degree has a well-paying job. These are averages, and the averages conceal a number of highly educated individuals in low-paying jobs who had other priorities than income, were unfortunate in their choice of college or field of study, or who were just plain unfortunate.

Only a handful of countries have a greater fraction of the labor force aged twenty-five to sixty-four with tertiary degrees, or higher average years of schooling in their population than the United States, yet its tertiary education premium resembles that in emerging markets like Turkey or the Czech Republic, which have a far lower fraction of the labor force with a tertiary degree.[28] Indeed, the OECD estimates that the total benefits to getting a tertiary education (relative to staying with high school education) for a man in the United States in 2013 to be $569,600, second only to Chile at $576,900.

Why is there such a gap between the demand and supply of the highly educated in the United States, as suggested by the wage premium? US colleges and universities are, by every ranking measure, including the number of foreign students they attract, still the best in the world—for instance, according to Shanghai Jiao Tong University's ranking of world universities, eight of the top ten, and sixteen of the top twenty universities in the world in 2017 were in the United States.[29] It is hard to argue the problem is with the quality of the universities, though, of course, not all are at the same level. Instead, the problem seems to be that too many students who enter college, especially those who do not complete high school and instead eventually get a General Educational Diploma (GED), are unprepared for higher studies and drop out before completing degrees.

In addition to inadequate preparation in school, though, the cost of tertiary education in the United States is high, and despite the availability of scholarships, student borrowing builds up quickly. This is especially the case if the student has to take a number of remedial courses to come up to speed, which then prolongs their stay in college and increases their eventual debt.

Both inadequate preparation and high costs contribute to a high dropout rate. In 2015, only 55 percent of students who entered US colleges graduated with a degree. The graduation rate was much higher for US women at 65 percent and was only 45 percent for men, with the lowest graduation rates in for-profit institutions.[30]

The problem in the United States thus seems to lie squarely not in its universities but in its schooling system, which once was the best in the world. Indeed, the inadequacy of schools—which we will see stems partly from the decline of economically mixed communities—may help explain the high college premium in the United States. If employers cannot trust that high school graduates know what they are supposed to have learned by the time they leave school, they may insist on a college degree just to be sure of basic skills. Indeed, as we will see, there seems to be an escalation in the credentials demanded of various jobs in the United States. With higher-than-warranted demand for job candidates with degrees and lower-than-desirable demand for candidates with high school diplomas, it is less surprising that the wage premium in the United States is higher than elsewhere despite the high average years of education.

THE ONE PERCENT AND THE WINNER-TAKE-MOST EFFECTS OF TECHNOLOGY

While incomes for those with a bachelor's degree, especially in technology and engineering, have grown relative to the rest, incomes at the very top have truly exploded in a number of countries. As economists Thomas Piketty and Emmanuel Saez have documented in various studies, in the United States, the top 1 percent of earners took only 8 percent of total income in 1970, but this grew to 18 percent by 2010.[31] In the United Kingdom, starting from similar shares in 1970, the top 1 percent earned about 15 percent of total income by 2010. Such an explosion of the incomes of the rich has not happened in continental Europe.[32] Each year, the top 1 percent have earned about 8 percent of total income in France since 1950, and about 11 percent in Germany over that period with little variation. Japanese top income shares have remained relatively flat at about 8 percent.

We should not rule out the possibility of mismeasurement here. For example, many of the very rich in Europe have closely held firms, and because of high taxes, may be unwilling to pay profits out as dividends. The wealth of these individuals may build as undistributed profit grows, but it may not show up as income. Instead, this would show up in rising inheritance amounts, and indeed inheritance as a share of total wealth has been rising in Germany and France over the last few decades while it has been relatively flat in the United Kingdom over the same period.[33] Thus top incomes may be understated in high-tax countries, and their rise may be a more general phenomenon across developed countries.[34]

The increase in top incomes is not because countries are dominated by the idle rich. Even for the richest 0.01 percent of Americans toward the end of the twentieth century, 80 percent of income consisted of wages and income from self-owned businesses, while only 20 percent consisted of income from financial investments.[35] This is in stark contrast to the pattern in the early part of the twentieth century when the richest got most of their income from property. The rich are now more likely to be the working self-made rich rather than the idle inheriting rich.

A recent study of tax returns from 2000 onward by my colleagues Owen Zidar and Eric Zwick, along with others, finds that the spurt in top incomes in the United States can be traced to the rising incomes of private business owners who manage their own firms.[36] The majority of top earners receive business income, and tend to be owners of single-establishment, skill-intensive, midsized firms in areas like law, consulting, dentistry, or medicine. These firms tend to be twice as profitable per worker than other similar firms, and the rise in incomes appears to be driven by greater profitability rather than an increase in scale. The study finds owners typically are at an age where they take active part in the business. The premature death of an owner cuts substantially into profitability, suggesting their skills are critical to income generation. The authors conclude the working rich remain central to rising top incomes even today.

In another study of the four hundred wealthiest individuals in the United States (the Forbes 400), my colleague Steve Kaplan with Joshua Rauh of Stanford find that the Forbes 400 today are less privileged than those in the past in that they are less likely to have been born wealthy.[37] They did get a good education when young (hence, they mostly come from upper-middle-class families) and entered rapidly expanding and scalable industries like technology, finance, and mass retail.

Perhaps more important than hard work and a good education, technological change helps explain the rise in inequality at the very top—it has created a "winner-take-most" economy. When a farmer wants his fruit plucked, the more workers the better (until the orchard becomes overcrowded). Each worker contributes, no matter how unskilled and how many fruits he picks, and can be paid accordingly. On the other hand, if the farmer wants to listen to music, one good fiddler is far preferable to ten mediocre ones. Furthermore, for such activities, the larger the accessible market, the more the performer will get paid.

As markets expand and become more integrated across the world, and communication becomes easier, the best singers and sportsmen can use myriad channels to reach households everywhere. While there is still some charm in watching a live performance by a moderately talented local artist in a small local theater, more of the household budget increasingly goes to watching supremely talented international superstars. Sherwin Rosen, the Chicago economist who first analyzed the growing superstar economy, noted that Elizabeth Billington, the star of the London Opera in the 1801 season, earned between £10,000 and £15,000.[38] When adjusted for inflation, that would imply an income of between £680,000 to £1 million, or between $825,000 and $1.25 million today. In comparison, Forbes reports that Taylor Swift, the top-earning music diva, pulled in $170 million in 2016, while Adele, the top UK female singer, grossed $80.5 million. Superstars earn far more today because, through technology, they go beyond merely the audience in the London opera house into a global market—Taylor Swift's hit single, "Shake It Off," had 2.4 billion views on YouTube at the time of writing.

The "winner-take-most" structure has spread beyond the performance arts to a variety of occupations. With improvements in communication, corporations can be more effectively managed even as they get bigger and access larger markets—Julie Wulf and I find that the span of control for corporate CEOs, as measured by the number of direct reports, has been increasing.[39] CEOs can manage more people, perhaps because much more communication and reporting can be routinized today, with the CEO able to act quickly on exceptions that are flagged up to her.

As corporate size increases, corporations also seek out the most capable suppliers of key inputs, magnifying the returns to small differences in talent. In corporate law, for example, international companies seek the same handful of lawyers to represent them in multi-billion-dollar lawsuits—why settle for anything less than the best when lawyer fees are small compared to the potential penalties for losing the suit? Differences in capability, even small ones, now can mean large differences in income. All this adds to the incomes for the very skilled or talented, who already benefit from the premium that skills command today.

How much of these superstar or top 1 percent effects are because of human responses to the liberalization and integration of markets, and not just to technological change alone? Probably some. The private sector's typical reaction to increases in competition, whether generated by shifts in technology or in policy, is to first become more efficient, and then figure out ways to limit the competition. This pattern has indeed replicated itself in the liberalizations since the 1980s. While there are some differences between the Anglo-American economies and continental Europe based on their different reform paths, ultimately practices spread. What follows relies heavily on studies in the United States, but the analysis applies more generally to developed countries.

THE PRIVATE SECTOR'S REACTION TO LIBERALIZATION

Both Ronald Reagan and Margaret Thatcher pushed back against the state. They believed this would imply a greater role for markets and ensure greater individual freedom. Rolling back state oversight did not free everyone. While too much government leads to privileges for some, so does too little government. Moreover, in the fervid evangelical individualistic environment they had unleashed, what was privately optimal for the individual could be detrimental to the community. Doctrinaire reform, as we will see, proved problematic.

A Change in Attitudes Toward Profit and Incomes

A stark example of the individualism that was being reasserted once more, partly as a reaction to the collectivist pressures that had dominated since the Depression, was the change in attitudes toward corporate profit and managerial incomes. In the postwar years of the expansionary state, the clamor in the United States for corporations to do more than simply focus on their business became louder. Influential commentators argued that corporations ought to work with the state to fulfill their corporate social responsibility, and some government officials in the 1960s even asked corporations to hold back price increases as their social contribution to the fight against inflation.

Economists who were drawn into this debate on the proper role of the corporation started by noting that the owners of the corporation, the shareholders, were the residual claimants; they were paid only after fixed claimants such as suppliers, workers, and creditors were paid. Given that they bore all the risk, economists argued, it was appropriate that they should have ownership and exercise control, and the corporation ought to be run in their interests.

What, though, were the owner's interests in the large professionally managed corporations with many dispersed small shareholders that now dominated the economy? With each shareholder owning a tiny fraction of the firm, whose interests should management, which itself had a tiny stake, focus on?

Milton Friedman was characteristically bold in his answer to these questions: "There is one and only one social responsibility of business—to use its resources and engage in activities designed to increase its profits so long as it stays within the rules of the game, which is to say, engages in open and free competition without deception or fraud."[40] Since profits are what go to shareholders, Friedman was saying management should maximize the value of the corporation's shares, allowing each shareholder the maximum freedom to use her valuable shares to fund causes dear to her heart. Let her support the local football team in her neighborhood or donate to the firefighters' fund if she chooses to, Friedman insisted; after all, it is her money, earned from bearing risk. Friedman's dictum had an "invisible hand" aspect to it—by maximizing the value of the only claim to the corporation that was not fixed, management would not just be maximizing shareholder value but also the corporation's value, and thus the corporation's contribution to society. Friedman firmly rejected any role for the corporation in helping the state do its job, for example, in containing inflation, or in undertaking charitable activities, especially if it impinged on its profitability.

Friedman's views had enormous influence, both in academia and outside. The notion that corporate social responsibility began and ended with the corporation maximizing shareholder value was very clear and was consistent with the growing ethic of individualism. Instead of being a sin, avarice was now a duty, in part because it could be spelled out clearly to firm management. With such straightforward marching orders, shareholders could evaluate performance without the noise, hypocrisy, and occasional self-aggrandizement introduced by social responsibility. It suggested three courses of action to put corporate management back on the right track.

First, management's incentives should be aligned more with shareholder interests by paying management for performance, preferably in stock. This view became particularly influential when a study by Michael Jensen and Kevin Murphy in 1990 found that for every $1,000 change in shareholder wealth in the United States, the wealth of top management went up by only $3.25.[41] The authors suggested it should be much more. Corporate chieftains obviously loved this message. Second, large activist shareholders ought to monitor firm management and push it to do the right thing for shareholders—a recent example was when the influential shareholders of the vehicle hire company Uber came together to depose the CEO, Travis Kalanick, whose aggressive management style and actions were apparently eroding Uber's business prospects. Finally, there should be an active market for corporate control, where raiders could take over the management of underperforming corporations, even if existing management resisted. The raiders would gain from bringing in their own management and increasing share value in the most poorly managed firms, while the fear of hostile takeovers would discipline behavior in even the better-managed firms.

In a postwar world that had gotten used to gentle competition and easy profits, management refocusing was indeed necessary in the more competitive liberalized environment. There were tremendous societal benefits if management increased profitability and reduced waste—and this would increase the long-run likelihood of the firm's survival to the benefit of all. Friedman's assertion that the business of business was only business was a valuable corrective for corporations that had lost their way. However, Friedman's dictum was theoretically valid in fewer situations than it was applied, so the courses of action that benefited shareholders were not always beneficial for society. Moreover, his caveats were frequently overlooked, undermining his message. Most important, his dictum, especially when some of the aberrant consequences were publicly highlighted, undermined support for corporations.

Shareholders are residual claimants and all others are fixed claimants only in a somewhat textbook view of the corporation where all inputs to the firm are essentially like commodities, bought in competitive markets and paid for through explicit short-term contracts. In practice, not all inputs are commodities and not all contracts are short-term or explicit. For instance, corporations enter into implicit contracts with their employees in many ways. They often ask employees to go the extra mile—work overtime on an express order or staff a difficult position temporarily—with the promise that the company will make it up to them later. Employees who expect to be with a corporation for a long time also invest in acquiring company-specific skills and in building relationships with other corporate employees, investments that may have little value elsewhere but make the company work better. There is usually an understanding that the company will compensate the employee for these investments, even if there is no written contract to the effect, and thus no legal power for the employee to enforce compliance.

When a corporate raider takes over a company where most employees have already made such investments, repudiates these implicit contracts, eliminates jobs and cuts wages, the raider benefits, as do shareholders. Workers take a large hit, though, and they, as well as future employees in the industry, may forever lose trust in management.

Harvard economists Andrei Shleifer and Larry Summers emphasized this point in the context of airline takeovers in the 1980s, after the industry was deregulated. When corporate raider Carl Icahn took over Trans World Airlines (TWA) in 1985, they argue that much of the value he squeezed out for shareholders came from abrogating wage agreements and renegotiating worker wages down.[42] To the extent that workers were overpaid because of lax prior management and strong union bargaining, this was beneficial for shareholders, but unless lower costs led to lower ticket prices and more travel, this was a wash for society since no additional value was created. To the extent that the renegotiation breeched employee trust, we may all have been the losers—it may have transformed airline workers from being customer-friendly and willing to go the extra mile for the airline to being suspicious of management, unhappy, transactional, and working only by the book. Even seen from the best interests of the corporation, let alone society, shareholder value maximization may be inappropriate in some circumstances.

In a sense, the principle of maximizing shareholder value strips transactions of their corporate and social context. This is a good starting point for deciding whether a transaction is worth doing, and is particularly useful when custom and tradition obscure underlying economic rationales. However, transactions do take place in the real world with all its incompleteness and uncertainties. The richer noncontractual addenda—relationships, implicit contracts, promises, trust—often improve outcomes, and have to be added back to understand whether the transaction is still worth doing. To focus only on the contractual is to be myopic, and this can serve the corporation poorly.

Coupled with the finding that CEOs earned so little of the value they created for shareholders, Friedman's arguments opened the way for boards to pay management enormous amounts of stock-based compensation. The rationale was that this would align management incentives with shareholders. In practice, this raised a number of concerns. There is no clear guidance on how much is enough. Usually, in a competitive market, a worker is paid on the basis of the value he adds. However, if a new CEO enhances the company's share price by $10 billion more than would normally be expected, does she deserve to be paid the entire $10 billion? How much growth is because of the unique assets and workers the firm possesses, which the CEO only pointed in the right direction as opportunities came along? With no real guidance, corporate boards could engage in a compensation race, which they often did by asking their compensation committees to make sure their CEO was paid more than the industry average. As many did this, the industry average escalated.

High CEO pay sent a strong signal to employees, and to society more generally, that money was the central measure of worth. To the extent that money could only be made by doing the right thing by society, Friedman's dictum was beneficial. There were many other ways of making money, though. Most immediately, if corporate management could "manage" their boards and their compensation committees, payouts could be enormous, and totally unrelated to long-term performance. Some indeed were.[43]

More problematic was that Friedman's dictum also encouraged misbehavior. Friedman was careful to add the caveat "so long as it [the corporation] stays within the rules of the game, which is to say, engages in open and free competition without deception or fraud." Yet, if management is given very high-powered incentives to make profits, and CEOs of highly profitable companies are accorded high social status, not everyone will make profits by respecting the rules of the game. Management of powerful corporations can break not only the rules, but it can also change them. The important question is whether the enhanced incentives for good behavior outweigh misbehavior. Unfortunately, misbehavior has not been negligible, especially after the easy steps to increase productivity and competitiveness in underperforming firms were taken in the 1980s and 1990s.

Pay for performance has encouraged deception, especially in the financial sector, where it is very hard to identify true performance in the short run. Management can always goose up performance for a while by taking on hidden risk, and unless compensation contracts are structured well, performance pay can fuel excessive risk-taking. Furthermore, when a dictum like shareholder value maximization takes hold of a firm, more nuanced understandings get lost, not just at the top but also as the dictum is pushed down to the operational level. The medieval proscription of the sin of avarice was, in part, to protect the poor rural peasant from exploitation by the traveling merchant, in a world where information was hard to come by. Even though many transactions today are governed by caveat emptor (let the buyer beware), society still does not take kindly to systematic exploitation of the vulnerable—the enormous fines levied on banks for misselling mortgages in the run-up to the Global Financial Crisis is a case in point. It is all very well to say that the principle of shareholder value maximization does not condone misselling—it truly does not—yet misselling can maximize profits in the short run. Implicit in rewarding employees for the profits they make is the

belief that this will be done legally, and not in a way that will hurt the corporation in the long run. Yet, in the mind of the employee, the size of the year-
end bonus can dwarf all these other considerations.

Pay for performance may also have motivated firms to seek the easy route
to profits; shutting down the competition. In a sense, this is no different from
Adam Smith's frequently articulated concerns about anticompetitive instincts of corporations, but there is a greater urgency about this threat today.
As new technology and global markets give firms enormous economies of
scale, large firms can get even bigger and more productive as a matter of
course. This gives them huge resources to influence the political process,
something my colleague and frequent coauthor, Luigi Zingales, writes about
in his perceptive book *A Capitalism for the People*. Writing in the early 1900s,
Ida Tarbell was appalled that despite their efficiency, Rockefeller's managers
felt the need to stifle the competition. We should similarly be concerned that
despite their productivity and advantages stemming from size and access,
some of the largest corporations still try to alter the system to shield themselves from competition or taxes.

Perhaps of greatest concern, if enough corporations follow Friedman and
focused solely on profits, they undermine the private sector's ability to be a
political force for social good. Friedman was right that a fair amount of corporate social responsibility substitutes for actions the state should take, and
panders to the specific charitable interests of a firm's top managers. This is
not beneficial for the firm. Yet the firm exists in the community; if there is a
local earthquake and the state is underprepared, the firm cannot keep its
earthmoving equipment off the roads, regardless of whether it will ever get
paid. More substantially, Friedman enjoined corporations to take the rules of
the game as given, which meant they ought not to protest if a government
turned authoritarian or despoiled the environment. Presumably, he believed
nothing so drastic would happen in the United States. Yet, when an enormous source of independent power, the private sector, is passive, or worse,
rendered suspect in the eyes of the community because its every action has to
be in pursuit of corporate profits, there are fewer checks on the arbitrary
power of the state. Clearly, corporations are not meant to be political organizations, and should not attempt to be so. Nevertheless, they ought to stand up
and be counted when the fundamental tenets of society are at risk, for in the

long run, this will affect everyone's ability to make profits. An overly narrow focus on firm profit maximization will ensure that when needed, many will be missing in action.

The renewed emphasis on individualism, on profits, and on rolling back the state, as exemplified by Friedman's dictum, certainly raised efficiency initially. The roll back has been selective, though, typically favoring powerful large private players at the expense of weaker smaller ones. This could affect economic dynamism in the longer run, further exacerbating inequality of opportunity and outcomes.

LOW ENTRY AND GROWING CONCENTRATION

According to the United States census, the pace of new business creation in the United States has fallen steadily since the late 1970s.[44] In contrast, the pace of exits—companies either being taken over or going out of business— has remained fairly constant, with peaks in recessions. Why is new company formation falling, when ostensibly a more liberalized and competitive environment should encourage more such activity? A clue may be available in a study by economists Xiaohui Gao, Jay Ritter, and Zhongyan Zhu, where they note the alarming decline in initial public offerings (whereby young companies go public) in the United States—from an average of 310 per year between 1980 and 2000 to only 108 per year from 2001 to 2016.[45] They argue that it is harder for small companies to make money—the uptrend in small public companies reporting losses started in the 1980s and continues. Perhaps as a result, and increasingly, small start-ups are selling out to large companies rather than staying independent and going public. In the last decade, Google bought over 120 companies, Monsanto over 30, and Oracle over 80.[46] It is easier to be part of a large public firm today than be small and independent. If the path to becoming big and profitable is harder, it would explain the decline in entry.

The average US public firm today is three times larger, even after correcting for inflation, than it was two decades ago.[47] As a number of studies have shown, US industries are becoming more dominated by a few large firms today—they are becoming more concentrated, in econ-speak.[48] For example, between 1982 and 2012, retail trade saw the share of the top four firms double from 15 percent to 30 percent. In the critical sector of information technology, media, and communications, the *Economist* magazine found the top four firms now accounted for nearly 50 percent of the revenue.[49]

Concentration has been made easier by a more lax antitrust environment, as argued by my colleague Sam Peltzman.[50] Right until the early 1980s, antitrust authorities were quite active in preventing mergers that increased industry concentration substantially. The legal scholar Robert Bork (yes, he of the failed Supreme Court nomination) argued in his book *The Antitrust Paradox* in 1978 that it is possible that rising concentration in an industry may reflect gains in market share for more efficient players rather than growing monopolization.[51] He urged antitrust regulators to focus on whether the consumer was better off rather than whether industry was dominated by a few firms. In a sense, Bork pushed for a focus on outcomes such as whether the customer got a better price rather than whether the industry structure and processes would allow it to be monopolized. This reflected an abiding faith that potential innovation and entry would keep monopoly practices under check. In 1982, the US Department of Justice bought this argument, and set out guidelines that would, in principle, allow merged parties to have very large and unchallenged market shares. As Peltzman writes, "the war against mergers was over, and Bork won." Certainly, antitrust action has fallen off in the United States in recent years. From 1970 to 1999, regulators brought sixteen cases against mergers on average every year; in the period 2000–2014, this had fallen below three.[52]

In recent years, a strong positive correlation has emerged between the concentration of industry and the profitability of firms in it.[53] As Bork argued, growing profitability in a concentrated industry need not be a sign only of monopolistic practices, it could be a sign of the greater efficiency of large incumbents that allows them to gain market share. Greater size itself could reduce costs if there are scale economies in the industry. Also, the size of the customer base could increase demand if there are network effects—where the product increases in value as more people use it. Compounding all these effects, large firms do seem to attract better management.[54]

It is hard for researchers to tell monopoly power from efficiency since an increase in a company's revenues for a given amount of input costs could be because the company has raised prices unduly or because it produces more, higher-quality output at the same costs. The former is a sign of monopoly, the latter a sign of productivity. At this point, it is fair to say that a mix of higher productivity and monopoly power is responsible for the higher profitability of industries that are dominated by large firms, with the importance of each explanation varying by industry.[55] Health care in the United States has more monopoly and less productivity, while consumer products are the reverse.

Regardless, as industry sales concentrate in a small number of firms— dubbed "superstar firms"—a substantial portion of the rise in inequality of worker incomes that we discussed earlier seems to be largely because highly paid workers work at firms that pay their average worker better: Productive, well-paid workers seem to congregate in profitable firms.[56] Growing inequality in profitability between firms is translating into inequality between the incomes of the employees of those firms. The relatively stagnant median wage problem actually seems to be a stagnant median firm problem. While some of this is because of economies of scale and network effects, indubitably some of this is also because large firms have altered the rules of the competitive game.

SCARING COMPETITION AWAY AND ALTERING THE RULES OF THE GAME

Economists since Joseph Schumpeter have argued that just because competition is weak today does not mean it will be weak in the future. In an economy where technological progress is rapid, competition does not just come from existing firms, it also comes from the possible firms of the future, who use entirely new technologies to upend incumbents. After all, Google's search engine took away the market from Yahoo!, while Facebook destroyed GeoCities (acquired, then closed, by Yahoo!) and Myspace (acquired, then eventually sold for a pittance, by News Corp).

However, once a firm comes to dominate an area after an initial flurry of competition, for example because consumers find it hard to switch away from it because it has their data, the market may come to believe in its continuing dominance. This could make the monopoly self-fulfilling, as Luigi Zingales and I argue.[57] In part, this is because the stock market will bid the firm's share price to stratospheric levels in view of its expected monopoly profits. The firm's high-priced shares will then give it the currency to buy up any threatening competitors, way before they get to a size where an acquisition might raise antitrust concerns. Indeed, in the pharmaceutical industry, firms even undertake "killer" acquisitions whereby they acquire targets only to shut down promising drug projects that would compete with their existing drugs.[58] If the competitor is stubborn enough not to sell out, the dominant firm could threaten a prolonged price war or blatantly mimic the competitor's product, secure in the knowledge that it has the resources to afford a lengthy court battle over intellectual property. Independent innovators will consequently have a lower incentive to innovate, knowing that their access to the customer is blocked by the dominant firm, and knowing they will eventually have their product replicated or be forced to sell out to it at a discounted price. Indeed, venture capitalists refuse to fund start-ups whose projects lie within a "kill-zone" that can be replicated or acquired by dominant platforms. This reinforces the platforms' dominance.

Dominant firms could also alter the rules of the game. For instance, the Dodd–Frank Wall Street Reform and Consumer Protection Act on financial regulation after the financial crisis certainly helped reduce risk in large banks, but it was also shaped by an army of their lobbyists to favor their interests. Compliance costs increased and disproportionately hurt small banks that had less business to spread it over. Similarly, large online platforms have protected themselves with both the Computer Fraud and Abuse Act and the Digital Millennium Copyright Act, which make it a crime punishable by prison for any outside firm to plug into their platforms. This holds back interoperability, which would allow others to benefit from the platform's network effects and let them compete on a more level playing field.

As worrisome as the effects on the incentives to innovate is the effect on the diffusion of knowledge. Patents and copyright laws protect the right for an innovator or artist to benefit from their innovation for a while. If granted overly long or expansive protection, though, the innovator can stand in the way of new innovation or creativity. This is why patents should be granted carefully, and should terminate after a reasonable period, as should copyrights. Moreover, the free granting of patents, especially for fairly obvious

ideas, creates a minefield for anyone who follows. Often, innovators unknow-
ingly follow similar paths. It is impossible for anyone to check everything
they do against the enormous stock of existing patents. This means any successful innovator is a target for an incumbent who holds significant patents
and can employ good lawyers.

Large firms also seem to have the ability to extend protections afforded by
the government. For example, every time Disney's copyright on Mickey
Mouse is scheduled to expire, a new act extends copyright protection.[59] Perhaps the United States would benefit if companies could not "evergreen" their
copyrights or their patents with minor improvements so easily. As Brink
Lindsey and Steven Teles argue, the United States established a Court of Appeals for the Federal Circuit in 1982, which lowered the earlier standard for
granting a patent.[60] It also extended protection to software, business processes, and even the human genome. Since then, the number of patents issued
has exploded. After moving up and down around a steady level in the two
decades before 1983, patents have grown over fivefold since then, from 61,982
in 1983 to 175,919 in 1993 to 325,979 in 2015, even while productivity—the
desired consequence of true innovation—has slowed.[61]

Yet another source of protection is non-compete agreements preventing
employees from quitting a firm to work at a competitor's, in part to prevent
them for transferring secrets to rivals. A number of states enforce these
agreements (California, one of the most innovative states, does not), and over
a quarter of American workers are bound by such agreements, even in innocuous industries like fast food.[62] As my colleague, Jessica Jeffers, shows, the
enforcement of such clauses favors incumbent firms at the expense of entrants, reducing worker quits in incumbents and enhancing investment,
while reducing new entry into the industry.[63] Such agreements constrain
worker freedom even as they reduce the diffusion of ideas.

There is some indication that diffusion of knowledge is slowing. In a study
of industries in twenty-three countries, an OECD study finds a growing gap
between the large profitable patenting firms at the frontier of productivity
and the rest within the industry.[64] A study in the United States finds that in
industries where technology diffusion fell by more (as reflected in the slowdown of patent citations), industry dominance by a few firms rose by more.[65]

Slower diffusion of knowledge from innovative productive firms to the rest would partly explain why productivity has not picked up in advanced countries even in the midst of seemingly frenetic innovation.

The broader point is that the liberalization that started in the 1980s in the United States has been uneven. While initially it incentivized corporations to become more efficient, it also opened the way for them to create new sources of protection through market dominance and excessive protection of intellectual property. The former may have been achieved by a pushback on antitrust regulation, the latter by an increase in patent and copyright regulation as well as non-compete clauses restricting employee mobility. The common theme has been to favor large incumbent corporations. The profitability of large corporations has been further enhanced by their ability to both influence the tax code, as well as to adopt multinational tax-avoidance strategies. All this may have created an uneven playing field, and when coupled with emerging advantages of size like scale economies and network effects in a globalized economy, could explain slowing small-firm entry.

OCCUPATIONAL LICENSING

When manufacturing was dominant, workers protected themselves through union membership, and unionized jobs paid a hefty wage premium. For a variety of reasons, including the decline in manufacturing and the rise of global competition, union membership has declined. Even while manufacturing workers have lost their premium wages, service professionals have built protections for their business. It is well known that doctors and lawyers need a separate license in each state of the United States to practice there, but manicurists and barbers are also licensed in fifty states, and athletic trainers are licensed in forty-six states.[66] Licensing grew from covering less than 5 percent of the workforce in the 1950s to nearly 30 percent in 2008, even while union membership declined from over 30 percent to just over 10 percent over the same period.[67]

The licensing authority typically consists of, or relies on, the professionals themselves. Much like the guilds of yore, the stated reason for licensing is to ensure adequate quality of practitioners, though a more plausible motivation for licensing seems to be to restrict entry into their professions and limit competition. Specifically, if licensing is so important for quality, it is hard to understand why a licensed security guard requires three years of training in Michigan, but only about two weeks in many other states.[68]

Economists Morris Kleiner and Alan Krueger find that occupational licensing elevates wages by about 18 percent. Some occupations seem to enjoy far higher rents.[69] Separately, Kleiner finds that the wage boost from licensing is highest for the highest quintile of earners—up to 24 percent, while it is less than 5 percent for the lowest quintile.[70] Higher earners seem to be better able to protect themselves against competition, though some of those higher earnings are because of the protection itself. US primary-care doctors, for example, earn $252,000 according to the Bureau of Labor Statistics, while the average for other OECD countries is $130,000.[71] We have already seen that the American Medical Association has consistently opposed attempts at universal health care in the United States because of fears that the government would curtail their earnings. The power of the doctor lobby in limiting the entry of new doctors even while protecting its freedom to price is, in part, why the United States spends the most among developed countries on ealth care, despite being one of the very few without universal health care.

THE PRIVATE SECTOR'S REACTION TO LIBERALIZATION—SUMMARY

The pushback against state encroachment helped enhance efficiency initially. It also seems to have protected certain forms of incumbency and all manner of property much better in the United States today. This may well have hurt competition and innovation. The little space left for the potential small entrant firm has been further reduced by onerous regulations that only large firms can navigate. This has especially disadvantaged small towns and semi-urban communities, where few large firms are headquartered.

As islands of privilege have emerged across the United States, there is a growing sense among those who do not have their own protections, or have lost their unionized protections, that the system discriminates. If significant aspects of private profit making are seen as unfair, the taint could spread to all of private profits. Without the support of the people, private-sector independence will be compromised, removing an important check on the power of the state. Conditions are all the more worrisome as large corporations dominate more and more industries. These corporations are indeed very efficient thus far, which reduces their need to depend on the state. There is no guarantee, though, that they will remain independent, especially as they rely on the state rather than continuous innovation to protect their intellectual property, and as ownership of data and networks, where the state has enormous influence in setting policy, is debated. Moreover, a few large corporations are easier to do deals with than many smaller ones of equal aggregate size. The distance between behemoth and leviathan is narrowing again.

THE EUROPEAN APPROACH

Europe's answer to slow growth, as we have seen in the last chapter, was to integrate to create a superstate with the hope that the expanded market would energize competition and growth. There were differences in outcomes, in part because the European Union bureaucracy in Brussels was not so averse to government as the dominant Anglo-American consensus. Nevertheless, global markets spread many practices across countries. Europe had some of the same problems as the Anglo-American economies, but it also had different ones.

MISTAKES NOT MADE . . .

The European Union was successful in enhancing competition, especially in manufacturing and finance. The harmonization of rules made it hard for countries to keep out companies from other European countries. Nevertheless, despite a more committed pan-European antitrust structure, the domination of industries within European countries by a few firms, as also of Europe as a whole, appears to have increased, though the evidence is less conclusive than in the United States.[72] This suggests technological forces are partly responsible for the increasing concentration across the developed world, though regulatory differences also have influence. The European Union has had a harder time breaking down national barriers in services—

licensing rules are probably as complicated and varied between the states of the Union as they are between the states in the United States. Overall, though, Europe today has a market that is more competitive in many sectors than the United States, something that would have been unthinkable a few decades ago.

At the corporate level, European corporations attempted to avoid the hard decisions taken by US corporations. They were typically less attracted to the idea of corporations maximizing shareholder value, and insisted on a fuzzier notion of enhancing stakeholder value—where stakeholders included everyone from employees to customers to society (and, of course, shareholders). Such a diffused objective essentially gave little direction to CEOs. Perhaps that was the intent. Indeed, the words of the early-twentieth-century German banker Carl Furstenberg still resonate: "Shareholders are stupid and impertinent—stupid because they give their money to somebody else without any effective control over what this person is doing with it, and impertinent because they ask for a dividend as a reward for their stupidity."[73] Most CEOs did not dismiss shareholder interests so rudely, but it was not their prime concern.

Nevertheless, practices did spread across the Atlantic. For example, there has been convergence in CEO pay levels.[74] There were also differences. European corporations were far more protective of employees at the expense of corporate efficiency. Continental Europe was less successful in closing down inefficient firms, or creating jobs for those who were not already in the system, especially its young people. Youth unemployment (for workers between ages fifteen and twenty-four) was 18.3 percent in 2000 across twenty-seven EU countries, 20.9 percent in 2010 following the financial crisis, and 16.8 percent in 2017. The United States treated its young far better, with youth unemployment rates of 9.2 percent, 18.3 percent, and 10 percent respectively.[75] Therefore, the better protections for European incumbent workers often came at the expense of outsiders like the youth and immigrants.

Finally, we should also note that the somewhat more diffused management incentives in Europe relative to the United States have not helped it avoid scandals. Volkswagen doctored emission test results for its diesel cars, while many European banks were also fined for misleading customers. In an integrated world, behavioral norms do spill over between leading firms. The larger difference between the Anglo-American economies and continental Europe is that the former elevated the deregulated profit-maximizing free market onto a pedestal, while the latter has been more skeptical of its behavioral aberrations. Europe has not gotten all the efficiency benefits that it could from the unfettered market, but neither has society been undermined as much by the accompanying ideology.

AND MISTAKES MADE . . .

Perhaps the most important mistakes Europe made were where it took the largest steps—on integration. Europe tried to integrate, taking for granted that countries would meet their responsibilities toward one another as "united" states, when in fact there was not enough empathy, solidarity, or trust between the peoples of the countries to warrant this belief. With the local community weakened by the effects of technology and trade, the sovereign powers that the Union attempted to arrogate further put people's backs up. As they looked for the national community to substitute, in part, for the local community, they found that it too was under threat by the Union. All this came to a head, as we will see, with the immigration crisis in 2015.

CONCLUSION

In the United States, the overemphasis on the market resulted in growing economic inequality; some caused by technology, some man-made. The elite-led European project had a crisis of legitimacy, as people had never really been asked to approve it. Both approaches were imbalanced.

The rise in inequality could have partly been tackled by a renewed emphasis on expanding people's capabilities, and partly by sensible government regulation. Yet the change in public mood, as countries tried to break from the collectivizing legacies of the Great Depression and Second World War, weakened the public response. When the ICT revolution, transmitted through the global market, exacerbated economic inequality, there was little to offset it.

Neither traditionally disadvantaged communities like the minorities, concentrated in city ghettos, nor newly disadvantaged workers from the majority community in semirural areas, have been able to take advantage of the liber-alized economy. Indeed, across the developed world, as we will see in the next chapter, an elite upper-middle class looked to its own interests while aban-doning the economically mixed community. From leading the fight against vested interests, the upper middle class became part of the vested interests. The unfettered market was now in ascendance, with an ideologically and fis-cally constrained state and a weakened community offering limited check. The developed world had opened itself to the risk of radical populism once again.

THE REEMERGENCE OF POPULISM IN THE INDUSTRIAL WEST

I n the last chapter, we saw that the natural and man-made underpinnings of inequality have been increasing as the ICT revolution has raised the importance of human capabilities. In this chapter, we will see that the resentment against the upper-middle-class elite has grown across the United States and Europe as they have insulated themselves from the economic forces they have unleashed, leaving everyone else to deal with them. The abandonment of the elites has hampered the broader community's ability to adapt to change.

With incomes stagnating for many people, and with policy makers bereft of new ideas to spread economic growth more widely, governments in the early years of the twenty-first century took a huge gamble—betting that borrowing in liberalized financial markets could be the engine of broad-based sustainable growth. Although it initially enhanced growth and kept the citizenry happy, debt-fueled growth is not sustainable. Eventually, the gamble failed, culminating in the Global Financial Crisis. Instead of a happy consumer, it created an overly indebted one. Instead of fiscally healthy governments, with their debt reduced by economic growth, it created yet more debt for already-strapped governments. Instead of an electorate hopeful that beneficial change was around the corner, it created one that feared change and did not trust the ruling upper-middle-class elite to look beyond their own interests. Populist politicians only needed an issue to fan the smoldering rage into flames. In the

United States, it was the Affordable Care Act, also known as Obamacare. In Europe, it was immigration. We will look at all this more closely in this chapter.

THE MANY FACES OF POPULISM

A populist movement, as we have seen, is one that believes the ruling elite are corrupt and undemocratic, that the masses have been treated poorly, and that the system ought to be changed because the general will of the people demands it. Populist protest movements, however nativist or racist in parts, can play a valuable role. They have little regard for the elite, and therefore are willing to challenge the elite's most cherished ideas and their coziest practices. Their criticism, as we have seen in the late nineteenth century, can be very constructive, bringing transparency and democracy to governance, and forcing traditions to be justified beyond the lazy, "this is how we have always done it." Populist movements, when focused and temporary, can be very healthy. On the other hand, they can also be sectarian, delusional, and dangerous as they point in every direction to the causes of their difficulties except toward themselves. They cannot be ignored, though.

At the risk of caricature, left-wing populists tend to see everyone other than the dominant elite as the oppressed. Their aim is not to overturn the system, but to get a greater share of the benefits for the masses. They do not seek revolution, only a reorientation of the system, with the government typically doing more and the market less. A left-wing populist leader like Bernie Sanders, who ran for the Democratic Party nomination in the 2016, saw free trade as hurting the American people. He wanted less of it. He also campaigned for universal health care and free public college education, and for more humane treatment of immigrants. Left-wing populists do not distinguish among people in the country; they typically want a better deal for all the oppressed.

Right-wing populists, on the other hand, are more discriminating in the objects of their ire. For instance, in the United States, right-wing populists do not necessarily target the very rich such as wealthy businesspeople.[1] Instead, they reserve their anger for the administrative, professional, and intellectual elites, the upper middle class, whom they believe have tailored public policy to favor themselves as well as their favorites—women, minorities, and immigrants—and elevated these above the native-born non-Hispanic white male. There is both an ethnic and a nationalist component in these views.

ETHNIC NATIONALISM

Nationalism, simply put, is a greater preference for what is inside the nation's borders, such as one's countrymen or culture, than what is outside the borders.[2] At the risk of oversimplifying, nationalism can be unifying by emphasizing the solidarity of the included, stressing common bonds that will allow citizens to accomplish greater deeds together. For example, the nation offers a seamless common market where everyone can work, produce, or trade anywhere. It has a common government budget that gets taxpayers in the richer parts of the country to fund schools, hospitals, industry, and infrastructure in the poorer parts so that everyone can grow together. National solidarity offers people in every corner of the country the expectation of help from elsewhere in the country if they are hit by a natural calamity or a severe localized economic shock. National empathy creates a robust safety net for those who are ill, disabled, elderly, or just unlucky. National pride generates a collective joy when the national team wins, as well as a collective celebration of accomplishments of the past.

The nation, in a sense, is like a medieval guild, bringing prestige, protection, and some rents to those who belong to a powerful one. For some adrift lonely individuals, it may be the only social group they feel any belonging to. The greater the size of a nation for a given level of homogeneity of its people, the greater are the benefits that can be shared by everyone within it. The more homogenous the population for any given size, the stronger are the natural, even evolutionary, bonds that draw forth mutual empathy and goodwill within the nation.

The precise traits that represent homogeneity and the "true" native in a nation are a matter of definition. Ethnic nationalists, for example, might focus on race, religion, or a common cultural heritage as the basis for nationalism. In a country with a homogenous population, ethnic nationalism can be unifying. In a country with a diverse population, it will invariably be divisive, with the natives defined more in terms of who is excluded, typically minorities and recent immigrants within the country. Moreover, many of the typical symbols of nationalism in a large civilized diverse nation—such as the national constitution—tend to be inclusive. In such countries, ethnic nationalists constantly fall back to fear or resentment of the excluded to unify their followers.

Populist Ethnic Nationalists

Right-wing populists are typically populist ethnic nationalists—that is a mouthful! For simplicity, we will refer to them as populist nationalists. In their view, the native-born from the majority ethnic group are "the people," those who have an innate sense of the nation's correct path. They have been betrayed by the elite who, in their own interests, support others such as for-eigners, immigrants, and minorities.

The populist nationalist leader recognizes that people fear that their prox-imate communities are disintegrating. She knows they are disoriented by the dizzying pace of technological change, even as they struggle to cope with the effects of global integration. She understands why they are resentful, as fam-ilies and communities, already stressed by economic forces and slipping in social status, are also shamed for not accepting the liberal values of the elite.[3] She plays up their fears about weakening social solidarity, as a more open multicultural society brings in outsiders who do not share a common under-standing of past cultural legacies. The alternative she proposes is meant to restore respect to her followers. She will anchor her people in an imagined national virtual community of ethnically or culturally homogenous natives, inheriting the warm sepia-tinged monochromatic glories of the past. She will filter out the alarming colors, languages, and prayers that make today's soci-ety so confusing. In contrast to the weak, fractured, and equivocal elite estab-lishment, her leadership will be strong and muscular, emphasizing popular beliefs as obvious truths. Those whose real communities are breaking down will have an alternative, something to believe in, to belong to, and to fight for.

Since populist nationalists want to reaffirm the majority ethnic group's innate superiority, they emphasize that the reason it is falling behind is be-cause of unfair policy—for example, needless affirmative action for groups that complain about being historically disadvantaged, or cheating by foreign governments on global trade rules. These justifications need not be accurate, but they are part of the narrative that gives those falling behind self-respect. Importantly, the justifications minimize the need for the majority group itself to adapt—once the un-level playing field is righted, the group will recover its natural place in the social order, or so they believe.

What the populist nationalist leader views as a program to level the playing field looks to others like a protectionist program to exclude those who come from outside the native-born fold. Not only will the typical populist nationalist leader's program, carried to its logical conclusion, allow identity to determine market participation and success, thus paving the way for cronyism, it will also divide society into a favored native group, with the rest excluded as undeserving not-quite-citizens. It is an appealing program for those who believe they will be on the inside, benefiting from the empathy of others in the national community like themselves, as they recapture the nation from the rootless multicultural aspirations of the governing elite. It is particularly attractive for those who are looking for a sense of identity, a sense of belonging, because their own proximate communities are in disarray. This is why rooted communities that are suddenly hit by economic adversity are prone to populist nationalist appeals as they lose trust in the establishment.[4]

WHY DOES POPULISM MATTER?

Populism, at its core, is a cry for help, sheathed in a demand for respect, and enveloped in the anger of those who feel they have been ignored. Both the left-wing and right-wing populists are right in their diagnosis—the elite have betrayed the people's trust in the past. Looking forward, there is a very real fear that workers are not prepared for the changes that are coming, yet the elite establishment is largely paralyzed, and does not see that the actions of its own class are part of the problem. While the populist leaders have a better understanding of public concerns, they are unlikely to have the right answers either, because every policy answer has to resonate with their followers.

Yet public attention spans are short, so the intended consequences of policy are seemingly straightforward—raising tariffs on steel imports will save steel jobs—while the unintended consequences—it could lose us many more jobs elsewhere—are harder to explain to the layperson in 140 characters. All this means that in a campaign between the tribune of the people and the expert for the attention of the people, the tribune will always win out, more so if the expert has lost popular trust. If populist answers have to meet the filter of popular approval, if they crowdsource all their solutions, they are unlikely to be effective—after all, this is why Madison preferred representative democracy to direct democracy.[5] There is wisdom in crowds, but it has to be distilled carefully.

In this chapter, we will draw on the economic developments we discussed in the previous chapter, as well as changes in the community and media, to explain why the electorate in developed countries has become more open to listening to radical politicians. At the heart of the problem will be that technological change is creating a meritocracy based on capability. At the same time, access to capabilities is narrowing as communities weaken and so are opportunities for the people in them. The situation is further complicated by issues of race and immigration.

THE GROWING DIVIDE

Surveys of people's values across developed countries suggest that people tend to have greater trust and affinity for strangers, as well as are more concerned about the wider world beyond their immediate families, when they are economically secure.[6] This partly explains why developed countries became significantly more open and generous to immigrants and minorities in the prosperous 1960s. The resulting policies, unfortunately, exacerbate domestic divisions today.

Developed country societies became progressively more socially liberal, as the well-educated children of prosperous 1960s middle-class parents became the tolerant vanguard of movements that pressed for the rights of the historically downtrodden, benefiting women, minorities, immigrants, and those in the LGBTQ+ community. In an insightful, satirical book, the *New York Times* commentator David Brooks labeled this new elite Bobos—bourgeois bohemians—because they had the work ethic of the single-minded Calvinist while retaining the social liberalism that only rebellious youth from a secure upper-middle-class background could have.[7]

Moderately educated male white workers, on the other hand, experienced the dwindling in decent job opportunities at the middle of the income distribution that we noted in the previous chapter. To the elite, immigrants and the newly empowered minorities were well-educated coworkers, sharing in the expanding numbers of high-quality jobs, and offering a daily testament of their own fair-mindedness. To the moderately educated worker, they were competition for scarce good jobs. As their economic security and social status became more fragile, the moderately educated became less able and willing to accommodate change.

There was a debate worth having about the merits of an open society—one open to trade, to new people, and to new ideas and values. It was not, however, a debate that took place, because the elite did not engage as they abandoned the integrated community. It was hard to fault their choice, though. The meritocratic markets now demanded it, and as they have throughout history, tested the community.

THE PARADOXICAL
IMPORTANCE OF PLACE

Why does location matter so much in this age of technological wizardry? Can't people in communities that lose jobs simply telecommute? After all, isn't one element of the technological revolution the increasing ability to work at a distance? My daughter seems to accomplish everything she can do in her office, even while staying a continent away from it. As another example, Mitchell Petersen and I found that the average distance between a small-business owner in the United States and the bank branch she borrowed from had been increasing steadily since the 1970s, and recent work has confirmed that this pattern continues.[8] The reason obviously is that banking transactions went from being conducted in person, to being conducted on the phone, then online, reducing the need to be nearby.

Somewhat paradoxically, though, despite being able to work at a distance, more and more skilled people seem to be attracted to places where there already are plenty of skilled people.[9] Perhaps this is because serendipitous human interaction still matters. Today, it is rarely the lone inventor, beavering away in his basement, who comes up with the revolutionary breakthrough. Instead, innovation emerges from teams of productive people spurring one another on. Perhaps they need to be in the same room to generate ideas. Perhaps teams are cross-fertilized by other competing teams of smart people nearby, through meetings in bars and parties, or by simply poaching their members. That the whole is greater than the sum of the parts when capable people congregate together is a form of what economists term "agglomeration economies."

This would explain why some regions like Silicon Valley or cities like London, New York, or San Francisco become magnets for the capable and talented, where they meet one another and become yet more successful. My colleague Chang-Tai Hsieh and Enrico Moretti from Berkeley estimate that the dispersion in wages across US cities in 2009 was twice as large as in 1964, in part because of the emergence of superstar cities like New York, San Francisco, and San Jose.[10] They argue that simply reducing the stringent zoning regulations in New York, San Jose, and San Francisco to that of the median US city, and thus allowing freer worker movement into those cities with a red-hot job market, would have increased GDP per US worker by an additional $3,685 in 2009.

Agglomeration economies in the workplace would suggest economic productivity goes up when the capable flock together. It is hard to estimate their size, but one credible study does so. It finds that in an industry that emphasizes creativity and innovation—academia—they seem to be small. Luigi Zingales, along with Han Kim and Adair Morse, examines academic productivity in economics faculties in elite universities.[11] In the 1970s, they find that a faculty member moving up from a non-top-five university to a top-five university would see her productivity (in terms of quality-adjusted papers published) increase 60 percent. By the 1990s, this effect had vanished. The authors argue that in the past, you had to be at an elite university to collaborate with someone there. Today, you can collaborate at a distance, which eliminates the need to move to an elite university. Indeed, they find that the percentage of papers coauthored by a faculty member from an elite university with someone from a non-elite university doubled between the 1970s and the early 2000s.

Interestingly, though, they do not find that faculty members at the elite universities are any less productive, relative to other universities, than in the past. Indeed, the productivity difference between faculty members at the top universities and elsewhere seems to have increased. Put differently, the most productive faculty do still choose to be at elite universities.

Academia may not be representative of the stereotypical highly skilled industry but this study raises an important possibility; perhaps the capable do not need to be physically proximate to be productive—agglomeration economies in the workplace may indeed have fallen as technology has reduced distance. Why, then, do the capable increasingly choose to move to the same places as do productive academics to elite universities? It may well be that the prestige of an elite university or a white-shoe investment bank still attracts them, but it is not obvious that prestige has gone up over time to offset the ability to work at a distance.

An alternative possibility, which we will now turn to, is that it is not so much the workplace but the attraction of the residential community full of other capable people that drives them together. More important than one's social taste for having people from a similar socioeconomic background as neighbors, is the economic imperative of giving one's children the best possible education in a world that emphasizes capabilities. Children do better in schools full of children from supportive family backgrounds, hence the imperative to move to school districts where there are largely such families. And regardless of what drives the capable to reside in a particular region, their presence will attract more good employers to set up in that region, attracting yet more capable workers. . . . Strong communities create virtuous circles that strengthen them further.

Observationally, we will see capable people working and living in the same superstar hubs regardless of whether there are agglomeration economies in the workplace or in the residential community. Of course, both may be present at the same time. The former would suggest an economy-wide benefit from the sorting, the latter would suggest a private benefit to the capable families that sort together, and a private cost to the communities who are deprived of their presence. Regardless of which effect predominates, many communities will see a narrowing of opportunity as the capable abandon mixed communities to live and work in communities full of their own kind.

THE GREAT RESIDENTIAL SORTING

As education became the great differentiator, and as women increasingly obtained degrees and became professionals, couples paired off based on education and incomes. The proximity of smart people was not entirely coincidental. They met at colleges, as they always used to, except there were more women now in colleges. Increasingly, as we have seen, smart workers also congregated together in interesting cosmopolitan cities (or green, affluent suburbs). High real-estate prices drove out any remaining smokestack industries and their workers from the cities, making the areas more gentrified and livable for the professional elite but also unaffordable for most others.

While earlier, doctors married their nurses and managers their assistants, now professors marry professors (as I did) and consultants marry consultants. These couples entered into marriage carefully, and sometimes hesitantly, but they had the dual incomes to take the economic stress and uncertainty out of daily life and make marriage work. Often, they planned children carefully. Importantly, they had the ability and desire to invest in them, thus maintaining the hope of progress for the next generation.[12]

The Importance of Capable Parents

The advantages capable parents give their children starts early on. For instance, one study finds that children of professional families hear more spoken words—about 2,100 per hour—compared to 1,200 per hour in working-class families and 600 per hour in families on welfare.[13] This means the child in a professional family typically hears millions more words every year than a child in a family on welfare, which naturally boosts both the child's vocabulary and its ability to speak relative to its peers.

The famous Stanford marshmallow test and follow-up studies suggest that professional families give their children more than just learning—they give them trust and self-control. In the early 1960s, Walter Mischel and his graduate students gave little children from Stanford University's Bing Nursery

School the choice between eating a marshmallow immediately, or waiting and getting a second marshmallow after fifteen minutes or so if they could hold out. Videos of the torments children go through as they stare at the marshmallow have been an enormous source of entertainment for adults, but Mischel found something more. Those who held out typically did better later in life, with higher SAT scores, less likelihood of substance abuse, and lower body mass index thirty years after the test.[14]

A later study at the University of Rochester qualified Mischel's findings.[15] Those researchers conjectured that for children in crowded homes, surrounded by predatory older children and with no adults around, the "only guaranteed treats are the ones you have already swallowed." In contrast, in a stable home where parents promise and deliver on treats, promises may be more credible, and children more willing to wait. To test this, the researchers divided children into two groups, one set to whom a researcher defaulted on a promise to give stickers, and the other to whom the researcher delivered on the promise. When these two groups were subjected to the marshmallow test, the group which obtained the sticker and thus found the researcher reliable waited four times longer before eating their marshmallow (many even waited until the researcher returned, thus earning the second marshmallow) than the group that had the unreliable researcher. It would appear, then, that self-control seems a learned attribute, emanating from a belief that the world is stable and reliable.

This belief is something professional families have a far greater ability to give their children. While Mischel's original study was conducted on children in the prosperous Stanford University community, its broader implication is that strong stable families prepare children better for life by giving them a healthier worldview. Indeed, not only does the Chicago economist James Heckman find that the early childhood environment, structured by the family and community, is essential for further learning and a successful career, he also somewhat ironically describes "the biggest market failure of all" is that of picking the "wrong" parents.

THE PRESSURES OF BRINGING UP
CHILDREN IN A MERITOCRACY

As we have seen in the last chapter, technological change has accentuated the income differences associated with capabilities, which is a mix of inherent intelligence and talents that we will call smarts, coupled with educational attainments, all tempered with a dose of experience. Today's job market favors those with higher capabilities while disfavoring those in the middle. Furthermore, the winner-take-all tendencies in globally integrated markets increase the returns to small capability differences among people at the top of the distribution of capabilities. The market has therefore increased the rewards to being very capable significantly compared to the past.

If the names of winners of top incomes in society were drawn from a massive urn containing everyone's names, people would be envious of the winners but not angry. Inequality, per se, is not divisive. After all, everyone had an equal chance. If the winners made it because of their proximity to the government and their privileged access to lucrative deals and contracts, people would resent their success because it would be tainted by corruption. It would not, however, make them look at one another as competitors. In either case, the newly anointed nouveau riche, picked by chance or corruption, would have little need to move out of their community. They might build mansions to flaunt their wealth to their neighbors, but that might be the extent of the change.

There is a specific problem with the extreme meritocracy created by the forces we discussed in the last chapter—top incomes are not handed out at random; they typically go to those who are more capable. Capable parents who want the best life chances for their children (and who would not?) will undoubtedly look for the best education that money can buy. As Richard Reeves writes in his perceptive book *Dream Hoarders,* having established a stable family and an instructive and interesting home environment for their children, highly educated parents will then complete the job by securing good schools for their children and providing them every other assistance— say resume-padding internships or tutors for college preparation—where needed.[16] The higher the socioeconomic status of the parents, the more all this matters, for it ensures their children will inherit their place in the emerging meritocracy.

THE IMPORTANCE OF COMMUNITY FOR LEARNING

What actually does matter for the quality of education a child receives? In 1966, sociologist James Coleman wrote a report on the state of America's schools, based on data collected from one of the largest social science surveys that had been conducted till then.[17] The study tried to understand how well children were learning, attempting to identify factors such as funding, teachers, fellow students, or family that influence educational outcomes. The conventional wisdom emphasized the criticality of a school's physical facilities and its funding. These were not unimportant, Coleman found, but far more influential in contributing to learning were the school's student body diversity as well as a student's home life. Coleman argued that children, especially from poorer backgrounds, performed better if the school brought together students from very different social and economic backgrounds, for a student's learning was a "function more of the characteristics of his classmates than those of the teacher." As important as what happened in school was what happened at home, where the family's educational background was the most important factor in bolstering what was taught in school.

Both James Coleman and James Heckman emphasize the importance of family education and environment for a child's subsequent learning. Smart, well-educated parents will likely give their children the necessary head start and continuing support that researchers believe is important for learning. Furthermore, Coleman's work suggests that the better the caliber of other students in school, the better an entering student's learning experience. So keeping other things constant, the more that other children in the school come from homes with smart, well-educated parents, the better the child's educational experience will be.

Montgomery County in Maryland, where my children went to school, has affordable public housing to which poor families are assigned by lottery. Over the period from 2001 to 2007, Heather Schwartz examined the performance of students from disadvantaged backgrounds who attended the district's most advantaged district elementary schools (in the sense of having the few-est children from economically disadvantaged backgrounds) and found they far outperformed in math and reading those children in public housing who attended the district's least-advantaged district elementary schools.[18] She also found that lower poverty in the neighborhood where students lived enhanced their performance, but only about half as much as the school effect.

So if we had a highly educated couple with substantial incomes looking for the best public schooling for their only child, what would they do? Obvi-ously, they would visit every school within fifty miles of their workplace, trying to gauge which one worked best (they are young competitive par-ents, after all!). Almost surely, they would end up choosing a school in a neighborhood with other upper-middle-class parents like themselves. The high incomes in the neighborhood would ensure almost every family would give its children the head start that Heckman finds so important to life chances; a class full of such students would learn more academically, with students challenging one another to do better; and there would be few lag-gards to hold everyone back and occupy the teacher's attention. For such rea-sons, choosy parents would typically move to the highest-income school district they could afford to live in.

The data are consistent with such choices. Residential segregation by in-comes has increased over the last four decades in the United States, even as the ICT revolution has increased the wage premium associated with capa-bilities. The proportion of families living in neighborhoods with median in-comes well above (1.5 times) or well below (0.67 times) the median income of their metropolitan area has grown rapidly since 1970.[19] In 1970, only 15 per-cent of all families lived in such neighborhoods, while 65 percent lived in middle-income neighborhoods. By 2012, 34 percent of all families lived in either rich or poor neighborhoods, more than double the percentage in 1970. Over the same time period, the proportion living in middle-income neigh-borhoods declined from 65 percent to 40 percent. Moreover, sociologist Ann Owens finds that such income segregation (that is, neighborhoods sorting by income) increases only for families with children, with it changing little for families without children.[20] This suggests that a big factor in residential sort-ing is parental desire for good schools for their children.

Neither family background nor community are dispositive. There are plenty of spoiled rich children who make little use of their good fortune, and plenty of children from families with modest resources who succeed despite the odds—two of the United States's recent presidents came from households of moderate means headed by single women (their successors, however, came from millionaire families). Furthermore, academic learning is not the only purpose of school; school, as John Dewey wrote, is also about preparing the child for the kind of society we want. All this is true, but beside the point. In a meritocracy, capabilities matter. As a general tendency, those with higher incomes will also be better educated and be able to give their children a better head start. So if the couple wants the best for their child in the job market of tomorrow, they should follow the money today. And they typically do. The responsibility to family proves stronger than the ties of community!

As more leave, the mixed community becomes even less attractive for the remaining upper-middle-class parents, even those who harbor a strong sense of community. With the middle class and lower middle class left behind, it is not surprising that the middle class would also start leaving the original community. Soon, the classes sort into different communities, as the data suggest.

Commentators like David Brooks, Christopher Lasch, Edward Luce, Charles Murray, and Robert Putnam have all noted such residential sorting in the United States, which greatly weakens less-well-off communities.[21] Less central to their narratives are the economic forces that drive the sorting. Sorting does not seem to have occurred because of some breakdown in egalitarianism and growing elite distaste for the company of the rest but more likely because of parental concern for children and their success, an economic consequence of our more meritocratic and capability-demanding economies. As we have seen repeatedly through history, the demands of the market weaken the community. We are all becoming amorally familial (as in Banfield's dysfunctional Montegrano).

Importantly, none of this sorting would happen if the less-well-off could follow the better-off into their enclaves. There would be no escaping the mixed, integrated community. In the United States, the price of housing, maintained at a high level by zoning laws that effectively limit the construction of low-income housing, keeps the unwanted lower classes out of a higher-class neighborhood or out of a desirable city. Conversely, in declining communities hit by trade, we have seen that the better-educated management workers move out, accelerating the decline in the remaining community. The net effect of all this is that in an economy that increasingly requires workers with stronger capabilities, access to acquiring capabilities has become highly unequal, with the children of those who already have strong capabilities more likely to secure them, and the children of those with modest capabilities unlikely to have much hope for their children. The market has subverted the community's role in providing equal access by creating unequal communities. We have moved toward a hereditary meritocracy.

Some Related Issues in Learning

None of the forces I have described are specific to the United States. They are a natural consequence of the technology-created need for capabilities, and the greater ability of richer families to move to acquire them. Only countries where housing is broadly affordable across the country, public transport is available and inexpensive, and public schools are well funded, can avoid the residential sorting by incomes that is the source of resentment. Some countries in Europe have such conditions, many do not.

There are ways some of this sorting can be mitigated. For the smart kid from a poor family, charter schools or scholarships offer the possibility of getting the same opportunities that richer kids get. It seems cruel to deny that child the opportunity, yet some well-meaning advocates would do that because when that bright child leaves, it further depletes the environment in the public school they were attending. Similarly, some public schooling systems create special classes or schools for the bright. In England, bright students are tracked into grammar schools at age eleven. A study finds that the performance of those who get into the grammar schools improves significantly by age sixteen, but the average performance of those left behind deteriorates so that such streaming has little overall effect.[22] Once again, such tracking helps the educational experience of the tracked at the expense of the rest. Even as I write, there is a raging debate in New York public schools because some schools have tried to assure higher preparedness and thus learning in their classrooms by instituting admission tests. Ultimately, the question is not whether a few poor smart kids should bear the brunt of society's failure to create adequate access for all, but how society as a whole will remedy this failure.

THE EFFECTS OF RACE AND IMMIGRATION ON SORTING

Any discussion of residential sorting, and city to suburb and back to city movements, in the United States has to also account for race. The changing situation of the historically disadvantaged African Americans has exacerbated the movements associated with everyone's desire for stronger capabilities for their children.

In the early 1950s, African Americans were still restricted to separate but unequal schools, where funding was significantly lower than in schools elsewhere. In the southern United States, where African Americans and whites lived side-by-side, schools were explicitly segregated. In the North and the West, where African Americans lived in segregated neighborhoods, segregation occurred de facto.

The law became the lever with which to change society. As challenges mounted against segregated and poorly resourced schools, in 1954 in *Brown versus Board of Education* the Supreme Court ruled that formal segregation in public schools violated the right to equal protection. The fight to integrate schools now had legal sanction. The passage of the National Defense Education Act in 1958 and President Lyndon Johnson's Elementary and Secondary Education Act in 1965 as part of his War on Poverty boosted federal funding for education tremendously. As this opened a pathway for the federal government into local school districts, courts began using the lever of federal education subsidies to implement district-wide desegregation programs.

Even as the government increased its intervention, the student body in many schools became less diverse. The reason was simple: As more disadvantaged minorities were admitted into public schools, the white parents who could, moved their children out. The share of minority students in schools that have over 90 percent minority children decreased after the Civil Rights movement through much of the United States, but has climbed back up since.[23] In the Northeast, it never decreased, and by this measure, the liberal

Northeast is the most segregated region in the United States today. It is easy to ascribe such actions to racism, and some of it indeed was. However, we should not dismiss economic fears of the kind outlined earlier—that the children coming from disadvantaged backgrounds would hold back upper-middle-class children. The problem was not necessarily the race of the students, it was that the move from separate and unequal schools to integrated schools was bound to be disruptive for all if the minority students were not given a chance and the means to catch up first.

The urban African American community itself experienced a loss of economic diversity when the Civil Rights movement made it easier for middle-class African Americans to move elsewhere. Sociologist William Junius Wilson argues in his seminal book *The Truly Disadvantaged* that the deteriorating social conditions of the poor urban black community in the 1970s and 1980s—with rising teenage pregnancies, an increase in single-parent (typically headed by women) families, exploding substance abuse, youth crime, and incarceration—is hard to understand, since this followed the successes of the Civil Rights movement. Wilson argues that even with the debilitating legacy of slavery and racism, black families and communities in the 1950s were not any less stable or supportive than similarly positioned white ones. Indeed, even though segregation was devastating in its overall economic effect, it kept the community together, much as we have already seen with the Quakers during the Industrial Revolution.

Talented and capable black teachers, for example, with few attractive outside opportunities, were a boon to underfunded African American schools, making them in effect somewhat less unequal. Wilson argues that a better explanation than the deleterious consequences of expanded welfare programs or racism for the social breakdown of black urban communities are two important factors. First is the loss of well-paying urban factory jobs in the big northern cities in the 1970s and 1980s, which disproportionately constituted the good stable jobs for the black community. Second is the departure of the black middle class from urban ghettos.

The first reduced job opportunities for black urban youth, who found it harder to switch to service jobs. It also put economic pressure on black families as breadwinners lost their jobs. As men lose access to steady decent-paying manufacturing jobs and become less-reliable earners, they become less-attractive marriage partners. Women might be more inclined to have children without marrying if marriage means tying themselves to a husband who may not be dependable. A reduction in job opportunities for men tends, therefore, to increase the percentage of unmarried mothers, as well as of children living in single-parent households. Interestingly, while Wilson offered this explanation for the social breakdown of poor black urban communities starting in the 1970s, recent studies document a similar social breakdown in the largely white semirural communities that we discussed in the last chapter.[24] Once again, albeit with a gap of a quarter of a century or so, the reason seems to be economic, as manufacturing jobs have disappeared because of trade and automation.[25] Without stable families, communities are greatly weakened. Too many men, without the anchor of family and responsibility, have turned to substance abuse and crime, resulting in an early hopeless death, both in the black community that Wilson analyzed, and in white semirural communities today. Community breakdown is hard to reverse—which makes it much harder for people to pick up again when economic activity returns.

With their stable jobs, the black middle class could have supported local stores with their custom, local institutions like schools with their volunteering and engagement, and served as exemplars for the young. They could have provided the networks that connected poorer youth to jobs. As outright racism and segregation diminished, though, they found they could move into jobs and communities that better matched their talents and socioeconomic aspirations, and move they did. While understandable, this left the urban black community poorer still.

None of this is to diminish the possible consequences of racism. The African American community still has too few of the opportunities other communities in the United States have. However, some of its disabilities may be economic rather than social, and may be more amenable to remedies, especially when the ailments it experiences are recognized to be more widespread.

Immigrants, especially unskilled ones, typically find they can afford to live only in poorer, working-class communities. It is striking how the earlier debate about the entry of minorities into neighborhoods in the United States and the anxiety it caused is now being replayed in the ongoing debate in Europe (and the United States) about the entry of immigrants and the tensions that arise. We will return to this shortly.

THE LOSS OF LOCAL CONTROL AND THE DECLINE IN SCHOOL QUALITY

In the United States, sorting by economic class into communities has had its effects on local control of schools, parental engagement, and ultimately once again, the quality of schooling. In the rich suburbs, the upper-middle-class parents still engaged with their public school, supporting it with their time and money. Local boards were significantly more empowered in such areas and schools reflected local needs. Parents truly did care about community, except it was a community of their own kind.

In communities where parents were poorer, less educated, and less able to engage, and where the state and federal government provided more funding, the federal and state educational establishment gained more power. With the loss of local control, the community outside the school also became less supportive. An increase in government funding was sometimes partly offset by a diminution of local funding. Some districts became unwilling to increase local property taxes to keep pace with the increasing requirements and costs of education. When asked by Ohio Public Radio why rural voters did not approve increased tax levies from the 1970s through the 2010s, some voters replied the teachers were already overpaid, and the schools were run by "elitist bureaucrats" while another acknowledged that "the trust is broken," and "it goes back to when several local districts were consolidated."[26]

One consequence of broken trust was the increasingly ugly political battle over what was taught in schools. Parents and the educational establishment fought over the teaching of evolution, sex education, feminism, and novels such as Dostoevsky's *Crime and Punishment* or J. D. Salinger's *Catcher in the Rye*. With parents and teachers angry or disengaged, the overall educational experience of their children suffered.

In the early 1980s, the Reagan administration tasked the National Commission on Excellence in Education to assess the quality of schools. In its widely read report entitled *A Nation at Risk,* the commission asserted, "If an unfriendly foreign power had attempted to impose on America the mediocre educational performance that exists today, we might well have viewed it as an act of war. As it stands, we have allowed this to happen to ourselves." It deplored "the rising tide of mediocrity" in schools, as "more and more young people [graduated] from high school ready neither for college nor for work."[27] Much of this is still true today.

The United States used to have the best publicly funded school system in the world, strengthened by community engagement and involvement. The pressure of the market, both in terms of the availability of local jobs and of residential sorting, has broken the economically integrated community. The quality of US schools is now much more varied, denying many students the equal opportunity that is central to the stability of American capitalism. All youth, by and large, got a chance at the same education. Now, they do not. No wonder their parents are angry.

LOW SCHOOL QUALITY AND CREDENTIAL INFLATION

The uneven quality of school education even within a school district has other ramifications. We noted in the last chapter the high-wage premium associated with degrees in the United States, and indicated it was a puzzle, given the high fraction of workers with degrees. Certainly, many jobs do require more skills as a result of technological change—the worker who used the machine lathe may be unprepared to program the robotic arm that now does the job. Nevertheless there seems to be something more at work in the high wage premiums—a study by researchers at Harvard Business School finds that in 2015, 67 percent of production supervisor job postings in the United States asked for a college degree, while only 16 percent of employed supervisors had one.[28] While companies may be trying to make up their skills gap with more-qualified new entrants, the difference in credentials between that of those employed and those sought in job postings seems too large to be accounted for by just catch up.

Companies seem to be rating jobs as requiring higher credentials, simply because schools are not teaching basic skills well; there is a greater likelihood of finding a capable candidate who writes reasonably and has simple numeracy skills among those who have completed college.[29] International assessments seem to verify the low average quality of US schooling. In the latest

PISA assessments of the quality of fifteen-year-old students across countries, the United States came in thirtieth in mathematics and nineteenth in science among the thirty-five-member OECD group of rich countries.[30]

A college degree is then valued because it signals the candidate's competence in high school skills, rather than any additional capabilities picked up in college. The degree may also signal the candidate's determination and ambition, as evidenced by her ability to survive the rigors of college. Indeed, at the risk of oversimplifying economist Michael Spence's Nobel Prize–winning theory of signaling, it was just this: College may teach students nothing of use in a job. It is particularly costly, though, to complete for those who do not have basic skills. Those who have solid basic skills can then separate themselves from those who do not by acquiring a college degree. The human resource departments of companies seem to believe something like this, and have simplified hiring by demanding a college degree even when it is not needed for the position they need to fill.

The harm done is worse than simply too much time spent by students who do not need degrees acquiring them at great expense, firms overpaying for qualifications they do not need, and a higher-education system that consumes enormous resources. It causes professions to inflate their own minimum credential requirements as they strive to gain in prestige—it would be nice for preschool teachers to have degrees in child development or education but would we not lose a lot of perfectly capable teachers by requiring it?[31] The barriers to getting good jobs increases for those who have basic skills but do not have the money, aptitude, or interest in college. It becomes nearly impossible for those who have been consigned to bad schools and never had a chance of acquiring basic skills.

THE CONFLICT OVER VALUES AND POLITICS

Even though the upper-middle-class elite seceded from the integrated community into gated ones, their social values were lobbed over the battlements for all to consider and adopt. To many among the elite, birth control and feminism became the nonnegotiable terms of their engagement with the rest of society, with liberals among them adding abortion rights and gay rights to their creed. Yet such new freedoms were not easy for those outside the walls to espouse.

Divorce would free the partners in an unhappy marriage, but as social commentators Ross Douthat and Reihan Salam argue, divorce is much costlier for a low-income family, where no parent individually has the resources to give children a comfortable upbringing.[32] Facing rising and costly social ills like teenage pregnancies and broken families, it was natural for the newly disadvantaged to remember a rosier past where families were stronger and bound together in a prosperous community. They had reason to hold on to religion and traditions in the hope that these would help reverse their deteriorating present. Conversely, they rejected the modern values of the upper-middle-class elite transmitted through mainstream media, not because their own social life was exemplary, but because they believed that religion and traditions were perhaps their last protection against total social breakdown. To the upper middle class, this seemed like hypocrisy. To the working class, this was survival.

The differences also translated to the political. Democrats have historically been the party of the state and the worker, while Republicans have been the party of the market and business. The social divisions gave the parties additional identities. The Democrats became pro-choice and the party for social liberals, the Republicans became pro-life, and thus more closely aligned with religious conservatives and traditionalists. The parties also divided on ethnic and racial identity. Ever since the Civil Rights movement, the Democrats have found their natural sympathizers among the traditionally downtrodden—racial and sexual minorities, immigrants, and women. The Republican Party, which ironically was the party that emancipated the slaves, has disproportionately attracted white voters who were upset with the Democratic Party's new leanings. Consider these numbers: In the 1976 presidential elections, white voters voted for Republican Gerald Ford over Democrat Jimmy Carter, 52 percent to 48 percent. In 2016, white voters chose Donald Trump over Hillary Clinton, 57 percent to 37 percent, the same twenty-point margin by which they had chosen Republican Mitt Romney over Democrat Barack Obama in the previous election.[33]

Perhaps the most dramatic example of the divide is a 2012 study that examines attitudes toward interparty marriage.[34] In 1960, only 5 percent of Republicans and four percent of Democrats felt "displeased" if their son or daughter married someone from the other political party. By 2010, fully 49 percent of Republicans and 33 percent of Democrats indicated they would be somewhat or very unhappy if their child married outside the party.

Many countries in Europe started with fewer of the problems experienced by the United States because of the greater ethnic and racial homogeneity of their populations. However, some of the undercurrents—especially of an elite increasingly divorced from the masses in favoring trade and immigration, and of domestic communities very differently affected by economic change— exist in continental Europe also. For instance, Marine Le Pen, the French nationalist leader, developed her political views while serving as a regional councilor in a constituency ravaged by the loss of factory jobs, and where constituents felt the mainstream parties in Paris no longer understood their concerns.[35] In Germany, the mainstream parties declared, after months of negotiation over their joint program in 2018, their intent to focus more attention on neglected small towns, and rural areas, many of which did not even have decent broadband access.[36] The lack of jobs for youth, and large income differences between the rich industrialized North and the poorer industrializing South in an ever-integrating Europe, are added complications. As we will see shortly, so is immigration.

Many of the causes for public anger have been growing for some time, as has populism. Why is it so strong now, both in the United States and Europe? Averaged across EU states in 2000, the populist vote was 8.5 percent. By 2017, it had moved up to 24.1 percent.[37] The United States elected a populist president in 2016. Certainly, the effects of technological change have coursed steadily through developed economies, and the consequent resentment has built. In addition, though, the Global Financial Crisis of 2007–2008 and its aftermath had an enormous effect on popular perceptions.

THE FINANCIAL CRISIS

Democracy does not allow politicians to ignore problems for long. In the early years of this century, it was clear something had to be done for those falling behind. The easy answer through much of the developed world seemed to be to paper the problem over with debt. In the United States, the government sought to boost housing demand in the pre-crisis years through easier housing loans. Not only did rising house prices encourage new construction, which created jobs for the moderately skilled who had been laid off by manufacturing, it also allowed the owners of the existing homes to feel richer, and spend more by borrowing against the higher value of the house.[38] Their stagnant paychecks were not so worrisome when their house was a piggybank that could support their consumption. Debt-fueled housing purchases offered the economy a new avenue for growth. The problem was that it was unsustainable.

In Europe, the move toward a common Euro currency allowed all countries to benefit from the low common nominal Euro interest rate. It was low because everyone trusted the inflation-averse European Central Bank to keep overall inflation low. Yet, in countries at the periphery that had historically not maintained a tight control over inflation, inflation was still high. This further reduced the effective cost of borrowing in those countries, for borrowers had inflated revenues to repay cheap Euro borrowing. Having endured the discipline (or cooked the books) to meet the entry requirements into the Euro, a number of countries abandoned caution as they found they could now borrow easily and cheaply. In Greece, the government splurged, expanding both government spending and government jobs.[39] Not all European countries that got into trouble relied on government borrowing and spending. In Spain, a combination of a private-construction boom fueled by easy credit and spending by local governments created jobs. In Ireland, it was primarily a bank-lending-fueled housing bubble that did the trick. Regardless, the common thread was easy borrowing.

The mix of rising credit and rising house prices was immensely risky, but the accompanying job growth took pressure off the politicians. Bankers, motivated by large bonuses to maximize short-run profits and lulled by easy financial conditions, took too much risk. Central banks across the world were too complacent, both about the consequences of the very low interest rates they maintained, as well as about the extent of risk-taking. The boom turned to bust, and seventy years after the Great Depression, the world looked like it was entering a new depression. Governments and central banks intervened very actively, including bailing out big banks and financial companies. They

helped avoid a financial sector meltdown, but they did not explain the necessity for their actions to the public other than saying the alternative would
have been Armageddon. It was a grave mistake because the rescues looked
like an unfair stitch-up to the angry public.

Judicial investigations in the United States and Europe have since revealed
how bank traders blatantly manipulated markets, ranging from securities to
foreign exchange. Nevertheless, these very banks received government assistance, even while ordinary people lost their jobs, their houses, and now saw
their taxes used to pay down the sovereign debt accumulated during the bail-
outs. Public anger was further aroused by the haste with which bailed-out
bankers went back to receiving large bonuses, and by the difficulty the judicial system had in putting any senior banker in jail for their behavior. Perhaps the government bailout was warranted in order to stave off a complete
collapse of the banking system. But should this not have resulted in more
severe prosecutions of unscrupulous bankers for putting public money at
risk? The public conclusion was the market was no longer evenhanded, with
one treatment for privileged bankers and another for the rest.

In Europe, the costs of the bank rescues, coupled with the increase in
spending during the Great Recession, weighed on government finances. As
governments in Greece, Ireland, Portugal, and Spain found markets unwilling to continue lending to them, they tottered on the brink of default. They
needed a bailout, and Northern European countries suddenly found that
their ant-like discipline—for example, Germany reformed its labor market in
the early 2000s by reducing unemployment benefits and job protections,
while restraining wage growth—made them responsible for bailing out their
more irresponsible grasshopper cousins. No one told the German people (or
the Dutch or the Finns . . .) that this would be a consequence of entering the
Euro. Equally, no one told the people in the countries that were being rescued
that part of the funds from the new borrowing they undertook from their
rescuers would flow out immediately to help their banks repay German (and
Dutch and Finnish . . .) banks. A Union where substantial transfers were to
take place between countries required trust, solidarity, and empathy. There
was precious little of these on display because the public had never really
been asked whether they wanted in. The lack of transparency on the European rescues, and the sense among each country that it was paying for the

mistakes made by others, created widespread dissatisfaction, both among the ostensible rescuers and the rescued.

Apart from its direct economic effects in slowing growth and increasing government indebtedness still more, the financial crisis destroyed the public's belief that developed country markets are largely fair and clean. Perhaps more problematic, the public lost faith in the governing elite and the system they had created. Why could they not see the crisis coming? Why did they take so long in pulling economies out of the recession that followed? Why did they not jail any prominent bankers? The growing consensus was that the elite must be both incompetent and biased toward protecting their own favorites. If so, everything in the postwar consensus was now fair game for questioning.

For instance, could biased policies be responsible for the cheapness of imports, the loss of the good old jobs, and the rising competition from women, immigrants, and minorities for jobs held by the majority-group male worker? With entrepreneurial political leaders sensing opportunity and articulating such grievances aloud, and social media making it easy for aggrieved groups to organize and spread messages that the elite would have disregarded or even blocked in the past, it was not surprising that many people were convinced the system was broken. Indeed, the financial crisis triggered two essential factors that researchers find explains increased votes for populism across developed countries—economic distress as measured by an increase in unemployment and distrust in the political institutions of the country.[40] All that was needed was a spark.

THE AMERICAN TRIGGER

In the United States, the Affordable Care Act, or Obamacare, was an important catalyst in the organizing of the Tea Party movement, a forerunner of the populist nationalist movement. Berkeley sociologist Arlie Russell Hochschild, who studied blue-collar workers in Louisiana, offers an account of Tea Party supporters' views. As she surmises through her interviews, the white Southern male believed he had been trudging steadily in line toward the American dream, respecting the rules of the game.[41] The line moved more slowly than it had in his father's days, as economic opportunity dwindled.

The worker was disappointed but not angry because he believed the system was fair. As he looked around, though, he saw others cutting in line ahead of him, complaining about their past victimization and suffering. Initially it was minorities, then women, and now immigrants. They were getting opportunities to go to college and earn better livelihoods, opportunities that he never had. Why, the worker thought, did he have to pay for the sins of his father, if in fact they were sins? As Hochschild writes, anxieties were heightened by the election of the nation's first nonwhite president:

". . . And President Obama: how did he rise so high? The biracial son of a low-income single mother becomes president of the most powerful country in the world; you didn't see that coming. And if he's there, what kind of a slouch does his rise make you feel like, you who are supposed to be so much more privileged? Or did Obama get there fairly? How did he get into an expensive place like Columbia University? How did Michelle Obama get enough money to go to Princeton? And then Harvard Law School, with a father who was a city water plant employee? You've never seen anything like it, not up close. The federal government must have given them money . . ."

Not surprisingly then, the Obama administration's effort to reduce the numbers of those without health coverage in the United States was seen as yet another attempt to benefit the undeserving clients of the Democratic Party, the poor, the minorities, and the immigrants, rather than as an attempt to bring the United States up to the standards of universal health care of the civilized world. What especially enraged the members of the Tea Party movement was the expansion in free health care for the poor, as well as the compulsion for all others to sign up for insurance plans. The proponents of Obamacare thought that compulsion would reduce overall health insurance premiums by reducing the extent of adverse selection (the phenomenon where the healthiest young people do not sign on because they least need health care). The angry Tea Party opponents instead felt they were subsidizing undeserving others through their own overly expensive premiums.[42]

Many among the Democratic leadership believed Tea Party members were protesting against their own interests, but they did not appreciate the extent to which the white majority had become angry about what they thought were the unfair privileges given to the clienteles of the Democratic Party, and the anxiety they had about their own slipping social status. Better, it seemed, that no one be helped, than undeserving get a free ride. It is easier, then, to understand why there is strong support among Tea Party supporters for entitlements they have ostensibly paid for like Social Security and Medicare (old-age health insurance) while Obamacare is anathema.

POPULIST NATIONALISM IN EUROPE

In Europe, the sovereign debt crisis brought to the fore the growing resentment people felt about increasingly powerful pan-European institutions that were dictating policy to nations. The undercurrents of anger were barely below the surface, and ran in every direction. Strong rich nations like Germany feared they would forever be paying for the profligacy of the rest of Europe. Angela Merkel was the first German chancellor born after the Second World War, and many in Germany believed it was time for the country to move on from paying explicitly or implicitly for Germany's past behavior. Slow-growing, economically vulnerable countries resented the tough economic conditionality imposed by European institutions in return for help. They saw the barely hidden hand of a resurgent Germany behind the conditionality, and complained that through the idea of Europe, Germany had finally obtained the hegemony it always desired. Small countries, having lost their veto over much of European policy, felt helpless in the face of policy determined by the large powerful countries.

All these resentments came to the fore with the immigration crisis. In 2015 and 2016, over a million refugees each year applied for asylum in Europe. The would-be migrants were largely Muslim and typically came from war-torn countries like Syria, Iraq, and Afghanistan. These were not, however, the only migrants. Droughts in Sub-Saharan Africa pushed many Africans to also try their chance, some as asylum seekers from conflict-ridden countries like Somalia, Sudan, and the Congo, but others simply as undocumented economic migrants. Many migrants sought to go to immigrant-friendly countries like Germany, Sweden, and the United Kingdom. European regulations required them to apply in the first country they arrived in. Greece, Italy, and Hungary were where many asylum seekers first entered the European Union. It was hard for these "frontier" countries to absorb the enormous inflows. As the number of refugees built up in Hungary, Austria and Germany opened their borders in September 2015. That year, Germany accepted over a million migrants.

Easier immigration when welfare benefits are high is bound to raise concerns about freeloading, especially when immigrants are economically and culturally distant. This is exacerbated by misperceptions. A detailed survey by Harvard researchers suggests the extent of misinformation about even legal immigrants is substantial. In Italy and the United States, where the actual population share of such immigrants is around 10 percent, the average perception is that it is 26 percent and 36 percent respectively.[43] Respondents systematically overestimate the share of Muslim immigrants and the dependence of immigrants on welfare, while underestimating immigrant education and employment. The extent of misinformation increases for the low-skilled who work with immigrants, the non–college educated, women, and right-wing respondents. Those who personally know an immigrant tend to have more accurate responses, while those in the United States who live in an area with more immigrants tend to have greater misperceptions. Finally, those who see immigrants as better educated and more hardworking tend to be more supportive of policies favoring immigration and redistribution.

The immigration crisis still roils the European Union, even though the numbers of potential immigrants has fallen dramatically. A number of countries like the Czech Republic, Hungary, and Poland, with strong anti-immigration movements, resented the imposition of immigration quotas by the Union, no matter how small they might be, and refused to take their shares. At the time of writing, the European Union is contemplating reducing its funding for the recalcitrant countries. In Europe, therefore, two concerns have come together in the immigration crisis. One is a fear of losing sovereignty and control, the other is the fear of being swamped by foreigners with alien cultures and religions, especially if they also tap into Europe's generous welfare state without having paid into it—a similar fear to that of the Tea Party in the United States.

In Britain, those who campaigned in the 2016 referendum to exit the European Union emphasized both these fears. More generally, while the initial idea of a European common market without customs or tariffs separating countries was widely accepted as economically beneficial, the push toward full integration was not. Presumably, Europhilic politicians and bureaucrats hoped that once people were in it together, empathy would build. The financial crisis, followed by the immigration and refugee crisis, tested the European project before strong bonds of empathy were built. Equally to blame were Eurosceptic politicians, who attributed all difficult national policies to an unelected bureaucracy in Brussels, while taking credit for all the benefits of an integrated market. So Europe remains an important, potentially valuable idea, but with only modest popular support.

CONCLUSION

A decade after the crisis, the world economy has recovered, in part by pumping up debt once again. Even as financial vulnerabilities build again, technology progresses further, and many people are still unprepared for the new economy. Society needs to rebalance. Both the state and community pillars have to give people the support they need to engage in global markets. Only then will they resist the urge to balkanize it with specific protections.

Unfortunately, far too many people now distrust the elite. The policies of openness that served the world well after the Second World War are now being questioned, and it is hard for the mainstream politician to explain in simple words why they still are relevant when confronted by the simplistic but more direct arguments of the populist. The value of the postwar trust enjoyed by technocrats was that they did not have to spell out these arguments to the wider public; they were generally trusted to do what was right. Now they are not.

Some commentators argue that deep divisions between mainstream parties, the demonizing by each mainstream party of the others, and their inability to cooperate, exacerbates the trust breakdown and pushes people to search for radical alternatives. Perhaps. Yet equally, too cozy an arrangement between mainstream parties can also make people upset because they feel establishment parties are all the same. When they are distressed and they have lost trust, the aggrieved masses are fertile ground for the radicals no matter what the configuration of the mainstream.[44]

These are dangerous times. If people have lost faith in their ability to compete in markets, if their communities continue to decline, if they feel that the elite have appropriated all opportunities for themselves, both by monopolizing the markets and by monopolizing access to capability build-ing, popular resentment can turn to rage. Democracy requires equal access, and when access is unequal, democracy reacts. More populist radicals will be elected. Of course, if these radical populist movements push for reforms that include rather than exclude, that tackle the cronyism and the usurpation of opportunity by the elite—as did the Populist and Progressive movements in the nineteenth-century United States—they would be very healthy correc-tives for restoring the balance.

More likely on offer are populist nationalist movements led by charismatic leaders who seek to exclude rather than include, and thus tend to skew rather than restore the balance. While the populist nationalist does not offer last-ing solutions, she still has the power to damage. Institutionalized checks and balances may contain new Napoleons for a while. Yet rare is the institution that can stand up to popular will for a sustained period of time, without sup-port from other sources of power. A key element of the populist nationalist's agenda is to undermine those sources.

Authoritarian crony capitalistic states, hostile to the ties between nations that come from trade and the flows of people and capital, hostile to any mul-tilateral agreements and multilateral governance, but nevertheless having to live together on this planet . . . Such a disunited world will inevitably revive the specter of global big power conflict that we hoped was a relic of the twen-tieth century.

8

THE OTHER HALF
OF THE WORLD

S o far we have focused primarily on Europe and America. Before we discuss solutions, we should examine the countries that will grow in the
future, including the countries currently labeled "emerging markets"—
such as Brazil, China, India, Mexico, Saudi Arabia, South Africa, Turkey, and
Vietnam—as well as the developing countries of Africa and Asia like Ethio-
pia and Myanmar. Any developed-country policy maker has to recognize
that while it may seem that trade and immigration are polarizing today, they
will be solutions to the problem of population aging that almost every developed country will have to confront soon. The future markets for developed-
country goods, the destinations for their citizens' excess savings as they
prepare for old age, and the source of the labor they will need to support an
aged society will lie in the growing and still-young emerging markets and
developing countries.

This is why it would be myopic for the developed world to erect high barriers separating themselves from the rest as it deals with its current political
problems. Moreover, problems that need global solutions, such as climate
change, which threatens the quality of our existence, and volatile global capital flows, which cause periodic crises, need global engagement.

Our existing structures for global governance are outdated. Developed countries account for less and less of global economic heft, yet they still hold all the meaningful reins in the institutions of global governance. Before the next decade is out, barring serious calamity, China's economy will be bigger than the United States's, while India's economy, already bigger than France's, will be the third-largest in the world. In the past, the belief that the large developed countries were responsible custodians of the global rules-based order that the United States built after World War II gave the rest pause in their demand for a more equitable sharing of power. Even though the system was designed so that the United States could break free of the rules, for the most part it acted as if it was bound by them. Now that it has shown it can elect administrations that do not respect norms, can the world accept any nation that is above the rules?

Yet, even though populist nationalists have no respect for global institutions, they will resist ceding power. This impasse is not good. Either the rest will stop respecting global institutions and create their own, or there will be a vacuum in global governance until the rest become powerful enough to take over global institutions directly. In the latter case, the largest emerging markets will inherit the skewed distribution of power that now favors the developed countries. Developed countries will regret their reluctance to reform if the emerging markets impose on them the power structure that is currently being imposed on the emerging markets.

There is always the possibility that we abandon the rules-based international order that has helped the world focus on collective mutually beneficial interests rather than self-interest. When every country wants to make itself great again, the zero-sum economic machinations of the pre–Second World War world will return. To make sense of these issues, the reader needs a view from the emerging and developing world. We will focus on the two largest emerging markets, China and India, partly to understand some of the challenges these countries face—including rebalancing the pillars in their own countries—and partly to understand how important it is for the world to engage these countries as responsible members of the community of nations.

ARE CHINA AND INDIA
AT ALL SIMILAR?

The Communist Party took over China after the Second World War. At about the same time, India became democratic and independent from the British Empire. In India, every government has to fight periodically for a renewed mandate, which has meant that the government is more constrained in its actions, not just by the power of democratic protest and numerous civil society organizations, but also by institutions like the judiciary and the opposition. Critics like Lee Kuan Yew, the creator of modern Singapore, have argued that poor countries cannot afford democracy. Indeed, in the race between China and India for growth, it would seem that authoritarian China beats democratic India hands down. Simple extrapolation then suggests India should never be spoken of in the same breath as China; China has an economy as well as a per capita income (since the two countries have about the same population) that is nearly five times as large as India's at market exchange rates.

Yet, there are more similarities between the two countries' growth paths than we allow for. Both China and India were government-dominated systems with weak markets at the beginning of their respective reforms. China's government, under the centralized control of the Communist Party, was more able to execute, while India's markets and private sector were a little stronger at the outset. The initial liberalizations, prompted by the end of Maoism in China and a financial crisis in India, greased by corruption since both systems were still overregulated, produced strong growth. China could suppress markets more, and repress households more, because it did not have to contend with democracy. This allowed it to generate faster growth, but its growth was more skewed—in favor of state corporations over households, in favor of savings and investment over consumption, and benefiting foreign investors more than citizens.

A variety of imbalances have built up in China—overcapacity in industries because of excess investment; excessive corporate and local government debt burdens as a consequence; and overdependence on investment and exports for growth. Also, China is close to catching up to the global productivity frontier in a number of industries. The state will find it hard to continue making economic decisions in such a modern complex economy, for these are best left to the market—China is trying to allow the market more freedom to make allocations and to reward or punish. It will have to move to a more constitutionally limited state if it wants the private sector to have the confidence to make investments. Yet China's Communist Party wants to continue to maintain its monopoly over political power, and there are signs that intraparty democracy is also weakening. Can China pull all this off?

India, with its more pluralistic and open-access political system, is better positioned for the community to create more separation between the state and markets. Its weakest pillar is the state.[1] To match what China has already done successfully, India will have to improve state capacity significantly, something that may come as a surprise to those who think India has excess bureaucracy. In reality, India has a plethora of rules and red tape, but it has relatively few officials employed by the state, given the nation's population (which is one reason why it takes so long to get applications cleared). Officials are all too often poorly trained or motivated, and the good ones are overburdened. Much of what an effective state should do, including providing public services and infrastructure, enforcing regulations, or clearing court cases, is left unattended because the state tries to do too much else with too few resources.

India also has a private sector that is still dependent on the state, which makes it a feeble constraint on it. So India has the paradox of having an ineffective but only moderately limited state. India's challenge in the years to come is not its democracy, which is probably the only way to keep a country with such varied communities together, but the need to strengthen both state capacity and private-sector independence. Will India make the transition to a liberal market democracy? Let us look for answers.

THE CHINA STORY:
MARKET LIBERALIZATION
UNDER PARTY CONTROL

Chairman Mao Zedong became increasingly erratic in the last two decades of his life. His Great Leap Forward (in which millions of Chinese died of hunger in the early 1960s as he tried to move rural areas away from food production into industry) as well as his Great Proletarian Cultural Revolution (in which many intellectuals were persecuted, humiliated, jailed, and killed in order to purify the Communist movement and purge it of capitalist tendencies) left the country traumatized. China's next leader, Deng Xiaoping, was determined that the country should not be dominated by a single person ever again. Deng, who had been purged by the Communist Party twice, and whose son was crippled by the Red Guards during the Cultural Revolution, gradually ratcheted up change after 1978.

THE PATH NOT TAKEN

The early reforms were often implicit—for example, the authorities turned a blind eye to private commercial activity even though it was technically illegal under the Communist regime. Growth picked up in rural areas, far from the reach of the central bureaucracy, for it was in the rural areas that the party had not entirely snuffed out the notion of private property. Under the Household Responsibility System, rural households contracted land and machinery from farmer collectives and kept any surplus they generated beyond a required payment. It was an important step toward greater agricultural productivity.

A number of private firms also started, cloaked in the permissible garb of collectives known as Town and Village enterprises.[2] Marxist ideologues had determined that these enterprises would become exploitative if they exceeded seven members, yet the rule was rarely enforced. Such enterprises produced a range of goods, from radios to refrigerators, and many farmers grew rich. Reforms even touched state-owned enterprises, where the better-performing ones were allowed to keep profits and pay their workers more. Growth soared, and with that came some political liberalization as the liberal faction of the Communist Party gained credibility. Villagers were allowed to elect their representatives. With growing prosperity, village governments acquired the funds for meaningful activity.[3] The rural community became the center of both economic revival and an emerging democratic spirit. The press obtained more access, with even foreign reporters invited to hobnob with Politburo members at the conclusion of the 1987 party congress.[4] Reformers like

Zhao Ziyang, the general secretary of the Communist Party and a Deng pro-
tégé, emphasized the need to distance the Communist Party from the government, a necessary first step toward a multi-party system.

Yet clouds were gathering. In a socialist economy, many prices are fixed,
and essential goods like grain are distributed through the public distribution
system. As the Chinese authorities sought to harness market forces, they allowed the prices of some goods to fluctuate. Speculators diverted goods to the
open market where prices were highest. As a result, shortages developed in
the public distribution system where prices were fixed at affordable levels,
especially as people, anticipating price rises, bought to hoard. Inflation
soared. Workers in poorly performing factories or in salaried sectors of the
economy started feeling the pinch, even as they feared further reforms would
take their jobs away. They also resented the access the party elite had to goods
in short supply. Growing evidence of party corruption, as local authorities
took bribes to overlook the breach of regulations by new enterprises, further
angered them.

Reforms had also raised expectations, but the market taketh even as it
giveth. Instead of obtaining the good jobs that students in elite universities
like Beijing University believed they were destined for, many experienced unemployment as the now profit-conscious, overstaffed, state-owned firms cut
back on hiring. Moreover, students were aware of the growing protests against
socialist governments in Eastern Europe, and the cracks that were emerging
in the Soviet empire. Somewhat optimistically, they believed that China's reformers, who seemed so open to economic change, might also support more
broad-based political liberalization. The death of Hu Yaobang, a leading re-
former who had been forced to resign for being too liberal, was the trigger for
protests in Tiananmen Square in Beijing in the spring of 1989, where unhappy workers joined students.

For a while, it seemed that the protesters might force the party to back
down. Students of the Central Academy of Fine Arts erected a statue of the
Goddess of Democracy in the square, facing the huge official poster of Mao
Zedong. Yet, when Deng was faced with a choice between political liberalization and continued Communist Party control, the man who had been purged
twice chose the party. The army was called in, and on a bloody June 4, 1989,
cleared out the square. Many students, workers, and their supporters died in

and around the square. A tank pushed over the Goddess of Democracy, and it was soon reduced to rubble. Key protest leaders were arrested, the worker leaders were tried and some executed, while the better-connected student leaders got jail terms. The liberals in the party such as the general secretary, Zhao Ziyang, were purged and hardliners gained influence. There was no longer any question of distancing the party from the government. The party would govern.

Deng was faced with terrible choices, though there was a cold-blooded logic to his decision. China had suffered enormously from internal chaos in the past when the center had been weak. The turmoil in the Soviet Union, where Gorbachev's *Perestroika* encouraged fissiparous forces without energizing economic growth, suggested what not to do. Deng rejected radical political liberalization so that he could orchestrate gradual economic reforms. The government would create the market in China, instead of allowing it to emerge spontaneously and unpredictably from the embers of a socialist economy. Perhaps his choice was right for the growth of the Chinese economy, but it postponed political freedom for the Chinese well into the future. By skewing the balance, it probably made it harder to move China away from the possibility of autocratic rule, one of Deng's aims. It was probably one of the most consequential decisions in recent world history.

For a while, further economic reform was put on the back burner. However, in 1992, Deng went on a tour of southern China, using the trip to reaffirm the necessity of continued liberalization. He is rumored to have said, "To get rich is glorious," and to have complained that the conservative elements of Chinese society were more dangerous than the liberalizing elements. Reforms took off once more, but they were profoundly different in character, as MIT economist Yasheng Huang argues. In the next decade, under the leadership of President Jiang Zemin, who had been the Communist Party boss in Shanghai, the epicenter of economic activity as well as government attention shifted to the large towns and cities in the coastal areas, to state-owned enterprises, and to encouraging foreign direct investment.[5]

At the same time, the small village communities, which had seen a whiff of political liberalization and democracy in the 1980s, had their powers, including budgeting, taken away by party bosses in townships in the 1990s.[6] The party bosses were appointed, not elected, so this was effectively a centralization of power away from the hard-to-control and numerous village communities.

FROM ENTREPRENEURIAL TO STATE CAPITALISM

So from the uncontrolled, near-spontaneous emergence of entrepreneurial activity in poorer, rural, and interior areas, China moved toward more state-led capitalism in the richer towns and cities and coastal areas. State-owned firms, especially the larger ones, were obviously easier for the party to control, but they were overstaffed and inefficient. Over the decade of the 1990s, China took three important steps to improve their functioning.

First, it adopted the policy of "grasping the large, letting go of the small." This meant selling or closing smaller state-owned firms across the country, many of which were unprofitable. Some of these were sitting on valuable assets like real estate. City or provincial party bosses captured the illegal gains as they sold these to cronies at bargain basement prices.[7]

As the government's ownership was pruned, it could focus its attention on the large, and significantly more important, state-owned enterprises. In 1990, the State Council enacted a policy of "two guarantees," which assured the large state-owned enterprises of access to cheap credit and underpriced inputs like commodities. The enterprises also obtained cheap power and land. Some of the inefficiencies of these overstaffed firms were offset as they invested in more modern capital stock, and other inefficiencies were masked by the lower costs of their inputs. Many of these companies were also allowed to list on domestic or foreign stock markets, which gave them access to equity capital and also brought on board large investors who could exercise some corporate oversight and improve productive efficiency.

Second, the state-owned enterprises were allowed to sack their surplus staff. Workers in China believed they would always have the "iron rice bowl"—the promise of lifelong employment with a guaranteed pension and other benefits such as housing. The Communist Party abandoned this implicit promise. The unemployment generated by the state-owned firms laying off nearly fifty million employees in the decade after Deng's southern tour was a tremendous shock, as traumatic as one any capitalist system would impose. It was made more brutal by it being unexpected.

Third, state-owned firms were consolidated where possible under common holding companies so that operations could be rationalized and they would get pricing power. For example, the Baosteel Group took control of six large steel manufacturers—three wholly owned by the group and three publicly traded.[8] The effect of all this was to increase output per worker and the profitability of the state-owned enterprises. Much of this improvement typically came from overinvestment of cheap capital, which was used very unproductively.[9]

The surplus workers fired from state-owned enterprises, as well as the migrants from rural areas who had been let go from increasingly mechanized agriculture, had to be employed somewhere, for the party could not ignore worker distress indefinitely. This reflects a paradox in China, and more generally with authoritarian regimes. Since they do not have legitimacy from the polls, they need legitimacy from policy choices that indicate they have the greater good of the people in mind, else the cost of maintaining the authoritarian regime against the wishes of the people would increase exponentially. Democratic leaders can admit to mistakes saying, "We messed up," and move on. In many cases, they can blame the previous administration. Authoritarian regimes, at least those that want to retain the consent of the ruled, cannot, since sound policy is the basis of their legitimacy. Nor do they have the luxury of blaming the previous regime—even if the decisions were made by different leaders, current leaders have to defend them, else it would suggest the regime is fallible and the people should have the choice of dispensing with it. We will return to this paradox of legitimacy-seeking authoritarianism shortly.

One solution was foreign direct investment, which was especially attractive to the Chinese authorities because it brought know-how, but very little political threat—any foreign firm that dared to interfere politically could be summarily expelled. Cheap and well-trained labor was an important attraction for foreign firms intending to manufacture and export from China to world markets. So was the ability to locate in the coastal areas, with easy access to ports. It was not easy, though, for foreigners with few local connections to comply with the myriad regulations that a reforming socialist economy imposed on business—even today, as economist Chang-Tai Hsieh emphasizes, China is only seventy-second on the World Bank's *Ease of Doing*

Business ranking. This is where the city mayor or regional party boss came in.

An Indian businessman told me how he had expressed an interest in investing in a middle-sized Chinese city in the early 2000s. When he went to visit the city, he was met at the airport by the deputy mayor on a Sunday, taken to visit a possible site that very day, then taken to the mayoral office where all the necessary permissions had already been prepared. Every difficulty could be dealt with; all he needed to do was to sign on the various dotted lines and bring in his money to start the project. The party eased the way for its favored businesspeople.

There were two other important motivations for foreign investors. One was a lower income tax rate relative to domestic firms. Second, starting in the 1990s, China worked to keep its exchange rate from appreciating even as its exports and trade surpluses increased. The undervalued exchange rate was effectively a subsidy to exporters, because dollar revenues were higher when translated back to renminbi. Many foreign firms set up production in China to take advantage of its abundant educated labor, its improving infrastructure, the willingness of suppliers to promise and deliver the impossible, and to a lesser extent, its undervalued exchange rate.

What worked for foreign direct investment also worked for local private investment, especially construction and real estate, which employed many unskilled workers and had the collateral benefit of creating infrastructure. The key input here was cheap credit, land, and permissions, all of which the mayor could secure. Land, especially farmland, could simply be expropriated from the current occupier for little compensation, especially since all land technically belonged to the state. The expropriated land could then be turned over to the real-estate developer, sometimes at a significant markup that added to the coffers of the city government. Such actions became increasingly necessary as the central government started retaining most of the tax revenues in the early 1990s, forcing city and provincial governments to become entrepreneurial in raising money. Invariably, some of the funds generated from such legally murky actions also went to bolster the personal income of the party officials as compensation for their "entrepreneurship."[10]

Corruption was not the only motivator. Many party bosses showed keen interest in such investment because economic growth in their region was an important consideration for their promotion up the party hierarchy. Others did so because the local government obtained shares in the start-up, which gave it a continuing stake in the company's growth. At any rate, the onerous rules and regulations as well as the relatively murky property rights were an important obstacle to any ordinary person setting up business, but were not a problem for those with party connections. The party thus fostered private enterprise while keeping control over who was allowed to open businesses or expand.

When the irrepressible ordinary citizen ignored these implicit norms and struck out on their own, they did so at their peril. For example, the Xiushui Market in Beijing was a thriving outdoor market, specializing in brand-name fakes (especially popular with foreign tourists).[11] The district government closed the market on grounds that it was a fire hazard and that it was selling fakes, and proceeded to evict the shopkeepers and demolish the market. A private entrepreneur was then given the rights to build and operate the new indoor Xiushui Market, and he proceeded to auction the more limited space there, with the highest bid for a stall reaching $480,000. The merchants who had built the name and reputation of the earlier market (no matter that it was built on fakes) had their own brand name expropriated from them, and only a third could afford stalls in the new market. Poetic justice some would say but not surprisingly, many of the stalls in the new market also sold fakes!

THE REPRESSED HOUSEHOLD

The subsidized inputs to corporations had to be paid for by someone—that was the ordinary householder. Given her productivity, not only were her wages lower than they would have been in a more developed economy (as in many developing countries, they were held down by massive surplus labor in agriculture), her taxes paid for the other subsidies granted to the corporate sector, she paid the high prices charged by local monopolists, and she received low interest rates on her deposits (the government capped the rates payable on deposits at a low level, in order to allow banks to profitably make cheap loans to corporations and developers).

Even while the household received miserable returns on its deposited savings, the government had taken away its promise of a safe job and guaranteed pension. Chinese labor unions did not really fight for worker wages or rights, except when signaled to do so by the government—they were essentially there to control and channel worker dissatisfaction. Furthermore, in 1979, China's one-child policy effectively mandated a maximum of one child per couple. It resulted in six adults—four grandparents and two parents—depending on that one child for support in their old age, if they did not have savings of their own.

The household had further challenges. Its most important property—the house and the land it stood on—was insecure, as we have already seen. Also, industrial growth, as well as the blind eye that was turned to violations of regulations, polluted the air people breathed, the water they drank, and the food they ate. China was becoming the workshop to the world, but its people were paying for it with a deteriorating quality of life as the country drew in the dirty factories and power plants that were closing everywhere else.

China therefore followed a unique growth path. Ordinary households bore a burden that would not have been possible in a more democratic environment. There were important compensations. Because the system generated very modern infrastructure and investment rapidly, the economy grew fast. Many new jobs were created, and the productivity of existing jobs increased quickly. So average wages grew fast, even though they were lower than the additional value each worker created. China was growing rich quickly, so it was easy to ignore the distortions.

Nevertheless, a large share of the income generated in the country ended up as savings rather than final consumption by the households—partly because it was locked up as corporate profits of state-owned corporations that were not paid out but reinvested and partly because households saved more, worried about the removal of the safety net and the insecurity of property. Chinese private consumption to GDP fell from about 50 percent in 1990 to about 47 percent in 2000. In the next decade, when China grew very fast, consumption fell further to a meager 35.5 percent of income in 2010. The Chinese household paid a price for the jobs that growth generated, but the growth was spectacular. Hundreds of millions of Chinese have been lifted from poverty into relatively comfortable middle-class lives since the reforms started.

Party Control and Crony Competition

The party therefore facilitated growth, not by opening access to all but by using its good offices to clear the path for select business. At the same time, it tightened its political control. A 2005 white paper by the party defined democratic government as "the Chinese Communist Party governing on behalf of the people."[12] This meant more than single-party rule, it meant extending the party's tentacles more directly into business.

Every large state-owned enterprise had a party cell, with the party boss often a more powerful figure than the company CEO.[13] The party decided overall strategy and senior appointments in the company. This ensured the party had firm control of the state-owned enterprises, and their enormous funds. Of course, this also enabled party members to do favors for one another, including appointing one another's children to cozy jobs.

Membership in the party was increasingly the route to success in China. Private-sector firms soon read the writing on the wall and created their own cells. In the internationally known consumer electronics and home appliances product company Haier, its CEO also served as the secretary of the company's Communist Party committee.[14] The party made it clear that it wanted both information and the ability to intervene in every organization that might be a possible threat to its political monopoly. The private sector complied.[15]

Such strong political control over business, without a vocal public community that can enforce separation between the state and business, raises concerns about inefficient crony capitalism and possible authoritarianism that we have discussed earlier in the book. Has China been special in avoiding these ills? In a sense it has . . . thus far . . .

As political scientist Daniel Bell argues, the Chinese Communist Party is in many ways a meritocracy, which trains and tests its members in the practice of governance.[16] Each of the nine members of the Standing Committee of the Politburo, the apex body of the party, has come up the hierarchy after proving themselves in regional or city governments. With an important element of their performance appraisal being how much they grew the local economy, local party bosses were ferocious in attracting potential investors to their locality, facilitating the set-up and growth of local firms, and protecting them against authorities elsewhere including at the center. Chang-Tai Hsieh points out that many of the big cities in China have taxis of only one make—the make produced by the automobile joint venture of the city government. By forcing local taxi owners to buy the favored brand, the local authorities support their local champion.

So there is extensive cronyism within a locality. Moreover, the subsidies to firms in a locality can keep them alive even if they destroy economic value. Also, the party has favorites at the national level, including some very large state-owned firms that monopolize the national market. Therefore, it is hard to call China a fully competitive market. Ferocious business competition is, however, sustained between the champions of the myriad localities. Competitive cronyism is probably a more appropriate term for Chinese practice. It has worked thus far. Does China have the right system for continued growth, though? To answer that, we have to understand the post–financial crisis change in China's model of growth.

The Need for Change

What China has managed in the last few decades is truly unprecedented in the history of mankind. Never have so many been brought out of poverty so quickly. Furthermore, China has some of the world's most technologically capable companies, its most competitive universities, its speediest transport and logistics networks, and its most vibrant cities. Chinese development has been near miraculous, growing at 8.7 percent a year between 1980 and 2015. However, China can no longer grow as it used to.

The model of growth that China followed in the 1990s and early 2000s, of lowering input prices for corporations while making households bear the costs, has its limits. For one, it relies on export growth as well as investment growth providing a significant portion of the demand for the goods it manufactures, since consumption, by design, has been relatively low. The Global Financial Crisis severely constrained developed-country spending, especially on imports, many of which come from China. Furthermore, as populist parties have gained strength across the developed world, it has also become clear that some governments will turn protectionist. As I write this, the United States and China are engaged in a tariff war. Finally, foreign firms that invested in China with the intent of exporting to the world now see the growing Chinese domestic market as very attractive. They used to defend Chinese exports (which often were from their own Chinese operations) into their countries. Now, they support protectionist threats from their governments, hoping this will force the Chinese government to lower tariffs and other barriers, and open the Chinese market to their goods. From China's perspective, the political environment in developed countries makes it risky for China to rely further on exports. That means China has to generate more demand for its production domestically.

Credit-supported domestic investment expansion was one way China goosed up domestic demand, but it is yielding diminishing returns. Debt has been mounting in the system, with a huge jump after the financial crisis. Moreover, continuing investment in infrastructure and housing is getting harder to justify. The premise behind Chinese infrastructure investment was "build it and they will come"—that once built, utilization of the infrastructure would pick up quickly. In the early years of investment, this proved true, given the enormous pent-up demand. There was little need to keep track of whether China needed the investment; it generally did. Now, almost every moderately sized city has a swanky airport and a shiny new metro. The absence of a market test of whether the investment is justified and the enormous subsidies that are given to every investment are leading to excessive investment. The costs of keeping new infrastructure running, given the modest local utilization, eats into local government budgets. Local governments have been permitted to borrow from the public markets in recent years, but their finances now look precarious, given their enormous debt loads and the mounting losses on their public investments. Similar concerns pertain to investment by state-owned firms, where subsidies allow firms to expand when they should instead be closed down.

That leaves the option of boosting consumption. The removal of the distortions that generated easy growth, such as unduly low interest rates on household bank deposits, will give households more income from which to consume. Moreover, households are growing more resistant to bearing the costs of growth. Even in the first decade of the century, indiscriminate and unfair land acquisition from households prompted thousands of protests across the country.

China also has a problem with inequality. Many households in rural communities have not benefited from development since employment growth has been unevenly distributed, with the best and most numerous jobs in cities, especially in the coastal areas. China has to address growing income inequality by creating good jobs in rural areas and in the internal provinces, a problem we have seen that developed countries also grapple with.

Finally, as a result of its one-child policy, and because it allows very little immigration, China is one emerging market that is aging rapidly. As labor-force growth has slowed, wages are rising rapidly, forcing some industries to shift to cheaper countries. Even though the one-child policy has been relaxed in recent years, the Chinese are increasingly reluctant to have multiple children. China, therefore, may grow old before it grows rich—which is why it has to plan for a future society where the resources it will have to support its elderly are far lower than what Western populations have.

In sum, China, having reached middle income and caught up with advanced economies in a variety of industries, has to move toward a more normal economy, repressing consumption less and subsidizing investment less. It must protect household property rights better. It has to move away from relying on the rest of the world to consume its additional production to consuming more of it domestically. It must move away from dirty manufacturing to cleaner high-tech manufacturing and to services. Finally, given the enormous increase in complexity of the Chinese economy, it ought to let market forces play a greater role, with the government retreating from guiding the economy at every turn. Indeed, all these objectives are part of the intended Chinese policy reset.

Yet it requires an enormous change in the Chinese way of doing business. Chinese firms will have to become efficient on their own steam, and win market share, without subsidized inputs or local government protection. Financial markets and competition, not the party, will guide who gets resources. Such a future China looks very different from the China of the past. Can China manage the change? Its greatest weakness may be its greatest strength so far, the Communist Party and its desire for continued control.

WHAT CHANGE ENTAILS

The Communist Party has obtained its legitimacy from its superb management of the economy, and its ability to create growth and jobs. It has lost legitimacy from the visible corruption of some of its members, both locally and at the center. The key elements of President Xi Jinping's agenda, when his term started in 2013, were to create growth that relied more on household consumption. He also wanted to improve the party's image by reducing corruption. Let us see what this implies.

Fighting corruption is popular, and the public has joined in. For instance, Chinese social media has brought down a number of officials who have been photographed wearing watches that are many times their annual salary (their defense, naturally, is that these are cheap fakes). Yet the anti-corruption campaign hits at a core element of the earlier growth success. By spreading fear and shutting down local sweet deals, it prevents local officials from helping business navigate the thicket of rules successfully. The solution is obvious. Lighter, clearer, transparent regulations will permit freer business entry, dispensing with the need for "door-opening" by powerful local party officials.

With innovative new entrants, and the adoption of new technology and efficient management practices by incumbents, China will be able to grow without weighing on households. Some Chinese firms such as Baidu, Alibaba, and Tencent are pushing the frontiers of what is possible on online platforms and payment systems, catering to Chinese youth who are much more willing to consume and take on debt than their parents. China, given its enormous access to data, is probably much further along in some aspects of artificial intelligence and machine learning than developed countries.

The bulk of employment is not in high-tech sectors, though, but in older legacy manufacturing such as automobiles and steel. This is where China needs new technologies—such as electric and driverless cars and battery storage. It could acquire them by requiring foreign companies to enter into joint ventures if they want to sell in China—and the enormous size of the domestic Chinese economy now makes it a very attractive carrot—or it could buy companies abroad. Yet companies and countries are growing increasingly wary of China's ambitions, realizing that the Chinese will improve upon any technology shared today to outcompete them tomorrow. Equally, Chinese firms are finding it harder to replicate or otherwise expropriate foreign technology, as developed country firms become more aware of the threat and protect their technology better.

China therefore has to innovate, using its increasingly well-trained students, many of whom receive advanced degrees abroad, as well as its diaspora, who can be attracted back with the promise of well-funded laboratories and comfortable lifestyles. Chinese research and development has been progressing fast, but it will take time to make a difference.[17] In the meantime, if China does give market forces more play, significant parts of its manufacturing sector will be uncompetitive without the explicit and implicit subsidies they have grown used to. When parts of the economy become uncompetitive, modern economies rely on the financial sector to identify troubled firms, shut them down, and reallocate resources from them to healthier ones. Thus markets, rather than the state, allocate resources, and they do so based on who can use the resources better in the future rather than on the basis of who has the best connections.

In sum then, China has to open up entry, remove subsidies for incumbents, allow free competition, and let the market close down underperformers. All this has to be done while the party retains control, which means it cannot allow the private sector to become too independent. What might it do?

The Challenge of Changing Party Behavior and Retaining Party Control

Freer business entry means local party bosses will have to shift from selecting which new firms will enter and opening doors for them, to leaving all doors open to anyone who may wish to enter. This requires an enormous change in mind-set, especially since it requires the officials to allow their incumbent local champions—the source of some of their revenues and even personal incomes—to be subject to competition. If local party bosses are unwilling to lower local entry barriers, and at the same time unwilling to go back to the old corrupt ways fearing a vigilant central leadership, there will be little entry and slow growth.

Suppose local party bosses do acquiesce to command from the center and free business entry. The party then has to ensure that those firms that grow can be trusted, since the new entry process does not filter the politically un-reliable out. The party already has a method of doing this—to place its cells in each large firm, whether private or public, to govern the political direction of the firm. Presumably, if entry is freed, party cells will have to go into firms at an earlier stage than currently the case, to compensate for the lack of initial vetting.

Given the party's power, party representatives will be tempted to influence the course of the business, if nothing else to improve local growth and em-ployment outcomes. That will make ostensibly private firms, which are typi-cally focused on efficiency and profitability, into softer state-linked firms. It will require enormous discipline for party appointees to avoid the allure of influencing business decisions, when they have the power and position to do so.

Even if they do not interfere, the existence of such powerful cells will tie the firms to the party in the minds of the people. That leads to yet another problem. In a growing and changing economy, some firms will have the wrong business model. The right business decision would be to let such a distressed firm go into bankruptcy, and even shut down. Given that every significant firm is believed to be under some party direction, the party's rep-utation for infallibility will be at some risk. The party's reputation can absorb the occasional corporate failure, not a cluster of them. An intrusive party will suffer from the classic soft-budget constraint that János Kornai postulated for socialist economies: It will not be able to shut down failing firms, especially if failures are bunched. Instead, it will rescue them and waste resources.[18] Control is not free, it comes with the people assigning responsibility to the party.

Can the financial market help ease the party's problem? Probably not—it will tend to make it worse. That the party-controlled state will intervene if there are a number of failures creates the classic moral hazard problem of "too many to fail." If markets know that the state will bail out firms or invest-ments so long as there are a sufficient number of them, it has an incentive to create that number and more, and stop worrying about risk. The party's desire for political control could, therefore, undermine the market's pricing of risk.

The investment behavior of Chinese households, which needs to augment

savings for retirement, does not help. The household is ever alert for opportunities to make higher returns domestically, given that there are significant
restrictions on investing abroad. Every time the government alters its policies
a little, allowing households new investment opportunities or signaling a
more relaxed attitude to credit, huge quantities of savings move to take advantage of the return differentials that might briefly be available. This flow
pushes up the prices of financial assets, creating asset price bubbles. The government, wary of antagonizing the many households who invest their precious savings, is then tempted to intervene to support financial asset prices if
they fall. If it does intervene, households come to rely on the government to
bail them out, thus ensuring the financial market underprices risks. If the
government does not intervene, it will have many unhappy households, and
undermine its reputation for economic management and thus its legitimacy.
Invariably, it chooses to intervene, ensuring the Chinese financial markets
remain an unreliable allocator of funds.

In sum, the party will be tempted periodically to substitute its wisdom for
the wisdom of the market. If so, the market will never be able to mature to
guide resource allocation and risk management. Real change will occur only
when Chinese financial markets are weaned off the state's protection. China
needs its investors to absorb the lesson that financial markets do not just go
up but they also go down. That is a painful lesson that the state finds difficult
to impart, for financial busts do raise questions about the competence of an
all-seeing and all-powerful party. For a party that is unelected, and has little ability to blame previous administrations, these questions are better
not asked.

As China moves to the frontier of innovation, its businesses will have to
make more mistakes. It will also have to close more of its old smokestack industries. The strength of markets is their ability to deal with mistakes and
failure. The desire of the party to stay in control could undermine that
strength.

The State, Markets, and Democracy in China

Democracy, as we will see in India's case, makes it harder for the state to act
in some cases. However, it also makes inaction easier. The party in power

does not have to take responsibility for everything, and it does not have to maintain a pretense of infallibility since it derives its legitimacy from elections, not perfection. That allows it to deal better with market ups and downs. Certainly, democratic governments also intervene in markets, but every market crash is not a referendum on the government. Democracy therefore creates a separation between the state and markets in yet another way than the one we saw in the Populist and Progressive movements. It allows the state to be more decoupled from markets, and allows each, then, to function better without any cross-linkages undermining their functions.

All this assumes that China will continue to have enlightened meritocratic leadership that enjoys the broad support of its people. In the absence of elections, the people have to rely on the internal processes within the party to produce the right candidates. There are important reasons to worry that the internal processes are being undermined.[19]

The anti-corruption campaign has had the collateral effect of centralizing power within the party, with those who have the ability to levy corruption charges. Since so many party officials and existing businesspeople are compromised by corrupt acts in the past, the anti-corruption campaign can be used selectively to quiet opposition within the party and among the private sector. Indeed, my Chinese friends refer to the "original sin," a term used to describe the legal compromises that almost every private Chinese firm of any size (and their relevant local regulators) made in its early days when rules essentially prohibited all business. The original sin then gives the anti-corruption authorities a handle with which to beat everyone involved if they step out of line. The absence of any uncompromised opposition clears the way for an authoritarian faction to assume control of the party, if it so chooses.

Furthermore, party procedures, including those that ensured a regular change in leadership, are being overridden. Deng was worried about the re-emergence of one-person rule. The evaluation of party candidates for promotion based on objective measures of performance, as well as competition between them, injected a certain amount of dynamism in the party. Deng also attempted to instill traditions that would prevent a Mao-like dictator from taking over. Apart from structures that promoted collective leadership, one tradition was a limit of two five-year terms for the national president. A second was that the current president's successor would be determined in the middle of his term so that the succession would be smooth. Both traditions have been abandoned recently, corroborating the point that without sources of power in the country that are independent of the state, such norms are unlikely to constrain a determined leader.

The party seems to be moving toward more control and centralization. A Communist Party memo in 2013 entitled Document No. 9 warns about the perils from Western constitutional democracy, a free press, and other "universal values" as ideas meant to undermine and even break up China.[20] In a related vein, China's "Great Firewall" prevents radical ideas from the internet from seeping into the country, while China's large internet platforms have to share their data with the government. China's proposed "social credit system" intends to combine all the data on a person through artificial intelligence to produce a score for each Chinese citizen, which will determine their access to private and social services. Whether political and social activity will be taken into account remains a source of worry. With facial recognition software, and ubiquitous cameras, there may indeed be no privacy for the citizen from the state, as well as no freedom from it.

Hopefully, China's commitment to economic growth will keep it from becoming an autocracy that does not enjoy popular support. In the longer run, China will grow only if it can harness the immense innovative capabilities of its people—that is the nature of growth at the frontiers. People innovate when they are confident that they can question, when they are free to make radical changes, and when they do not fear reprisal for it. In China, such confidence can only come from continued trust in the leadership. While democracy is one way to verify that trust, and to delink the state from markets, perhaps China will find a different path. If so, it will be the first large country to do so.

China needs a more appropriate balance. The party dominates the state and markets have been repressed. The old pathways to growth are no longer viable. The new ways to grow require more of an accent on innovation and efficient resource allocation, less on financial repression and corruption. They require decentralization, but with clearer rules at the regional level, not the exercise of discretion.[21] All these, however, require the party to let go, to allow more freedom and independence to the market. The community will also have to be allowed more freedom and choice, both to sustain innovation and to maintain the separation between the state and markets. Whether all this can be done while the party retains its monopoly is the key question in China's central dilemma.

INDIA'S STORY: HOW TO HARNESS THE STRENGTHS OF A VIBRANT BUT CHAOTIC DEMOCRACY

India has grown at 7 percent a year for the last twenty-five years, a number that looks small only compared to China. Under its first prime minister after independence, Jawaharlal Nehru, India drew inspiration from the extraordinary development story of those times, the Soviet Union, which had transformed itself from peasant economy to industrial giant in the span of a generation. Following Lenin's dictum, Nehru reserved the "commanding heights of the economy," including critical industries like steel and heavy machinery for the state sector. Development economists at that time believed that poor countries would grow only through massive investment in critical industries that produced machines or infrastructure. This would increase their productive capacity and thus income. They should neither produce "frivolous" luxury goods for consumption, nor should domestic households consume much beyond basic necessities themselves. Only thus would they be able to husband savings for productive purposes, or so the thinking went.

SOCIALISM WITH INDIAN CHARACTERISTICS

Nehru's India did not actively suppress the private sector. Instead, a system of industrial licensing—that became known as the License Permit Raj—was put in place, ostensibly to use the country's savings carefully. Bureaucrats refused to grant licenses for industries that they believed were making unnecessary consumption goods (even durable ones such as cars), and instead encouraged investment in sectors that could support future growth such as the production of heavy machinery.

The consequence of licensing was that incumbents, typically private firms

from established families that were connected enough to procure early licenses, were protected from competition. The government also erected barriers against foreign competition—the idea was this would give a respite to
India's infant industries, allowing them a nurturing environment while they
matured and became competitive. However, no incumbent, having become
profitable behind barriers, had any incentive to allow the barriers to come
down. The protection India offered its infant industries thus became an excuse for the companies to become "Peter Pans"—companies who never grew
up. There were only five different variants of the Ambassador car, India's
only large car, over its nearly four decades of commercial production, and all
that seemed to change through much of this period were the headlights and
the shape of the front grill. After growing rapidly during an initial period of
post-independence industrialization, India got stuck at a per capita real
growth rate of about 1 percent—dubbed the "Hindu" rate of growth. The
private sector was inefficient and hugely indebted to the government for
protection. Cronyism was rife—the state and markets coalesced into one.

Did democracy not make a difference? Unfortunately not! India held elections every five years or so, but this did not mean that democracy gave a
significant voice to the people. The Congress Party had led the fight for independence and people trusted it for a while, so the party dominated elections
in most states. The lack of competition proved problematic. As Congress
Party affiliation, rather than local policies, seemed to be more important to
winning elections, decision making became more centralized. Indira Gandhi, the prime minister who probably arouses the most varied emotions
among Indians, both positive and negative, appointed her chief ministers
with a greater emphasis on their personal loyalty to her than on their competence or integrity. Strong independent regional politicians left the Congress
Party for the political wilderness, while party positions were filled with sycophants. With the delivery of public services in India abysmal because of India's ineffective state, patronage politics and public apathy that we encountered
earlier in the book dominated.

By the early 1970s, much of the wealth in the economy was either in the
state sector, controlled by it (many banks were nationalized in 1969), or held
by pliant private-sector magnates, so there was little power independent of
the state. The Congress Party itself was bereft of intraparty democracy. There

were still a few nonpartisan institutions, but most were powerless against a determined prime minister. When, in 1975, a high court disbarred Indira Gandhi from holding office because of an election violation, she invoked emergency powers and abrogated civil liberties, jailing much of the opposition. The constitution was amended in 1976 to make India officially a socialist republic, reflecting India's continued distrust of markets and its longing for a stronger state. That amendment also reduced the power of the inconvenient judiciary, thus taking India further down the road of economic and political illiberalism.

Though the power of the Indian state was almost unlimited, its performance in areas like the public provision of services was abysmal. In 1950, Indians had, on average, 0.92 years of education, somewhat better than the then Chinese average of 0.65.[22] By 1970, after twenty more years of democracy, India had crept up to 1.24. In contrast, China's population at that time had 2.77 years of education, nearly three times its earlier level. Apathetic uncompetitive democracy did not do much for the well-being of its people! Indian sham socialism merely gave top politicians, bureaucrats, and businesspeople a fig leaf with which to engage in cronyism—a reason to restrain the private sector with red tape so that it could selectively be peeled off.

INDIA AWAKENS AGAIN

India did move away from this path, though later than China did. Indira Gandhi ended the Emergency in 1977 and announced elections. Her party suffered a resounding defeat, suggesting that when roused the Indian electorate did vote their mind. India was back to being a chaotic democracy. After the opposition failed to make a go of it, Indira Gandhi returned to power in 1980, and India began a hesitant process of liberalization.[23]

Over the next two decades, India took some important steps toward becoming a liberal democracy. It did reverse some of the illiberal constitutional changes that had taken place during the Emergency. There were other developments that helped contain some of the arbitrary powers of the state. First, the Congress Party was no longer the electorate's inevitable choice. With the space opened for political competition, a number of regional and caste-based parties emerged to challenge the Congress Party. With such parties in power in different regional states, India effectively became more decentralized in its structure. Parties representing the lower castes, people who had historically been ignored by the elite, saw the need to develop the capabilities of their supporters. These parties pushed for an expansion in public services like health care and education in their states. Well-governed states started growing much faster.[24] Between 1970 and 1990, the average years of education in the Indian population more than doubled, from 1.24 to 2.96, and nearly doubled again from 1990 to 2010, to 5.39.

In the early 1990s, India decentralized further by formally creating a third level of governance at the village or municipal level.[25] Each village had to have an elected headman (the *sarpanch)* and a governing committee (the *panchayat*), and elections took place every five years. While state governments and local governments still tussle for resources and powers, decentralization continues.

Even as India was decentralizing and strengthening the community roots of democracy, a financial crisis marked the beginning of the end of sham socialism. India's external finances deteriorated so much over the 1980s that it had to go to the International Monetary Fund for emergency funding. The crisis made it abundantly clear that the system was not working, that the small reforms since 1980 were insufficient. China's tremendous progress over the previous decade made India's excuses for not liberalizing—that it worked only for small countries, and would empower predatory capitalists—seem like ways to justify continuing cronyism. The Congress Party realized India had to change. In his historic budget in March 1991, which started the process of dismantling the whole License Permit Raj system, Dr. Manmohan Singh said, "Let the whole world hear it loud and clear. India is now wide awake." His comment was a play on Jawaharlal Nehru's speech on India's gaining political independence, when Nehru said, "At the midnight hour, while the world sleeps, India will awake to life and freedom. . . ." Essentially, Dr. Singh heralded India's economic independence, as it threw off the economic shackles it had imposed on its own people.

The reform process had started in earnest, twelve years after China, but there were strong interests who opposed it. Once bureaucrats become used to helping businesspeople navigate the thicket of rules that they themselves have created, they do not let go easily. An Indian government bureaucrat explained it to me as "the sting of the scorpion." In any move toward liberalization, the bureaucrat plays along, but at the end, after all is debated and the thicket of earlier regulations consigned to the dustbin, he inserts an innocuous-looking-but-impossible-to-fulfill clause that reintroduces the need for bureaucratic discretion. Such resistance meant corruption did not go away. Nevertheless, the liberalization was genuine, steady, and significant. Growth picked up strongly as India's faith in markets grew.

Import tariffs were drastically reduced, subjecting Indian firms to greater competition. As with any liberalization, this did cause job losses in incumbent firms. Studies show that in trade-affected districts in India, the incidence of poverty was relatively higher, as was violent crime and property crimes.[26] Interestingly, these studies of the negative impacts of trade competition in trade-exposed areas appeared before the studies we described in Chapter 6 that were done in the United States. The reality is that trade, while typically beneficial overall, has a distributional impact. Emerging markets have long known this, but decided to embrace openness because of the overall positive benefits. It is ironic that having done so and absorbed the costs, they find some developed countries backing away from practicing what they used to preach. The costs of economic policy do become more real when they hit at home!

As business expanded, India did not just need to prune the old rule book, it needed new regulatory structures and processes. In the first decade of this century, the demand for, and value of, resources such as mineral deposits, land, and spectrum exploded. The government, which owned these resources, continued to give them away in an informal and nontransparent way, lining the pockets of the politicians, bureaucrats, and businesspeople involved. In the past, the apathetic public had not paid much attention. The India of the twenty-first century was very different, though, from the India that had folded supinely under Indira Gandhi's Emergency. As corruption became blatant there was clear pushback from the community.

It helped that a number of the public's watchdog institutions started asserting their independence. This was not based on a concerted decision by the elite establishment to give up its discretion and become better regulated. It was more a matter of happenstance, with the right person in the right place deciding to reform their watchdog institution so that it actually carried out its function. They were undoubtedly aided by a more decentralized and politically competitive India, which had become much more favorable to open political and economic access. So a chief election commissioner, a chief justice, or a comptroller and auditor general, refusing to accept the status quo, and urging their institution to perform their role effectively, could make a difference. As the economic and political system became increasingly pluralistic, it allowed such individuals to create space for their institutions, space that survived their departure. Even if the system pushed back a little, the institution had developed a tradition that it had to live up to, and that their successors could not neglect.

Therefore, as corruption assumed worrisome proportions, India's institutions such as the comptroller and auditor general and the judges of the Supreme Court investigated, publicized, and prosecuted the instances. Public outrage grew. Populist parties such as the Aam Aadmi Party (Common Person's Party) contested elections on an anti-corruption platform, emphasizing their willingness to listen to their constituents and work transparently on their behalf. Indeed, corruption was one of the two central issues in the 2014 general elections (the other was jobs). The ruling United Progressive Alliance lost decisively to the National Democratic Alliance.

THE STATE, MARKETS, AND DEMOCRACY IN INDIA

India is therefore different from many of the developed countries we have seen earlier in that it was a democracy before it industrialized, before it had a strong state, and before it had an independent private sector or healthy markets. While democracy was apathetic initially, political decentralization has revived political engagement, and has helped strengthen democratic institutions. It is hard to think of any system that would work in India other than democracy. Given the multiplicity of languages (twenty-two major ones and over seven hundred dialects), religions (India has fewer Muslims than only Indonesia and Pakistan), castes, and ethnicities, India needs a system that allows grievances to be expressed through democratic protest and dialogue, rather than one that bottles them up so that they explode later. India's raucous democracy alleviates pressures, and allows the country to be governed.

India's problems stem from the other two pillars. First, unlike the United

States, where a still-independent private sector criticizes government policy, including on social and political issues that are not directly related to their business, the Indian private sector—the market pillar—largely applauds all government policy. A determined government, despite being ineffective in most areas that benefit the public, can still cow the private sector and the press with threats, or bribe them with credit or government contracts. Even decades after liberalization began, there is still a sense among the public that the largest magnates have gotten where they are because of their ability to manipulate the system. The leaders of the party in power know the private sector's poor reputation well. Since there is usually some past sin buried in a magnate's past, as in China, which can be investigated and publicized if the magnate is uncooperative, very few are willing to speak out against the government of the day, let alone take steps to oppose it. This also means that when the party in power needs election financing, it only has to ask.

As a result, the opposition parties at the center find it harder to be heard, especially if the ruling party has a strong majority since both private-sector financing and press attention tend to dwindle after an election for fear of upsetting the government in power. This means the government's deficiencies and authoritarian tendencies are primarily checked only by the judiciary, by democratic institutions like the Election Commission, and by governments at the state level run by opposition parties.

An interesting event brought home to me the lowly status of the private sector in government eyes in India. President Obama was visiting Delhi, and the entire Indian elite was invited to meet him at a reception in the Indian president's house. True to form, the bureaucrats running the reception had identified everyone's precise place in the political hierarchy, and lined them up to shake President Obama's hand. It was a long line, starting with the Indian prime minister, the former prime minister, cabinet ministers, the leader of the opposition, military chiefs . . . retired dignitaries from the ruling party, ministers from various states . . . the Indian president's grandson, serving bureaucrats . . . and at number eighty-three, the chairman of India's largest private-sector group, accounting for over $100 billion in market value, followed by other tycoons and bankers. Admittedly, public service should be rewarded with higher status, to compensate for its lack of monetary rewards, but is not number eighty-three in the hierarchy for India's top businessman alarmingly low? This is not to say that power and dependence flows only one way. Ironically, after they retire, many of the bureaucrats who preceded the tycoons in the line will be working for them.

This has to change. Elections are not enough, it is what happens between elections also that make for a vibrant democracy. If India is to bury the specter of authoritarianism and cronyism, if Indian democracy is to be better informed and a stronger check on the state and corruption, India needs a more competitive, and thereby independent, private sector with higher public status. It needs many more small and medium enterprises to grow and flourish, providing competition to the established business houses.

That brings me to the deficiencies in the state. The state, while retaining the power to be arbitrary on occasion, is still not very effective; it tries to do too much with too few resources. Fortunately, the Indian state is also trying to reform itself. It is trying to bring professional expertise in laterally, and it is trying to use information technology to streamline delivery of its services and its monetary transfers to the public. These are important steps, but India has some way to go, especially in withdrawing from activities the state has no business being in.

Perhaps an anecdote will make the point: When I worked for a while at the Indian Finance Ministry as the chief economic adviser, I was shocked by the heavy paper files that came across my desk—shocked first that we still used paper files in the twenty-first century, and second at the amount of back papers I had to read to understand the note tagged on to the front of each file that required my comments and signature. Once I commented and signed, of course, my comments would become required reading for the next recipient of the file.

As I complained about this to a veteran bureaucrat, he gave me a simple solution backed by impeccable logic and experience: "Spend the least time on the thickest files. They are issues going nowhere, which circulate back and forth across desks, with everyone wasting each other's time by adding yet more comments. That is why they are so thick. Devote all your time to the thin files. Those are fresh issues where a cogent opinion may actually make things happen."

He was right but there is a broader message here. India needs to drop the thick files, and focus more on the thin files. The state can do more by trying to do less.

WHY INDIA HAS NOT DONE
AS WELL AS CHINA

China and India used to be sleeping Asian giants, but China awoke first. They used to be equally poor, but now China has raced ahead. China's initial advantages of a healthier and better educated workforce were perhaps more important in the early flush of liberalization, and its lack of a competitive market or private property rights were not disadvantages—indeed, they allowed the state to push favored industries.

Construction is probably the most important sector in the early phases of industrialization. It is a sector that employs unskilled workers—and hence can absorb many that leave agriculture. It is also a sector that contributes to the growth of other sectors, as businesses spring up to make use of the infrastructure. For example, it is quite magical in India to see the economic growth of a village as a good all-weather road is built connecting it to the city. The road allows trucks to transport goods to the city quickly, so farmers undertake new activities like dairy and poultry farming and horticulture. As they get richer, shops selling packaged goods and clothes open up in the village. Soon a kiosk starts selling prepaid cell phone cards, and not too long afterward, the village gets its first bank branch. Construction thus multiplies jobs and facilitates development.

Perhaps the most obvious consequence of their starting conditions is that China has been able to expand its construction sector enormously, while India has been less successful. China has moved ahead because it has been able to fund construction projects with cheap credit, and land acquisition has not been problematic because all land belongs to the state. In India, by contrast, credit comes at market rates. More important, any new project requires a painful and long acquisition of the necessary land from owners. If land rights are not well established, it can take even longer. The time delay involved itself undermines the economics of the project. While the law permits forcible land acquisition for public projects like roads and airports, opposition politicians, sensing the political opportunity, are always willing to organize protests against these. India's well-developed civil society, with each organization fighting for a special cause, often joins in. If the Indian state were effective, then these elements would provide an appropriate check on its power—indeed, Indian land acquisition laws are models of trying to balance the rights of the owner against the imperatives of development. The state, however, is ineffective, so land acquisition, and hence construction, is unduly delayed. India's infrastructure projects are, for the most part, too little and too late. In the early stage of growth, China has had an advantage.

India needs to speed up land acquisition. It would be tempting but short-sighted to lighten protections for the land owner. That would only bring the politician in to agitate against acquisitions that are deemed arbitrary in the court of public opinion. Instead, India needs to make the land owner a partner in development by giving them back a share of the developed land, as some Indian states are doing successfully. It could also focus some of its limited state capacity on establishing clean property rights in land, thereby easing ownership and sale, while giving up other activities it does less well, such as running an airline or bank. If it does this, India has plenty of easy catch-up growth still ahead of it, building roads, ports, railways, airports, and housing. Moreover, if it continues improving the education of its youth—and the quality of their learning needs to be the focus going forward—it will have the low-cost labor and the infrastructure to establish a larger presence in manufacturing, to add to its capabilities in services. Given the right reforms, India can still grow strongly for a long while. And with its vibrant democracy, it is probably better positioned than China for growth once it closes in on the frontier. It needs to get there first, though.

THE THREAT OF POPULIST NATIONALISM

Continued growth will put pressure on both China and India to liberalize further and become more market-oriented. Almost inevitably, this will make them look more like successful advanced economies, making global engagement and dialogue easier. Much slower growth, though, could lead them in more worrisome directions.

Leaders have an alternative to moving toward a liberal open-access society. And that is to exploit the populist nationalistic fervor that is latent in every society, especially as economic fears grow and disenchantment with the corrupt traditional elite increases. Both China and India have large numbers of people who have left their village community, and have moved to cities in search of work. These large young migrant populations, both tantalized and shocked by city life, and yet to be integrated into solid new communities, are ideal raw material for the populist nationalists' vision of a cohesive national community. They become especially malleable in times of slow job growth, as they see the incredible opportunities that the better-educated upper-class elite obtain. Rural village communities are also not immune to modernization. They too are intrigued and simultaneously repelled by the images they see on television of the lifestyles of the liberal urban rich.

In India, the Hindu nationalist movement tries to tap into such people's desire to anchor themselves in tradition. It also attempts to focus them on grievances that will shape them into a committed following. It exploits the sense among the majority Hindu population that they have bent over backward to appease minorities, especially Muslims. As with all populist nationalist movements, it portrays a glorious if mythical past, where Hindu India shone a beacon for the world to follow, while dismissing the entire period of Muslim rule over large parts of India as an aberration. For the rootless migrant from the village, the movement offers membership in organizations like the Rashtriya Swayamsevak Sangh (RSS), a volunteer paramilitary nationalist group, which drills its uniformed members and gives them a community, an ideology, and a sense of purpose. The truly committed majoritarian Hindu leader, drawn from a young age into the RSS, is usually personally austere—which endears him to those who dislike corruption—and committed to the cause, which makes him ruthless in his methods. They are a serious threat to a liberal tolerant innovative India, especially because they are more single minded than other groups, and thus effective in using their periods in power to infiltrate India's institutions with their sympathizers.

India faces serious challenges if global markets were to close. As it is, manufacturing exports are becoming more difficult as developed countries automate to compete with cheap labor elsewhere. Some developed countries are making it harder to provide cross-border services, which India has developed a strong presence in. An increase in tariff and nontariff barriers to goods and services will make the export-led path to growth much harder for India.

There is a protectionist streak among some Hindu nationalists, fueled by their business backers (they do have ties to business despite their seeming austerity), which will use the excuse of protectionism elsewhere to make India more protectionist once again. The private sector will then become yet more dependent on government favor. Therefore, the actions of populist nationalists elsewhere can weaken India's democracy and strengthen its destructive populist nationalism. Democratic, open, tolerant India will be an important, responsible contributor to global governance in the decades to come. Populist nationalism around the world will make this less likely.

Deng's dictum to China was that to prosper, it should "hide [its] capabilities and bide [its] time." China seems to believe that the time for that dictum is over. As President Xi stated in October 2017, "the Chinese nation has gone from standing up, to becoming rich, to becoming strong."[27] A great fear in Washington is that China is rapidly becoming able to challenge the United States, not just economically, but also militarily and politically. Hence its concern about the "Made in China 2025" program, which aims to increase China's presence in advanced manufacturing industries like aviation, chip manufacturing, robotics, artificial intelligence, and so on. While the United States still has a substantial technological lead in some of these industries, it worries that China will coerce US firms to part with technology and steal any technology it still needs. Similarly, new China-sponsored multilateral financial institutions like the Asian Infrastructure Investment Bank make the United States concerned that China is undercutting existing multilateral institutions that the United States dominates. China's hard power, as demonstrated by its militarization of islands in the South China Sea, and its soft power as evidenced by its One Belt, One Road initiative to build out infrastructure connectivity across land and sea from China, causes yet more unease in Washington.

The reality is that China's rise cannot, should not, be stopped. China has to be accommodated, especially in global governance structures. In turn, China also has to recognize global concerns about the means by which it has grown, especially its subsidies to industry and its appropriation of intellectual property. China has to become more responsible, now that it is becoming a substantial creator of intellectual property itself. It also has to assuage its neighbors' concerns about how their territorial disputes will be resolved, and make clear its intentions about respecting the global rules-based order as its power increases. There is a dialogue to be had which can reduce concerns on all sides, though the rise of a new power, challenging an earlier hegemony, is always difficult. That dialogue becomes much harder if China suspects the developed world is ganging up to prevent its natural development as well as if China becomes more repressive politically. Chinese populist nationalism, centered around the Han Chinese population, and driven by a sense that developed countries have historically exploited China with unfair treaties, will be strengthened by acts precipitated by western populist nationalists. China has its own minorities such as the Tibetans and Uyghurs, who have already experienced the oppressive weight of Chinese nationalism. A more virulent populist Chinese nationalism is not a development anyone, inside or outside, will want to see.

PART III

RESTORING THE BALANCE

You must be the change you wish to see in the world.

Mohandas Karamchand Gandhi

C onsider the sources of the imbalances we face today. Surging markets, enabled by the liberalization and integration that was necessary to reignite growth, and fueled by technological change and lower trade costs, have increased the potential for competition everywhere. This has created groups of winners and losers in every country. Semirural communities in developed countries, dependent on one or two large local employers, have been particularly affected by the factory closures and dislocation induced by trade. At the same time, even urban communities have been affected by the flight of the capable into enclaves of their own. Vibrant communities that used to have a mix of economic classes are left with less social capital, worse community institutions such as schools, and less wealth with which to raise the capabilities of their members. Disadvantaged groups are turning against one another as they find their economic and social status slipping.

Well-to-do incumbents have reacted to the increasing competition in markets by attacking its sources. For instance, they have raised barriers to entry through patents, copyrights, and licenses. This has further narrowed opportunities for the modestly educated, whose jobs in declining regions and industries have disappeared. As a few large firms dominate each industry, the potential for monopolization is increasing, while the independence of the private sector from the state is at risk. The state, burdened with debt and large entitlement promises made in happier times, is strapped for funds. It is also paralyzed in many countries, with discredited establishment parties at each other's throat, and challenged by radicals of all kinds.

In the meantime, technology rolls on, threatening to automate many more jobs, while not yet producing the growth that will help address society's difficulties. With society's values having turned more individualistic, and with little empathy available to paper over differences in already diverse societies, there is none to spare for new immigrants. Nevertheless, population aging is already shrinking labor forces in many countries, so they may well need to encourage immigration. And even as countries turn inwards, bent by the weight of domestic problems, there are very visible signs that climate change, which will require global cooperation to a degree we have never seen before, is upon us. We need to act now, both domestically and internationally, but the will and ability to act is weak.

Astute populist nationalist politicians see their chance amid this turmoil and respond. They emphasize an exclusive national identity, which serves as a replacement for the enfeebled community identity. They rally the native-born against minorities, immigrants, and the ceding of powers to international bodies. They suggest erecting tariffs against trade, much like the mercantilists of old, though they reserve for themselves the right to decide which industries will be protected and which will not. By accumulating such arbitrary powers to help or hurt the private sector, they will exacerbate the tendency towards cronyism.

When many countries engage in nostalgic nationalism, each pining for an era when they were strong, international relations become a zero sum game, and cooperative international action an impossibility. As countries assert a muscular nationalism, nations come closer to conflict. For this reason, the natural offset to an expansion in the market cannot be an expansion in the powers of the state, it has to be more a strengthening of the community through local empowerment. The centripetal forces within the local community have to be enlisted to offset the centrifugal forces of the global market.

We turn in these last five chapters to propose potential remedies. Specific plans will vary by country and location, and their details will have to take into account the difficulties of implementation. Rather than focus on details, I will explain why my proposals go in the right direction, given the analysis thus far.

I will explain how inclusive localism may contain many of the answers large diverse nations need, and what we can do to achieve it. The state will have the responsibility of creating an inclusive framework at the national level, using open-access markets to include and connect a diverse set of local communities. We will examine the kind of national constitution that will work well in a diverse country. I will describe localism: the process of decentralizing power to the local level so that people feel more empowered in their communities. The community, rather than the nation, will become a possible vehicle for ethnic cohesiveness and cultural continuity.

As markets have globalized, the power and resources to act have also drifted up, from the community to the region to the state and even to the superstate. Some legitimate national powers are now circumscribed by international agreements. Within nations, far too much is centralized, when there is little rationale for doing so. Localism therefore means returning power back to the people, from the international sphere to nations, and within nations from the federal to the regional to the community level. It means following the principle of subsidiarity strictly—powers should stay at the most decentralized level consistent with their effective use. Empowerment will force each one to take some responsibility, and make it harder to succumb to apathy or finger pointing. It will allow groups the possibility of maintaining identity, cultural continuity, and cohesiveness.

Many fear that empowered communities could become shelters for racists, easily hijacked by corrupt cronies, and prone to oppressive obscurantist traditionalism. All this is possible even in today's communities, but could become worse if the communities have more powers. Yet inclusive localism does not mean community powers will be unchecked—they will be balanced by the other two pillars, the markets and the state, which will force openness and inclusion. Federal law will ensure the community will be open to goods and services from across the nation, though the community itself will have substantial say over regulations governing local production. Moreover, the free flow of people, both in and out, will be guaranteed by law. Communities can still try to be narrow and parochial, but the economic costs of being so, especially given the possibility of benefiting from the flows of trade and people across its borders, will limit how unproductive or oppressive the community will get.

Development efforts in economically weaker communities will be driven by community leadership whenever available, but also supported by the state. The community will be aided in building out infrastructure, helped in improving the quality of its schools and community colleges, and subsidized to provide community-based tailored support to those in need. Technology will help the state monitor lightly, even while decentralizing much to the community. Likewise, technology will help community members keep a check on local government. Many of these technological solutions are scalable and, once developed, can be reused across multiple communities, with some local customization whenever needed.

To further inclusiveness, the state will break down barriers to opportunity and mobility that have built up over the years. For instance, barriers to building in some areas, which have made property prices prohibitive to newcomers, should be brought down. Some of this will interfere with community powers, but when inclusiveness goes up against localism, inclusiveness should always triumph. This is consistent with the theme throughout this book that when we have to choose between competition and property rights, we should invariably choose competition. More generally, though, markets have to be made more accessible, and the actions of market players more acceptable to the community. The first requires actions by the state, and the second requires a rethinking of the values of market players such as corporations.

Will the populist nationalists ever retreat from their mission of taking over the country and remaking it in their image? Will they accept enclaves within the country if they feel they can have the whole country? Any serious analysis of large diverse rich countries will suggest to even the most committed populist nationalist that diversity will continue to increase despite a strict clampdown on immigration, simply because the existing poorer minorities in the country have higher fertility rates. Unless the majority group is willing to impose a draconian apartheid regime, maintained by violence, the character of the country will naturally change. If some in the majority genuinely fear being swamped culturally, inclusive localism gives them a way to maintain their culture through monocultural communities, even while the rest of the country celebrates multiple cultures. In aging countries with fast growing minority/immigrant populations, some accommodation like inclusive localism may be the only civilized option.

I am hopeful that fear or resentment of the other will not be a permanent feature of our societies. Inclusive localism is not intended as an end condition. Instead, it will help alleviate pressures, giving everyone in society time to appreciate the value of diversity and figure out ways to manage it. We need to build a society for the future, when our peoples will be far more intermingled than they are today. We do not want to forget our cultures, our traditions, our very identities. At the same time, we do not want them to come in the way of embracing a broader humanity. Inclusive localism is a stepping stone to achieving both.

Let us not underestimate how difficult all this will be. Nation builders—ranging from benevolent democratic ones like India's Ambedkar and Nehru to murderous dictators like Russia's Stalin—have found it easier to break down community identities, to resist localism rather than to let it thrive. Yet they could not do away with the hold the community had on people. Perhaps it is time to try another approach, especially as technology makes decentralization of governance, and communication between communities, easier.

Similarly, Marxists have argued that the markets are based on destroying identity, on making everything commodity-like and transactional, while the community does exactly the opposite. They argue that markets and community can never be compatible. Yet although we have seen the tension between markets and the community repeatedly in this book, they do coexist. We trade anonymously in the market but then go home to volunteer for the school annual day festivities. We have multiple identities, as Amartya Sen emphasizes—trader during the day and deacon in the community church in the evening. Moreover, technology gives us the means to create more identity in the market, while giving us new ways of binding the community better together. Without minimizing the difficulty of our task, let us take hope from seeing that we undertake it in a different world than worlds past.

9

SOCIETY AND INCLUSIVE LOCALISM

One of the most contentious issues facing developed countries today, as we have seen, is the diversity of their populations. Many developed nations already have ethnically diverse populations. Many will get more diverse because of fast-growing minority groups, as well as inflows of immigrants and refugees. There are costs associated with diversity. These include the burden of absorbing poor immigrants initially, which falls disproportionately on poorer domestic communities and the lower mutual empathy between communities once the nation becomes more diverse, which leads to less support for a national safety net. Ethnically homogenous countries also fear a loss of their cultural heritage. Nevertheless, for many countries, there is no turning back. Even if they stop most immigration, they will get more diverse unless they choose to become authoritarian and illiberal toward their minority and immigrant populations, thus imperiling their liberal democratic ethos. Moreover, there are also enormous benefits to diversity, as we will see. How do countries reconcile the prospect of increasing national diversity with the majority group's genuine fear of being swamped, of losing cultural coherence and continuity? One way is through inclusive localism.

For some Populist nationalists, immigration is their key worry. For others, it is existing minorities. For many, it is both. Let us focus on immigration issues for now, though much of what follows pertains to minorities also—after all, today's immigrant is tomorrow's minority—and the terms will often be used together.

The life chances of a citizen of the United States are vastly different from the life chances of a citizen of the Democratic Republic of the Congo. Citizens benefit from national borders. Borders protect the rents citizens get from the country's wealth, institutions, and power. In effect, nations are the last of the guilds. By restricting decision-making largely to those living in the demarcated land, borders give the citizens a sense of self-determination and political control over their lives, and an ability to protect their cultural traditions. By only allowing people in who share something common, such as values or ethnicity, they allow for collective national efforts and engender the mutual empathy that allows the country to create support structures such as public schools, safety nets, and disaster relief. Therefore, while borders get in the way of productive efficiency, they may be necessary for the structures that help citizens manage modern life. It would be nice to go toward one borderless world—where we feel empathy for one another as citizens of the world, even while celebrating our specific cultural traditions—and some of what I suggest later will be small steps in that direction. But we are not ready for it yet.

Whether the lottery of birth that distributes citizenship is a fair one is a debate we will leave for global ethicists, and we will not enter the question of whether citizenship should be a right for those who have paid their dues—such as fighting in wars—or a gift to be bestowed by the citizenry who obtained their rights merely by birth. Taking the desire of citizens to control entry as legitimate, what factors should determine it? Let us start first with the benefits of a diverse population.

THE BENEFITS OF GREATER POPULATION DIVERSITY

THE GLOBAL SEARCH FOR TALENT

The very diversity of immigrants and minorities adds substantially to the pool of talent in a country. I teach about two hundred very capable M.B.A students at the University of Chicago's Booth School every year. The best students each year include many Americans (they account for two-thirds of our intake) but also a number from across the world. My most memorable students—in that they stood out distinctly from their cohort with their sheer capability—have been Chinese and Nigerian women. Talent knows no national, gender, or racial boundaries.

Moreover, given the winner-take-most nature of business, countries that can attract the most capable people from within the country and from around the world to work for them will have an edge. Singapore, for instance, has a scholarship program that hunts for the best students in China and brings them into Singapore schools at an early age. The education minister told me that every time he went back to his constituency, native Singaporean parents complained, "These kids come in knowing no English and are at the bottom of the class in the first year, in a couple of years they have learned English and have caught up with many of our children, and when they graduate from school, they are at the top. Is this fair?" After hearing them out, he responded, "Look, these kids are undoubtedly phenomenal, but they also now have our values—they are Singaporeans. Ten years from now, would you like to have them working on your side, or competing against you?" The complaints died down . . .

Apart from having a wider pool in which to search for raw talent, people from different cultures bring different perspectives and capabilities to teamwork. One culture may emphasize individualism and personal drive, while another may be better at building consensus. So long as teams have a basic understanding that allows them to communicate and engage, the whole can be better than the sum of the parts. Diversity, as many firms are recognizing, may aid performance.

Yet another value of skilled immigrants is that they facilitate ties between their home and host countries, thus increasing economic activity on both sides. Many cross-border investments by US companies in emerging markets are championed by US managers who have emigrated from those emerging markets and now help bridge cultural and trust gaps. Australia has grown steadily in recent decades by attracting skilled immigrants. In doing so, it has changed its ethnic character, from largely white to Eurasian. The foreign-born account for 28 percent of the population, with those from Asia accounting for more than 10 percent.[1] Not coincidentally, Australia has strong economic links with Asia today.

ADDRESSING THE CONSEQUENCES OF POPULATION AGING THROUGH IMMIGRATION

As nations get wealthier, women have fewer children, and have them later. Wealthy populations are, therefore, aging. As the population ages, the labor force shrinks, and fewer and fewer workers support more and more retirees. Forty countries now have shrinking working-age populations, including China, Japan, and Russia.[2] Fear naturally sets in as middle-aged citizens wonder who will pay for their retirement.

Japan is in the forefront of population aging, with its working-age population falling at 1 percent per year, and nearly four hundred schools shutting every year.[3] Thus far, it has adapted in two ways. Its workers are staying in the workforce longer, beyond the normal retirement age, and women are working outside the home at a greater rate. At some point, these additional sources of labor will reach their limits. Recognizing this, Japan also plans to automate more, using robots to substitute for the lack of workers. For example, Pepper, a big-eyed humanoid robot made by SoftBank, can lead exercise activities for a group of the elderly, talk to lonely patients in nursing homes, and patrol corridors at night.

There is another solution, though: Allow more immigration. After all, humans are still considerably more flexible than robots in accomplishing a variety of tasks. Immigrants have children who can add to the shrinking labor force and stabilize it, well before the burdens of supporting the elderly become impossible. They also spend their wages on consumption, something robots do not do. Because societies that are aging and shrinking suffer from weak domestic demand, immigrants can help out, especially with demand for goods that cannot be imported, such as housing and haircuts. Finally, humans supply humanity. Are we likely to be happier surrounded by unfeeling machines, programmed to make us think they are sentient, than by people, of a different ethnicity no doubt, who nevertheless listen, talk, laugh, cry, and are irrationally, unpredictably, gloriously human?

The United States, which has had substantial immigration and higher fertility rates among women (the two are not entirely unrelated—poor immigrants tend to have higher fertility rates), has much less of an aging problem than Japan. Yet Japan has resisted immigration, fearful of immigrants gaining political rights and affecting their culture. In a homogenous society like Japan, this is indeed an important and difficult decision—whether to age and decline alone as a society while retaining cultural purity, or, open more to immigration, become younger but also changed. Japan is trying to attract more foreign guest-workers even while debating whether to open up even more.[4]

Aging countries will have to decide whether to offset aging with immigration, for their wealth allows them the choice of immigrants today. If a country decides to proceed with immigration, it is probably wise for it to have steady and moderate immigration over time, so that immigrants can be integrated, and aging somewhat mitigated by births to immigrants. If the country waits till it experiences severe aging, immigrants may be scared off by the prospective size of the burden of supporting the elderly with taxes. A country which has not built structures to facilitate integration will also find it more difficult to absorb a large inflow of immigrants at that time of need.

Since aging affects the entire workforce regardless of skills, a country that decides to open up more to immigration to offset aging (rather than just to attract the best global talent) will draw immigrants from a broader set than just the most capable. Indeed, since low-skilled jobs like caring for the elderly are low-paid and physically taxing, they are likely to draw young poor immigrants. When immigrants fill jobs across the spectrum, there is less likely to be a concern among the native born that immigrants have privileged access to good jobs.

THE COSTS OF GREATER POPULATION DIVERSITY

Immigration, and more broadly, population diversity, is not always a blessing for the host country. People have to learn to live with diversity, and it takes more time and effort. In the meantime, they are less willing to support one another. As we saw with the Harvard study on immigration described in Chapter 7, people's intrinsic suspicion of immigrants is compounded by misinformation on their numbers, their skills, and their dependence on welfare. For the host country, the cost of greater diversity may well be a thinner and uneven public safety net, even for the native born.

Furthermore, the benefits of immigration are highest when a country can allow entry selectively to the kind of immigrants it needs. Countries like Canada, protected by oceans and distance from poorer countries, have the ability to be selective, and typically welcome immigrants. A country has no ability to be selective if a large fraction of immigration is undocumented or when it faces a huge wave of refugees. Following years of drought in Sub-Saharan Africa, farm workers and their families in recent years have braved stormy seas in rickety overcrowded boats as they look for refuge in Europe. Many have died on this perilous journey. Such immigration raises legal, moral, and humanitarian issues, not just economic ones, for pushing the starving, the fearful, or the persecuted back at the borders is simply inhumane. It may also create a wider security problem if stateless youth, with little to lose, take up arms and vent their anger against the unsympathetic world. And in these volatile times, today's reluctant host could be tomorrow's refugee. One of the most hospitable countries currently to Venezuelan refugees fleeing a venal incompetent regime is Colombia, which remembers how Venezuela took in Colombians when they were fleeing violence.

Nevertheless, the inflow of undocumented immigrants and refugees gives a number of countries only a limited ability to be selective. Typically, there is a mismatch between the skills and credentials these arrivals have and the skills and credentials that are needed, which means they are, in the short to medium run, effectively unskilled. There is a long and inconclusive debate about whether immigrants displace moderately skilled domestic workers or not. While the perception is that they do, the reality may well be that they compete with earlier immigrants for jobs that few native-born want. What is less in dispute is that the cost of hosting immigrants is also unevenly borne. Immigrants, typically being poorer, gravitate toward poorer areas where housing is cheaper, adding to the burden of public services there. Across countries with substantial unselective immigration, the working class is angry that the upper-middle-class elite enjoy the benefits of cheaper immigrant nannies and household help, even while their own children learn less because their teachers struggle with schools full of immigrant children who do not speak the national language. While this would suggest allocating more resources to create public services in areas that absorb more immigrants, few countries do this well.

Our views of immigration should, of course, not be based solely on a cost-benefit analysis to the receiving country. Immigrants themselves benefit tremendously, and this is typically ignored in cost-benefit analyses. Also, the emigration of skilled talent is a drain for the sending countries, for the talented typically do not return, and this is also ignored. Often, the sending country has spent enormous amounts in educating these students in its best schools to fill critically understaffed positions. When a doctor leaves Guinea, which had one doctor for every ten thousand people in 2016, to settle in the United Kingdom, which had twenty-eight doctors for every ten thousand people, she and the United Kingdom's stretched National Health Service certainly benefit, but Guinea probably does not.[5]

Most developed countries would benefit from a program of allowing immigrants in steadily and selectively. In practice, some have far less control than they would like. Immigration and refugee flows can overwhelm, especially if the country has accessible, porous, borders, bringing large numbers of people in who are poorly matched to the country's needs. Over time, these immigrants will learn and adapt, as immigrants have throughout history, but the process can take time. Ideally, countries should gain some control over their borders so that the flows are manageable, even while they improve their processes to absorb immigrants. To deal with the humanitarian problem of refugees overwhelming some countries, the world needs to create a better system, where its safer countries can share the burden with each accepting some immigrants as part of their international responsibilities. This is an issue we will return to later. In the long run, only peace and widespread development will reduce the flow of refugees and undocumented immigrants. Populist nationalism goes in exactly the wrong direction!

WHAT WILL CITIZENSHIP LOOK LIKE?

There is a fond hope among the populist nationalists that they will make the nation pure again by shutting off the flow of immigrants (except immigrants like themselves). Furthermore, they will impose a majoritarian template on existing immigrants and minorities so that they will be forced to shed much of what is different and alienating (and interesting) about them.

Race and religion are hard for immigrants and minorities to shed, but once they conform their other attributes to the template, these differences will only define their second-class status. The secret hope of the more extreme populist nationalists is that life will become so difficult for everyone who is different that they will "self-deport," returning to their "own" country. The most extreme actually want to initiate expulsions or ethnic cleansing that will make the country "pure." Obviously, for minorities who have been in the country for centuries, and for the children of immigrants, for whom the country has been the only one they have known, there is nothing to return to. The extremists do not care, and do not see that their legitimacy as citizens is no stronger than that of these minority citizens whom they want to push out—for, after all, everyone's ancestors came as an immigrant, ultimately from Africa.

Why the Populist Nationalist Dream Cannot Work

No one is happy with a second-class existence, so if the populist nationalists push, the minorities and immigrants will be forced into taking a stand, to push back. In this twenty-first century, where the civilized norm is that every citizen in a country has the right to determine their destiny and they have equal political rights, people will fight for the norm. The attempted tyranny of the majority in a country with a significant minority and immigrant population is a recipe for escalating conflict and increasing authoritarianism.

Some populist nationalists in countries with a substantial immigrant and minority population fear that their culture will be swamped. They want to preserve it by imposing it on everyone through national mandate. Hence, for example, the seemingly trivial debate in the United States on whether everyone should say "Merry Christmas!" while "Feliz Navidad!" or "Happy Holidays" are discouraged, and the related discussion about whether schools should be allowed to be bilingual. Yet such cultural imposition seems extremely shortsighted for countries where the identity of the majority group will almost surely change within the next few decades. Would the new majority also not use the same powers, fortified by precedent, to impose its culture? Is it not better to protect minorities and their culture better, by allowing

cultural diversity between communities under an overall national framework of common values, given that the day when the majority shifts to being
a minority is not so far away?

If the populist nationalist approach cannot work without creating an authoritarian apartheid regime, what can? If a country does need to attract immigrants over time and wants to give full opportunity to its minorities, how
does it balance this need against the concerns of those in the majority group
who fear their culture will be swamped?

Toward an Inclusive Civic Nationalism

One of the reasons populist nationalism appears to be spreading today is because alternative sources of social solidarity, such as the neighborhood or
community, seem to be tenuous, especially for those with lower incomes and
sliding status. For example, the World Values Survey indicates that in the
United States, only 57 percent of low-income respondents trusted people
from their neighborhood, while 85 percent of upper-middle-class respondents did so.[6] Similarly, when asked whether they saw themselves as part of
the community, there was a thirteen-percentage-point lower response for
low-income respondents than for those who saw themselves as upper-middle-
class. When asked whether they saw themselves as part of the nation, though,
responses were much closer together at 92 percent and 98 percent respectively. In general, upper-middle-class respondents seem more confident of
their membership and relationships in social structures than low-income respondents, but the sense of belonging to the nation is very strong at all income levels. This suggests that nationalism may persist when other social ties
fray, and may indeed substitute for them.

Instead of allowing the populist nationalist agenda to hijack the nation
entirely, it is better that their concerns be addressed at two levels. There are
certain attributes that an immigrant or minority cannot change, like their
race. There are also certain attributes that are so central to one's identity that
it would be extremely difficult for anyone to abandon, such as one's religion
and certain aspects of one's culture. At the national level, we therefore need a
concept of nationality that does not exclude anyone based on ethnicity or
religion but is based on shared values.

German philosopher Jurgen Habermas proposes that countries should aim for a constitutional patriotism, where the loyalty of the citizen is to the principles, ideals, and justice enshrined in the nation's constitution.[7] In addition, most nations have some founding narratives that give color and meaning to the values that formed the nation, and that stir the soul of citizens. These could offer a backdrop to the agreed covenant. For example, India's freedom struggle against British rule, led by Gandhi and Nehru, is the narrative that appeals to all Indians and gives meaning to the constitution and citizenship.[8] Countries such as Australia, Canada, France, India, and the United States, which embrace such civic nationalism, are inclusive in that anyone from anywhere can theoretically become a citizen, provided they satisfy residency requirements and sign up to the nation's values. They offer a nationalism that can hold a diverse country together and still inspire the great deeds that nations are capable of.

In addition, there are a lot of other ways in which an immigrant can and should integrate, including learning the local language and going along with important local customs and manners, sprinkled whenever beneficial with their own traditions. The intent at the national level should be integration, not submission.

So where does ethnicity and cultural continuity, which populist nationalists care about, get expressed? At the community level. If more powers are delegated from the state to the local community level (the "localism" in inclusive localism), a community can shape its own future better, and will have more control over it. Some communities will have a specific ethnic concentration, and community culture will gravitate toward that ethnic group's culture—the Pilsen community described in the Preface emphasizes its Mexican links and its Hispanic culture. A strong local community could satisfy people's need to live in a cohesive social structure with others of the same culture or religion. It would also slake their desire to preserve, celebrate, and pass on their heritage. The large number of communities where the majority group is concentrated will be ones where the populist nationalists can emphasize the ethnic aspects of nationalism that they care about. None of this implies exclusion—having monocultures that satisfy the tastes of those who want monocultures is as important as having multicultures.

This does raise the specter of a country dotted with segregated communities, each with its own race, national origin, and cultural traditions, and totally barred to outsiders. We must make sure that this is not the default outcome, not by forcing people to mix, but by emphasizing—if necessary, through laws—that in a nation, all communities are open to flows of people, goods, services, capital, and ideas, both in and out. Some communities will be thoroughly mixed, especially in the cosmopolitan cities, because of the myriad advantages of mixing. At the same time, many neighborhoods, even within cities, will be more representative of a certain religion or national origin, simply based on the choices of who moves in and out, without any overt discrimination.

As Canadian writer and politician Michael Ignatieff observes of the multiethnic neighborhood of Jackson Heights in Queens, New York, it is possible for communities to live side by side amicably, provided there is a fair institutional framework and policing structure that enables mutual trust and reciprocity.[9] Indeed, studies show that developed countries, which have a better ability to create such frameworks, can use diversity better to further growth.[10] Such communities thrive on their ethnic cohesion, but also see themselves as an integral part of the host nation. Streets will be closed for community celebrations, which will include both festivals from the host country and the favorites of the ethnic majority in the community. And over time, communities will mix, for familiarity first breeds comprehension then cohabitation.

Will the majority settle for communities while giving up the nation? In a sense, some diverse nations have already informally made the transition. Sanctuary cities in the United States, dominated by an immigrant electorate, refuse the diktats of the federal administration. Populist nationalism is then a rearguard action, attempting to reverse what has already largely changed. What is needed is a compromise, where communities have substantial autonomy, but respect national laws. That is what inclusive localism implies. In other countries, Populists nationalists still believe they can recapture the nation, and are applying discriminatory authoritarian polices to do so. How much of the country's soul will its citizens be willing to give up in order to maintain its ethnic purity? For some countries, unfortunately, the answer may be, "A lot!"

ENABLING THE DISADVANTAGED

Finally, what about affirmative action, a red rag to populist nationalist groups? Most large diverse countries have minority groups that have been discriminated against, are disadvantaged, and are underrepresented among the elite. Most such countries have scholarship and admission preferences in schools and colleges for these underprivileged minorities, as well as quotas for government jobs and preferences for government contracts. While not all these supports work well, in my previous job as the governor of the Reserve Bank in India, I had firsthand experience of the positive difference affirmative action could make.

Our lowest tier of employee was the *chaprasi*, or office peon, a position that essentially involves managing the flow of visitors to the office and carrying messages and files from the manager to other offices. This job requires only basic educational skills, but lots of diplomacy. Most of our peons had little education and came from underprivileged segments of Indian society (whence they qualified for affirmative action). The pay, benefits, and job security in public-sector jobs at the lower tiers typically exceed private-sector pay significantly, so getting a public-sector job is a form of affirmative action benefit. Our peons could send their children to decent schools and then to college. At periodic gatherings at my house, where I got to meet the families of office staff, the peons proudly introduced their children—here a bank manager, there a software engineer, everyone able to speak managerial English. The children had made it to comfortable middle class in a generation. It is hard to imagine this would have been possible without their father's public-sector job. When there is a hunger to take advantage of opportunity, affirmative action seems to work.

The problem, of course, is who should be allowed to take advantage of such preferences and for how long. From an economic perspective, it is not very helpful to see affirmative action as a righting of the historical wrongs suffered by an ethnic group. Instead, it is best seen as a way of righting current disabilities that hold groups back—and affirmative action should therefore also apply to subgroups within the majority group that are struggling economically and are socially unconnected to the elite. For instance, the bestselling book *Hillbilly Elegy* describes one set of groups among whites in the United States that should well qualify.[11] When the underprivileged group's path into higher positions in society is eased—for example with admission preferences into elite colleges—their successful members can demonstrate their capabilities and earn respect and acceptance for the group, they can serve as exemplars for young members within the group as well as mentor and aid them, and they can create networks that support group members. Easing the way for a few can create a pathway for many.

To succeed, affirmative action also requires affirmative support—the coaching and hand-holding that someone from an underprivileged section of society, thrown into the competitive elite world, needs, because they have not had the same privileges growing up as the others. Else, affirmative action risks reinforcing stereotypes. In a similar vein, while organizations should consider a broad variety of relevant skills and capabilities while deciding on promotions, eventually everyone ought to meet those standards for promotion. Else, the underprivileged who are promoted will always be under a cloud—did they get promoted because they met the standard or because they are underprivileged? Such uncertainty hurts them in the informal relationships that build in every organization, and thus in their ability to be chosen to lead exciting projects, get challenging clients, or attract good subordinates. If, however, an organization does not succeed over time in improving diversity at the top, it has to ask itself whether its systems and processes create blind spots that make it harder for it to nurture or recognize capabilities in others. Otherwise, it is all too easy for monocultures to maintain themselves by saying, "They just did not meet the bar."

In the interests of leveling the playing field, affirmative action for a minority group should eventually end. But when? Some early beneficiaries from affirmative action do well enough to put their children into good schools and colleges, as did our peons at the Reserve Bank. Should affirmative action end for their children (the peon's grandchildren)? The answer, India has decided, turns on whether the grandchildren continue to be disadvantaged or discriminated against, and whether their parent's higher incomes are sufficient to get them out of the trap of disadvantage. For groups that do not suffer social discrimination, affirmative action ends once parents have a middle-class income. For those who still continue to face social discrimination—in India the lowest castes and tribes are still discriminated against socially, including being treated as untouchables in some areas—affirmative action does not end even when the family attains decent incomes. How India will gauge when social discrimination has ended remains to be seen, but for now, this seems to be an acceptable answer in the world's most raucous democracy. It may well be worth examining by others.

CONCLUSION

It may seem naive to discuss the need for continuing immigration when countries seem unable to absorb existing flows and are dealing with fiery populist nationalist movements. All too often, though, the debate focuses too much on the here and now, and does not take a realistic view of the future, given where nations are headed. It is hard to imagine that the trend of increasing diversity in developed countries can be reversed without them losing their fundamental character as liberal democracies. Unlike ethnically homogenous countries like Japan that still have a choice of whether to become more diverse or not, civilized democratic countries with sizeable immigrant and minority populations really do not. For nations where the majority, because of differential birth rates, is slated to become a minority, populist nationalism is a tempting but mistaken diversion. Inclusive localism is a better, feasible alternative.

Many countries that are grappling with diversity already have much of the structure proposed in this chapter, including a citizenship framework that implies civic nationalism. Their task is to decentralize powers to the community, even while encouraging flows of trade and people between communities so that through contact, they eventually appreciate and welcome their differences. In the next chapter, we will examine how the state can help create bridges between communities. Nation building, under the umbrella of civic nationalism, is a task that never ends.

10

REBALANCING THE STATE
AND THE COMMUNITY

In the last chapter, I argued for bringing back the largely self-governing community as the locus of self-determination, identity, and cohesiveness, taking pressure off the nation to fulfill much of that role. Stronger communities will make it easier for diverse groups within countries to express their identities even while coexisting peacefully. Through localism, countries can also bypass the divisive policy gridlock that a number of them now experience at the federal level, as suggested by Bruce Katz and Jeremy Nowak in their book *The New Localism*.[1] Since some of that gridlock is because of identity politics, localism can even alleviate it.

An interesting historical study by Luigi Zingales and others highlights the long-term benefits of localism.[2] They find that Italian cities that achieved self-government in the Middle Ages have higher levels of social capital today—as measured by more nonprofit organizations per capita, the presence of an organ bank (indicating a willingness to donate) and fewer children caught cheating on national exams. They conclude that self-governance instilled a culture that allowed citizens to be confident in their ability to do what was needed and to reach goals. Decentralizing powers to communities may thus reduce apathy and force their members to assume responsibility for their destinies rather than blaming a distant elitist administration.

However, communities left on their own may resemble the isolated, vulnerable, unproductive, and sometimes oppressive manors of medieval times rather than the vibrant Northern Italian cities in the aforementioned study. We therefore need well-connected inclusive communities for the modern age, which is where the markets and the state come in. How might they work together?

National markets will provide competition to community producers as well as offer alternative possibilities for community consumers and workers that will keep the community from descending into cronyism and inefficiency. Any rules and regulations the community decides to impose will have to meet the market test: Does it create an undue burden on producers or consumers? If it does, the community will have to reconsider them or see its producers or consumers leave for a more hospitable community. Community members will tolerate small rents and inefficiencies that keep the community together, not large ones.

The state will make possible national markets by creating bridges between communities—literally, by building out the connecting physical and communications infrastructure, but also figuratively by keeping communities open to trade flows and people flows using national laws. In doing so, it will ease mobility for people, which will prevent any community from getting overly oppressive. The state can also create bridging vehicles such as national social or military service, secular national festivals, and national sports teams. It can encourage collective national efforts around hosting a major event like the Olympics or achieving a major environmental or developmental goal.

The state will monitor community governance lightly, investigating and prosecuting grand corruption, and ensuring civil rights are protected. Conversely, communities, aided by new communications technologies, will come together through the democratic process to influence the state and its policies. Finally, the state will provide some central support to communities, not just during periods of widespread economic distress when community resources are overwhelmed, but also to prevent any community from falling too far behind.

This last requires elaboration. The state still has the responsibility of holding the country together, which requires it to ensure that communities do not grow too far apart economically. Economic diversity creates differences in economic opportunity, and divisions in how communities see policy and one another. At the crudest level, if most students drop out of high school in one community, while they typically go on to university in another, the two communities will have very different views on federally funding public universities, on incentivizing entrepreneurship, and on welfare transfers. Of course, some level of economic diversity will always exist, but when it grows beyond a certain point, policy differences increase within the country, and it is harder to find compromise policies that satisfy most people. While decentralizing policy will help foster engaged policy action at the community level, nations cannot dispense with federal policy.

A critical federal problem in diverse countries is the unwillingness of well-off groups to support transfers to less-well-off and ethnically different groups.[3] Would such reluctance not get exacerbated when ethnically diverse communities are empowered? Perhaps! Yet, much of the reluctance to support transfers arises from the belief that they go to the "undeserving" poor to support a life of indolence. Transfers here would be aimed at community economic development, such as building public infrastructure, which would enhance the community's opportunities and help it contribute to everyone else's growth. Since policies would be nondiscriminatory, transfers would also go to poorer communities largely populated by the majority group. If carefully designed, with appropriate federal and community monitoring to ensure funds are spent well by the community, there could be broader support, especially if there are early positive results.

All this requires a balance of powers between the state and the local community government—not so much power with the state that the community has little sense of self-determination, and not so little that it cannot discipline obviously corrupt local governments, reduce the economic inequality in opportunity between communities, or create the common assets that drive a strong nation. We will consider the appropriate distribution of power between the state and community in three important spheres: the provision of public goods, the creation of capabilities, and the maintenance of a sound safety net. The key in each sphere will be to combine the resources and national reach of the state with the local information and engagement of the community, harnessing new technologies whenever possible.

LOCALIZING POWERS AND THE PROVISION OF PUBLIC SERVICES

Even though common national rules reduce community autonomy, some may be necessary to preserve the benefits of trade and freedom of movement.

PREVENTING ANTICOMPETITIVE BARRIERS BETWEEN COMMUNITIES

Different communities will have different views on business—for example, the kind of business they want operating in their communities. Some will want big-box retailers like Carrefour or Walmart, while others will prefer small local main-street grocers and shops, even if they cost more. Communities should have the power to determine the nature of local production (such as the production of retail services through big-box or small mom-and-pop stores), provided they do not directly impede domestic trade in goods and services.

Local business will attempt to influence decisions on which kind of businesses can locate in the community, and they will do so keeping in mind their profits. Yet there will be two checks on these influences being excessive. First, so long as local residents can travel outside the community to patronize businesses elsewhere, and so long as they can order goods and services from around the country, the extent of profit local businesses can make will be limited by locals' preference for convenience and timeliness. Second, the democratic decisions of the community will trade off the desire to help local businesses and preserve local ambience and jobs against the higher costs of goods and services. If the latter become excessive, the community can always allow more competition. So long, therefore, as there is no explicit barrier such as a tariff wall set around the community, the community should be allowed to determine business zoning decisions.

In addition to zoning, there are a variety of regulations local community government can impose if allowed. These can be extremely protectionist and impede the inward flow of goods and services from elsewhere. The general principle (in the spirit of the Commerce Clause in the United States Constitution) should be that the community has substantial say over the regulations governing the production of goods and services in it (within the scope allowed by national law, of course), but it cannot impede national trade by imposing tariffs or nontariff barriers. Therefore, for instance, the community may require a minimum wage to be paid by local businesses (a regulation on production), even if there is none at the national level, but should not be able to mandate that only gluten-free or organic products be sold locally (a nontariff barrier to trade). Put differently, communities can use their democratic influence over national regulation if they want to prohibit some products or mandate minimum standards on others, but no community should be able to impose restrictions on its own—else the national market will be fragmented to everyone's detriment. That said, in a Jewish neighborhood, shops may simply not order nonkosher food, but that will be by choice, not because of a trade barrier.

Discouraging Sorting of Residence and Communities by Income

Let us turn from production to residence, specifically the issue of residential sorting, which we encountered earlier. While nations have the right to control the inward flow of people, communities should not have that right, else that risks perpetuating inequality and segregation within the country. Yet many well-off communities, while ostensibly open, set zoning rules in a way that effectively discriminates against less-well-off people. For example, some communities forbid the construction of apartment buildings, rental occupancies, or single-family homes smaller than a certain size, thus keeping out anyone who cannot afford high housing costs. Effectively, they keep out lower-income folk through a nontariff barrier.

Economic segregation ensures those with lower incomes do not benefit from the institutional, social, and intellectual capital that the more well-to-do create for themselves—such as better schools. The individual's desire to sort is understandable, but it will exacerbate inequality of opportunity, and increase potential social conflict. Indeed, the more that zoning creates moats and battlements that protect the upper classes, the less incentive they have to worry about what happens to the rest. A state intent on creating more equal-opportunity communities should offset some of these incentives to sort, by ensuring the poor can follow the rich anywhere.

One way to get more economically diverse communities is to eliminate some of the most egregious constraints on what can be built, especially when local house prices are high. A bill introduced by a California state senator, for example, would allow all housing being built in California within a half-mile of a train station or a quarter-mile of a bus route to be exempt from regulations regarding the height of the building, the number of apartments, the provision of parking spaces, or specific design standards.[4] This is a bill that local property owners hate because it will create more housing supply and depress the value of their homes, but it will be tremendously beneficial for economic inclusion.

Every such solution has some downsides since they interfere with community choice but, I repeat, in the trade-off between inclusion and localism, inclusion should be given more weight. Consider some other possibilities. The state could mandate that some fraction of the residences in any community, say 15 percent, should be affordable for low-income residents. If the community would like to maintain its aesthetic look and allow only large single-family residences, then a sufficient number of these should be rented or sold to low-income families, with the rest of the community bearing the cost of making these affordable. Such a solution works most easily for new developments, where "set-asides" can be mandated for low-income housing. The city of Chicago negotiates set-asides for new developments, but certain states in the United States prohibit set-asides, perhaps because developers do not want to be burdened with the cost. Moreover, set-asides will be harder to mandate for established older communities, where there may be little vacant land for development.

Another way of encouraging mixing, or at least discouraging sorting, is through the tax code. For instance, high-income households whose children are enrolled in public schools in low-income districts could be given a tax rebate, essentially because of the positive spillovers that their children are likely to contribute to their classes. Private incentives could also help. For example, top universities could give incentives to students studying in public schools in low-income districts by allocating a fraction of admits to each public school in the state. Not only will this incentivize the less-well-off to apply to the elite universities, it may also be the carrot for some well-to-do parents to stay or even move into those school districts so that their children will have a leg up in admissions. While this may seem like a violation of the spirit of the plan, the presence of these well-prepared children and their pushy highly educated parents in the schools will be beneficial to all. In this vein, some states in the United States are already allocating some places in the state university to the top students in each public school.

Much of the incentive to sort comes because students coming from different households are at very different levels of educational and social preparation. Attempts to mix students with very different preparation—for example through state-mandated busing from poor communities into well-off communities—obviously leads to resentment and dissatisfaction on all sides. The students who are bused in feel inadequately prepared and fall behind, while the students in the receiving schools feel they are being held behind. The problem is the differential preparedness, which needs to be addressed before mixed classes can work. Early childhood programs that attempt to equalize preparation could be enormously beneficial, especially if they are then followed by mixed classes in public schools which ensure differences in educational capabilities do not build. Accelerated remedial education programs could also help, though the later they are in a child's life the less effective they will be. New technologies that can allow teachers to address students with different levels of preparedness (see later) can also help the process of equalization.

Countries that have a severe sorting problem could build in stronger tax incentives to mix, including residential congestion taxes that require rich households to pay higher taxes if they stay in communities with other rich households, and lower taxes if they stay in low-income communities. There are plenty of ideas, some more problematic than others, but we have to be open to experimentation if we want to avert the hereditary meritocracy emerging in many countries.

Ensuring that Communities Are Connected

It is essential that communities are connected to centers of economic activity so that they are economically viable. Connectivity includes fast physical

connections like roads, railways, and airports, but also cheap power, as well
as fast connections to the data highway.

With connectivity, a whole variety of economic activities becomes possible. For instance, with broadband connectivity, and with the support of logistics firms to transport goods quickly, small handicraft makers in remote
rural areas can advertise their wares on e-commerce platforms, thus reaching a global market. Retired schoolteachers can remain engaged by tutoring
children in the community without leaving home, music teachers can have
pupils around the world, while angel investors from elsewhere can mentor
local entrepreneurs. The death of distance makes so much more possible in
remote communities. Connection to the national market also ensures communities are connected with one another.

Not all developed countries are equally well connected. According to a
Pew survey, in 2018, over 89 percent of US adults use the internet, including
66 percent of those over 65.[5] Only 65 percent of households, though, have access to broadband—accounting for 73 percent of households using the internet. Not surprisingly, minorities, the elderly, and rural communities are less
well connected. For instance, only 58 percent of rural communities have access to broadband, while 70 percent of the typically richer suburban communities do. In contrast, in the European Union, 97 percent of households with
internet access had a broadband connection in 2016.[6] Europe's population is
more densely packed than that of the United States, which makes it easier to
service, but communities without broadband connection are severely handi-
capped in the information age, and providing for this is an essential role of
the state.

The US Federal Communications Commission has been subsidizing the
private sector to provide universal broadband service. Unwilling to wait, a
number of municipalities have decided to wire their own communities.[7]
Fearing a loss of business, cable and telephone companies have persuaded
state legislatures to ban or restrict municipal broadband. The United States
needs to do better in providing all its citizens fast access to the information
highway, for many of the solutions to community revival lie there. Indeed,
allowing communities, rather than large private companies with distant
headquarters, to take responsibility for some of the local connectivity infrastructure may solve two problems—it prevents the community from being at

the mercy of a monopoly private provider, and it draws some economic activity and responsibility into the community. Similar approaches could be tried for other infrastructure. For instance, as decentralized solar or wind power becomes cheaper, more remote communities could manage it, relying on the grid only for balancing power.

Improving Community Control over Local Government

The information highway can make it easier for people to engage with their government. This allows both for the decentralization of power to the community and the devolution of tax revenues to it. Historically, a concern about such devolution has been the lower capabilities of local government officials (after all, the federal government has its pick from the entire nation), as well as their greater susceptibility to local influence and corruption. Even if local officials are less capable intrinsically, they are more aware of local conditions and have greater flexibility to tailor policies to them since they are not crafting policy for the whole nation. In addition, they can turn to local people for advice and the locals can monitor their performance.

Two other ingredients can be very helpful in successful decentralization. The community should have full information about the sources and uses of the funds flowing through local officials so that it can assess whether the funds are spent fully and well on public services rather than on the officials themselves. To be able to act on its monitoring, it should have full democratic control over its officials, with the ability to terminate them for cause. The federal or state government's ability to post and access information online, as well as the local community's ability to draw its members into monitoring and posting on their experience with local government, makes effective decentralization more feasible today than in the past.

For instance, an app called SeeClickFix allows community residents to report potholes, broken streetlights, abandoned vehicles, building violations and other civic complaints, using their GPS location to pinpoint where the problem is.[8] The community webpage then displays the complaint for all to see, and reports when the local government actually fixes it. Citizens who lodge the most genuine problems can be acknowledged on the app, and even awarded prizes by the community. Apps like this allow local government to get to know of problems more quickly, involve the community, and make the performance of the local government more transparent to all. Even as I write, three open complaints have been closed in the City of Chicago SeeClickFix website. City officials could not find a car that was reported abandoned (perhaps not surprising because the officials arrived a month after the report was filed) and two instances of graffiti were removed (within a couple of days of the reports).

Local government misbehavior and corruption can also be more easily identified through community action, though it is important that citizen monitoring does not turn into vigilantism. For example, the body cameras on police officers help assess their behavior in difficult situations, protecting good officers who take reasonable actions while outing officers who do not. The ubiquitous cell-phone camera is also a way for people to record and report official misbehavior, with actions from intemperate words to rank brutality recorded for posterity, and broadcast widely on the internet. This helps redress the balance of power between the people and their public officials.

In India, the I Paid A Bribe website encourages people to report situations where they had to pay a bribe, situations where they refused to pay a bribe, as well as recognize honest officers who did not ask for bribes (in some government offices, meeting someone who does not ask for a bribe is surprising enough to be commented upon).[9] The website started by community activist Swati Ramanathan also produces reports on areas and communities that are most prone to corruption, and has a network of retired senior government officials who help publicize and rectify the problems the website has uncovered from its analysis of citizen reports.

The broader point is that the ICT revolution allows for more effective decentralization of state functions because the community can become more informed and engaged with local governance. Federal agencies should also monitor the use of funds, and have the ability to intervene when they detect gross malfeasance. This should be done with a light touch so that it does not effectively recentralize policy. Preemption laws, of the kind that states currently use to prevent specific communities from undertaking activities they disfavor, should be used lightly and primarily to enforce inclusion.[10] Effective decentralization is critical for empowering communities within the broader framework of civic nationalism.

IMPROVING THE BUILDING OF WORKER CAPABILITIES

The ICT revolution has altered the capabilities people need. Equally important, it also allows for different ways to meet these needs. We need to embrace technology as we prepare our students to face the challenges posed by technological change. In this section I will refrain from entering old and unresolved debates on how education needs to be reformed—debates such as school funding, teacher evaluations and salaries, teacher tenure, teacher unions, charter schools, and so on. I will also take the student body as given.

Instead, I will focus on how the relationship between the community and the state can be altered to improve capability building. The ICT revolution does not require everyone to get PhDs but it does require everyone to have a solid basic education, which prepares them for lifelong learning. New technologies allow a different mode of teaching, which permits teachers to tailor learning individually to each student. This will make it easier for teachers to teach classes with students from varied backgrounds and preparation, to ensure each student learns what is required and gets the basic education. These technologies can help reduce the incentive for residential sorting. They also allow federal, state, and district authorities to monitor class performance remotely, and thus feel more confident that funds are used well. Consequently, responsibility for course content can be delegated to the teachers in well-performing schools, thus allowing parents to engage with teachers once more. This will make the school a stronger focal point for community engagement. The state can also play a supportive role in improving both the certification process and the availability of information about educational and career opportunities. It can also make it easier for students to finance their learning.

Start with the Basics

It is easy to get overwhelmed by the prospects of technological change. Many jobs will indeed be automated, but which ones will they be? Experts believe there will continue to be a role for human empathy, flexibility, and creativity and that human combined with machine will probably beat human or machine alone.[11] The average human therefore requires the skills to be able to complement the machine. Computers can read out loud, take dictation, spellcheck, and do any mathematical calculation we ask them to perform, but we are still needed for them to communicate, stringing words into sentences, sentences into paragraphs, and paragraphs into an informative or persuasive message. Similarly, humans are needed to break down a problem into specific steps that our computers can perform. All this requires the human to have basic skills such as reading, writing, and arithmetic. Yet, even in developed countries, basic skills are not taught well to all students in schools today, so too many have no capacity to complement machines.

The ICT revolution does require some to learn far more so that they have the additional skills to come up with breakthrough new ideas, processes, and programs that the rest of us will use. There will be a premium to higher education. All too often, though, we are looking for higher education for everyone—a recipe for failure. Instead, in this environment, schools should prepare students with a solid understanding of the basics so that they have the flexibility to move between industries and jobs as the machines and environment change.

Teach Differently

In the traditional model of teaching, the teacher holds forth in the classroom, and students listen with varying degrees of attention. Since not all are at the same level, teachers are in a quandary. Should they teach to the smartest kid, the laggards, or the child in the middle? Any of these choices loses some kids, either to boredom or incomprehension, and reduces the learning experience for all. As we have seen, this is one reason we see residential sorting.

New tools like digital learning platforms—essentially a package of recorded lectures, reading materials, videos, question banks and assignments, and assessment programs to measure and keep track of student progress, all available online—allow the teacher to flip the classroom and homework in order to enhance learning across all students. The key resource in class is the teacher, and the key constraint is student time and attention. Rather than sitting passively in class, listening to the teacher lecture, the student could do that at home, perhaps even listening to nationwide star teachers assigned by the curriculum. By preparing for class at home (or in study hours at school if the students' home environment is too disturbing), students can replay digital content as many times as they need to absorb difficult sections—new face-tracking technologies can also indicate to the teacher whether videos have been watched. Each student can learn at their own pace. The platform can assess their understanding regularly, and offer supplementary material either to challenge them or to remedy deficiencies. Individualized adaptive teaching is thus easy with well-designed platforms, sparing the teacher the quandary of whom to teach to.

Class time is freed for the teacher to motivate students with interesting projects, help students as they go over assignment problems individually or in groups, and go over any issues the students find particularly difficult. Students will learn in class from one another and the teacher, and in the process fill in the gaps in their understanding. Since the teacher works closely with the students, she gets to know who is falling behind, if she does not already from automated assessments.

The teacher's role changes from lecturer to coach and designer, who combines the triad of human, machine, and process to create a better experience for her students. For the less-than-capable teacher, the school system could offer ready-made lesson plans and the associated resources such as lectures by star teachers so that course design is easy—communities could easily share what works with one another. As the teacher gains confidence, experience, and knowledge, she may become a star teacher in her own right. In contrast, the already capable teacher can pick and choose from the system, uploading her own lectures and problems when she thinks they offer more immediate and relatable content for the students, and using the system's content when adequate. Parental engagement is also much more feasible as the teacher takes up design.

JUDICIOUS DECENTRALIZATION

It is easy now to see how the state or district board would decentralize to the schools and the teachers. The central authorities could, together with the various communities, set out broad minimum objectives of education at each level and for each subject, leaving the specifics of how those objectives will be achieved to the schools themselves. It could also offer schools and teachers pedagogic tools that they could use, including the learning platform. Teachers and schools would pick and choose their curricula, based on the confidence they have in their own ability to make judicious choices. For those who don't believe they have the ability, the central authorities would provide a default curriculum. Decentralization allows teachers and schools to figure out the approach that works best for their students and community, while engaging parents in the process. Finally, schools can feed regular automated assessments of student performance to administrators to assure them that their funding is being used well.

None of this is "techno hype." Versions of this kind of learning model are used in very poor school districts across the world, including by Pratham, an organization working with slum children in India. An important virtue is the model is largely scalable (except for local customization), so most of the costs can be incurred centrally.

The promise of new technologies should not obscure other very real problems that hold back schooling systems everywhere such as student preparedness and motivation. As discussed earlier in the book, nurture during early childhood plays a very important part in a child's subsequent health and development. Many countries do little to support the child at this stage of its development, expecting families to do so. Many poor or broken families are unable to provide the young child the environment it needs. Once again, the community is in a better position to identify needy young children, and provide them the necessary support at that early stage, so that far costlier and less-effective remedial interventions are unnecessary later. In these and other aspects of education, such as student motivation and discipline, student delinquency, and student safety, community effort is critical.

Informing Employers and Students

As students develop solid foundations in the basics, and as platforms develop reliable student assessments, the excess search for credentials we discussed earlier will wane. If employers know that the high school graduate indeed knows what a high school graduate is supposed to know, and this is verified by a reliable certificate, they have no need to ask for extra credentials. The state could play an important role by ensuring uniformity in assessments by learning platforms.

Some students will want to go on to higher studies. In many poor communities, students have no one to turn to for advice on what they should learn, and where and how they should apply. Too many students end up in the wrong courses and with too much debt. Coalitions between local governments, unions, nongovernmental organizations, and corporations can help fund college and career counseling. Technology can also reduce costs—employment-oriented platforms can deal with routine counseling cases, while professional career counselors can handle the difficult ones. The state can also help students and their counselors choose by mandating that educational institutions post data on graduation and placement rates so as to weed out low-quality credential shops.

Paying for Learning

How much of skill acquisition and education ought to be state-subsidized? It is tempting to argue that free public education should be available to all until the highest degrees, as it is in France or in India. The United States has limited free public education through high school, though a number of US states are pushing to make community college free. It seems reasonable to set the bar for free education at a level at which most of the population can take advantage of it—in the United States, that may well be the community college today. Setting the bar higher could exacerbate credential inflation, overcrowding colleges even while diverting students into pathways that do not contribute to learning or jobs.

Any student or worker who wants to learn more should be able to map their specific needs, equipped with both information and counseling. A mix of grants and loans should be available to fund this. Innovative student loan plans across the world now tie repayment to a modest fraction of the student's subsequent earnings as verified by the tax authorities (thus charging high earners more and low earners less). They allow loan forgiveness after a number of years, especially if the recipient takes lower-paying community or public-sector jobs. Some allow borrowers who are servicing their loans to borrow more for additional training over their lifetimes. Some companies allow employees to build up credits toward a paid sabbatical or for outside courses. So do some governments; as part of its Skills Future program, Singapore gives every citizen above the age of twenty-five an annual S$500 credit that can be used to pay for training courses provided by any of list of approved providers. The intent is to get citizens into the habit of lifelong learning.

We need to be creative about such programs, making it easier for all to learn when warranted by the job market or intrinsically desired by the individual for personal interest or development, but not cross the line into forcing everyone to continue reenlisting in unnecessary higher education. We should not overvalue the credentials produced by education, and should not prioritize work with the mind over work with the hands or with people. After all, who knows where technological progress will take us?

DRAWING THE COMMUNITY INTO THE SAFETY NET

Let us turn finally to the safety net. In order to function without constant fear of destitution, there should be a basic level of unconditional federal economic support for those faced with unemployment or old age. It should be enough to manage a "Spartan" living as suggested by the Beveridge Report (discussed in Chapter 4). Over and above this basic level, individuals should pay for social insurance programs (such as social security in the United States) or private insurance (such as employer-supported pension plans).

Health care should be universal and funded by tax revenues (even if privately provided) on the grounds that no civilized democratic society should allow its members to be unable to participate fully in life simply because they cannot afford care. Democracy means each person counts, and they cannot count if they are debilitated by illness. Of course, income-linked co-payments should be asked of all so as to prevent overuse and there should be limits on reimbursements for costly experimental therapies. Nevertheless, nearly everyone will get all the care they need to be functioning members of society.

Before we end this chapter, we need to discuss three issues. First, to what extent should some of the support beyond the Beveridge level of care, for those who have not saved money or paid for insurance, be decided and administered by the community? Second, should we prepare for increasing technological unemployment with schemes like a universal basic income? Third, how do we pay for the entitlements that have already been committed to, as well as the outstanding government debt, even before we embark on creating new entitlements?

COMMUNITY-DETERMINED ADDITIONAL SUPPORT

The basic level of economic support in case of unemployment, disability, or old age should have no conditions attached. Neither should social or private insurance that has been paid for through past premiums. Some people will not have anything more than that basic level of support. The country may want to add a little more, especially if the basic level of support is far below community standards of living.

Could the community not be more closely engaged in determining the conditions under which the additional support will be given? For instance, the able-bodied unemployed could work on community-identified projects that will ease their way back into employment. The able indigent elderly could help staff community libraries or conduct local tours, for instance. As nations age, the elderly will need more care. All too often, love and affection from the caregiver are as important as the actual care, especially as many more of the childless grow old and outlive their partners. Perhaps the community could play a role here—could the elderly who are only moderately incapacitated be allowed to nominate a caregiver, who will be paid a modest sum by the community authorities, to tend to the elderly person's few needs, but also more generally to visit periodically and keep an eye on them? The sum need not be so large that professional caregivers are put out of work or that the elderly are swamped with unwanted attention as everyone cozies up to them begging to be chosen. It should also not be so small that it is a mere token and does not help the community rally. Money cannot, and should not, buy love, but it can help reward those who keep up the spirit of the community and spread love around. Many of these may be the formerly unemployed and unemployable in the community.

For single or poor parents with children, community support may not involve any conditions other than the presumption that it is spent in the interests of the family. Indeed, once locals know who the overburdened families are, they may pitch in to help with child care.

Some might see the conditions the community imposes for additional support as demeaning, intrusive, and paternalistic. There is certainly the possibility of abuse. Yet it is helpless dependence that is most demeaning for individuals. Aid administered by a faceless central bureaucracy is both anonymous and distant, which community support will not be. Some recipients might prefer anonymity, but it also leads to apathy. Community awareness can result in well-meaning community engagement, as in Elberfeld described in Chapter 4, and attempts to eliminate the conditions that brought about the need for aid. Federal regulations governing community-imposed conditionality coupled with the possibility of appeal to courts could provide some safeguards against excessively paternalistic or intrusive conditions. Properly structured, though, the design of such additional support could draw the community together, even while ensuring the recipient remains a contributing member to the community.

An Agenda for Support

Today, in the richest large country in the world, the United States, there is no explicit basic level of public support at the federal level, except for temporary assistance for families with children and assistance for the disabled. For everyone else who falls on hard times, there are a variety of programs—such as soup kitchens and homeless shelters—which are strung together with the help of the state government, the local government, private efforts, and charitable funds. These provide an informal and inadequate alternative to basic public support. Of course, people very rarely die from hunger or cold, and even then more because they are unwilling to seek out help or are incapable of doing so, rather than because help is not forthcoming. Nevertheless, too many go hungry and shelter is often insecure.

It would not be much costlier to replace informal support with formal Beveridge-level support since it would indeed be at a basic level. For the same reason, such support would not raise significant public concerns about "undeserving" others getting help. Nevertheless, it would constitute a reliable safety net, a necessity for a civilized society in the possibly volatile days ahead, especially if it has not fostered basic capabilities in all. No rich country should create uncertainty among its people about whether they will have enough to live.

If there were political appetite for more support, it could be delivered through the community to those who have resided in the community for a while (and to preserve mobility, the community would bear responsibility for a while for those who move out, with any conditionality porting to the beneficiary's new location). Community support should be relatively equal across proximate communities—else beneficiaries could swamp communities where the benefits and conditions are most favorable. Communities should bear a share of the cost of benefits so that they have skin in the game, with the share increasing in average community incomes. Who would pay the rest? Ideally it would be regional or state governments, who are close to the communities and can monitor performance. In countries where regional or state governments tend to discriminate against certain communities, the federal government would have to monitor flows or take over.

Finally, could community benefits be a fount of local corruption? Could local government abuse the system, picking their favorites for benefits, and denying them to those they do not like? Yes, but these are problems with any government plan. The more discretion local government has, the more programs can be tailored to local conditions, but also the more abuse is possible. Some rules will be necessary to limit abuse, but importantly, the community needs to be engaged and informed. The people in a number of countries are apathetic about local government today. As local government gains more power and funding, though, community members will increase their engagement and oversight. Not only do locals have the awareness that stems from proximity, they have an incentive to be involved because some of their own tax payments are at stake. As we have discussed, the ICT revolution also allows for a greater flow of information to the state, which can offer a second line of defense against corruption.

A MORE COMPREHENSIVE GOVERNMENT SUPPORT PLAN?

Some want to go much further in providing support. One proposal has been gaining currency as societies anticipate massive joblessness from technological change. It is to give every adult in the country a universal basic income (UBI), which will be enough to live a decent life, with no questions asked. The difference from the basic support we discussed above is that UBI would be set at much higher levels, and paid to everyone regardless of need. There is an ongoing debate about whether those who fear technological unemployment are too pessimistic, underestimating the ability of markets and human ingenuity to find productive uses for unemployed humans. History suggests the optimists have been right thus far, but this time could be different.

UBI, in principle, is extremely simple. Each adult would get a monthly check for themselves and their dependents. If, let us say, it takes $20,000 net of taxes for a single person to live a modest but not difficult life in the United States, then a total of about $6.5 trillion will have to be distributed to the US population of about 328 million persons. Assuming (very crudely) that the 140 million taxpayers bear the burden of paying for the transfers they get (which are therefore a wash), as well as the amount transferred to the rest of the 188 million who do not pay taxes. In that case, taxes for the payers, net of UBI transfers, will have to go up by $3.76 trillion. This is approximately the size of all US federal revenues today. Even if UBI substitutes for other transfers like food stamps, disability, and unemployment payments, it will not reduce interest payments, defense expenditures, health care, and social security spending, the biggest elements of expenditure today. More modest proposals (I have assumed the same transfers per child as per adult, and some may argue $20,000 per person is too much) will require lower tax revenues, but in general any worthwhile UBI will require a significant rise in tax rates. Indeed, if it does not provide a reasonable living, it is easy to imagine journalists interviewing people living in squalor despite the intent of UBI, and fueling agitations for an increased UBI.

There are other problems than just the political acceptability of a significant rise in taxes. UBI is an all-or-nothing scheme, and as such, suffers from the traditional difficulties associated with such a scheme. UBI essentially assumes that most people will not have a job, and there will be no point in them searching for one or attempting to retrain themselves since no new jobs will be possible. It is a counsel of despair not just for job seekers but also for job creators, because after UBI is implemented, any new job will have to be more attractive in pay and responsibilities than paid leisure, a difficult hurdle for any job to cross. Put differently, in the years to come it is quite likely that trucks become self-driving. If we do introduce UBI at that time, will we not prevent truck drivers from retraining as medical diagnostic practitioners (those who interview patients to elicit symptoms) or tax preparation assistants? These jobs do not pay enormous amounts, but they need to be done by humans, supported by computer algorithms. However, if the pay required to draw a person on UBI back into the labor force is high (yes, the income from the new job will be supplementary, but it will be taxed, and the erstwhile truck driver may already be fairly comfortable at home), then these new jobs will not be created, and the associated services will not be produced. Society will be poorer for it.

Alternatively, we could wait till we reach a point where it is clear that no new jobs will be created. It will be impossible to be certain, for future new technologies may require ordinary human involvement again, so it will be tempting to wait a really long time, until it is a near certainty that there are really no jobs for ordinary labor. If we wait, though, what happens to the truck drivers who really cannot adapt?

The proposal of community-based assistance, with attached conditions, could serve as an alternative, flexible way of achieving some of the aims of UBI. For those with poorly paying jobs or no job and large responsibilities, the community could offer a monetary top-up to basic income in exchange for the beneficiary performing some community services. This would not discourage the recipient from taking a better-paying job if one materialized. The community would be in a much better place than the federal government to identify local work opportunities, and could also nudge beneficiaries into private-sector jobs as they materialize. In a generalized deep downturn, or if there is actually widespread technological employment, the community would be overwhelmed. In such situations, the state would have to step up with innovative solutions, but for a range of lesser eventualities, community-based assistance should be effective.

How Will We Pay?

Ever since the 1970s, government debt in developed countries has been rising. With the population aging, the government's pension and health-care obligations have also been rising. In the United States, the Congressional Budget Office projects that government debt will hit 100 percent of GDP by 2028, from around 80 percent today. The trust funds for Medicare run out in 2029, and for Social Security in 2035, meaning that after those dates, spending under those heads will have to be financed entirely from the premiums paid each year as well as budgetary resources. Since the number of workers relative to retirees will continue falling with population aging, we should expect future workers will not just pay premiums for their own retirement benefits, but also make up the shortfalls in our retirement benefits. And the United States is far from the most indebted country among developed countries.

Think, then, about some of the legacies we leave our children. Debt—that we have built up by spending more than our means, even in normal times, on grounds that growth is too slow for our taste. No saved funds to pay for our retirement and certainly none to help them with theirs. Political paralysis. Climate change, which we have done precious little to reverse. Automation, which by causing great fear of the future, has unleashed the beast in many of us . . .

We can hope that the positive aspects of technological progress will enable us to offset these legacies; it will enhance productivity growth and overall growth without eliminating jobs on net; allow us to pay down debt and support entitlements; and give us new tools to fight poverty, disease, and reverse climate change. We cannot, however, place all our eggs in the technological basket.

For a start, we cannot continue to run up debt, hoping the future will take care of it. We have to be more careful about spending borrowed money to boost growth, especially if growth is tepid for reasons other than weak demand. We also have to look closely at all the unfunded promises we have made to ourselves, and reset them in such a way that they do not exceed what is fair to ask future generations to pay, given the world we will leave them.

The sooner we act to renegotiate promises—for instance, extending retirement ages, increasing social security insurance premium payments, and reducing cost-of-living adjustments—the more cohorts can share the cost of giving up some benefits. The longer we delay because politicians fear the political cost of touching the "third rail" of entitlements, the more the burdens will be felt by our children's generation, and the more likely that instead of a smooth renegotiation, they will simply default on supporting us.

The changes proposed in this chapter and the previous one are intended to help our system stay intact, to allow for trade, innovation, and reasonable levels of immigration through an inclusive national framework, even while skilling the workforce and creating a better safety net. They focus on preserving widespread access—to markets, to jobs, to capabilities, and to the safety net—while decentralizing power to the community so that people feel empowered. For these reasons, an apt description of the agenda is inclusive localism. Some of these proposals will save money, others will require spending. Undoubtedly, we will have to choose carefully, given overall scarce resources. We must remember, though, that worse than unfunded liabilities is to hand our children a broken system.

CONCLUSION

In this chapter, I have argued for a devolvement in powers from federal government through the regional government to the community. This will be an important step in rebalancing. Much as many small- and medium-sized companies help to distribute economic power and keep the unholy coalition of behemoth and leviathan from forming, the empowerment of many small communities helps distribute political power and creates another independent check on the unholy coalition. Vibrant communities also help build a sense of identity and purpose in a world where global markets and distant government are sucking out the air from social relationships. They also help diffuse the allure of divisive majoritarian national identities, which tend to also increase frictions between nations. Unfortunately, many communities are dysfunctional across the world, primarily because their old economic basis has disappeared. In the next chapter, we will examine how dysfunctional communities can be repaired.

11

REINVIGORATING THE
THIRD PILLAR

I n the last chapter, we discussed the importance of inclusive localism—of an inclusive nation that decentralizes many decisions to the local, physically proximate community. However, most people identify with a variety of communities and belong to a number of virtual communities. Why do we care about the local, physically proximate community?

The benefits of a vigorous physically proximate community include less divisiveness in nations with diverse populations when ethnic identities are expressed in communities rather than at the national level; greater social engagement in community institutions; a greater sense of self-determination for ordinary citizens, as power is decentralized back to the community; stronger local bonds that allow neighbors to fill in the gaps in formal structures of support; more room for political and economic experimentation, as well as political influence; and a structure to create meaningful local work that is not remunerated by the market. Let me elaborate on some of these.

The community can be a particularly useful way to preserve specific identities or affiliations in a country with a diverse population. While many communities will be thoroughly mixed, with people of all hues and affiliations living together, some people may choose to live with others they identify with, so as to preserve a particular religious or cultural identity. The hopeful future of many a diverse nation may lie in a variety of communities, both mixed as well as concentrated ethnic ones, all living peaceably side by side, governed by the common law of the land, and coming together in the national market, in national endeavors, as well as national celebrations. It certainly offers a less oppressive and divisive alternative than one where a dominant monoculture, fearful of being swamped, imposes itself on all other cultures, generating permanent divisiveness and conflict.

When members are in close physical proximity and work together for the community, they build a stronger community. As people run into one another, as they have to work with one another for local projects, social capital—as embodied in mutual understanding, empathy, and reservoirs of goodwill—accumulates. Social capital can be useful in building community institutions, overcoming ethnic divisions, as well as in filling in the holes left by more formal structures such as market contracts or social safety nets. Friendship will be what holds the communities of the future together when the older bonds of economic necessity weaken.

Communities also allow a multiplicity of venues to experiment with economic and political governance within a country—a thousand different solutions can be attempted to a problem. Experimentation allows for learning. Not only will some solutions turn out to be more effective than others, different communities will choose different mixes of solutions given their greater knowledge of their specific problems. So long as there is a single market for goods and services, the country obtains the benefits of a common market but also gets some resilience from the variety of chosen strategies—one common economic strategy does not dominate the country, leaving the country vulnerable to its weaknesses.

The community offers a venue to debate political positions, and when there is sufficient consensus, it provides the numbers to have political influence. Thus the community constitutes a ready-made mechanism for democratic political engagement. In many countries, local politics also becomes a learning ground and a stepping stone to national politics.

Finally, the jobs of the future, as goods production and certain services are automated, will have a much greater social, perhaps even nonmarket, component. In the really long run, any profitable production of goods or services may well be done by machines, with humans needed only to innovate and to fill some gaps. Many people will live on incomes generated by government redistribution. Rather than many becoming employees of a national government, which could lead to the potential for authoritarian governance, far better that governmental powers and revenues be distributed to local governments in communities. Not only will these be a check on national government, they can also identify nonmarket local jobs that will allow those being paid by the local government to retain a sense of self-worth.

What about the downsides of community? Every community generates competition for social prestige. Such competition is not always bad—it can incentivize activities such as neighborliness that are not rewarded by the market. Nevertheless, it can also incentivize wasteful one-upmanship—a recent study suggests that bankruptcy filings for neighbors go up if a household wins a lottery, presumably as the neighbors try to keep up with the Joneses.[1] Also, a community breeds jealousies, and even hatreds. It fosters conservatism. While we cannot presume that the good outweighs the bad in every community, members of a modern community have the option of leaving it if it turns out to be too oppressive. In general, communities will have to offer enough benefits to everyone so that they want to stay. That limits how bad communities can get.

In this chapter, we will start by examining why virtual communities, professional associations, religious associations, and other such structures will allow for some of these functions of the physically proximate community but not all. We need vibrant physically proximate communities, and central to their existence is the presence of viable economic activity—nothing erodes a person's self-worth faster than a sense that they have nothing productive to contribute. Despair, combined with alcohol, drugs, or violence, can erode the social fabric significantly. Even those who continue to hope may leave rather than succumb to the melancholy that surrounds them. In much of the rest of this chapter, we will discuss how weak communities in developed countries can recover from economic adversity. In many ways, their challenges resemble the developmental challenges that poor countries face, though there are important differences.

VARIETIES OF COMMUNITIES

I have focused on the physically proximate community through much of the book. We have more sources of identity than just the neighborhood we live in, and thus more communities we belong to. I am a resident of Hyde Park, a neighborhood in Cook County in Chicago, a city in the United States. I have other affiliations also. I am a citizen of India and a professor at the University of Chicago. I am a Tamilian Hindu; I speak English, Hindi, French, and Tamil with varying degrees of fluency; and I am a member of various organizations, both professional ones like the American Finance Association and those with a policy focus like the Group of Thirty. I am a member of various chat groups, including family and college alumni groups. Not only do we have identities that come to the forefront at different times, these identities can imply varying degrees of engagement and support.

Nevertheless, few groups that we identify with engage and support us in the many ways that the ideal proximate local community and its constituents— our family, friends and neighbors, kin, colleagues at work, church, etc.—do. Many of us do not live and work in an ideal local community, though. That is why we look to other communities for our sense of identity. Some find it in religion, others in nationalism, yet others in criminal gangs or extremism. For those without strong ties to a real, grounded, community, these weaker ties to imagined, virtual, or criminal communities may become important sources of identity.

DOES COMMUNICATIONS TECHNOLOGY ADD OR SUBTRACT FROM COMMUNITY?

While virtual communities may not substitute satisfactorily for a robust physically proximate community, does information and communications technology weaken community or strengthen it? In general, the evidence seems to be that, if anything, it strengthens it.

For example, the internet and social media clearly allow mass demonstrations to be organized quickly when many people are angry or resentful. The Arab Spring, a series of protests that rolled across the countries of the Middle East starting in late 2010, was a movement that relied on the internet and social media for mobilization. It has been followed by many others—as I write, an impromptu nationwide strike by Brazilian truckers, which has brought the nation to a standstill, was organized on WhatsApp. Technology can create temporary and largely spontaneous mass engagement. It enables easy affiliations and temporary commitments. However, the failure of many of these movements to generate sustained political reforms suggests that organizations of the committed, such as political parties or mobilized communities, are needed to keep people engaged and pushing for real change.

A combination of technology and commitment may work even better. Communications technology can allow a core group of the committed to continue staying in touch with the more loosely affiliated, even when separated by some distance. Technology can offer those on the periphery a greater sense of participation, allowing them to innovate and propose new directions. If the committed channel the energies of the merely affiliated effectively, they can create powerful social or political movements such as the recent #MeToo movement against sexual harassment and assault.[2]

Nevertheless, the dominant narratives on the advent of new communications technology are that they either turn people inward, making them spend more time on private leisure activities within the home and less on sociable or public activities, or they create a whole new form of distant virtual community, which again detracts from the physically proximate community.[3] To examine the validity of these narratives, in the late 1990s researchers Keith Hampton and Andrew Wellman studied a new development in a Toronto suburb. They called it Netville to disguise the actual location.[4] Around 60 percent of the homes were wired to high-speed internet with videophones, an online jukebox, online health services, local discussion forums, and a variety of other entertainment and educational applications. Due to some glitch, the rest of the homes were not wired, which gave the researchers an ideal experiment to measure the effects of connectivity.

They found that relative to the residents who had not been connected, the wired residents recognized three times as many neighbors, talked to those neighbors twice as often, made four times as many phone calls to neighbors, and communicated further with them by email. As one member said, "I have noticed a closeness you don't see in many communities." Essentially, the local network allowed easy introductions, quick organization of events like barbecues, and rapid response to emergencies like missing pets. The wired net lowered the cost of traversing physical barriers like shut doors.

Indeed, the wired neighbors organized to petition the developer to rectify defects in his construction, and to continue the high-speed access to the network when the trial ended. The developer was forced to acquiesce to their demands to some extent, though not entirely. Consequently, dissatisfied residents successfully petitioned the town to stop him from working on a second development. The researchers concluded that "based on his experience with Netville, the developer acknowledged that he would never build another wired neighborhood." The network did seem to increase people power in this case, much to the discomfiture of the developer!

The point is that new communications technologies offer opportunities to create, strengthen, and maintain real-world ties. My children keep in much closer contact with their school and college friends and even acquaintances than my generation ever managed to. Technology certainly has the power to strengthen the proximate community.

Does Technology Polarize Community?

Another concern seems to be that the new communications technologies tend to polarize communities—given the easy access to diverse opinions, people might dwell on the opinions or websites that most accord with their prejudices, and see their opinions reaffirmed by the comments therein. Therefore, for example, conservatives frequent the Fox News website, which today highlights the spiraling cost of the Mueller investigation into the alleged collusion between President Trump's campaign and Russia, while liberals turn to the MSNBC website, which headlines the expansion of the Mueller investigation to friends of President Trump's son-in-law. According to the view that the internet polarizes, few would turn to CNN, which is more middle-of-the-road.

Economists Matt Gentzkow and Jesse Shapiro examined whether people are indeed isolating themselves from contrary opinions as they visit the internet.[5] They computed an isolation index, which is the difference between the average conservative share of websites visited by self-reported conservatives and the average conservative share of websites visited by self-reported liberals. Therefore, crudely speaking, if conservatives visited only Fox News while liberals visited only MSNBC, the isolation index would be 100; if both visited only CNN, it would be zero. Interestingly, they found the average conservative's exposure to conservative content was 60.6 percent, similar to a person who gets all her news from usatoday.com. The average liberal's exposure was 53.1 percent, similar to a person who gets all her news from cnn. com. The isolation index for the internet was thus only 7.5 percentage points. Contrary to popular belief, if a consumer did indeed get news exclusively from Fox News, she would consume news more conservatively than 99 percent of internet news users.

The reasons are interesting. Most online news is obtained from relatively centrist news sites. Moreover, most consumers who tend to view politically extreme websites tend to be consumers of a variety of websites, and visit the opposite extremes also (some perhaps to reinforce their opinion of how depraved the other side is). Indeed, people are more eclectic in their choice of which websites to visit than in their choice of residential neighborhood or their friends. The authors report the isolation index for neighborhoods to be 18.7 percent, and for friends to be 30.3 percent. We choose to live in neighborhoods that think more like us, and to have friends who are especially likely to share our opinions. Indeed, for most people, access to the new communications technologies may broaden, rather than narrow, their sources of news and opinion.

Gentzkow and Shapiro conducted their study before the rise of the Tea Party and way before the polarizing 2016 election in the United States, so behavior may have changed. Moreover, internet users may be younger and more flexible. The elderly may prefer TV and may switch channels less. Nevertheless, their study does suggest the effects of technology may not be so straightforward as sometimes postulated. Moreover, as with any new media, the establishment is now getting to understand it better, and putting in filters to screen out its worst social effects.

CAVEATS?

There are at least two possible additional caveats to a view that technology enables stronger, more broadly informed proximate communities. First, technology is improving and becoming more immersive, luring those who are vulnerable to its charms away from the real world. My colleague Erik Hurst, along with others, notes a decline in the United States of market hours worked by young men in the age group of twenty-one to thirty of about 203 hours per year over the period 2000–2015.[6] Fully 15 percent of these young men did not work at all in 2015, compared to 8 percent in 2000. The declines in hours worked started before the Great Recession, accelerated during it, and have tapered somewhat since. The declines are more precipitous than for older men in the age group of thirty-one to fifty-five. Hurst and his coauthors argue that part of the explanation is that young men are spending more time in gaming and computer leisure use—around 99 hours more per year, on average.

It is hard to conclude from this study, though, that gaming is socially damaging. While young men do seem to spend more time online at the expense of paid work, they seem happy with their choice, and are spending more time at home (perhaps to the discomfiture of their parents). They also did not reduce the amount of time they spent socializing. In sum, while they might work less, there are some compensations. Indeed, to the extent it keeps some of them off the street and socially destructive activities, it may even be beneficial.

More generally, dire predictions of the demise of community engagement as technology offers more entertainment choices may be overstated. For instance, Robert Putnam argued in his influential book *Bowling Alone* that civic association in the United States has been declining since the 1970s, in significant part due to the advent of television, but also because of the decline in civic consciousness since the generations that came of age before World War II. Putnam pointed to the decline in the number of bowling leagues, among other indicators, to demonstrate the decline in engagement. However, as Princeton historian Daniel Rodgers asserts, ". . . other associations held their own or flourished. Volunteering rates among teenagers rose, megachurches boomed, and advocacy groups of all sorts grew dramatically . . . the agencies of socialization were different from before, but they were not discernibly weaker."[7] In sum, we do not have strong evidence that information and communications technology makes it hard for the proximate community to engage, though we have to be vigilant about the possibility.

The second caveat is that while technology may not increase polarization, it can allow extreme elements in society to find one another and organize. A number of impressionable youth have been converted to Jihadist ways over the internet, and drawn into committing terrorist acts. Similarly, incels or involuntary celibates are an online subculture that consists of men unable to find a romantic or sexual partner. They have spurred one another on through the internet to commit a number of mass murders in North America, particularly of women. In various emerging markets, lynch mobs have been provoked by inflammatory messages to commit murders. The internet and social media are not always beneficial for the civilized community. Nevertheless, the balance of evidence seems to be that ties in the proximate community have not been weakened, and may even have been strengthened, by the direct effects of communications technology.

REVIVING THE PROXIMATE COMMUNITY

At the same time, we do know that enhanced trade and technological change transmitted through markets have led to the loss of middle-income jobs and weakened the economic basis for the community in many parts of the developed world. It may be this, coupled with the flight of those who can leave, that is more responsible for the social disintegration of the community.

How do we revive the proximate community? There is no magic solution to creating local jobs, but as one examines case studies of what has worked, some key factors emerge. Once again, we will see the importance of technology as part of the solution. Let us start with two case studies. First, let's look at a project that revived community spirit, and in the process made the community more attractive and livable. It took place in Indore in India.

Cleaning Up Indore

Indian cities are colorful, vibrant, noisy, and . . . dirty. The commercial hub of the state of Madhya Pradesh, Indore, was no exception.[8] People treated it as a vast public garbage dump. After eating food on paper plates bought from stalls at the famous Sarafa food market, customers simply threw their plates and any residue on the ground. People were no more careful with their domestic garbage, dumping it anywhere in the proximity of overflowing dumpsters, which were rarely emptied. Stray animals—dogs, cows, goats, and pigs—roamed freely, eating the garbage and adding their excrement to the mix. Some poor people, who did not have access to toilets, defecated in the open, in vacant fields or near public drains. All in all, it was a perfect breeding place for flies, mosquitoes, and, therefore, disease.

Into this mix were thrown two abnormal individuals, Malini Gaud, who had been elected mayor of Indore on a plank of cleanliness, and Manish Singh, the municipal commissioner. There was also one dedicated NGO, Basix, which had experience in effective waste management. Basix wanted more waste for poor rag pickers, who make a living separating out metals, paper, plastic, and glass from waste, and recycling it. The reformers realized that part of the solution was to make it easier for people to dispose of their garbage. That meant placing public garbage cans at every needed place throughout the city with its location geo-tagged for easy collection, collecting domestic garbage directly from every home, and constructing over ten thousand toilets in places where people used open spaces.

The municipal cleaning staff now had to collect the garbage. The 5,500-person staff was used to collecting pay and not much more. Attendance was a miserable 30 to 40 percent. The municipal commissioner decided to apply both carrot and stick. Staff were given smart uniforms, and their cycle rickshaws replaced with motorized GPS-fitted trucks. Each vehicle was given about one thousand households or bins to collect from every day, and its location and performance was monitored. Most employees actually were unhappy with their poor image. They did want to do a good job once they realized the mayor and commissioner were serious about change and apathy would no longer be the order of the day. Some did not want to change, and the stick was applied to them. Biometric attendance was introduced, and after discussion with the union and due notice, three hundred still-recalcitrant employees were suspended, and six hundred were terminated.

The householder was happy that garbage was collected regularly at her doorstep, and soon agreed to pay a regular monthly fee for collection, offsetting the municipality's additional costs. Shops and eateries installed garbage cans outside, incentivized by a stiff fine if they lacked one. One knotty problem was that some people still preferred answering the call of nature in the open rather than in an enclosed toilet. The municipality adopted the innovative idea of drum squads—these would search stealthily for open defecators and then flush them out by drumming loudly when they were found. Open defecation ceased, and disease seems to have fallen significantly since.

Cleaning up a city seems small in the larger scheme of community revival, but it is an essential component of change, especially in a world where the ability to attract talented people with improved livability is an important source of competitive advantage. Moreover, it offers a very visible sign of community effort and engagement. According to Indian magazine *Business Today,* there is something strange about the Sarafa market today: "There is no leftover food, no dirty plates, no garbage to be seen—anywhere." Indore was ranked the cleanest city in India in 2017 (after coming in at 149th in 2014). Its citizens take pride in its ranking and, according to Vijay Mahajan, the chairman of Basix, are working hard to maintain it.

Reinventing Galena

Consider our second example of community revival, this time in a developed country. The population of Galena, Illinois, rivaled that of Chicago in the nineteenth century. Galena witnessed one of America's first mineral rushes as it had extensive deposits of lead sulfide, but the town declined steadily into the twentieth century as the demand for lead slowed and the Galena River became more difficult to use because of erosion. The population fell steadily from the 1950s until an enterprising mayor in the 1980s, Frank Einsweiler, decided to emphasize its tourist attractions. The boarded-up old houses on Main Street were refurbished—and a seedy downtown became a charming nineteenth-century vintage attraction virtually overnight. Soon a variety of restaurants and retailers of handicrafts, as well as purveyors of luxury goods, opened on and around Main Street, adding to tourist interest and local jobs.

The town also emphasized its links with the famous Union Civil War general and United States president Ulysses S. Grant, who worked in his family tannery and leather-goods shop in Galena before leaving for the war. On his victorious return in 1865, he was presented a brick house, which is now an important historical attraction in Galena.

An annual county craft fair started bringing in thousands of visitors, and in 2010 a Vision 2020 campaign began implementing new ideas for the future vitality of the town. Many Chicagoans now own second homes in Galena, and in 2011, TripAdvisor listed Galena among its top-ten "Charming Small Towns." Even though a number of venerable downtown pharmacies and grocery stores have closed, Galena's population has stabilized. Many residents now have jobs in the tourist industry.

Galena's example is worth noting because many examples of revival center around new technologies. Galena's does not. Indeed, in every developing country I visit, some ministry is putting together a plan to make their country a power in artificial intelligence, robotics, and financial technologies like cryptocurrencies and blockchains. Yet, few have the research base or the human capital to make the plan a success just yet. Far better to figure out realistic strengths as well as gaps, and go about exploiting the strengths and filling in the gaps, much as Galena did.

COMMON THEMES IN COMMUNITY REVIVAL

There are many examples of communities that have revived, some after the loss of a dominant industry (think Pittsburgh and steel) and others a major employer (the region around Lund and Malmo in Sweden after the Kockums shipyard downsized and closed in the 1980s).[9] There are also many failed attempts at revival that we hear very little of. The revival of declining communities resembles the development of nations in many ways, especially in that economists understand very little about either process. After a success, we can look back and see certain factors that seem to be associated with it, yet simply putting those factors together do not assure success again. Nevertheless, this is what we have to go on.

The common themes in successful episodes of community revival seem to include the following: a small and enthusiastic team leading the effort; a coming together of different players in the community; the identification, utilization, and improvement of key assets in the community, including human capital; a focus on changing the image of the community by remedying critical weaknesses; and importantly, the engagement of the community as they see some signs of success and start taking pride in it.

LEADERS

Where do good leaders like Mayor Malini Gaud of Indore or Frank Einsweiler of Galena come from? This is probably one of the most important unanswered questions in the social sciences. We simply do not know. Case studies suggest successful community reform could be led by a local politician or administrator, by a businessperson or philanthropist, by a university president or academic, indeed by anyone who simply steps up in a failing environment to take charge.[10] It helps if they have credentials and some explicit source of power, but these are neither necessary nor sufficient. For in the beginning, no one really has sufficient authority for broad reform.

Typically, any would-be leader has to bring together a team of key players in the community, such as the bureaucracy, the political establishment, business leaders, union leaders, church leaders, respected individuals, and the leaders of voluntary organizations, and unite them with a vision for change. Any such vision has some constants, but the path to it is rarely clear or static. Good leaders continuously adjust their strategies to the facts on the ground, taking advantage of any opportunities that come their way.

The vision often has to be sold hard because it is rarely self-evident—if the path to revival were so obvious, would the community not already have embarked on it? In a failing community, it is possible that the usual resistance to new ideas or change is weaker, and key players care less about preserving their own turf than about avoiding collective extinction. Yet, this is not a given, and any plan for revival benefits from early successes that reaffirm the leader's vision and creates greater solidarity and trust in their team.

IDENTIFYING, REVIVING, OR ATTRACTING ASSETS

Strategies for revival are often built around identifying and uncovering valuable key assets. The old run-down houses on Main Street in Galena suddenly became historical, quaint, and valuable tourist assets. Many towns across the developed world have charming streets that, with a little sprucing up, become "olde towns" full of luxury shops and pricy restaurants selling a collective experience to tourists. Other communities have "hard" assets such as power stations producing cheap power without much demand, plentiful cheap land, old industrial buildings that can be repurposed as space for start-ups or loft residences, biking and hiking trails for the health-conscious, and so on.

Sometimes the assets are human. The community may have rich entrepreneurs or philanthropists who might be looking for ways to give back to the community that made them. Underutilized well-educated or highly skilled workers might already exist, or might like to return to the community if they see opportunity. With the right vision, even young unskilled workers, capable of being trained and willing to start with moderate wages, are assets.

Often the assets are organizations such as a government or defense establishment, a large locally headquartered firm, a hospital, good schools, a community college, or a university—after all, Daniel Patrick Moynihan once quipped "If you want to build a great city, create a great university and wait 200 years."[11] When strong organizations exist in the proximity of declining communities, they typically are shielded off from it—else the community would typically not be declining. One of the tasks for the team engaged in revival is to find ways to bring down the shields.

The assets the leadership team identifies often need further investment to make them viable or accessible. As we saw in the last chapter, connectivity, such as a fast broadband network, or roads, railways, ports, airports, and power can help. Legacy assets may also hinder new activity. For instance, railway tracks or highways that separate parks or waterfronts from the community need to be rerouted, and vacant warehouses repurposed or demolished; as a town shifts from producing goods to producing ideas and services—its key concern is no longer cheap logistics but livability. When a city sets up a business park where it hopes to incubate new manufacturing firms, it can make the park more attractive if it has a workshop with state-of-the-art production facilities, like large 3D printers, so that start-ups can fabricate and test prototypes at low cost.

As important, the assets will need to be coordinated with one another. A community college can add substantial value to students if it has state-of-the-art equipment on which to train them.[12] Often, the leadership group finds a large local employer to contribute some of that equipment and train faculty as needed. In turn, the employer benefits from a more-skilled applicant pool. In a similar vein, the entrepreneurs in Chicago's incubator for ICT start-ups (named "1871," after the year of the Chicago fire that led to an earlier revitalization of the city) benefit from the city's ability to get venture capitalists and other financiers to set up office on the same floors of Chicago's huge Merchandise Mart, near the heart of downtown Chicago. It is easier to pitch your idea when you bump into a financier in the line for coffee than when you have to set up a formal appointment!

More generally, distressed communities typically start with an important advantage because of their recent loss of economic activity: They have a number of underutilized assets, which are available cheaply. Furthermore, as the community's leaders draw in more firms, they reduce their collective costs because they jointly enjoy scale economies—for example, logistic firms reduce what they charge for transport if there is sufficient volume emanating from the businesses in the community. Of course, if community revival is wildly successful, it starts experiencing congestion costs, as firms bid up the price of employees and real estate, while traffic jams and long commutes start eroding livability. Indeed, Janesville, the town that GM left, will soon start issuing parking tickets again to mark its revival. Most declining communities would love to have these problems, though!

Some local and regional governments offer long tax holidays to attract foreign investment. These may sometimes be warranted if the investor is an initial anchor investor, who bears all the risk of being a first mover and potentially seeing no one else follow. The first mover makes the community more attractive to others and "crowds-in" more economic activity. Often, though, such tax holidays leave the community strapped for resources. The community empowerment we discussed in the last chapter will allow community leaders to create infrastructure and regulations that make the community an easier place to do business. Communities should compete on the business environment they offer, which is often cheaper to make attractive, rather than waste future tax receipts that could be better devoted to funding schools, affordable housing, and topping up the safety net. One concern is that if communities compete for new investment by offering more business-friendly regulation, they could engage in the proverbial race to the regulatory bottom. However, communities have to live with the regulations they promulgate, so oversight by community members is a check on deregulating to the community's detriment. As long as national environment, product, and worker safety standards are respected, communities ought to have enough leeway to compete.

PEOPLE AS ASSETS

Some communities will not have any valuable hard assets, but they will have people. Even if domestic firms from elsewhere in the country are not interested in relocating, a community may still parlay its location within a large or rich country to lure foreign firms. They could be enticed to set up facilities there, especially if the community can make it easier for the investor to do business. Community leaders could well learn from the Chinese local government officials we described earlier, who work hard to assemble attractive investment packages for foreign investors, requiring them to stop at only one window (the local party boss's office) to collect all regulatory permissions.

Some communities will need to attract skilled people if they do not have enough. The skilled foreigner may be easier to attract than citizens from elsewhere in the country, especially if a period of residency in the distressed community can mean an easier path to permanent residency. This may be an important way for a distressed community to attract talent when it has few other attractions. Perhaps, then, a portion of the immigrants a country plans to let in could be allotted to distressed communities. Communities could advertise their needs—engineers, doctors, computer technicians, teachers, coaches, and so on—while would-be immigrants would signal their interest. When there is a two-way match (online employment platforms offer a ready-made template for such immigration services), the immigrant would get a visa, renewable at the end of each year if the immigrant is still employed and staying in the community. As is the practice in Canada, a host family in the community could help ease the immigrant family's transition and integration. After a reasonable number of years, the immigrant would get permanent residency and the freedom to stay and work anywhere in the country. A fair number might well put down roots in the community—at any rate, they would have served it and helped build its human capital. A small influx of capable immigrants may indeed demolish stereotypes about the ugly immigrant and thus enhance mutual understanding.

Another underutilized human asset is the nation's elderly, who will grow in number as the nation ages. Recently retired empty-nester professional couples often look for different challenges. Some could spend the early vigorous years of their retirement in needy communities, helping the revival. A retired accountant could serve as a mentor for a fledgling small-business owner, figuratively holding her hand as she acquires skills. Even if they are reluctant to move to the community, some could mentor online at a distance. In many countries today, healthy retirees want to have a meaningful retirement, not one spent entirely in travel or playing bingo. National governments, together with communities, could set up Mentorship Corps, programs whereby screened retirees and fledgling business owners could be brought together. Once again, platforms could help reduce the cost of search and two-way matching.

Another source that can be tapped is the highly capable stay-at-home parent, who does not want to do a full-time job but can contribute for a few hours a day. Similarly, there are many who want to step off the career treadmill and do something that is more rewarding at their own pace. Once again, ICT technology allows their capabilities to be tapped, for it enables the community and the volunteer to make contact.

Filling Gaps

Many communities will have critical gaps that need filling and they will need to undertake remedial measures before anything will work. This is why coordination across key players is important, since just one important deficiency in the business environment—the absence of a good school, for example— can derail other efforts.

Some of these gaps have a chicken-and-egg character. For instance, crime and drug abuse will have to come down if a community is to be remotely attractive to business, but the availability of decent jobs is key to keeping people from drifting into crime and drug abuse. Similarly, schools will become better as they attract smart new kids, but smart kids will come only if there are good schools. As with any chicken-and-egg problem, a quick solution requires a big push and the favor of the gods. For instance, a large firm could miraculously move into town, employing some locals directly as well as catalyzing economic activity that indirectly employs others. With growing prosperity, crime and drug abuse would fall. The employees the firm brings in from outside would send their children to local schools, thus helping to improve their quality, and so on. . . .

Absent such luck, though, the solution to such problems takes time, and requires virtuous circles. A concerted push against crime brings down the crime rate enough to attract a few bold businesspeople who create enough jobs and income that the crime rate falls a little further, drawing in developers who refurbish abandoned houses to rent them out, which reduces the crime rate still further. . . . Community revival is a long, drawn-out process in such cases, which is why it requires steadfast leadership and commitment.

Engaging the Community

Community revival has a much greater chance of success if the residents are stirred out of the apathy, cynicism, and despair that characterizes many distressed communities and start believing in their own prospects. When the residents of Indore started remonstrating with unthinking visitors who simply dropped their dirty plates on the ground, or when the residents of Galena started thinking of how they could generate income from the tourists who visited, was when the reforms gained a momentum that made them hard to reverse.

Change is particularly visible and motivating if it happens around important public spaces where the community congregates, such as the public library or schools. Indeed, in their book, *Our Towns: A 100,000-Mile Journey into the Heart of America,* James Fallows and Deborah Fallows declare that in the library, they "could discover the spirit of a town, get a feel for the people's needs and wants, and gauge their energy and mettle."[13] And later, ". . . we would ask what was the most distinctive school to visit at the K–12 level. The question served a similar function to asking who in town made things run. If four or five answers came quickly to mind, that was a good sign. If not, the reverse."

Therefore, an important task for the leadership group is to engage the community, so that they feel a part of the revival process. The crime prevention by residents of Pilsen, the actions by the residents of Indore to challenge those who still littered, and the attempts by the citizens of Galena to improve the tourist experience, all contributed to community pride and revival. Technology can help create a sense of engagement and participation, especially if the leadership group is comfortable with a certain amount of decentralized decision making, with residents taking ownership of some reforms and driving them in innovative directions.

THE ROLE OF THE STATE

Federal governments across the world are generally strapped for cash, and may have difficulty favoring specific communities, even if that were politically feasible. In the last chapter, we discussed the relative division of responsibilities, powers, and funding between federal and local government. Here we ask what else, if anything, the federal government can do to encourage development in distressed communities through its tax and spending policies.

There is a long history across the world of private enterprises being given tax incentives to locate in more remote or distressed areas. Many countries in Europe as well as in emerging markets follow such practices and the United States is attempting it again by designating certain areas as opportunity zones.[14] When unaccompanied by a collective local effort to attract business and reduce the costs of doing business, such incentives typically do not offset the higher cost of doing business in remote or distressed areas. As a result, even if companies do locate in the distressed area, they often try to game such incentives by only placing a skeleton operation there. Even though they do much of the work elsewhere, they show through clever transfer pricing that the value is added in the distressed area, so that they can collect the incentives.

Therefore, tax incentives are usually useful only as part of an overall package of measures that a community takes to improve its attractiveness to businesses. In practice, though, the federal government finds it hard to single out communities where a serious revival effort is under way. When it simply gives incentives to all firms that locate in distressed communities, the federal government ends up subsidizing bogus skeleton operations, firms that were going to invest there anyway, and firms whose investment does not add value, along with small quantities of genuine new useful investment. Most studies find the jobs created through location-based tax incentives come at a high cost to the taxpayer.[15]

An alternative might be to subsidize job creation directly through measures like the US Earned Income Tax Credit (EITC), which effectively gives a federal top-up to worker pay at low levels of income. The top-up rises with income over a range, stabilizes, then tapers off as the individual's income rises further. In order to encourage job creation in distressed areas, the EITC could be enhanced for jobs there, though there are obvious difficulties in measuring where exactly a job takes place, and there is some risk of fraud.[16] This is why the top-ups that we discussed in the last chapter, paid through the community, may be more useful. Perhaps, though, the most effective government intervention might be to support community efforts to retrain its adults. Most countries have a plethora of programs attempting this, and most programs are spread too thinly and are uncoordinated. Neither the affected people nor the communities have a full understanding of what is available and how to use the funds.[17] If the available funds are aggregated and made available to the community and the leadership team, it could utilize it in a way that could most serve the needs of the people in the community. In some communities, these funds could bring in career counselors who can chart out a plan of action for each person. The funds could also subsidize tuition for the courses each one needs to take. In other communities, funds could go to setting up evening nurseries where children are looked after while parents study, and in yet others, it could buy machines, or hire specialized faculty for the community college. The point is that most communities know what is needed, and apart from ensuring funds are spent transparently and effectively, the federal government should give them the freedom to choose.

FINANCING COMMUNITY REVIVAL

The problem with too much easy money is that it tends to get wasted. One of the biggest hurdles in financing local governments is the lack of transparency about their revenues, their spending, their assets, and their liabilities. One of the first steps in community revival is therefore to clarify the community's financial situation and to make its budget and accounting fully transparent. Once this is done, the leadership team, community members, as well as investors, will have a much better sense of how much room there is to raise more money.

Much of the funding for community revival should be raised from sources that offer a second pair of eyes as to how it is spent. This does not mean that all the finance has to be on market terms. Philanthropists and foundations are often willing to provide patient seed money or long-term low-interest loans, as are social-impact funds. Pension funds increasingly are willing to finance long-term infrastructure projects as they look to match their assets with their long-term payout liabilities. Many countries have community-development institutions that focus on community support, and some have mandates for large financial institutions to reinvest in communities from which they raise deposits. Local banks and finance companies have a very close relationship with community businesses. All these can be sources from which the community can raise funding.

While the bulk of funding can come from outside investors, some projects will require the community to put up equity, and this is where it will have to draw on friendly sources like philanthropies or its own saved resources. To enhance these own resources, some of the community's assets can be commercialized and used to raise money, without compromising the people's access to public services. For example, parks can do double duty after closing hours for private parties or gatherings. Certain superfluous assets, such as parking lots or excess community-owned land and buildings, can be leased out and eventually sold as the revival gains steam. The sales receipts can be the equity to catalyze the building of more needed assets.

The community can also raise money against future increases in tax receipts, especially if it needs to make large up-front investments. For example, it is natural that property prices and taxes would rise as the community's investments in the neighborhood's public assets like schools and parks pay off. Increments to tax receipts could be securitized and sold.

DEALING WITH FAILURE: GIVING UP, GETTING ACQUIRED, LEAVING

Much of this chapter has been about how the community can get up and running when it has leadership that allows it to find its inner strengths. What if that leadership does not emerge? What if there is no viable economic value in the local area? What if people have become irretrievably apathetic, cynical, and self-destructive? Every country will have pockets of such despair, communities that were once normal but now seem beyond redemption. It is important not to give up easily. Nevertheless, some communities may simply not have the administrative or economic capabilities, or the social will, to survive independently.

Some of these may still find a future by merging with another, more vibrant community. They may lose some powers, but may retain a feeling of self-determination because of their voice in the larger community. Some communities may, unfortunately, be so distressed that they have no hope of survival, and no one has any desire to absorb them. As countries age and resist immigration, some communities will literally die out. Other communities may be too small or too remote to have a chance, but may also have young people. Rather than spending enormous amounts of money to preserve such communities, it may well make sense to ease the way for the young to emigrate to other, more vibrant communities. Too many people across the world are trapped by non-portable unemployment benefits, health insurance, or just the support of a warm, even if impoverished, community. The safety net should be portable across the country, and indeed countries and communities should explore the possibility of subsidizing moves by the unemployed from high-unemployment communities to elsewhere in search of employment. Out-migration may indeed be the best future for some declining communities.

CONCLUSION

It seems paradoxical that as technology is bringing the whole world to us, the proposed solution to some of our problems is to embrace what is near—the community—rather than what is far. What is near anchors us, a necessity as our experiences become more virtual. Reviving what is near is therefore essential to ensuring our continuing humanity. As we work to improve the troubled world, that has to be our lodestar.

12

RESPONSIBLE SOVEREIGNTY

The two Opium Wars, the first fought between 1839 and 1842 and the second fought between 1856 and 1860, were among the most shameful of wars in humankind's long and sorry history of wars. The primary protagonists were the British and the Chinese. In the early 1800s, British traders imported large quantities of silks, porcelain, and tea from China. China seemed to want few British goods in return, in part because China restricted foreign merchants to doing business only out of Canton. Not surprisingly, traders found it hard to sell British manufactures to the Chinese. As British gold and silver disappeared into China in payment for Chinese exports, British traders tried desperately to find something they could sell to China. Opium, procured in India by the British East India Company, was the answer. Opium was addictive and its exports grew quickly as it morphed from an indulgence of the rich Chinese into a debilitating affliction for the masses. Fearing economic and social breakdown, the Chinese emperor banned the opium trade, and his agents confiscated the opium that British traders intended to smuggle into China. In response, the British sent warships and soldiers, ostensibly to recover their merchants' goods and protect their trading privileges. Thus started the First Opium War.

The real British objective, recognized even then in parliamentary debates in England, was more sordid. The British were protecting their freedom to peddle dope to the Chinese masses. When the war ended with China's defeat, these "freedoms" were embedded in the humiliating Treaty of Nanking. The Second Opium War expanded European and American trading rights further. It is obvious today that the Chinese were the wronged party in these wars, that the British trampled over their sovereign right to ban the opium trade to protect the Chinese people. Chinese national resolve today is understandably shaped by the desire to never again be at the mercy of foreign powers as they were then.

Nevertheless, and though it was well within their right, was there a cost to the Chinese of restricting European traders to Canton? Did they do themselves harm? Despite being the source of momentous inventions like gunpowder and the compass, China was technologically and militarily far behind Western Europe by the time of the Opium Wars, which explains its resounding defeat. Might China have been better able to stand up to the British if they had bought more modern European muskets for all their soldiers, and if they had a better awareness of European military tactics through deeper contacts with the outside world? Indeed, China's willingness to absorb good ideas from anywhere in the world today may reflect learning from its historical experience of the consequences of isolation. At any rate, all these questions are even more relevant today.

THE INTERCONNECTED WORLD

It is commonplace to say the world is now much more interconnected. In addition to cross-border trade and capital flows, many countries have had to figure out how to deal with economic migrants as well as refugees from conflict. Our ancestors also experienced trade, capital, and people coming from across the seas, though perhaps to a lesser degree. In addition, though, we have new sources of interconnections. As a result of the ICT revolution, information and disinformation now flows across borders in real time. With the possible exception of China, no country has found a way to filter or censor the information its citizens receive over the internet. Data too traverses borders in massive quantities—Google knows more about the use of Indian roads through its map app than does the Indian government, while fitness apps can reveal the location of secret military bases around the world, since military personnel are the few in remote areas who are fitness buffs.[1] Cybercrime, where hundreds of millions of dollars can be stolen in seconds, is a whole new area of opportunity for the malevolently intelligent, as the ICT revolution has brought vast unprepared populations within easy reach of cyber villains.

Another new form of cross-border flow is service activities—the ICT revolution enables tasks such as real-time human monitoring of a building's security cameras or mathematics tutoring to be done at a distance and across borders. Laws too, such as those governing intellectual property, now are applied across borders. Environmental damage also traverses borders, as carbon emissions generated anywhere in the world contribute to more volatile climatic conditions everywhere.

How much control should countries exercise over cross-border flows? I have argued thus far that when policy is set by smaller political entities such as the community, which are closer to the individual, individuals are more likely to have a sense of agency. It is important to enhance such empowerment when markets and technological change tend to do just the opposite—make the individual feel they are buffeted by forces beyond their control. The decentralization of powers should apply as much at the international level as at the national and sub-national level, indeed more so because individuals have very little sense of ownership of decisions made at the international level.

At the same time, for localism to be inclusive it has to be open to flows from, and to, the outside. So how should a country balance these two concerns? How much freedom should a country retain over policies, especially governing cross-border flows, and how much should it let itself be bound by international agreements and treaties? How much should it let its policies be driven by its global responsibilities? These are the questions we will examine in this chapter.

RETAINING SOVEREIGN POWERS TO CONTROL FLOWS

If the democratically elected representatives of the people exercise control over a country's borders to avoid sudden, overwhelming flows, and to shape other flows so that they are beneficial and timely, citizens have a stronger sense of control. Populist nationalism has fewer grievances to exploit, while communities feel more in control. To the general principle that countries should control cross-border flows, I will add two caveats.

First, while a country should retain powers to manage or deflect a particularly pernicious kind of flow, it is in its own interest that it should not protect itself permanently from engagement. No country can hope to remain an island forever, isolated from the rest of the world. Indeed, as China's earlier experience suggests, the longer a country remains isolated, the further it falls behind the rest of the world and the greater the pain it faces on reconnecting.

Second, there are categories of flows where the world is generally better off when most countries are open to them—and where countries may be tempted to choose wrongly when the decision is left to them. In such situations, the world has an interest in nudging countries to be open to them. Trade in goods and services is one such category in which the benefits of free flow across borders for countries that have reached a certain stage of development are clear, but in which these countries left unconstrained are apt to put up barriers. In the short run, free trade creates losers who are likely to oppose any reduction in trade barriers forcefully. Countries need to find better ways of compensating them. Revitalizing the community that is adversely affected by trade, as we have seen, is an important mechanism to mitigate its effects. The losses of a few, though, should not be allowed to derail the gains to many.

Free trade creates a global market, and takes us a long way toward efficient global production. We thus save on global resources and limit environmental despoliation. In addition, though, free trade disciplines domestic producers and keeps them competitive. It diminishes the possibility of cronyism between government and private sector since foreign producers are outside the control of the government and hard to cartelize. As we have seen, all this is necessary for the independence of the private sector which, in turn, limits the arbitrary powers of government, protects property rights, and indeed protects democracy itself. External trade can also strengthen other domestic markets by limiting the influence of anticompetitive domestic interests; for instance, Luigi Zingales and I find that a country's financial markets tend to be more developed when the country is more open to trade.[2]

Low tariffs are an essential precondition for free trade and a global market, and its benefits are large enough that all countries ought to be willing to give up much of their right to limit cross-border flows of goods and services if they can be assured that others will also do so. No doubt, some countries that have been closed to trade for a long time will benefit from reducing tariffs gradually so that their people and corporations can adjust, while others that are hit by a sudden loss of competitiveness may want to raise tariffs temporarily. Yet there are always corporate interests and some professional or labor interests in every country that will use the excuse of costs of adjustment to resist ever freeing trade—free trade and competition is good, they say, but for everyone else, not for us. Even with the best democratic intent, it may be hard for a country to agree to, and stay committed to, low tariffs. A little international nudge is therefore often warranted to push countries into reducing tariffs—a nudge admirably given first by the General Agreement on Tariffs and Trade (GATT) and subsequently its successor, the World Trade Organization (WTO).

By engaging in protracted international negotiations, these organizations have convinced countries to agree collectively to not raise tariffs above a (low) maximum pledged amount. When such an agreement is approved by a country's parliament, it has other benefits. By signing on to a negotiated common tariff structure, a country avoids lobbying by powerful domestic interests to protect themselves through selectively high tariffs. Also, to the extent that countries continue adhering to international agreements when the government changes—which will be the case if there are significant costs to domestic industry of withdrawing from commitments—it gives firms across the world predictability of tariffs over time, and thus a stronger incentive to invest. As we have seen, such a low tariff regime has proven so attractive that a number of emerging markets have lowered tariffs significantly so that their producers can become part of global supply chains. All this is to suggest that we should resist the populist nationalist turn to protectionism, and redouble our efforts to lower tariffs globally.

The merits of cross-border flows other than those of goods and services are more uncertain and contingent on circumstances. As a series of financial crises have shown us, capital flows into a country are not an unmitigated blessing, especially if the flows are short-term in nature, and the country has poorly developed financial markets and institutions. Even rich countries like Ireland and Spain found such flows difficult to handle prior to the Global

Financial Crisis. Likewise, the flows of information and data across borders can be benign, but they can also be used to manipulate or blackmail domestic residents. The recent controversy over disguised Russian involvement through social media in influencing voters in the 2016 US Presidential elections is just one example of what is possible, because bits and bytes do not have national identity stamped on them.

Unlike trade, such flows are not so unconditionally beneficial that countries should be pushed to accept them. These flows have to be managed more judiciously and contingently, so a country's people have to have stronger democratic control over their management. International agreements that peremptorily take away a country's flexibility here seem a step too far. This is not to argue at all that these flows should be stopped, but that countries have a legitimate role in deliberating and determining policy without an international presumption that there is one best way that all countries should adopt. In other words, agreements on these issues should be bottom up rather than top down.

NONTARIFF BARRIERS
AND HARMONIZATION

There is a further consideration even with trade. Countries do not just impose tariffs on imports, they can alter domestic taxes, regulations, safety standards, property rights, and so on. Some of these may effectively become nontariff barriers to trade. For example, in the 1980s, Japanese officials argued for keeping out US beef because Japanese digestive systems were different, US pharmaceuticals because they had not been tested on Japanese subjects, and US-made skis because Japanese snow was unique.[3] While such arguments are so patently protectionist that they border on the facetious, and thus can quickly be called out for their protectionist intent, some countries have genuine reasons for the differences in their markets.

Most commercial poultry farms in the United States crowd chickens together in tight spaces, with little light or ventilation. This raises the risk of disease and contamination, which is why US chickens are disinfected by washing them in chlorine. The unscrupulous poultry farmer can also use chlorine to "freshen" up stale meat.

In the European Union, minimum space and ventilation standards for poultry rearing reduce the risk of disease, and thus allow poultry farmers to achieve the applicable local health standards by washing chicken with only water. The European Union bans the sale of chlorine-washed chickens, even though there is no clear evidence that the chickens thus treated are a health risk.[4] The ban serves two purposes. It reflects European discomfort with harsh rearing methods that create the necessity for chlorine washes. It also reduces the risk that improperly washed contaminated birds or "freshened" stale meat get into the European food chain. Clearly, the prohibition on chlorine-washed chicken can seem to be a protectionist targeting of US-produced chicken. Instead, it may reflect the genuine preferences of Europeans or the concerns of their food administrators.

To avoid such situations, some countries have pushed for the harmonization of rules and regulations across countries to prevent the possible erection of nontariff barriers to trade. This will make it easier for corporations to traverse borders and do business everywhere. They want every country to feel and behave alike. Indeed, such harmonization can be taken to comic levels: European Commission Regulation No. 2257/94 required all bananas sold in stores within the Union to be "free of abnormal curvature" and at least 14 cm in length, and all cucumbers to be "practically straight" and bent by a gradient of no more than one-tenth.[5] It is easy to imagine the anger of a Portuguese grocer, cursing foreign-imposed idiocy as she measured her vegetables with ruler and protractor. These regulations were eventually laughed out, but even when the attempt at harmonization is more serious, it is often a step too far, as emphasized, for example, by the economist and Financial Times commentator, Martin Wolf.[6]

For one, it tramples over the preferences of citizens of small countries. When countries get together to decide whose rules will prevail, typically, the voices of small countries are drowned by larger and more powerful ones. Moreover, the views of negotiators from large powerful countries are shaped all too often by what will favor their largest corporations, rather than what can genuinely benefit their own country, let alone the world. This need not be because large corporations have corrupted their government's negotiators. The reality is often more prosaic. Large corporations have smart specialized analysts who can understand the possible consequences of new rules and regulations, can figure out what configuration will benefit their corporation, and can feed the analysis in a persuasive way through lobbyists to their country's official negotiators. Since these negotiators have little data or analytical support of their own, it is not surprising they will use what they are fed.

The push toward lower tariffs is not complicated—lower is typically better for everyone for every good and service. By contrast, the direction in which to go to harmonize business environments across countries is less clear. Should one adopt the United States's preferences on washing chickens or the European Union's preferences on giving chickens space? And do the negotiators for the United States reflect the preferences of their people or of the chicken-producer lobby? Do the representatives of poorer countries have equal say in, or equal understanding of, the negotiations? Typically, the outcomes of these negotiations to harmonize regulations are profoundly undemocratic, both within nations and across the community of nations.

Moreover, much of the benefit of a common global market can be had with low tariffs but without harmonization. If a common standard is of the essence to attract business, then countries will sign up to it without being coerced. Blatant attempts at protectionism through differentiated rules, standards, or regulations can be thwarted by taking the potential violator to an international dispute resolution mechanism like the WTO court. If the court rules that the ostensible violation was not primarily protectionist in intent, it should be permitted. That will preserve a country's democratic space to be different.

Indeed, differences in environment between countries simply mean that exporters have to work a little harder to address the market, not that they are shut out. American chicken producers who want to export to Europe will not be able to rear their poultry in the same crowded pens as they rear poultry for the American market—they will have to give the chickens intended for Europe more space and light. This is not entirely a bad outcome, since it can make their European consumers happier. Indeed, multinational companies do not assume consumer preferences in each country are the same—they alter their products, their marketing, and their financing to suit each market, even while drawing on their global economies of scale to address each market more cheaply. Why can't they also adapt to differences in taxation or regulation? Put differently, what the world needs is predictable, low-cost access to markets in different countries. What is less important are harmonized taxes or regulations or safety standards. . . . Why should people not have more control over these issues, which might make them more willing to accept free trade?

There is virtue to diversity. Often, we have no idea what production environment or standards will be best going forward. If we insist on uniformity across countries, we preclude the possibility of experimentation, which could throw up better alternatives than the current consensus. We also run the risk of coordinating on a set of rules that prove disastrous. Therefore, even if harmonization was driven with the best interests of the world in mind, it might still make sense to leave decisions to countries so that a variety of environments emerge, so that there is competition between environments, and the global system develops both resilience and better practices.

There are certainly areas where a common global standard adds significant value. For example, common protocols may be necessary in communication networks to ensure interoperability. There is virtue in competition even here. If a set of standards is negotiated, it should be up to every country to decide whether to opt in, and no presumption that any country that does not do so will be excluded by everyone else. That will allow countries to experiment with alternative standards, so that a superior standard could emerge. Enforcing a monopoly here, as almost everywhere else, is bad.

Finally, the alert reader might note a seeming inconsistency in my proposals. I argued earlier that communities should not be able to impose their own regulations to keep out goods and services from elsewhere in the country. I have just proposed that countries should have the right to impose regulations such as the ban on chlorine-washed chicken, so long as their primary purpose is not protectionist. The difference is that communities in a democracy can shape national regulation on the goods and services that can be sold. Once the national policy is set, though, communities should abide by them so that the national market is seamless, to everyone's benefit. In contrast, international agreements, such as those on the harmonization of regulations, are rarely arrived at in a democratic spirit, as I have argued. This is why I believe countries should have a more bottom-up deliberative process on what they regulate and what they adhere to, and the ability to pick and choose in most such agreements.

RACE TO THE BOTTOM . . .

One concern countries have is a race to the bottom. If there is no harmonization of regulations, will countries that adopt the lowest standards benefit their firms, giving them a competitive advantage? This danger is emphasized, often by countries that fear their preferred position demands too much of their own firms. They prefer everyone to be disadvantaged by onerous regulations, rather than their firms alone. This becomes a way for powerful countries to create and export their bad regulations everywhere, and for everyone else to adopt unnecessary and inappropriate regulations.

Take, for example, bank capital regulation. Banks do benefit from operating with little capital, especially when markets are buoyant and financing is easy. For instance, before the financial crisis, some banks were operating at debt-to-equity ratios of 50 to 1 or more. This leaves very little room for error, as the financial crisis proved. Moreover, the leverage that is best for each bank's profits may be excessive for the system collectively. Therefore, regulators have rightly seen a need to mandate minimum capital requirements.

However, each country's optimal minimum capital requirements for its banks may differ depending on its stage of development and the kinds of activities its banks undertake. If the banks in a country are sophisticated, can take on sizable, exotic risks, and are large relative to the country's size—as for example in Switzerland and the United Kingdom—it is natural that those countries should impose higher capital requirements on their banks, because the risk to the country of the failure of these large banks is enormous. On the other hand, there is no reason why a small developing country with a fledgling banking sector should impose the same requirements on its banks. Nevertheless, the Basel Accords attempt to harmonize capital requirements across countries. While these accords do require more capital of large sophisticated banks, it is not clear that there is adequate differentiation allowed between countries.

Moreover, under the guise of harmonization, countries or regions with special requirements try and impose them on everyone else. During the recent European crisis, European regulators worried that governments in southern European countries like Greece and Italy were pressurizing their domestic banks to buy domestic government bonds so as to ease government access to new financing. Given that the fiscal situation of these countries was far from healthy, there was a possibility the strapped governments would default on their bonds. The banks that bought more of their own government's bonds were increasing the chances of their own default, and because Europe would eventually pay for the rescue, transferring the costs to Europe.

One way to prevent such a problem recurring would be for European regulators to impose a higher capital requirement on any European bank that bought government bonds issued by distressed countries; Greek banks would quickly stop buying if they had to raise more equity capital for each Greek government bond that they bought. Yet, instead of agreeing to a European solution, European regulators tried to impose this across the world. Emerging markets would be at a particular disadvantage with this proposal since the bonds issued by emerging market governments are not highly rated, and would require their banks to hold more capital against them. The problem that Europe faces is not a problem for an emerging market. There is no one waiting to bail out an emerging market government, and no one it can shift costs to. If the European proposal were adopted, emerging market banks would hold costly additional capital for a nonexistent problem, even while these banks had other important financing needs they could not meet.

It may be that Europe believed that by getting international agreement, it avoided a thornier negotiation within Europe. Moreover, once everyone was similarly disadvantaged, the costs to the southern European countries of agreeing would be smaller—at least so the thinking might go. It may be that this was a Machiavellian attempt by supporters of southern European countries to torpedo the entire move by escalating it to international levels. Regardless, the episode highlights the problems with harmonization—regulators cartelize and spread unnecessary and inappropriate regulation across countries, preventing competition between jurisdictions from highlighting the costs of such regulations.

Finally, what about the race to the bottom? Regulators agreed to common bank capital requirements in the various Basel Accords because they feared that if given the flexibility, some regulators might impose inordinately low requirements on their banks. Yet this fear is questionable. If higher bank capital reduces risks, why wouldn't the bank regulators in each country internalize the need to set capital requirements for their domestic banks at adequate levels? Moreover, if regulators feared competition in their markets from inadequately capitalized foreign banks, they could always require that such banks operate domestically through entities that meet domestic capital standards.

There is one other plausible reason for a harmonized international capital standard; the fear that each country's regulators, left to themselves, will not be able to set an adequate capital standard domestically—the domestic bank lobby will be too powerful for them. By meeting in Basel, far from domestic lobbies and democratic pressures, regulators can set capital requirements closer to the level they feel comfortable with. Arguing, then, that their hand has been forced by the international bargains they have had to make, they avoid the need to justify the standard at home. If so, regulators are essentially asking their people to trust them to get it right. But such agreements are not free of perverse influence, and they reinforce the popular belief across the world that too much is decided far away behind closed doors. International agreement and pressure on tariff reduction is warranted because the objectives are transparent and the outcomes generally beneficial to all. Few other technocratic international agreements meet these standards. They should be used sparingly given the democratic tolerance for such agreements is narrowing. Domestic democratic oversight, flawed as it may be, is better than the alternatives.

WORKER RIGHTS . . .

Another area where there is often talk of harmonization is worker rights. Some countries, especially developing ones, do not have strong unions and adequate worker protections. The concern, then, is that this allows firms in that country to underpay workers or to underinvest in their working conditions, thus giving them a competitive advantage. The proponents of harmonization argue for keeping out the country's exports until it improves its treatment of workers.

One problem is that the low pay of workers in developing countries may reflect their low productivity, not exploitation by owners. If those firms are required to pay significantly more, they may be forced to fire their workers and close down. Similarly, worker-safety regulation is naturally better in advanced countries. While developing countries should work continuously to improve worker safety, if owners are suddenly required to implement safety measures at rich country levels, they may find production uneconomical once again. More generally, given their circumstances, a steady job and the accompanying income may do more for worker health and well-being in a poor country than workplace safety measures. Having both jobs and safety would be even better, but the country may be forced to choose. Is it not in the best position to make this choice? In short, could insistence on harmonization of worker pay or worker rights risk turning into protectionism?

Some argue that instead of focusing on specific worker-friendly measures, countries should harmonize their treatment of worker organizations like unions. Once unions are in place, they can figure out what is best for their members. This form of institutional harmonization is both impractical and intrusive—impractical, because developed countries treat unions and protect union rights very differently. Scandinavian countries place unions on a much higher pedestal than, say, the United States. Indeed, even in the United States, the eastern states offer a far more union-friendly environment than the "right-to-work" southern ones. Whose standard should be applied? And will application of these standards not be intrusive? Don't developing countries, even ones that are not fully democratic, have the sovereign right to decide what environment they create domestically?

All countries should, of course, respect universal human rights, including refraining from using slave labor or child labor. Consumers in developed countries should be free to pay more for fair-trade coffee or to boycott clothing produced by exploited labor elsewhere. Multinational firms should also feel free to set better standards for their operations than local requirements. Should powerful countries additionally impose their preferences on others through internationally determined rules? Probably not.

INTELLECTUAL PROPERTY

Yet another area where harmonization has been controversial is intellectual property. Historically, countries have been more lax on protecting intellectual property until they developed enough creativity of their own.[7] Nearly every developed country, in the early stages of its development, appropriated intellectual property from elsewhere. Like the power to levy taxes, the right to define what is property is a sovereign power. Property rights in intellectual property ought to be determined by each country, deciding what it wants to define as protectable intellectual property, and how long it wants to protect it.

While countries should certainly pay for the intellectual property they use, the more contentious question is the duration and breadth of intellectual-property protection. Countries that generate intellectual property, such as the United States, obviously want to apply the long duration and extensive protection granted in their own countries everywhere else. The argument is that such protection will give innovators greater profits and therefore greater incentive to innovate. As we have seen with the debate over patents, it can also reduce innovation by others in the industry, whose way is blocked by earlier patents.

Such problems are accentuated in developing countries. Domestic firms in developing countries primarily consume intellectual property as they try to catch up, and their ability to innovate would benefit from wider availability of intellectual property. Josh Lerner from Harvard University finds, after examining the patent policy of 60 countries over 150 years, that an enhancement in patent protection in a country enhances patent filing by foreign firms while reducing filing by domestic firms.[8] The absence of any positive effect of strengthening patent protection on patenting by domestic firms is particularly pronounced in developing countries, suggesting they benefit little from such laws, which may deter domestic innovation.

Through the Trade Related Intellectual Property Rights Agreement (TRIPS) negotiated under the auspices of the World Trade Organization in 1994, developed countries have pushed stronger intellectual-property protections on all other countries. TRIPS specifies long periods of protection even in areas where intellectual property rights protection is controversial. Rich pharmaceutical companies in developed countries lobbied their governments to effectively create more lucrative property rights for them in the poorest countries, arguing this was essential to enhance innovation. Developing countries acquiesced for fear of being excluded from trade. Such agreements coerce poorer countries into accepting an intellectual property rights regime that is far stricter than one they themselves, fearing a slowing of domestic innovation and growth, might enact.

TRIPS creates a uniformity of regime across the world that limits competition between jurisdictions. It may be that long duration intellectual property rights protection makes sense once countries reach a certain level of development, but not before. It may be that protection never makes sense. We may have chilled innovation in a number of countries to protect existing intellectual property in rich countries. We will never know, for we have shut out the possibility of regulatory experimentation and trampled on the right of countries to choose.

To summarize, there are tremendous benefits to some cross-border flows, especially trade. Undoubtedly, we have to support the losers from trade in each country better, which most countries do not do well. An important source of dissatisfaction with the plethora of international agreements, though, is that they try to do too much, and much of that activity is hidden away from democratic oversight. While small poor countries get the worst deal from the intrusive agreements that are crafted, the interests of the broader population in developed countries are also not necessarily well represented. In order to make globalization more sustainable, we ought to do our best to keep cross-border trade open everywhere by lowering tariffs, but be far less intrusive on the shape the markets take in each country. We should aim for fewer international agreements, and more democratic inputs over policy governing cross-border flows, even as we puzzle over how to deal with newer flows like data and information.

INTERNATIONAL RESPONSIBILITIES

Thus far, we have focused on how countries should treat flows. Consider now country policies. What among a country's policies does the international community have a legitimate interest in? How might it try and shape those policies?

Economist Dani Rodrik of Harvard University suggests economic policies fall into four broad buckets when seen from the perspective of cross-border flows.[9] Some policies have purely domestic effects. They may help or hurt the country but for the most part do not translate into flows elsewhere. For instance, raising taxes on the rich so as to cut taxes for the middle class will largely have domestic consequences, with only the rare billionaire deciding to up stakes and become a citizen of Monaco. Our emphasis on the need to preserve sovereignty would shield such policies from international influence, unless they are so bad that the country and its people risk becoming an international burden. The proper channel for transmitting international advice even in these dire cases should be through multilateral institutions that are seen as impartial, transparent, and fairly governed. We will come back to this shortly.

Then there are policies, such as raising tariffs on imports, which typically have adverse effects on the rest of the world, but also have serious adverse effects on the country imposing the tariffs. The jobs protected by steel tariffs typically are outweighed by the jobs lost everywhere else.[10] Rodrik calls these policies "beggar thyself" policies because they are driven by domestic special interests or constituencies but hurt the national interest also. We have already argued that both countries and the international community have an interest in treaties that keep tariffs everywhere low, and in creating an international adjudication mechanism that can declare nontariff barriers that have primarily a protectionist intent illegitimate. There should be little room for such "beggar thyself" policies.

Consider next policies that became known as "beggar thy neighbor" policies during the Great Depression. For example, when a country intervenes directly in exchange markets or through unconventional monetary policies to keep its exchange rate undervalued, or when it subsidizes an exporting sector heavily, it tends to make the country's exports hypercompetitive, driving down profits in competing countries. This leads to factory closures and unemployment in those countries. A country may engage in such behavior because it believes it will gain a permanent and profitable presence in production when factories elsewhere close, or because it fears the domestic political costs of slow growth and high unemployment. Regardless, the country's growth comes at the expense of everyone else. Indeed, if others retaliate, as they did during the Great Depression, everyone is worse off.

In the fourth bucket are policies that affect the well-being of all countries by altering commonly held resources, collective resources, or the environment. Overfishing on the high seas affects catches everywhere. The reluctance to vaccinate all children domestically allows the scourge of polio to reemerge, threatening children around the world once again. Refugees could also be seen as altering the global "commons." Much like carbon emissions, policies affecting the global commons are felt everywhere.

Rodrik's classification of policies has little place for idealism, but the world periodically rediscovers it. As we have seen, the United States helped rebuild Europe after World War II with Marshall Plan funds. Good Samaritan policies such as grants for reconstruction, or other forms of humanitarian aid, can benefit recipients tremendously, but they result from democratic deliberations within countries. Apart from highlighting the benefits of such policies and coordinating efforts across coalitions of willing countries, there is little role for the world.

In contrast, the outside world has an important role to play in influencing domestic policies that affect the global commons. Unlike the attempt to harmonize regulations, which are largely unnecessary, the world has an interest, indeed a duty to future generations, to reduce carbon emissions or overfishing on the high seas. It also has a humanitarian duty to absorb refugees. Binding international agreements are extremely important, but any effort to reach such agreements will be plagued by the asymmetric power, expertise, and information between countries, as well as the absence of democratic engagement from within countries. Perhaps when agreements are complicated with uncertain costs of compliance, they should start with "best efforts" pledges, with country-specific binding targets nailed down over time as domestic constituencies for commitment strengthen. In this light, the "best-efforts" Paris Agreement on climate change in 2015 seemed more sensible than the Kyoto Protocol in 1997, which tried to impose binding targets. Paris has a chance of success if countries debate their responsibilities domestically, and embed their democratically arrived consensus eventually in international commitments. Hopefully, the US withdrawal from the Paris Agreement will not be permanent, and simply reflects the need for greater domestic consensus.

The most difficult bucket of policies to address are those that have positive domestic effects but adverse international effects—the "beggar thy neighbor" policies. For instance, most central banks have domestic mandates—typically, they are required to keep inflation at around 2 percent. In normal times, central banks achieve this target through conventional monetary policy— raising or lowering interest rates—which has few sustained adverse external effects. In bad times, when their economies are mired in deflationary conditions, central banks may undertake actions, including unconventional monetary policies, which have the primary effect of depreciating the country's exchange rate and drawing demand from other countries. Today, nothing prevents a central bank from doing this, and it can be a source of misunderstanding and friction between countries. For instance, as I write this, there is considerable ire in Washington that Japanese monetary efforts in recent years have been primarily transmitted through a depreciated yen. Washington believes Tokyo is playing unfair by stealing growth from other countries, including the United States. Concerns about currency manipulation are part of the reason why Washington has recently slapped tariffs on Japanese aluminum and steel.

The reality is that with the world becoming more interconnected, more hitherto domestic policies will have international effects. While no country has a duty to undertake policies that help the world more than it helps the country, it does have a responsibility to avoid policies that do significant harm to others. No country will agree to place its central bank's policies under international supervision. It is also hard to imagine that policies can be coordinated among central banks so as to reduce such sources of tension. The Federal Reserve will set US monetary policy based on how it sees US conditions, while the Bank of Japan will do its best for Japan. Coordination will only cause confusion on what each central bank is trying to do.

Nevertheless, there is a possible improvement on the status quo, drawing on the idea that good fences make good neighbors. Countries could agree to a set of rules that will circumscribe what their central banks can do, eschewing policies that have serious or sustained adverse effects for everyone else.[11] Policies that have zero or positive effects outside the country should be given a free pass—conventional monetary policy will fall in this category. Policies that primarily have adverse external effects should be prohibited—sustained efforts to keep the domestic exchange rate depreciated would fall in this category. Finally, there would be a gray zone of policies that have large positive domestic effects and small negative external effects. These could be allowed temporarily. A considerable amount of work will have to go into identifying and negotiating rules. Unlike other global negotiations where the asymmetric capabilities among negotiators typically bias the outcomes, this would involve the largest central banks and finance ministries in the world, who all have strong capabilities.

A critical requirement in agreements of this kind on rules of the game, though, is for an impartial arbitrator to weigh in on difficult cases. Such an arbitrator should be able to enforce its decisions. Can any of the multilateral institutions play this role? Let us turn to that next.

MULTILATERAL INSTITUTIONS AND GLOBAL GOVERNANCE

As we saw earlier in the book, the victors in World War II, led by the United States, designed the postwar architecture that would govern international economic and political relations between countries. They naturally gave themselves extra powers, whether it was a permanent seat on the United Nations Security Council, veto powers over decisions in that Council, or large voting quotas at the International Monetary Fund. Even among the victors, the United States was supreme—for example, it alone, because of its large quota, enjoys a veto over important decisions by the International Monetary Fund.

The system worked reasonably well, so long as the United States felt confident of itself economically and militarily, for it could afford to be benevolent and not use the system too much to further its own interests. When the Soviet Union collapsed in 1991, the United States became the sole economic and military hegemon in the world. For a while, the structure of postwar institutions and the actual structure of power mirrored each other once again. While multilateral institutions like the United Nations General Assembly or the International Monetary Fund occasionally criticized the United States, in part to assert their independence, on important matters it was clear that the United States was the court of last resort.

In this environment, any rules in place constrained everyone else except the United States. Its views were dispositive because through a group of like-minded G7 nations—Canada, Japan, and the big Western European powers—it had enough votes to push through any measure, and through its funding, it controlled the purse strings of most multilateral organizations. This was not entirely bad, for the United States had a clear global agenda, where global interests coincided with its domestic interests; it worked toward a more open global system and took responsibility for delivering on that agenda, including ironing out the mini-crises that periodically shook markets.

There are reasons that this benevolent hegemony will not work as well going forward. The United States's relative economic superiority has eroded significantly over time. Increasingly, it is likely to be one of the players involved in disputes over monetary policy or trade or investment, and can no longer serve as the disinterested arbiter. Moreover, its political divisions that we discussed earlier in the book are turning it inward, and it is no longer likely to assume responsibility for international solutions or be as generous with its money. The periodic frustration in the United States about being the world's policeman (and paying the costs thereof) is now combined with the sense that others have caught up and are not paying their share of policing costs. Its populist nationalists seem to be intent on using the United States's immense economic and military power to extract every advantage from its relationships with allies, eroding the trust and goodwill that the United States had built up since World War II. Yet this kind of behavior makes the United States no different from the rest. Why then, countries ask, should it continue to have a privileged position at the center of global institutions, especially when it elects administrations that seem intent on undermining them?

Perhaps most important, with China growing rapidly, it is clear that the United States will not remain the largest economy in the world for much longer.[12] China wants more recognition and say in multilateral institutions. Indeed, it would be natural for it to want to take the place that the United States carved out for itself postwar. The privileges are many. For instance, in the International Monetary Fund's founding statutes, Article VIII, Section 1 states that the principal office of the Fund shall be located in the territory of the member having the largest shareholding, which typically goes by economic heft. So, by right, the Fund's head office should move soon from Washington to Beijing. The view of global economics from the Grand Canal in Beijing will look very different from what it seems from the shores of the Potomac in Washington.

With privilege, though, comes responsibility and costs. It is hard to see China slipping into the United States's position as benevolent hegemon smoothly, both because China's position is very different from that of the United States just after the war, and because the world is very different. No matter how we count and what we count, the world has become multipolar. Economically speaking, we have at least three big blocks, the United States, China, and the European Union. Militarily, we should add Russia. In this multipolar world, our institutions of global governance that have been structured for a unipolar world could get paralyzed if we do not reform them.

There is a window of opportunity as the structure of global power shifts, in which global institutions can be remade to serve the multipolar world better. These organizations have to become more independent of any single country or block, which requires reexamining shares, votes, and vetoes. Their recruitment and funding has to become more varied. Rather than depend on the will of a benevolent hegemon to resolve conflicts, they have to work out norms of international behavior or rules of the game in the key areas where international spillovers of policies cause frictions. Finally, they have to create impartial structures that can arbitrate disagreement. In other words, international organizations have to become more transparent and democratic.

All this requires a change in the behavior of countries also. Countries can no longer leave it to the United States to take responsibility for the system working. As they gain more power, large emerging markets have to take more responsibility. Some of these responsibilities will be embedded in the rules that evolve, but rules cannot cover all contingencies. Some responsibilities will be unspecified and vague—a general responsibility to step up and work with others in case of global calamity. This will require some countries to become comfortable with not having undisputed say, while others have to compromise so as to reach reasonable solutions. Global citizenship will imply both sovereign rights and international responsibilities.

There is a window of time in which developed countries legitimately have majority say in multilateral organizations because of their economic heft. They should not waste this time by trying to hang on to power—the world is changing and their relative economic weight will inevitably wane. They cannot become great again—if greatness means relative superiority—but they can share in a greater, better, world. They should use this period to alter the governance structure of these organizations to be more representative, democratic, and inclusive, so that when power actually shifts, they do not become a minority with little say. Democratization now is in their self-interest.

EUROPE: TO MOVE AHEAD, STAY, OR MOVE BACK?

Any discussion of integration obviously has to address Europe. It is now obvious that Europe moved faster and further than its people were ready for—certainly, once the costs of economic integration became apparent after the Global Financial Crisis.

Perhaps Europe's mistake was to go much beyond a common market in goods and services before solidarity had built up. The optimists want to move forward, integrating more so as to make it even more costly to exit the Union or the Euro, and hoping that European solidarity builds before the next crisis. The pessimists want to roll back past measures so that the extent of integration matches the solidarity that is currently available. The optimists fear that once momentum is lost, the dream of a united Europe will forever remain that. The pessimists don't want to lose everything that has been gained by overreaching, and forcing more countries to exit.

The pessimists are more practical, but the idea of Europe, indeed of world citizenship, is as much about idealism as it is about practicality. After all, empathy builds only when people get to know one another—European officials and students, who travel and work much more in other European countries, are far more sympathetic to the idea of Europe than those who travel little. That idealism needs to be more widely shared. Perhaps it is best to take small steps forward to keep the idea of the United States of Europe alive, but to wait till there is more solidarity among the peoples of Europe for large steps. And perhaps it would be wise to ask them this time!

CONCLUSION

Dani Rodrik from Harvard University has argued that globalization, democracy, and national sovereignty constitute a trilemma that are impossible to reconcile. Countries can have two but not all three. As with all supposed trilemmas, though, the difficulties of reconciling different objectives simply means that we cannot find doctrinaire or esthetically pleasing solutions. Most policies will have trade-offs, and countries will have to find ways of muddling through.

Attempts at globalization have gone too far in two ways. We have tried to encourage cross-border flows that are not strictly necessary for all countries to prosper, such as financial flows. Allowing them freely may indeed do damage to some countries. Decisions on whether to allow or disallow cross-border flows should largely be left to countries, with a few exceptions such as trade in goods and services, where the long term benefits for all (with a few narrow caveats) are clear. Here, there is a role for multilateral organizations to nudge countries to continue on the path of reducing tariffs on goods and services and binding them to be low. The benefits of a global competitive market are not just greater efficiency, but stronger and more independent private sectors in each country, and potentially stronger democracies.

At the same time, we should be less eager to harmonize rules and regulations across countries unless absolutely necessary to avoid high transactions costs. The process of setting these rules at the international level is not transparent and is undemocratic. Furthermore, harmonization reduces variety and competition between jurisdictions. Binding international agreements reduce the sense people have of self-determination, and should be used sparingly—to secure low tariffs but rarely to force harmonization of other rules and regulations. This is one way to reap the benefits of globalization while respecting democracy and national sovereignty.

Turning to domestic policies, countries should have a free hand except in two regards. First, we should evolve collective agreements or rules on the legitimacy of policies that have sustained adverse effects on other countries. Such policies should be flagged and the country asked to cease and desist, with the full weight of international bodies descending on defaulters. Second, actions such as creating carbon emissions or overfishing that affect the global commons should be subject to globally agreed limits, but through a process that engages the people of the countries in the targets to which they agree.

Globalization has to be managed. Countries have to regain the tools to manage it, which means steadily delegating back to countries the powers that international agreements have usurped. Even as sovereign powers to act are enhanced, countries have to accept they have international responsibilities. As countries obtain more control over globalization, the push toward self-interested nationalism could well be tempered by a realization that we do have to live together in the only home we have.

13

REFORMING MARKETS

Markets endanger themselves when they stop working for the broader citizenry, because it may rise up to shut them down. Today, some people are disenchanted because they feel large firms are closing opportunities for small firms and individuals. Others are angry because they have suffered painful losses of wealth and incomes and see little support forthcoming from the community or state. Yet others fear their jobs will be displaced by technology or foreign competition. For far too many, the markets have been disappointing. We must take actions to restore public faith in the power of markets to improve well-being.

Growth in the economic pie, which requires innovation and competition, will help. To enable this, barriers that currently protect dominant incumbents must be brought down so that markets are accessible by all. Everyone's ideas and products can then compete to generate that growth. Widely accessible markets are also less likely to be seen as only vehicles for the rich to grow richer. Within markets, powerful participants must be trusted to do the right thing by society. The right explicit objectives and monetary incentives for such participants will help, but so will community-provided social rewards for those who behave admirably. In this chapter, I will suggest three steps to help restore faith in markets and make them more reliable vehicles for sustainable inclusive growth.

First, people need to believe once more that corporations can be trusted to take the right actions for society's well-being. The mantra of shareholder value maximization worked well to dissuade the government from insisting that private corporations were extensions of government departments. Unfortunately, it has also led important constituencies, especially labor and the general public, to worry that top management is out to rip everyone off in the interests of shareholders. We need a better objective that promotes not just efficiency but also trust.

Second, a market dominated by a few is unlikely to create opportunities for the many. Competition today in an industry is the best way to guarantee society is benefited, not just today but also in the future. We have to examine and reduce barriers to competition, including new forms of incumbent property rights that have built up in recent years.

Finally, policies can help jump-start adjustment but both the market and the community will also adjust on their own over time. They should be given the space and time to do so.

CHANGING FROM PROFIT MAXIMIZATION TO VALUE MAXIMIZATION

We have seen that along with the search for more productive efficiency, shareholder value maximization also encourages aberrant behavior, such as violating implicit contracts with employees. Can corporations not do better? If the private sector is to be trusted by the community, and if it is to be a reliable check on the state, it does not just have to be well behaved, it has to be seen to be well behaved. At the same time, though, the private sector cannot give up its hard-nosed focus on productive efficiency, for that is an important contribution markets make to society. How can these varied goals be reconciled?

Maximizing the Value of the Firm

Shareholders are only one set of claimholders on the firm. One possible alternative is to ask top management to maximize the value of stakeholders in the firm, as is sometimes suggested to corporate bosses in Continental Europe. Yet this prescription needs, at the very least, to be fleshed out. Who exactly is a stakeholder? If a customer is one, is not one way of maximizing her value to give her everything she wants free? If so, how will the firm survive?

Here is a better alternative.[1] It may seem a small tweak, but it would alter firm behavior significantly in some situations. Not only would it increase firm value, but it would increase public understanding and support for the public corporation. Specifically, let the objective set for firm management be to maximize the value of the firm, but define firm value to be more than just the value of the financial investments in the firm. Let it also include the value of specific investments made in the firm by those who have a long-term attachment to it. So, for example, the investment made by an employee in learning a hotel's culture of hospitality is a specific investment. It is specific in that it has little value in another hotel with a different culture, and it is an investment because it takes time and effort for the employee to learn it. The value of that specific investment is the stream of additional profits the hotel will generate from the great customer experience provided by its long-term employees specialized in that culture. Others who make specific investments include long-term suppliers who have built a relationship with the hotel and have specialized personnel and equipment catering to it. In contrast, one-off suppliers who are protected by contract or price-conscious customers who flip-flop between hotels would not be deemed to have made specific investments in the hotel.

By taking as its objective the maximization of the value of financial and specific investments, management inspires greater trust in key constituents, offers a more socially acceptable picture of the corporation and, in fact, maximizes the economic value of the firm.

Why is this last statement true? Think of it this way. When management is bringing together the people and entities that make up the firm, it has no need to worry about those who have a passing relationship with the firm, or who are protected by contract. In Milton Friedman's framework, everyone but the equity holders were protected by contract. Hence, he postulated that management would maximize economic value by maximizing the value of equity. If the only unprotected entities in the firm were equity holders, our proposal would be consistent with that dictum. In practice, though, debt holders are unprotected when the hotel gets near financial default. Worse, those who have specific investments in the firm are rarely protected by contract, even in good times.

In many situations, our objective of firm value maximization would elicit similar behavior from management as when the objective is shareholder value maximization. Consider a couple of situations where it produces a better outcome. When the hotel is highly levered, management has an incentive to invest in riskier but high-yielding projects, which may even destroy value on net. The reason is that if the projects succeed, equity holders benefit from the substantial upside, while if they fail and the hotel goes into bankruptcy, highly levered equity has little to lose, and the losses are borne by the debtholders and the long-term employees. If hotel management were governed by our proposal, they would incorporate the loss from bankruptcy to creditors and employees in their assessments, and be more cautious in their investment.

Consider now an investment in training long-term employees in the specifics of the hotel's business and culture that generates more revenue for the hotel than the training costs. Assume that trained long-term employees can bargain for higher wages (because they now are better trained), and the increase in revenues is not enough to cover both the training costs and the increase in wages. The shareholder value maximizing management would not undertake the training because it negatively impacts profits. The firm value maximizing management would train, because it would see the higher wages going to long-term employees not as a cost, but merely a transfer from one set of firm investors (shareholders) to another (long-term employees). It would see the positive increase in revenue net of training costs as the total benefit to the firm.

The shift to firm value maximization is not just good for society (in that a value-enhancing investment takes place, regardless of how the fruits are shared), it is good for employees (since their wages go up), and it is even good for shareholders. This may seem strange since shareholders suffer a direct loss in profits from training the employees. This is where the words "specific investment" and "long-term" come in. If employees are expected to make substantial specific investments in the hotel's culture over time, they know they are tied to it because they would be reluctant to leave the hotel's employment and lose the additional wages that come from their specialization. Conversely, hotel management knows these are long-term employees.

When management commits to fair treatment of its investors, including employees, the expectation of fair treatment is then priced into the dealings they have. When employees join the firm initially, they have alternative choices. If they join a firm where management maximizes shareholder value only, employees know that when forced to choose between investing in employees and enhancing shareholder value, the firm will choose the latter if there is a conflict. Rationally, employees will know they will not see the increment to their wages if that firm had to make the training decision. They will therefore require additional compensation, equal to the prospective foregone increase in wages, to join a firm that does not invest in training relative to one that does. Consequently, the shareholder value maximizing firm saves nothing in wages over time. However, because it foregoes the additional net revenue from the investment in training, it is worse off economically. Put differently, the firm value maximizing firm will be valued higher, both by the stock market and by long-term employees, because it makes decisions that benefit both rather than playing one off against the other.

The law in some countries already urges management to behave in this way. In the United Kingdom, for example, the Companies Act requires the consideration of interests other than shareholders, including employees, customers, and suppliers provided it ultimately "promotes the success of the company."[2] Nevertheless, uncertainty over what exactly management will do in various situations can prevent the firm from benefiting fully from a clearly articulated objective. If the proposed objective is mandated in board policy and filters into managerial compensation structures, stock market investors will be able to predict management actions. They will bid up firm value appropriately. Equally, such commitment will enhance the legitimacy of corporate activity in the eyes of the public.

The firm value maximizing management will continue to take hard decisions, a necessity if the firm is to stay competitive and survive. If, for example, employees are overpaid, management has an incentive to negotiate employee salaries down. So long as the rationale is carefully explained and employee morale is not depressed significantly, not only will this benefit shareholders, it will benefit other key stakeholders, including employees, by ensuring the survival of the firm. The corporation also has no incentive to hold prices down to help the government, one of the fears that prompted Milton Friedman's article. Firm value maximization will ensure a continued separation between the corporate sector and the government. Tough decisions will continue to enhance productive efficiency, a key contribution of private corporations.

Will the firm desist from political lobbying? Lobbying is sometimes needed to correct truly misguided legislation, or to ensure that legislators have the full picture while framing legislation. These legitimate rationales for lobbying can undoubtedly serve as cover for more self-interested lobbying that benefits the corporation at the expense of society. A ban on lobbying would be near impossible to enforce, though. Far better, then, to follow Madison's cure for the problem of political interests—have enough corporations lobbying that no interest dominates and they compete to keep each other honest. This is one more reason to not have any industry or country dominated by a few large firms, a matter we will return to shortly.

Finally, what about corporate social responsibility? Firms should focus on business in normal times, maximizing the value of the firm while obeying the law. Broader social responsibility should be left to the state and the community, enriched by the value the firm creates and the taxes it pays—the only exception is if the firm operates in a society where both the state and the community are totally dysfunctional. This is not to discourage actions firms take to attract a certain kind of employee or to improve their public image. For example, some firms will allow their employees to devote some of their time to voluntary social work. To the extent that this enables them to induct the right kind of employee, or allows employees to stay motivated by seeing a larger purpose in their jobs, and to the extent it allows the firm to be more acceptable to the community, it actually increases firm value. However, movements that want corporations to have a "social conscience" beyond this will risk undermining their hard-nosed focus on productivity, and thus their key contribution to the economy—producing a useful product at the least cost and sold cheaply, thus benefiting consumers and creating jobs. Overburdening the corporation with what truly should be done by the community and the state ensures it will do none of these tasks well.

Even in a functional society, though, the corporation must act in extraordinary times. When fundamental principles of society such as rule of law, fundamental rights, and democracy are being threatened, a corporation cannot stick to business and free-ride on the political activities of others. If every corporation does that, an enormous source of power is neutered, and society's underpinnings are more likely to crumble. At such times, corporations that do not use their power are much like those who keep earth-moving equipment under lock and key as society copes with an earthquake. In extraordinary circumstances—and it is a difficult judgment call for corporate boards and management to decide when such a situation prevails—corporations should act even if they do not enhance firm value directly, simply because of the power society has entrusted them with. In doing so, they maximize societal value, not just economic value.

ENHANCING COMPETITION TO BUILD TRUST IN MARKETS

A second aspect of markets that needs attention is the degree of competition in them, and the increasing dominance of large firms in each sector. Let us start first with competition.

Industry Dominance and Market Power

The benign view of an industry dominated by a few large firms has much to do with the Austrian economist Joseph Schumpeter. He believed that competitive discipline did not come from existing competitors in the market at a point in time, but from the disruptive innovator who would strike "not at the margins of the profits and their outputs of the existing firms but at their foundations and their very lives."[3] Schumpeter's view was that a monopoly firm's paranoia about possible future threats to its monopoly profits would be the spur to innovation, and the reason it would give its customers a good deal. The continuation of its monopoly would be its reward.

However, as argued earlier, the stock market may reward an incumbent monopolist with the high share price and fund-raising capacity that allows him to threaten anyone who enters with a bruising fight, and to buy out any innovator. Perhaps, then, the presence of other incumbents who have similar resources may prevent the stock market from anointing any one incumbent, and may prove better for competition, both on current prices and on innovation. Put differently, while the prospect of maintaining a monopoly is a spur to innovation, being forced to start the race for that prize at the same starting line, rather than many paces in front, is an additional spur. Schumpeter's theory about the irrelevance of current industry structure is not fully persuasive—competition today may be necessary for competition tomorrow.

THE CASE AGAINST GIGANTISM

Is there anything else that can guide us? Are there any other dangers to industry dominance by a few large firms? Our discussion throughout this book suggests that the larger and fewer the firms in an economy, the easier it is for them to do deals with the state to protect their position.[4] Conversely, a state that seeks to concentrate power in its hands needs to persuade only these few large players with carrots or sticks. Perhaps the most successful examples of outside interventions to create liberal democracies were the postwar transformations of defeated fascist Germany and Japan. A key step there was the insistence by the American-occupying authority that big business cartels and combines be broken up. Indeed, the Celler-Kefauver Act passed by the United States Congress in 1950 attempted to reduce the dominance of any industry by a few firms within the United States, in part because "centralizing of corporate control also threatened to destroy a democratic system requiring decentralized private as well as political power."[5]

Society cannot afford to be complacent. Democracy requires constant vigil, and the need for corporate independence from the state suggests a mild bias against corporate gigantism, especially if it does not come at the expense of corporate efficiency. In this vein, the owners of small and medium enterprises or well-to-do professionals are the modern equivalent of the seventeenth-century British gentry. They are not large enough to do individual deals with the state or to monopolize their industries. They are rich enough, though, to not depend on government support, and indeed can fund movements pushing their favorite causes. This independent small-holder group needs open access and a level playing field. It constitutes the vanguard of any movement for broader economic and political opportunity. Therefore, any economic system has to also be judged by whether it preserves room for new entrants and fast-growing small and medium firms. As we have noted, the pace of new business creation is falling in the United States, as are the number of start-ups that stay independent.

A final, and separate, rationale for encouraging new entrants and fostering dynamism is that small and medium enterprises also tend to be contained within specific communities and can do more for those communities.[6] In work that I have done with coauthors, we find that large banks are more able to lend to large firms that have good accounting records, while small banks are much more able to lend to small nearby firms that operate more informally.[7] Intuitively, decisions by small banks can be made by the owner or manager assessing the trustworthiness of the potential borrower through direct meetings, and substantiated with information from the local grapevine—while decisions by loan officers of large banks have to be sufficiently supported with hard records so that they pass muster with headquarters, or can be checked by inspection teams.[8] Small banks are therefore better at local, informal, lending. Indeed, such studies validate the Pilsen community's strong desire to rescue its local community bank (discussed in the Preface).

So what does all this mean for antitrust policy? Antitrust authorities should examine mergers for the possibility of industry dominance, not just from the perspective of whether the customer is better served today, but also whether competition will be irretrievably altered. For instance, acquisitions that have the primary objective of closing an innovative competitor, or absorbing a rival who might prove a competitive threat, should be prohibited. Preserving competition today may also be essential so that the stock market does not give a dominant incumbent the resources with which to shut out competition tomorrow. The pragmatic solution is to adopt once again the clear and defensible *rules of thumb* of the past, whereby antitrust authorities opposed corporate actions that increased a single corporation's dominance of any market beyond a preset specified point, no matter what the claims about greater efficiency and consumer welfare were. Antitrust authorities must be broad-minded about what constitutes the relevant market and competition, recognizing that technology can bring product and geographic markets together that were separated in the past. However, arguments that innovation or entry by rivals will make the market more competitive in the future should be met with some skepticism—today's dominance can allow the incumbent to alter conditions so as to make it much harder for rivals to get their foot in the door in the future.

The economic costs of rule-of-thumb antitrust enforcement may not be large as information technology improves, and as contracting and monitoring costs fall. Instead of a company owning the entire supply chain, we could get a more nimble, competitive supply chain consisting of many corporations contracting with one another. Instead of a company merging with all competitors who produce a product, ostensibly to obtain economies of scale, we could instead retain many competitors who cooperate on specific projects through alliances whenever the economies of scale of doing so are really significant. Put differently, corporations will adapt to effective antitrust enforcement, and given the improvements in contracting and communications, we will likely get both competition and productive efficiency at the same time.

INTELLECTUAL PROPERTY AS A SOURCE OF MARKET POWER

In the new economy being created by the ICT revolution, information, knowledge, creative works, and ideas—broadly termed intellectual property—are the key assets. Such intangible assets are nonrival—if I sing or listen to a song, it does not preclude you from singing or listening to that same song. If a song could be sung by anybody, the songwriter could never benefit monetarily from her creativity; without legal protection, intellectual property, especially property that needs to be used publicly, would have no value.

In addition to being nonrival, though, intellectual property is often essential and unique. These two characteristics make protected intellectual property a very great source of monopoly power, far greater than that obtained from physical property, for which there typically are substitutes. Moreover, because intellectual property gets its value from past innovation and government protection rather than necessarily the owner's continued innovativeness or efficiency, it tends to make the private sector more dependent on the government for protection than would be the case with physical property; it draws behemoth and leviathan closer.

One example of such protection is patents, which aim to encourage innovation. It is unclear that the patent awardee has a strong incentive to innovate further after acquiring the patent. Economists Michele Boldrin and David Levine, strong critics of the patenting system, argue that bursts of innovation start out in competitive industries.[9] Patents are typically filed after a substantial amount of time has passed. The filings tend to obscure key steps so as to keep competitors from stealing a march, even though this defeats the purpose of patenting—which is to reveal the underlying secrets for all to build on in exchange for a period of government-protected monopoly. By the time patents are approved, the flurry of innovation that moved the industry to new heights has abated. As a result, they argue, patents typically serve to protect the positions of incumbents against entrants and rivals, rather than spur additional innovation.

The patenting process has to manage the tension between two fundamental aspects of the free enterprise system—the need to protect property rights as a reward for past effort and the need to preserve competition as a spur to current initiative. Too much patent protection, and we chill competition. Too little, and we may deter effort. It is unclear whether patent protection achieves the right tradeoff in the United States today, but clearly small innovators are disfavored in a number of ways. Even if they are awarded a patent, single patents are easy for large firms to navigate around or to challenge. Few good lawyers are willing to work to defend a single patent on a contingency fee basis (where the lawyer gets paid only when the plaintiff wins), and most small entrepreneurs cannot afford to pay legal fees otherwise.

A more effective strategy is to develop a cluster of patents that will trip up a violator no matter how they contort themselves to explain their strategy, but such extensive patenting is something that typically only large firms can afford. Indeed, large firms often seem to use their patents not so much to protect their innovations but as a possible counterthreat against rivals who sue for patent infringement. Given the thicket of patents that have been awarded in recent years, corporations have invariably violated one another's patents. In such cases, patents, like nuclear weapons, are valuable primarily because they can be used to threaten mutually assured legal destruction. If so, would all sides except lawyers not be better off with no patents? In sum, in an environment where corporate dominance of industry and rising concentration of income are important sources of concern, it is probably wise to reduce the contribution of patents to market power, even while monitoring closely the effect of these changes on innovation.

The reforms that should be considered include being more careful about what can be patented—Apple received a patent for the shape of the iPad, while drug companies received patents for genes.[10] The first trivializes patenting, while the second gives drug companies too much power for something that already exists in nature—which is why such patents were eventually denied by the Supreme Court.[11] In general, patent offices should adhere to their mandate of granting patents for nonobvious bigger ideas rather than allow every minor extension of existing ideas to be patented. Furthermore, patents should not be for longer than necessary to give the inventor a reasonable profit. Today, all patents last for twenty years, driven in part by drug companies, which take a long while to test their drugs and get approval before they go to market. An alternative could be to allow a patent to expire twenty years after filing or (say) eight years after a product using the patent is sold in the market, whichever occurs first. This will limit the extraordinary profits that accrue to software producers, who need little time to reach the market and enjoy nearly twenty years of protected sales.

Finally, given the criticality of the patenting process to innovation, it is important that more well-trained talented people should be hired into government patent offices. It may be relevant to note that one of the examiners in the patent office in Bern, Switzerland, between 1902 and 1909 was a certain Albert Einstein.[12]

Data as Market Power

Information is power today. When an e-commerce platform like Amazon or Alibaba collects data on the sales and receipts of a merchant selling on their platform (and perhaps buying on it), they have a good sense of the merchant's cash flows, and thus his creditworthiness. This allows them to lend to the merchant. Over time, when the platform sees the merchant service loans regularly, it can entrust him with larger loans, thus allowing him to grow his business. Given its privileged access to the information, the platform can charge a hefty interest on the loans. In other words, if the platform owns the merchant's data, it can refuse to share it with others (and his own records may neither be well maintained nor credible). It has a lock on him. The data are both essential and unique, which gives the platform tremendous economic power.

What if the merchant owned the data he generated? What if the platform were forced to send data (in standardized digital form) on the merchant's

sales and receipts as well as his loans and repayments, to any entity the merchant directed it to share with? The platform would lose its information monopoly. It would still collect the information, hoping the merchant would
borrow from it, but it would have to compete with other possible financiers
on service or ability to analyze the data, rather than get a step up based on its
privileged information. The change in property rights, from the data being
implicitly owned by the platform to it being explicitly owned by the merchant, changes the allocation of power and profits from the platform to the
merchant. Indeed, the European Payment Services Directive that came into
force in January 2018 requires banks to share their depositors' current account transactions data with any third party specified by the depositor, thus
freeing customers from the hold of their bank.

In this Information Age, therefore, the individual or small business needs
to own their own data if they are to be free economically.[13] The one exception
could be when firms invest substantial amounts in gathering and processing
data into usable form, when some kind of profit-sharing arrangement from
the use of the data ought to be worked out.

Customer ownership of their own data is not an impossible ideal, especially given the advances in data processing. If the interface between the customer and the application, the application itself, and the customer data it uses
are all separate, any data collected on a customer could be maintained in
standardized but decentralized fashion. Any designated recipient could re-
create structures like the web of social relationships the individual has, and
their likes and dislikes.[14] Most of us would not be able to manage our data,
but if there is a need, the market will respond. It is easy to visualize the emergence of trusted information utilities, with no ties to firms that use the data.
The individual could authorize the utility to map out where the individual's
data lie, what is used and how. The utility could partition data into various
buckets depending on their usefulness for different purposes, enabling the
individual to grant or withdraw usage permission (a potential financier does
not need to know her dating preferences, even if they could be marginally
useful in the decision to approve her loan application).

Once the individual controls her data, she will have the option to sell portions of it to firms, or enter into longer-term arrangements where firms would
provide her services in return for the use of her data. Some of what is implicit

today would become explicit, the difference is it would be controlled by the user. Indeed, new technologies like blockchains will help decentralize this process, and bargaining bots can help routinize data acquisition for a fee when corporations need vast amounts of data to train their artificial-intelligence applications.[15]

Another important source of power that e-platforms or social media have is their ownership of the network. If an individual leaves a network, her access to it, and to the many relationships she has built on it, are cut off. This causes many to stay on even if they dislike the network and its services. In other words, as the size of the network grows, the degree to which people are attached also grows (since more of their relationships are on it), and the more value is extracted by the network.

Some countries deal with this problem by placing the ownership of the network in the public domain. For instance, in India, electronic retail payments are made over a bridge called the Unified Payments Interface (UPI), which has been developed by a corporation owned by all the banks. An individual with an account in a bank or platform like Google, WhatsApp, or Alipay, can make payments over the bridge to anyone who has an account in any other bank or company. No entity owns the network, but all benefit from it.

Public ownership of the network is not necessary so long as a country mandates interoperability between networks. If an individual wants to leave social network A and go to social network B, she should still have access to all her relationships in network A, and they should have access to her in network B. The networks may not have exactly the same functions and features, but much as calls are connected between networks run by different mobile companies, social networks should also be interconnected. Of course, the networks will negotiate some interchange fee based on the net requests for connections.

The objective in all this is not to eliminate the profitability of innovation, but to reduce the economic power corporations and platforms acquire through intellectual property, data, and network externalities that tie users in. By redefining ownership of intellectual property and the data, and shifting more of the latter into the hand of the users who create it, as well as by requiring networks be interoperable, power will be rebalanced. As the temptation to acquire monopolies is reduced, corporations and platforms will have to compete harder on the products and services they provide. This is as it should be.

REDUCING REGULATIONS THAT LIMIT COMPETITION

Regulations are not necessarily bad. For example, the presence of the Food and Drug Administration and the knowledge that it has vetted a new food producer allows consumers to have more confidence in the safety of the food produced, and thus facilitates entry by new food producers. Large incumbent firms have more of an ability to deal with regulations, though, and regulatory bureaucracies have an incentive to churn out more regulations to justify their existence. The *New York Times* estimated a total of about five thousand restrictions and rules that applied just to an apple orchard, including a large number on how precisely a ladder should be placed.[16] Lighter, more meaningful regulation that does not overly burden small and medium enterprises and chill entry has to be a reform priority.

Non-compete clauses, which prevent individuals from moving to rival firms that value them more, are a restraint on individual choice, and may prevent the diffusion of knowledge that helps elevate productivity in entire industries and keep them competitive. California, one of the most innovative states, does not have them. Why should others?

Just as corporations have tried to protect themselves against competition by merging, professionals, especially the more skilled ones, have tried to protect themselves against competition by licensing entry strictly into their professions. One reason we get so much occupational licensing is because every local jurisdiction has its own licensing authority. They have to justify their existence by claiming local professional needs are special, hence the need for a separate local license to practice. In addition, the licensing authority are often practicing professionals. Giving them the power of determining licensing requirements is much like putting the fox in charge of chicken coop security. Both features of occupational licensing must change.

For most professions, except the ones where local requirements are actually different, there should only be a national license. In the spirit of allowing local decision making, communities could be free to set local licensing norms, but those norms should not be stricter than national norms. In other words, a locality, intent on increasing employment, could allow manicurists with less training than the national norm to practice locally, but the locality should not be able to set the norm for training at a stricter level than the national norm so as to keep out manicurists from elsewhere. This is in the spirit of keeping internal borders open to trade in goods and services that we discussed earlier. Finally, if there are significant local differences in conditions that require local licensing, these should be addressed through a supplementary local license that only tests for the ability to handle the additional local issues. Furthermore, it would be best that national licensing norms are set by panels of laypersons who are advised by the professional experts, much as any kind of legislation is written. That would place some public oversight over the licensing process, and ensure it is not set by the professionals for the professionals.

ALLOWING THE MARKET AND COMMUNITY TO ADJUST

Not every aberration or distortion needs policy action. Sometimes the market itself creates the incentives for correction. For instance, the wage differential between the skilled and the moderately skilled has stopped growing, as we noted earlier. The high wages of doctors attract more youngsters to become doctors (supplementing any natural inclination toward medicine). It also creates strong monetary incentives for tech firms to create artificial-intelligence medical diagnostic systems, where ordinary doctors could be replaced by nurse practitioner interviewers with far less training. The competitive market targets those who benefit the most from it since the profits these entities make are most worth disrupting. Therefore, even as the quality and quantity of health care expands significantly, and even as countries grow older and richer, the need for doctors could moderate, normalizing their wages and reducing income inequality.

Similarly, the abundance of machine-made or foreign goods, and the fall in local wages, could also prompt a shift in taste toward goods with more human and local content. We already see some of this. The more accurate but cheap quartz or digital watch has been displaced by painstakingly hand-crafted and intricate mechanical watches at the high end of the luxury scale.

Local farmers markets pop up like mushrooms in rich suburbs or cities in the United States, as customers abandon the supermarket for local produce. Consumer tastes could shift. Jobs that require working with one's hands rather than with one's mind or that require local work could reemerge, once again reducing the wage premium to education.

Markets or Community?

That said, some of the adjustment will also come from communities adjusting the reach of the market and limiting where the market will go. Consider a situation that Harvard philosopher Michael Sandel describes: Some companies in the United States pay the unemployed to stand in line for free public tickets to congressional hearings.[17] They then sell the tickets to lobbyists and corporate lawyers who have a business interest in the hearing but are too busy to stand in line. Public hearings are an important element of participatory democracy. All citizens should have equal access. So selling access seems a perversion of democratic principles, which is why Sandel criticizes it. How should we see his example in the light of this book?

First, let us be clear what is at stake. The fundamental problem is scarcity. We cannot accommodate everyone who might have an interest in a particularly important hearing in the room. Therefore, we have to ration entry. We can either allow people to use their time (as they stand in line) to bid for seats, or we can auction seats for money. The former seems fairer, because all citizens seemingly start with equal endowments of time—we all start with twenty-four hours in a day. However, is a single mother with a high-pressure job and three young children as equally endowed with spare time as a student on summer vacation? Is society better off if she, the chief legal counsel in a large corporation, spends much of her time standing in line for hearings?

Whether it is better to sell entry tickets for time or for money thus depends on what we hope to achieve. If we want to increase society's productive efficiency—the realm of the market—people's willingness to pay with money is a reasonable indicator of how much they will gain if they have access to the hearing. Auctioning seats for money makes sense—the lawyer contributes more to society by preparing briefs than standing in line. On the other hand, if it is important that young impressionable citizens see how their democracy works, if it is important that we build social solidarity by making corporate executives stand in line with jobless teenagers—in short, if we want to build a sense of community—perhaps we should make entry tickets nontransferable and make people bid with their time by standing in line. If we think that both objectives should play some role, perhaps we should turn a blind eye to some operators hiring those with spare time to stay in line in lieu of busy lawyers, so long as they do not corner all the seats.

The appropriate answer, therefore, depends on the conditions in society. In an environment where we worry about the overly strong association between incomes and capabilities, and the unequal access to acquiring capabilities, it is probably wise to emphasize community relative to markets. There are undoubtedly times and places where the reverse may be true, something Sandel does not emphasize.

More generally, though, one of the community's reactions to a meritocratic ladder few can climb is to establish other ladders that more people can climb. Reducing the range of things that money can buy can increase the space for such nonmarket activity. Engagement with the church, in community leadership and service, in government or military service, with charitable organizations, and with the family and kin, are alternative ladders that are respected in their own right. By imposing clear limits on the market—one cannot buy public office, professional accomplishments, military glory, unconditional love . . . and even seats for a congressional hearing—a community allows nonmarket pathways to self-actualization. When the community honors other achievements than the accumulation of wealth, the wealthy are envied less and imitated less, and the community is cohesive despite some wealth inequality.[18] Sandel is right that economists should not be too hasty in attempting to monetize everything!

THE ROLE OF COMMUNITY VALUES IN CHANGING THE TOLERANCE FOR MARKETS

As we have seen through history, community values are not static, they do respond over time to take advantage of opportunities created by the market, or to offset the problems it creates. This will be part of the necessary change. In India, for example, over my lifetime a very socialist distrust of markets has given way to a grudging celebration of its benefits. In the Hindi movies I saw in my childhood, the arch villain was typically a businessman, usually found at the horse races with a glass of whisky, a cigar, and a moll clinging to his arm, even while his henchmen evicted the poor hero and his mother from their humble abode. Today, the hero is often likely to be a successful software entrepreneur, jet-setting across the world to woo his equally accomplished love interest. The move away from sham socialism in India since the early 1990s has made market success more worthy of emulation than in the past.

In contrast, Hollywood has typically had a somewhat suspicious attitude toward business, perhaps to offset the more celebratory views of capitalism that prevail in the mainstream United States. It is worth noting, though, that this view may be turning yet more jaundiced today, consistent with a belief that the market has overreached. Even a children's film, *The LEGO Movie,* whose intent was, in part, to increase the sales of LEGO toys to small children, has "Lord Business" as its villain.[19] Society is not better informed when the individualistic clean-cut entrepreneurial heroes of Ayn Rand's novels are transmogrified into Lord Business. Both extremes are caricatures, targeted at the impressionable. Nevertheless, they do reflect, each in its own time, attempts to change social attitudes toward the market, attempts that can indeed help in restoring the balance. They are not unhealthy for society.

In a similar vein, we have seen a shift in public attitudes toward big technology companies across the developed world. Their size and profitability, their ability to target individuals with features and feeds that hook them into staying connected, and their power to influence the political opinions of large numbers of people directly would have been alarming in the past. Nevertheless, they escaped both careful scrutiny and regulation, because people seemed entranced by their ostensibly free products, the enormous wealth of their youthful entrepreneurial bosses, their idealistic corporate vision statements, and their seeming innocence of the sordid real world. The reality that these are profit-maximizing corporations, which have been careless about the degree to which they have intruded on customer privacy, and that have let their access and trust be misused by third parties, has come as a public shock. It is prompting the usual zeal by authorities to punish and overcorrect after having been asleep at the wheel. The public suspicion of these companies now matches the broader concern about the behavior of large corporations in traditional industries. As we move back to balance, we will also undoubtedly figure out the right mix of credulity and suspicion with which to treat these companies.

CONCLUSION

The temptation when imbalances arise is to hack all the pillars down to the lowest height among them. This typically will bring back equilibrium, but at a much lower level for society. Far better to push a pillar down only if absolutely necessary, and instead, focus on elevating all pillars to the greatest common level. That is the only way society will progress. In this vein, the temptation today will be to constrain competitive markets to give communities a chance at recovery. That might unleash other forces such as cronyism that would be hard to reverse. Instead, it is better to improve the functioning of the market, even while also refocusing the state and strengthening the community.

EPILOGUE

The three pillars that support society—the state, markets, and the community—are in constant flux, buffeted by economic and technological shocks. Society perpetually strives for a new equilibrium, through a rebalancing of the pillars. The ICT revolution, accompanied by the Global Financial Crisis of 2007–2008, has once again highlighted the need for rebalancing. Recent elections across the developed world suggest people are deeply dissatisfied with the current state of affairs.

The ICT revolution has created a meritocracy, which is close to hereditary in some developed countries. Moreover, in reaction to the competition generated by global markets, those who can, such as large corporations and professionals, have created protected enclaves for themselves, further enhancing the benefits of being part of the higher meritocracy. For the rest, outside the walled and moated enclaves, competition from man and machine from across the globe has been fierce. For the unprotected, new opportunities, preserved for the privileged by walls of credentials and licenses, have been hard to access, in part because educational ladders have been too short and rickety. In part, they also have been inaccessible because the greatest opportunities have emerged in global cities, where limited space and zoning laws have made residence unaffordable for most. As economic activity has moved away from rural and semi-urban communities, despair and social disintegration has moved in. With the establishment discredited, there is widespread desire for new answers. The demagogues of the left and right propose answers people want to hear, not what they should hear. All too often, there is someone else or something else to blame, which then imposes the burden of change elsewhere. That is comforting to their audiences but dangerously misleading. The reality is that we all are part of the problem, and we all can be part of the solution.

In the last five chapters, I have laid out a possible path to a new balance, a way to resist the seemingly inexorable diminution of the community, even while preserving the open access that markets provide us. The intent is to build the pillars up, rather than reduce them to the lowest common denominator. The essence of this new balance is inclusive localism. We can use the tools we have obtained through the ICT revolution to empower communities more, to give people more of a sense of control over their futures, in the process creating and distributing economic and political power. At the same time, I argue for a national framework that is inclusive, in that all ethnicities are seen as part of the nation, and the nation does not entrench differences in economic opportunity between ethnicities or classes. Inclusive localism breaks down gigantic walls protecting privilege, while encouraging tiny walls to preserve community character.

The hope is that such a path helps us hold on to the best aspects of a system that has contributed to global prosperity—primarily the open access and competition stemming from global markets—while dealing with the inequality and fear generated by technological change. Specifically, for some of us, inclusive localism fulfills at the community level the natural human instinct to congregate with others similar to us. It thus heads off more divisive and artificial attempts in diverse nations to fulfill that tribal instinct at the national level through populist nationalism. Also, by enhancing the local infrastructure, the means of building capabilities, and the safety net at the community level, inclusive localism attempts to broaden and equalize opportunities. It allows each community's members to participate in, and benefit from, global markets.

The proposed path builds on what we have. I do not advocate dispensing with any of the pillars—I neither recommend eliminating markets and private property nor do I suggest putting everything, including governance, for sale. The state is necessary, but has to cede power to the community and can be much more effective. The community is essential for us to express our humanity, but it needs to carve out space from both markets and the state to

flourish. Even if seemingly moderate, the reform path is ambitious for it es-
chews easy but often wrong solutions.

We also need to recognize realities. Deep down, the vast majority of us
recognize the human in one another. Yet we need to come close enough to do
that, and all too often, we label at a distance. Understanding and tolerance of
other cultures is not a weakness, not a sign of inadequate patriotism, not an
indication that we are rootless "citizens of nowhere." In reality, it reflects our
preparation for the world of tomorrow, where we will become ever more
mixed as peoples, even as we study, value, and preserve our collective cultural
heritage. The world is not there yet. Therefore, we need to take smaller, easier
steps, where there is room for all as we develop a better understanding of one
another. The strengthening of proximate communities will not just allow a
diversity of views, including the most tribal and the most cosmopolitan, to
exist. It will also allow us to preserve direct social interaction, which may well
be where more of the jobs of the future lie, as automation depletes jobs in sectors that produce commercial goods and services.

It may be that the changes that are about to hit us will be more extraordinary than anything we have seen. Maybe most of us will be unemployed in a
decade, rendered redundant by robots and generalized artificial superintel-
ligence. I doubt it—ever since the 1950s, experts have been predicting that
generalized artificial intelligence, that is algorithms that can replace humans
fully, is less than a couple of decades away—but I also do not fear that outcome, so long as we preserve the balance. That we are unemployed will mean
that machines are doing our work more cheaply, that the cost of goods and
services will fall, and their quality increase, to reflect the greater productivity
of machines. As Keynes argued nearly a hundred years ago, we will be freed
to contemplate the finer elements of our existence, to create and cherish great
art and beauty, to value goodness rather than just commercial success.[1]

Many of us fear that we will not have the incomes for such a fine life, since
the machines will be owned by a few, and all income will flow to them. Yet as
our excursion through history suggests, social values change. We glorified
the victorious warrior, we then turned to praise merchants and bankers,
today we place successful entrepreneurs on a pedestal, and we may exalt community workers tomorrow. If the distribution of wealth becomes skewed towards a very few, the few may decide their accumulation of wealth unseemly

and find ways to give it back. Society will aid that process by muting its applause for the captains of industry who only accumulate, while increasing it for those who distribute wisely. Indeed, this already seems underway with the Giving Pledge, where billionaires across the world have pledged to give away at least half their wealth.

Even if values do not change, the feared outcome of mass poverty amid productive plenty will not come to pass if we maintain our democracy, and the separation between behemoth corporations and the leviathan state. For property rights are a social construct, created and enforced only with the tolerance of the people. If incomes and wealth do get more skewed toward a few owners, democracy will turn from protecting the property of the few to preserving opportunity for the many, as it has done before. Only the coalition of the behemoth and the leviathan, subverting democracy to enforce the property rights of the few and the poverty of the many, can stand in the way. This possibility is still in the future, and we need to ensure we never get there by keeping our democracy strong and vigilant, and the realm of the market and government separate. The path I propose will help us do this.

A more immediate problem many countries face is population aging. In the near future, some countries will have a surfeit of jobs they need to fill, rather than too few jobs. They will have excess physical capital—infrastructure, plant and machinery, buildings and houses—that will go waste. For countries like Japan that have largely homogenous populations, the temptation will be to use more machines, thus avoiding the problems of coping with the diversity that stems from immigration. That is a choice aging countries with homogenous populations will have to make—to choose loneliness for their elderly or to accept initial culture shock and then adaptation. For aging countries with already diverse populations, the responsible choice ought to be steady and controlled immigration, with the objective of integrating immigrants and making them full and active citizens. Once again, the path I propose offers ways to attract and integrate immigrants, while maintaining the support of the native-born population.

I have said little about one of our most pressing problems, climate change and associated problems like water scarcity. It may well be that technological change will allow us to address this more easily in the future. For instance, cheap renewable energy like solar or wind power, storable in large batteries and powering our cars, trucks, and factories, can help us reduce carbon emissions significantly. If it also powers reverse osmosis plants generating fresh water from sea water, and helps pipe that water inland, we can solve problems of water scarcity, and transform many a desert into lush farmland. We must also be prepared, though, for the possibility that technology develops too slowly, and we do have to deal with climate change through more painful collective measures. We cannot afford self-interested, zero-sum nationalism if the fate of the world is in question. Instead, we need responsible internationalism. By weakening our propensity for jingoistic nationalism, inclusive localism will allow us to embrace responsibility as a nation.

Finally, the historical excursions in this book suggest hope. Our values are not static—they change. Dr. Martin Luther King Jr. said, "The arc of the moral universe is long but it bends towards justice." When seen over short stretches, it seems that history repeats, that racism and militant nationalism erupt periodically in the world to sow hatred and spawn conflict. Yet the society that experiences these movements is not the same, it trends toward being more tolerant, more respectful, and more just. Around that trend line, we do go up and down. We may be down today, and we have a long way to go, but the distance we have come should give us hope. Let us not let the future surprise us. Instead, let us shape it. There is much to do. We have to, we must, choose wisely if we want to live together well and in peace. I am confident we can.

ACKNOWLEDGMENTS

This book is a collective effort, even if it has a single author. My wife, Radhika, has been with me every step of the way, debating, correcting, criticizing, and always encouraging. This book has come together only because of her, and is as much a product of her effort as it is mine. My children have constantly challenged my thinking and forced me to sharpen my ideas. I also owe any appreciation of modern sensibilities and social media that I have to them. My mother-in-law passed away suddenly during the writing of this book. She was always eager to engage in debate, and taught me much, even while showering me with love. She will be deeply missed. My parents have, as always, been supportive, and I thank them every day for the childhood they gave me that, alas, too few children in this world get.

I owe many of the ideas in this book to the stimulating environment at the University of Chicago's Booth School of Business, where I have spent the best part of my academic life. The work I have coauthored with Luigi Zingales is central to some of the ideas in this book. Work with Rodney Ramcharan has also been enormously relevant to some of the themes in this book. Both were very generous with their comments on an earlier draft. I have also benefited from discussions with, and comments from, Marianne Bertrand, Steve Davis, Douglas Diamond, Eugene Fama, Rob Gertner, Chang-Tai Hsieh, Erik Hurst, Steven Kaplan, Anil Kashyap, Yueran Ma, Bhanu Pratap Mehta Lubos Pastor, Sam Peltzman, Eswar Prasad, Ram Shivakumar, Amir Sufi, Chad Syverson, Richard

Thaler, Rob Vishny, and Eric Zwick. Rohit Lamba and Prateek Raj were especially kind in going through the early chapters and giving me detailed useful comments. Krishna Kamepalli and Adarsh Kumar provided very helpful research assistance.

I had very useful conversations with Douglas Baird, Marshall Bouton, Mark Carney, Dipesh Chakrabarty, Raj Chetty, John Cochrane, Matt Gentzkow, Rakesh Kochhar, Prachi Mishra, David Nirenberg, Josh Rauh, and James Robinson over the course of this book.

Max Brockman, my agent, has been very supportive of this project from the outset and helped get the book into the hands of my editor, Scott Moyers. Scott is the ideal editor, always encouraging while shaping early drafts of the book into something far better. I also am grateful to the team at Penguin Random House, including Christina Caruccio (who did a fine job copyediting the book), Mia Council, Sarah Hutson, and Christopher Richards.

Finally, I thank the Center for Research on Securities Prices, the Stigler Center, and the Initiative on Global Markets, all at the University of Chicago's Booth School, for funding support.

NOTES

PREFACE

1. Anne Case and Angus Deaton, "Rising morbidity and mortality in midlife among white non-Hispanic Americans in the 21st century," *Proceedings of the National Academy of Sciences* 112, no. 49 (November 02, 2015), doi:10.1073/pnas.1518393112.

2. This is from dictionary.com. http://www.dictionary.com/browse/community?s=t. According to *Merriam-Webster* online, a community is "the people with common interests living in a particular area." https://www.merriam-webster.com/dictionary/community

3. Raj Chetty and Nathaniel Hendren, "The Impacts of Neighborhoods on Intergenerational Mobility I: Childhood Exposure Effects," rev. ed. NBER Working Paper No. 23001, May 2017.

4. See Hannah Arendt, *The Origins of Totalitarianism*, (Orlando: Harvest, 1994).

5. The term "imagined community" is associated with Benedict Anderson, *Imagined Communities: Reflections on the Origin and Spread of Nationalism* (London: Verso, 1983).

6. University of Illinois, Chicago Great Cities Institute, *Pilsen: October 2017 Quality of Life Plan,* October 2016, https://greatcities.uic.edu/wp-content/uploads/2015/10/FINAL-Pilsen-QoL-Plan-Full.pdf.

7. Robert Sapolsky, *Behave: The Biology of Humans at Our Best and Worst* (New York: Penguin Press, 2017), 311.

8. "My Neighborhood Pilsen—Safety," WTTW (website), accessed August 07, 2018, https://interactive.wttw.com/my-neighborhood/pilsen/safety.

9. See, for example, Allen Berger, Nathan Miller, Mitchell Petersen, Raghuram Rajan, and Jeremy Stein, "Does Function Follow Organizational Form? Evidence from the Lending Practices of Large and Small Banks," *Journal of Financial Economics* 76, no. 2 (2005): 237–269.

10. Raghuram G. Rajan, *Fault Lines: How Hidden Fractures Still Threaten the World Economy* (Princeton, NJ: Princeton University Press, 2010), 45.

11. Daniel Burnham (1907) quoted in Charles Moore, *Daniel H. Burnham, Architect, Planner of Cities.* Volume 2. (Boston: Houghton Mifflin, 1921), 147.

INTRODUCTION: THE THIRD PILLAR

1. See Amartya Sen, *Identity and Violence: The Illusion of Destiny* (New York: Norton, 2006).

2. Ferdinand Tönnies, *Community and Society—Gemeinschaft und Gesellschaft,* trans. Charles P. Loomis (Mineola, NY: Dover Publications, 2002), 65.

3. See Stephen Marglin, *The Dismal Science: How Thinking like an Economist Undermines Community* (Cambridge, MA: Harvard Business Review, 2010). This excellent book also points to the fragility of the community in the face of advances by the market and the government; he is more skeptical of the broader role of markets.

4. See, for example, Robert Sapolsky, *Behave: The Biology of Humans at Our Best and Worst* (New York: Penguin Press, 2017).

5. See Sebastian Jung, *Tribe: On Homecoming and Belonging* (New York: Twelve, 2016), 37; Desmond Morris and Peter March, *Tribes* (London: Pyramid Books, 1988), 34–35.

6. Elenore Smith Bowen [Laura Bohannan, pseud.], *Return to Laughter* (New York: Anchor Books, 1964), 47, 131.

7. Kaivan Munshi and Mark Rosenzweig, "Networks and Misallocation: Insurance, Migration, and the Rural-Urban Wage Gap," *American Economic Review* 106, no. 1 (January 2016): 56, http://dx.doi.org/10.1257/aer.20131365.

8. Avner Greif, "Reputation and Coalitions in Medieval Trade: Evidence on the Maghribi Traders," *Journal of Economic History* 49, no. 4 (December 1989): 857–82.

9. Douglas Oliver, *A Solomon Island Society* (Cambridge, MA: Harvard University Press, 1955), 454–55, cited in Marshall Sahlins, *Stone Age Economics* (Chicago: Adline-Atherton, 1972), 197.

10. Robert C. Ellickson, *Order without Law* (Cambridge, MA: Harvard University Press, 1991), 61–62.

11. Ellickson, *Order without Law*, 60.

12. Edward C. Banfield, *The Moral Basis of a Backward Society* (Glencoe, IL: The Free Press, 1958), 10.

13. Banfield, *Moral Basis,* 22.

14. Banfield, *Moral Basis,* 92.

15. Banfield, *Moral Basis,* 17.

16. Banfield, *Moral Basis,* 17.

17. Banfield, *Moral Basis,* 19.

18. Banfield, *Moral Basis,* 18.

19. Mitchell A. Petersen and Raghuram G. Rajan, "The Effect of Credit Market Competition on Lending Relationships," *Quarterly Journal of Economics* 110, no. 2 (May 1995): 407–43.

20. Peter Mathias, *The First Industrial Nation: An Economic History of Britain 1700–1914* (New York: Charles Scribner, 1969), 158–160.

21. There is a long literature that worries about the damage to community caused by change, including the appearance of market forces. Thinkers like Edmund Burke, Justus Moser, Karl Polanyi, Jean Jacques Rousseau, and, of course, Karl Marx and Frederick Engels have commented on the destruction of the community and its culture. For an excellent overview, see Jerry Muller, *The Mind and Market: Capitalism in Western Thought* (New York: Alfred Knopf, 2002).

22. This paragraph draws on Mathias, *First Industrial Nation.*

23. Duncan Bythell, "The Hand-Loom Weavers in the English Cotton Industry during the Industrial Revolution: Some Problems," *The Economic History Review* 17, no. 2 (1964): 339–53.

24. Ellen Barry, "In India, a Small Band of Women Risk It All for a Chance to Work," *The New York Times*, January 30, 2016, https://www.nytimes.com/2016/01/31/world/asia/indian-women-labor-work-force.html; Ellen Barry, "'We Will Not Apologize': Chronicling the Defiant Women of India," *The New York Times*, January 30, 2016, https://www.nytimes.com/2016/01/31/insider/we-will-not-apologize-encountering-the-defiant-women-of-india.html.

25. See Avinash Dixit, "Governance Institutions and Economic Activity," *American Economic Review* 99, no. 1 (March 2009): 5–24, for an example where the community is worse off as its size grows because of the difficulties of sharing information.

26. David de la Croix, Matthias Doepke, and Joel Mokyr, "More than family matters: Apprenticeship and the rise of Europe," *Vox, CEPR Policy Portal,* March 2, 2017, https://voxeu.org/article/apprenticeship-and-rise-europe.

27. Joel Mokyr, *A Culture of Growth: The Origins of the Modern Economy* (Princeton, NJ: Princeton University Press, 2017).

CHAPTER 1: TOLERATING AVARICE

1. Kautilya, *The Arthashastra*, ed. L. N. Rangarajan (New Delhi: Penguin Books, 1992), 426.

2. Edward L. Glaeser and José Scheinkman, "Neither a Borrower Nor a Lender Be: An Economic Analysis of Interest Restrictions and Usury Laws," *Journal of Law and Economics* 41, no. 1 (April 1998): 1–36.

3. Clyde G. Reed and Cliff T. Bekar, "Religious Prohibitions against Usury," *Explorations in Economic History* 40, no. 4 (October 2003): 350.

4. R. H. Tawney, *Religion and the Rise of Capitalism* (New York: Mentor Books, 1963), 39.

5. See Henri Pirenne, *Economic and Social History of Medieval Europe*, trans. I. E. Clegg (New York: Harvest, 1937), 7–8.

6. Ibid., 9.

7. R. H. Tawney, *The Agrarian Problem of the Sixteenth Century* (London: Longmans, Green and Co., 1912), 264.

8. Alan Macfarlane, *The Origins of English Individualism* (New York: Cambridge University Press 1979), 18.

9. See ibid., 124–26, and H. J. Habakkuk, "English Landownership 1680–1740," *Economic History Review* 10, no. 1 (February 1940): 2–17, for comments on the hostility of courts to entails.

10. Douglass C. North, John Joseph Wallis, and Barry R. Weingast, *Violence and Social Orders: A Conceptual Framework for Interpreting Recorded Human History* (Cambridge, UK: Cambridge University Press, 2009), 84.

11. Much of this paragraph draws on Jack Goody, *The Development of the Family and Marriage in Europe* (Cambridge, UK: Cambridge University Press, 1983), 118, 132.

12. Reed and Bekar, "Religious Prohibitions," 352.

13. D. N. McCloskey, "English Open Fields as Behavior Towards Risk," ed. P. Unselding, *Research in Economic History* 1, cited in Reed and Bekar, "Religious Prohibitions."

14. See Reed and Bekar, "Religious Prohibitions."

15. See Harold J. Berman, *Law and Revolution, The Formation of the Western Legal Tradition* (Cambridge, MA: Harvard University Press, 1983).

16. Goody, *Development of the Family*.

17. Aristotle, *Politics*, trans. Benjamin Jowett (Kitchener, Canada: Batoche Books, 1999), 17.

18. Albert O. Hirschman, *The Passions and the Interests: Political Arguments for Capitalism before Its Triumph* (Princeton, NJ: Princeton University Press, 1977).

19. Tawney, *Religion and the Rise of Capitalism*, 36.

20. C. Dyer, "Standards of Living in the Later Middle Ages" (Cambridge, UK: Cambridge University Press, 1989), 141–42, cited in Reed and Bekar, "Religious Prohibitions," 363.

21. Barrington Moore Jr., *Social Origins of Dictatorship and Democracy: Lord and Peasant in the Making of the Modern World* (1966; repr., Harmondsworth, UK: Penguin University Press, 1974), 460–64.

22. E. L. Jones, *The European Miracle*, 3rd ed. (1981; repr., Cambridge, UK: Cambridge University Press, 2003), 57–58.

23. Pirenne, *Economic and Social History*, 53.

24. Jones, *European Miracle*, 130.

25. Jones, *European Miracle*, 130.

26. Geoffrey Parker, *The Military Revolution*, 2nd ed. (1988; repr., Cambridge, UK: Cambridge University Press, 1996), 18–19.

27. Immanuel Wallerstein, *The Modern World-System I: Capitalist Agriculture and the Origins of the European World-Economy in the Sixteenth Century* (New York: Academic Press, 1974).

28. Parker, *Military Revolution*, 1.

29. Jones, *European Miracle*, 130.

30. Pirenne, *Economic and Social History*, 83.

31. Pirenne, *Economic and Social History*, 118–19.

32. Jared Rubin, "Bills of Exchange, Interest Bans, and Impersonal Exchange in Islam and Christianity," *Explorations in Economic History* 47, no. 2 (April 2010): 213–27.

33. Goody, *Development of Family*, 165.

34. Nicholas Carr, "Is Google Making Us Stupid?," *The Atlantic*, July/August 2008, https://www.theatlantic.com/magazine/archive/2008/07/is-google-making-us-stupid/306868/.

35. Timothy Egan, "The Phone is Smart, but Where's the Big Idea?," *The New York Times*, July 7, 2017, https://www.nytimes.com/2017/07/07/opinion/iphone-apple-printing-press.html?smprod=nytcore-ipad&smid=nytcore-ipad-share&_r=0.

36. Lester K. Little, *Religious Poverty* (Ithaca, NY: Cornell University Press, 1978), 57.

37. Tawney, *Religion and the Rise of Capitalism*.

38. Max Weber, *The Protestant Ethic and the Spirit of Capitalism*, trans. Talcott Parsons (London: Routledge, 1992), 32.

39. Cited in Benjamin Nelson, *The Idea of Usury: From Tribal Brotherhood to Universal Otherhood* (Chicago: The University of Chicago Press, 1969), 75.

40. Nelson, *Idea of Usury*, 75.

41. James Ackerman, "Interest Rates and the Law: A History of Usury," *Arizona State Law Journal* 27, no. 61 (1981): 78.

42. Tawney, *Religion and the Rise of Capitalism*.

43. See Reed and Bekar, "Religious Prohibitions," for a development of this theory.

44. See, for example, the articles in Michael Duffy, *The Military Revolution and the State 1500–1800* (Exeter, UK: University of Exeter, 1986); Jones, *European Miracle*; and Charles Tilly, *Coercion, Capital, and European States AD 990–1992* (Oxford, UK: Blackwell, 1992).

CHAPTER 2: THE RISE OF THE STRONG BUT LIMITED STATE

1. This section draws on Raghuram G. Rajan and Luigi Zingales, *Saving Capitalism from the Capitalists: Unleashing the Power of Financial Markets to Create Wealth and Spread Opportunity* (Princeton, NJ: Princeton University Press, 2003), chapter 6.

2. Lawrence Stone, *The Crisis of the Aristocracy, 1558–1641* (Oxford, UK: Clarendon Press, 1965).

3. Stone, *Crisis of the Aristocracy*.

4. S. E. Finer, *The History of Government*, vol. 3 (Oxford, UK: Oxford University Press, 1999).

5. Frederick C. Dietz, *An Economic History of England* (New York: H. Holt, 1942).

6. Ibid.

7. Stone, *Crisis of the Aristocracy*; also see R. H. Tawney, "The Rise of the Gentry, 1558–1640," *The Economic History Review* 11, no. 1 (1941): 1–38.

8. See Tawney, "The Rise of the Gentry," and Stone, *Crisis of the Aristocracy*.

9. C. V. Wedgwood, *The Great Rebellion: The King's Peace, 1637–1641* (London: Collins, 1956), 367.

10. Indeed, if the fear of expropriation was rife, none would buy, being at most willing to pay a rental from the annual income from the property as compensation. A substantial fraction of the seized monastery property was indeed let out for long tenures rather than sold. There was little point in taking these away from the current efficient tenants and looking for new ones.

11. See, for example, Douglass C. North, John Joseph Wallis, and Barry R. Weingast, *Violence and Social Orders: A Conceptual Framework for Interpreting Recorded Human History* (Cambridge, UK: Cambridge University Press, 2009).

12. Stone, *Crisis of the Aristocracy*.

13. See, for instance, Rajan and Zingales, *Saving Capitalism*, chapter 6, and Andro Linklater, *Owning the Earth: The Transforming History of Land Ownership* (New York: Bloomsbury, 2013).

14. Robert C. Allen, *Enclosure and the Yeoman* (Oxford: Clarendon Press, 1992).

15. S. E. Finer, *History of Government: Empires, Monarchies, and the Modern State*, vol. 3 (New York: Oxford University Press, 1997).

16. See Linklater, *Owning the Earth*.

17. J. R. Green, *A Short History of the English People* (London: Macmillan, 1888).

18. Peter Mathias, *The First Industrial Nation: An Economic History of Britain 1700–1914* (New York: Charles Scribner 1969), 41.

19. Cited in Sheilagh Ogilvie, *Institutions and European Trade: Merchant Guilds, 1000–1800* (New York: Cambridge University Press, 2011), 8.

20. See Dietz, *Economic History of England*, 264.

21. See, for example, Ogilvie, *Institutions and European Trade*, 163.

22. This is essentially a restatement of David Hume's price–specie flow mechanism, which is contained in his book *On the Balance of Trade*, published in 1752. Also see Robert W. McGee, "The Economic Thought of David Hume," *Hume Studies* 15, no. 1 (1989), 184–204. http://www.hume society.org/hs/issues/v15n1/mcgee/mcgee-v15n1.pdf

23. The quotations are from Dietz, *Economic History of England*, 270.

24. This paragraph draws on E. L. Jones, *The European Miracle*, 3rd ed. (1981; repr., Cambridge, UK: Cambridge University Press, 2003), 98–102.

25. Jones, *The European Miracle*, 98.

26. Adam Smith, *An Inquiry into the Nature and Causes of the Wealth of Nations* (Chicago: University of Chicago Press, 1976).

27. Jones, *European Miracle*, 114; Eric Evans, *The Forging of the Modern State: Early Industrial Britain 1783–1870* (London: Longman, 2001), 32, conjectures that even in the late eighteenth century when government was more capable than earlier, fully one-fifth of all imports were smuggled.

28. See Ogilvie, *Institutions and European Trade*, 18.

29. See Bruce G. Carruthers, *City of Capital—Politics and Markets in the English Financial Revolution* (Princeton, NJ: Princeton University Press, 1996), 37.

30. Finer, *History of Government*, vol. 3, 1341–43.

31. This paragraph draws on Douglass C. North and Barry R. Weingast, "Constitutions and Commitment: The Evolution of Institutions Governing Public Choice in Seventeenth-Century England," *Journal of Economic History* 49, no. 4 (December 1989), 816–17.

32. John Brewer, *The Sinews of Power* (London: Unwin Hyman, 1989), 66.

33. See North, Wallis, and Weingast, *Violence and Social Orders*.

34. See Carruthers, *City of Capital*, 75.

35. See Brewer, *Sinews of Power*, 125.

36. North and Weingast, "Constitution and Commitment."

37. See Rajan and Zingales, *Saving Capitalism*.

38. See Dani Rodrik, Arvind Subramanian, and Franceso Tebbi, "Institutions Rule: The Primacy of Institutions Over Geography and Integration in Economic Development," *Journal of Economic Growth* 9, no. 2 (June 2004): 131–65.

39. See Rajan and Zingales, *Saving Capitalism*.

40. On corruption, see Linklater, *Owning the Earth*, 225–26.

41. Rodney Ramcharan, "Inequality and Redistribution: Evidence from U.S. Counties and States, 1890–1930," *Review of Economics and Statistics* 92, no. 4 (November 2010): 729–44.

42. Raghuram Rajan and Rodney Ramcharan, "Land and Credit: A Study of the Political Economy of Banking in the United States in the Early 20th Century," *Journal of Finance* 66, no. 6 (December 2011): 1895–1931.

43. Stanley L. Engerman and Kenneth L. Sokoloff, "Factor Endowments, Inequality, and Paths of Development Among New World Economics," NBER Working Paper No. 9259, October 2002.

44. Barrington Moore Jr., *Social Origins of Dictatorship and Democracy: Lord and Peasant in the Making of the Modern World* (1966; repr., Harmondsworth, UK: Penguin Press, 1974), 462–63.

45. Linklater, *Owning the Earth*, 117.

46. See Moore, *Social Origins*.

CHAPTER 3: FREEING THE MARKET . . . THEN DEFENDING IT

1. Quoted in Edward Cheyney, *An Introduction to the Industrial and Social History of England* (New York: Macmillan, 1916), chapter 8.

2. Adam Smith, *An Inquiry into the Nature and Causes of the Wealth of Nations* (Chicago: University of Chicago Press, 1976), 90. Page numbers are from the Kindle edition of this text.

3. Smith, *Wealth of Nations,* 176.

4. See, for example, Smith, *Wealth of Nations,* 493.

5. Smith, *Wealth of Nations,* 314.

6. Smith, *Wealth of Nations,* 482.

7. The quotes from Mill in the paragraphs that follow are from John Stuart Mill, *On Liberty* (London: Walter Scott Publishing; The Project Gutenberg ebook, released in 2011), https://www.gutenberg.org/files/34901/34901-h/34901-h.htm.

8. Jerry Z. Muller, *The Mind and the Market: Capitalism in Modern European Thought* (New York: Anchor, 2002).

9. Karl Polanyi, *The Great Transformation: The Political and Economic Origins of Our Time,* 2nd ed. (Boston: Beacon Press, 2001).

10. H. W. Brands, *American Colossus: The Triumph of Capitalism, 1865–1900* (New York: Anchor Books, 2011).

11. Brands, *American Colossus.*

12. Ron Chernow, *Titan: The Life of John D. Rockefeller, Sr.,* 2nd ed. (New York: Vintage Books, 2004); Brands, *American Colossus.*

13. Chernow, *Titan.*

14. Ida Tarbell, *The History of the Standard Oil Company,* vol. 1 (Glouchester, MA: Peter Smith, 1904), 65, cited in ibid., chapter 8.

15. Chernow, *Titan.*

16. Chernow, *Titan.*

17. Karl Marx, *The Poverty of Philosophy,* rev. ed. (1847, 1982), 109, cited in John E. Roemer, *Free to Lose: An Introduction to Marxist Economic Philosophy* (Cambridge, MA: Harvard University Press, 1988), 112.

18. See, for example, Michael Kumhof, Romain Rancière, and Pablo Winant, "Inequality, Leverage, and Crises," *American Economic Review* 105, no. 3 (March, 2005): 1217–45.

19. Leon Trotsky, "The world economic crisis and the new tasks of the Communist International," in *The First Five Years of the Communist International,* vol. I (London: New Park, 1973), 252, cited in Stuart Easterling, "Marx's Theory of Economic Crisis," *International Socialist Review* 32 (November/December 2003), https://isreview.org/issues/32/crisis_theory.shtml.

20. Frederick Engels, "Outline of a Critique of Political Economy," paragraph 48, cited in Easterling, "Marx's Theory of Economic Crisis."

21. This paragraph draws on Stanley Engerman and Kenneth Sokoloff, "The Evolution of Suffrage Institutions in the New World," *Journal of Economic History* 65, no. 4 (December 2005): 891–921.

22. See, for instance, Paul Foot, *The Vote: How It Was Won and How It Was Undermined* (New York: Viking, 2005).

23. Engerman and Sokoloff, "Evolution of Suffrage."

24. See, for example, Alessandro Lizzeri and Nicola Persico, "Why Did the Elites Extend the Suffrage? Democracy and the Scope of Government, with an Application to Britain's 'Age of Reform,'" *Quarterly Journal of Economics* 119, no. 2 (May 2004); 707–65.

25. See, for instance, Engerman and Sokoloff, "Evolution of Suffrage"; Daron Acemoglu and James A Robinson, "Why Did the West Extend the Franchise? Democracy, Inequality, and Growth in Historical Perspective," *Quarterly Journal of Economics* 115, no. 4 (November 2000): 1167–99, https://doi.org/10.1162/003355300555042; and Lizzeri and Persico, "Why Did the Elites Extend the Suffrage?"

26. Engerman and Sokoloff, "Evolution of Suffrage."

27. Acemoglu and Robinson, "Why Did the West Extend the Franchise?"

28. Edmund Burke, "The importance of property," in *Reflections on the Revolution in France* (1790), part 1.

29. See Eric J. Evans, *The Forging of the Modern State: Early Industrial Britain, 1783–1870,* 3rd ed. (New York: Routledge, 2001); Foot, *The Vote.*

30. Foot, *The Vote.*
31. See Lizzeri and Persico, "Why Did the Elites Extend the Suffrage?"
32. Engerman and Sokoloff, "Evolution of Suffrage."
33. Oded Galor, Omer Moav, and Dietrich Vollrath, "Inequality in Land Ownership, the Emergence of Human Capital Promoting Institutions, and the Great Divergence," *Review of Economic Studies* 76, no. 1 (January 2009): 143–79.
34. See, for example, Alexander Hamilton, James Madison, and John Jay, *The Federalist papers* (1788), available at https://www.congress.gov/resources/display/content/The+Federalist+Papers, especially Federalist 10, "The Same Subject Continued: The Union as a Safeguard Against Domestic Faction and Insurrection."
35. Douglass C. North, John Joseph Wallis, and Barry R. Weingast, *Violence and Social Orders: A Conceptual Framework for Interpreting Recorded Human History* (Cambridge, UK: Cambridge University Press, 2009).
36. Edward Glaeser and Claudia Goldin, "Corruption and Reform: An Introduction," in *Corruption and Reform: Lessons from America's History,* ed. Edward Glaeser and Claudia Goldin (Chicago: The University of Chicago Press, 2006), 14.
37. See, for example, John Joseph Wallis, "The Concept of Systematic Corruption in American History," in *Corruption and Reform,* ed. Edward Glaeser and Claudia Goldin (Chicago: The University of Chicago Press, 2006).
38. Hicks, *Populist Revolt: A History of the Farmers' Alliance and the People's Party* (Minneapolis: University of Minnesota Press, 1931).
39. See Barry Eichengreen, *The Populist Temptation: Economic Grievance and Political Reaction in the Modern Era* (New York: Oxford University Press, 2018).
40. Hicks, *Populist Revolt,* 25–26.
41. Hicks, *Populist Revolt,* 32.
42. Richard Hofstadter, *The Age of Reform* (New York: Vintage Books, 1960).
43. See, for example, George Stigler, "The Economic Effects of Antitrust Laws," *Journal of Law and Economics* 9 (October 1996).
44. Chernow, *Titan,* chapter 22.
45. Chernow, *Titan,* chapter. 27.
46. Michael McGerr, *A Fierce Discontent: The Rise and Fall of the Progressive Movement in America* (New York: Free Press, 2003).
47. Indeed, a persuasive study shows that as news of McKinley's condition on his deathbed waxed and waned, so did the price of stocks most subject to antitrust action, suggesting the change in leadership was both unexpected and important to the course of history. See Richard B. Baker, Carola Frydman, and Eric Hilt, "From Plutocracy to Progressivism? The Assassination of President McKinley as a Turning Point in American History," September 2014, https://economics .yale.edu/sites/default/files/hilt.pdf.

CHAPTER 4: THE COMMUNITY IN THE BALANCE

1. Marshall Goldman, *Petrostate: Putin, Power, and the New Russia* (New York: Oxford University Press, 2008).
2. Goldman, *Petrostate.*
3. See Andro Linklater, *Owning the Earth: The Transforming History of Land Ownership* (New York: Bloomsbury, 2013).
4. Franz Neumann, *Behemoth: The Structure and Practice of National Socialism, 1933–1944* (New York: Octagon Books, 1963).
5. See Enrico C. Perotti and Ernst-Ludwig von Thadden, "The Political Economy of Corporate Control and Labor Rents," *Journal of Political Economy* 114, no. 1 (February 2006): 145–75.
6. Shanker Satyanath, Nico Voigtländer, and Hans-Joachim Voth, "Bowling for Fascism: Social Capital and the Rise of the Nazi Party," *Journal of Political Economy* 125, no. 2 (April 2017): 478–526, https://doi.org/10.1086/690949.

7. Fareed Zakaria, "The Rise of Illiberal Democracy," *Foreign Affairs,* November/December 1997, https://www.foreignaffairs.com/articles/1997-11-01/rise-illiberal-democracy.

8. This section stems from long discussions with friends who are members of parliament in India. They shall remain unnamed.

9. See, for example, the description of Democratic machine politics in Richard Hofstadter's classic, *The Age of Reform* (New York: Vintage Books, 1960).

10. See Robert Nozick, *Anarchy, State, and Utopia* (New York: Basic Books, 1974).

11. See John E. Roemer, *Free to Lose: An Introduction to Marxist Economic Philosophy* (Cambridge, MA: Harvard University Press, 1988).

12. See John Rawls, *A Theory of Justice* (Cambridge, MA: Belknap Press, 1971).

13. See Robert J. Gordon, *The Rise and Decline of American Growth: The U.S. Standard of Living Since the Civil War* (Princeton, NJ: Princeton University Press, 2016).

14. Klaus Schwab, "The Fourth Industrial Revolution: what it means, how to respond," *World Economic Forum* (January 14, 2016), https://www.weforum.org/agenda/2016/01/the-fourth-industrial -revolution-what-it-means-and-how-to-respond/.

15. Gordon, *Rise and Decline of American Growth.*

16. Carlotta Perez, *Technological Revolutions and Financial Capital: The Dynamics of Bubbles and Golden Ages* (Cletenham, UK: Edward Elgar, 2002).

17. Michael Signer, *Demagogue: The Fight to Save Democracy from Its Worst Enemies* (New York: Macmillan, 2009), 38–40.

18. See John Rury, *Education and Social Change: Contours in the History of American Schooling,* 5th ed. (New York: Routledge, 2016), 44.

19. Claudia Goldin and Lawrence F. Katz, *The Race between Technology and Education* (Cambridge, MA: Belknap Press, 2009), 139.

20. See Nancy Beadie, *Education and the Creation of Capital in the Early American Republic* (Cambridge, UK: Cambridge University Press, 2010), for a detailed picture of the early school.

21. Rury, *Education,* 61.

22. See Campbell F. Scribner, *The Fight for Local Control: Schools, Suburbs, and American Democracy* (Ithaca, NY: Cornell University Press, 2016), 28.

23. Goldin and Katz, *Technology and Education,* 163.

24. Tom Dietz, "From High School to the High Court," *Michigan Bar Journal* (July 2016): 18–19, http://www.michbar.org/file/barjournal/article/documents/pdf4article2909.pdf.

25. Cited in Goldin and Katz, *Technology and Education,* 193.

26. Goldin and Katz, *Technology and Education,* 180.

27. Goldin and Katz, *Technology and Education,* 164.

28. See, for example, Scribner, *Fight for Local Control,* 40.

29. Scribner, *Fight for Local Control,* 35–37.

30. Michael McGerr, *A Fierce Discontent: The Rise and Fall of the Progressive Movement in America* (New York: Free Press, 2003).

31. C. S. Benson, *The Cheerful Prospect: A Statement on the Future of Public Education* (Boston: Houghton-Mifflin, 1965), 51, cited in Scribner, *Fight for Local Control,* 99.

32. Klaus Desmet, Ignacio Ortuño-Ortín, and Romain Wacziarg, "The Political Economy of Linguistic Cleavages," *Journal of Development Economics* 97, no. 2 (2012): 322–38.

33. Michael B. Katz, *In the Shadow of the Poorhouse: A Social History of Welfare In America,* 2nd ed. (New York: BasicBooks, 1996), 57.

34. The description of the Eberfeld system draws on Larry Frohman, *Poor Relief and Welfare in Germany: From the Reformation to World War I* (New York: Cambridge University Press, 2008), 89–95.

35. E. P. Hennock, *The Origin of the Welfare State in England and Germany, 1850–1914: Social Policies Compared* (Cambridge, UK: Cambridge University Press), 2007), 53.

36. Frohman, *Poor Relief,* 96.

37. Ibid., 97.

38. See Daniel Rodgers, *Atlantic Crossings: Social Politics in a Progressive Age* (Cambridge, MA: Belknap Press, 1998), 223–26.

39. Rodgers, *Atlantic Crossings*, 223.

40. Katz, *Shadow of the Poorhouse,* 147.

41. Katz, *Shadow of the Poorhouse*, 240.

42. See Rodgers, *Atlantic Crossings,* 260–64.

43. Katz, *Shadow of the Poorhouse*, 150–51.

44. See Franklin D. Roosevelt, "1932 Democratic National Convention acceptance" (speech), July 2, 1932, Democratic National Convention, Chicago, transcript, http://www.danaroc.com/guests _fdr_021609.html.

45. Franklin D. Roosevelt, "Message to Congress on the Objectives and Accomplishments of the Administration," June 8, 1934, transcript, http://www.presidency.ucsb.edu/ws/index.php?pid =14690; also see David M. Kennedy, *Freedom from Fear: The American People in Depression and War, 1929–1945* (New York: Oxford University Press, 2005), 245.

46. Kennedy, *Freedom from Fear,* 267.

47. John B. Judis, *The Populist Explosion: How the Great Recession Transformed American and European Politics* (New York: Columbia Global Reports, 2016).

48. Katz, *Shadow of the Poorhouse,* 240; Rodgers, *Atlantic Crossings,* 443.

49. Katz, *Shadow of the Poorhouse,* 240.

50. Alberto Alesina and Edward Glaeser, *Fighting Poverty in the US and Europe: A World of Difference (The Rodolfo De Benedetti Lecture Series)* (Oxford, UK: Oxford University Press, 2004), 148.

51. Milton Friedman and Rose Friedman, *Free to Choose: A Personal Statement* (New York: Penguin, 1980), 135.

52. James Poterba, "Demographic Structure and the Political Economy of Public Education," *Journal of Policy Analysis and Management* 16, no. 1 (1997): 48–66.

CHAPTER 5: THE PRESSURE TO PROMISE

1. Tony Judt, *Postwar: A History of Europe Science 1945* (New York: Penguin Books, 2005), 236.

2. Robert J. Gordon, *The Rise and Decline of American Growth: The U.S. Standard of Living Since the Civil War* (Princeton, NJ: Princeton University Press, 2016), 120.

3. See Tyler Cowen, *The Great Stagnation: How America Ate All the Low-hanging Fruit of Modern History, Got Sick, and Will (Eventually) Feel Better* (New York: Dutton, 2011).

4. See Harold James, *Europe Reborn, A History 1914–2000* (New York: Routledge, 2015), 231–33.

5. Markus K. Brunnermeier, Harold James, and Jean-Pierre Landau, *The Euro and the Battle of Ideas* (Princeton, NJ: Princeton University Press, 2018).

6. Judt, *Postwar,* 338.

7. Computed from Ibid., 340.

8. "Transport > Road > Motor Vehicles per 1000 People: Countries Compared," NationMaster (website), accessed August 06, 2018, http://www.nationmaster.com/country-info/stats/Transport/Road/Motor-vehicles-per-1000-people.

9. David Banister, *European Transport Policy and Sustainable Mobility* (London: Routledge, 2000), 42.

10. Judt, *Postwar,* 330.

11. The following paragraphs draw on Daniel Rodgers, *Atlantic Crossings: Social Politics in a Progressive Age* (Cambridge, MA: Belknap Press, 1998). Bernard Harris, *The Origins of the British Welfare State: Social Welfare in England and Wales, 1800–1945* (Houndmills, Basingstoke: Palgrave Macmillan, 2004).

12. Harris, *British Welfare State,* 290.

13. Ibid., 291.

14. See Kenneth Scheve and David Stasavage, *Taxing the Rich: A History of Fiscal Fairness in the United States and Europe* (Princeton, NJ: Princeton University Press, 2016); "Historical Highest

Marginal Income Tax Rates," Tax Policy Center (website), March 22, 2017, http://www.taxpoli cycenter.org/statistics/historical-highest-marginal-income-tax-rates.

15. Judith Rollins, *All Is Never Said: The Narrative of Odette Harper Hines* (Philadelphia: Temple University Press, 1995), 119; "African Americans in World War II: Fighting for a Double Victory," National World War II Museum: New Orleans (website), accessed August 7, 2018, https://www.nationalww2museum.org/sites/default/files/2017-07/african-americans.pdf.

16. Martin Luther King, "I Have A Dream . . ." (speech), "March on Washington," Washington, D.C., August 28, 1963, transcript, https://www.archives.gov/files/press/exhibits/dream-speech.pdf.

17. See Sidney M. Milkis and Jerome M. Mileur, "Lyndon Johnson, The Great Society, and the 'Twilight' of the Modern Presidency," and Frances Fox Piven and Richard A. Cloward, "The Politics of the Great Society," in *The Great Society and the High Tide of Liberalism,* ed. Sidney M. Milkis and Jerome M. Mileur (Amherst: University of Massachusetts Press, 2005); as well as the excellent biographies: Robert Caro, *The Path to Power* (New York: Vintage, 1982) and Doris Kearns Goodwin, *Lyndon Johnson and the American Dream* (New York: St. Martin's Griffin, 1982).

18. Daniel P. Moynihan, *Maximal Feasible Misunderstanding: Community Action in the War on Poverty* (New York: Free Press), 168.

19. Milkis and Mileur, *Great Society.*

20. Judt, *Postwar,* 334.

21. Enoch Powell, "Rivers of Blood" (speech), Conservative Association meeting, Birmingham, UK, April 20, 1968, transcript, http://www.telegraph.co.uk/comment/3643823/Enoch-Powells -Rivers-of-Blood-speech.html.

22. Gordon, *Rise and Decline of American Growth*; Cowen, *Great Stagnation.*

23. Gordon, *Rise and Decline of American Growth,* 13.

24. Paul A. David, "The Dynamo and the Computer: An Historical Perspective on the Modern Productivity Paradox," *The American Economic Review* 80, no. 2, (May, 1990): 355–61.

25. James, *Europe Reborn,* 390–91.

26. See Chad Syverson, "Challenges to Mismeasurement Explanations for the U.S. Productivity Slowdown," *Journal of Economic Perspectives* 31 (Spring 2016): 165–86.

27. Judt, *Postwar,* 541.

28. James, *Europe Reborn,* 362.

29. Brunnermeier et al, *The Euro.*

30. James, *Europe Reborn,* 368.

31. James, *Europe Reborn,* 400.

CHAPTER 6: THE ICT REVOLUTION COMETH

1. See, for example, David H. Autor, Frank Levy, and Richard J. Murnane, "The Skill Content of Recent Technological Change: An Empirical Exploration," *The Quarterly Journal of Economics* 118, no. 4 (2003): 1279–1333.

2. "Amazon Go," Amazon, accessed August 08, 2018, https://www.amazon.com/b?node= 16008589011.

3. Liz Alderman, "In Sweden, a Cash-Free Future Nears," *The New York Times,* December 26, 2015, https://www.nytimes.com/2015/12/27/business/international/in-sweden-a-cash-free -future-nears.html.

4. James Bessen, "Toil and Technology," *Finance & Development* 52, no. 1 (March 2015).

5. Luis Garicano, "Hierarchies and the Organization of Knowledge in Production," *Journal of Political Economy* 108, no. 5 (2000): 874–904.

6. David H. Autor and David Dorn, "The Growth of Low Skill Service Jobs and the Polarization of the U.S. Labor Market," rev. ed., NBER Working Paper No. 15150, May 2012.

7. Maarten Goos, Alan Manning, and Anna Salomons, "Job Polarization in Europe," *American Economic Review* 99, no. 2 (2009): 58–63.

8. Daniel M. Bernhofen, Zouheir El-Sahli, and Richard Kneller, "Estimating the Effects of the

Container Revolution on World Trade," *Journal of International Economics* 98 (January 2016): 36–50.

9. Ibid.

10. E. H., *The Economist* Explains, "Why Have Containers Boosted Trade so Much?," *The Economist*, May 22, 2013, https://www.economist.com/blogs/economist-explains/2013/05/economist-explains-14.

11. Bernhofen et al., "Container Revolution."

12. Chance Miller, "iPhone X Said to Cost Apple $357 to Make, Gross Margin Higher than iPhone 8," 9to5Mac (website), November 6, 2017, https://9to5mac.com/2017/11/06/how-much-iphone-x-costs-apple-to-make/.

13. Richard Baldwin, *The Great Convergence* (Cambridge, MA: Harvard University Press, 2016).

14. Lisa Goldapple, "Cipla: India's Robin Hood of Drugs," *Project Breakthrough*, September 19, 2018, http://breakthrough.unglobalcompact.org/briefs/cipla-indias-robin-hood-of-drugs-yusuf-hamied/.

15. Elena Crivellaro, "The College Wage Premium over Time: Trends in Europe in the Last 15 Years," in *Inequality: Causes and Consequences*, ed. Lorenzo Cappellari, Solomon W. Polachek, Konstantinos Tatsiramos (Bingley, UK: Emerald, 2016), 287–328; Robert Valletta, "Recent Flattening in the Higher Education Wage Premium: Polarization, Skill Downgrading, or Both?," NBER Working Paper No. 22935, December 2016.

16. Alan Blinder, "How Many US Jobs Might Be Offshorable?" *World Economics* 10, no. 2 (April 2007): 41–78.

17. Martin Neil Baily and Barry P. Bosworth, "US Manufacturing: Understanding Its Past and Its Potential Future," *Journal of Economic Perspectives* 28, no. 1 (2014): 3–26.

18. Daron Acemoglu, David H. Autor, David Dorn, Gordon H. Hanson, and Brendan Price, "Import Competition and the Great U.S. Employment Sag of the 2000s," *Journal of Labor Economics* 34, no. 1 (January 2016): 141–98.

19. Peter S. Goodman, "More Wealth, More Jobs, but Not for Everyone: What Fuels the Backlash on Trade," *The New York Times*, September 28, 2016, https://www.nytimes.com/2016/09/29/business/economy/more-wealth-more-jobs-but-not-for-everyone-what-fuels-the-backlash-on-trade.html?_r=0.

20. David Autor, David Dorn, and Gordon Hanson, "Untangling Trade and Technology: Evidence from Local Labor Markets," NBER Working Paper No. 18938, April 2013.

21. David Autor, David Dorn, Gordon H. Hanson, and Jae Song, "Trade Adjustment: Worker Level Evidence," *Quarterly Journal of Economics* 129, no. 4 (November 2014): 1799–1860.

22. "Selected Data From Social Security's Disability Program," Social Security Administration (website), accessed August 7, 2018, https://www.ssa.gov/oact/STATS/dibStat.html.

23. See Amy Goldstein, *Janesville: An American Story* (New York: Simon and Schuster, 2017).

24. "Median usual weekly real earnings: Wage and salary workers: 16 years and over," Federal Reserve Bank of St. Louis (website), accessed August 7, 2018, https://fred.stlouisfed.org/series/LEU0252881600A.

25. Congressional Budget Office, "The Distribution of Household Income, 2014" (March 19, 2018), retrieved from https://www.cbo.gov/publication/53597#interactive-graphic2.

26. Paul Beaudry, David A. Green, and Benjamin M. Sand, "The Great Reversal in the Demand for Skill and Cognitive Tasks," *Journal of Labor Economics* 34, no. 1 (January 2016): 199–247.

27. OECD, *Education at a Glance 2017: OECD Indicators* (Paris: OECD Publishing, 2017), https://doi.org/10.1787/eag-2017-en.

28. OECD, *Education at a Glance 2017*, 107.

29. "Academic Ranking of World Universities, 2017," Shanghai Rankings (website), accessed August 7, 2018, http://www.shanghairanking.com/ARWU2017.html.

30. "Table 326.10," Digest of Education Statistics, National Center for Education Statistics, accessed August 7, 2018, https://nces.ed.gov/programs/digest/d16/tables/dt16_326.10.asp.

31. See Thomas Piketty and Emmanuel Saez, "Income Inequality in the United States, 1913–1998," *Quarterly Journal of Economics* 118, no. 1 (2003): 1–41; Anthony Atkinson, Thomas Piketty, and

Emmanuel Saez, "Top Incomes in the Long Run of History," *Journal of Economic Literature* 49, no. 1 (2011): 3–71; Thomas Piketty, *Capital in the Twenty-First Century* (Cambridge, MA: Belknap Press, 2014).

32. Piketty, *Capital.*

33. Tobias Buck, "German Inheritance Wave Stokes Fears over Inequality," *Financial Times,* May 2, 2018. https://www.ft.com/content/894689c2-4933-11e8-8ee8-cae73aab7ccb; "Taxing inheritances is falling out of favour," *The Economist,* November 23, 2017, https://www.economist.com/briefing/2017/11/23/taxing-inheritances-is-falling-out-of-favour?frsc=dg%7Ce.

34. Annette Alstadsæter, Niels Johannesen, and Gabriel Zucman, "Tax Evasion and Inequality," NBER Working Paper No. 23772, September 2017; and Annette Alstadsæter, Martin Jacob, Wojciech Kopczuk, and Kjetil Telle, "Accounting for Business Income in Measuring Top Income Shares: Integrated Accrual Approach Using Individual and Firm Data From Norway," NBER Working Paper No. 22888, December 2016.

35. Piketty and Saez, "Income Inequality."

36. Piketty, *Capital.*

37. Steven N. Kaplan and Joshua D. Rauh, "Family, Education, and Sources of Wealth among the Richest Americans, 1982–2012," *The American Economic Review* 103, no. 3 (May 2013): 158–62.

38. Sherwin Rosen, "The Economics of Superstars," *The American Economic Review* 71, no. 5 (December 1981): 845–58.

39. Raghuram Rajan and Julie Wulf, "The Flattening Firm: Evidence from Panel Data on the Changing Nature of Corporate Hierarchies," *The Review of Economics and Statistics* 88, no. 4 (November 2006) 759–73.

40. Milton Friedman, "The Social Responsibility of Business Is to Increase Its Profits," *The New York Times Magazine,* September 13, 1970.

41. Michael Jensen and Kevin J. Murphy, "Performance Pay and Top-Management Incentives," *Journal of Political Economy* 98, no. 2 (April 1990): 225–64.

42. Andrei Shleifer and Lawrence H. Summers, "Breach of Trust in Hostile Takeovers," in *Corporate Takeovers: Causes and Consequences,* ed. Alan J. Auerbach (Chicago: University of Chicago Press, 1988), 33–68; Luigi Zingales, "In Search of New Foundations," *The Journal of Finance* 55, no. 4 (August 2000): 1623–53.

43. Marianne Bertrand and Sendhil Mullainathan, "Are CEOs Rewarded for Luck? The Ones without Principles Are," *The Quarterly Journal of Economics* 116, no. 3 (August 2001): 901–32.

44. See, for example, William A. Galston and Clara Hendrickson, "A Policy at Peace with Itself: Antitrust Remedies for Our Concentrated, Uncompetitive Economy," Brookings, January 5, 2018, https://www.brookings.edu/research/a-policy-at-peace-with-itself-antitrust-remedies-for-our-concentrated-uncompetitive-economy/.

45. Xiaohui Gao, Jay R. Ritter, and Zhongyan Zhu, "Where Have All the IPOs Gone?" *The Journal of Financial and Quantitative Analysis* 48, no. 6 (December 2013): 1663–92, https://doi.org/10.1017/S0022109014000015.

46. See Galston and Hendrickson, "Policy at Peace with Itself."

47. Gustavo Grullon, Yelena Larkin, and Roni Michaely, "Are US Industries Becoming More Concentrated?" August 31, 2017, available at https://pdfs.semanticscholar.org/138f/249c43bfec315227a242b305b9764d57a0af.pdf. Of course, average size would also increase if small firms no longer enter.

48. See Sam Peltzman, "Industrial Concentration under the Rule of Reason," *The Journal of Law and Economics* 57, no. S3 (August 2014): S101–20.

49. "Too Much of a Good Thing," *The Economist,* March 26, 2016, https://www.economist.com/briefing/2016/03/26/too-much-of-a-good-thing.

50. Sam Peltzman, "Industrial Concentration."

51. Robert Bork, *The Antitrust Paradox: A Policy at War With Itself* (New York: Basic Books, 1978).

52. "AT&T and Time Warner Are Cleared to Merge," *The Economist,* June 16, 2018, https://www.economist.com/news/leaders/21744068-more-consolidation-will-follow-consumers-ought-worry-att-and-time-warner-are-cleared?frsc=dge.

53. Grullon et al., "Are US Industries Becoming More Concentrated?"

54. See John Van Reenen, "Increasing Differences Between Firms: Market Power and the Macro-Economy," paper presented at the Jackson Hole Economic Policy Symposium, August 2018, https://www.kansascityfed.org/~/media/files/publicat/sympos/2018/papersandhandouts /824180729van%20reenenpaper.pdf?la=en.

55. See, for example, Nicolas Crouzet and Janice Eberly, "Understanding Weak Capital Investment: the Role of Market Concentration and Intangibles," paper presented at the Jackson Hole Economic Policy Symposium, August 2018, https://www.kansascityfed.org/~/media/files/publicat /sympos/2018/papersandhandouts/824180810eberlycrouzetpaper.pdf?la=en.

56. Jae Song, David J. Price, Fatih Guvenen, Nicholas Bloom, and Till Von Wachter, "Firming Up Inequality," rev. ed., NBER Working Paper No. 21199, June 2015.

57. These remarks are based on ongoing work with Luigi Zingales.

58. Collen Cunningham, Florian Ederer, and Song Ma, "Killer Acquisitions," Working Paper, Yale School of Management, 2018.

59. Steve Schlackman, "How Mickey Mouse Keeps Changing Copyright Law," *Art Law Journal*, February 15, 2014, https://atp.orangenius.com/how-mickey-mouse-keeps-changing-copyright-law/.

60. See Brink Lindsey and Steven Teles, *The Captured Economy: How the Powerful Enrich Themselves, Slow Down Growth, and Increase Inequality* (New York: Oxford University Press, 2017).

61. "U.S. Patent Statistics Chart Calendar Years 1963–2015," United States Patent and Trademark Office, accessed August 07, 2018, https://www.uspto.gov/web/offices/ac/ido/oeip/taf/us_stat .htm.

62. Alan Krueger, "Reflections on Dwindling Worker Bargaining Power and Monetary Policy," Luncheon Address at the Jackson Hole Symposium 2018, https://www.kansascityfed.org/~ /media/files/publicat/sympos/2018/papersandhandouts/824180824kruegerremarks.pdf?la=en.

63. Jessica Jeffers, "The Impact of Restricting Labor Mobility on Corporate Investment and Entrepreneurship," Working Paper, University of Chicago—Booth School of Business, 2018.

64. Dan Andrews, Chiara Criscuolo, and Peter Gal, *Frontier Firms, Technology Diffusion and Public Policy: Micro Evidence from OECD Countries*, vol. 2 (Paris: OECD Publishing, 2015).

65. David Autor, David Dorn, Lawrence Katz, Christina Patterson, and John Van Reenen, "Fall of the Labor Share and the Rise of Superstar Firms," NBER Working Paper 23396.

66. See Lindsey and Teles, *Captured Economy*.

67. Morris M. Kleiner and Alan B. Krueger, "Analyzing the Extent and Influence of Occupational Licensing on the Labor Market," *Journal of Labor Economics* 31, no. 2 (Part 2, April 2013): S173–S202.

68. "A Lapse in Concentration," *The Economist*, October 1, 2016, https://www.economist.com /node/21707838/print.

69. Kleiner and Krueger, "Occupational Licensing."

70. Morris Kleiner and Evgeny Vorotnikov, "Analyzing Occupational Licensing Among the States," *Journal of Regulatory Economics* 52, no. 2 (2017): 132–158.

71. "Occupational Licensing Blunts Competition and Boosts Inequality," *The Economist*, February 17, 2018, https://www.economist.com/news/united-states/21737053-how-high-earning-professions -lock-their-competitors-out-market-occupational?frsc=dge.

72. See, for example, John Van Reenen, "Increasing Differences Between Firms: Market Power and the Macro-Economy," presented at the Jackson Hole Conference, 2018; and Germán Gutiérrez and Thomas Philippon, "Declining Competition and Investment in the US," NBER Working Paper no. 23583, July 2017.

73. Martin Hellwig, "A Critique of Corporate Governane Theory" (presentation), GCGC Conference, Stockholm, June 10–12, 2016. Powerpoint presentation can be accessed at http://gcgc .global/presentations/contracts-versus-institutions-a-critique-of-corporate-governance -theory-2/.

74. Nuno Fernandes, Miguel Ferreira, Pedro Matos, and Kevin J. Murphy, "Are U.S. CEOs Paid More? New International Evidence," Working Paper, University of Southern California, 2011.

75. "Employment and Unemployment (LFS)–Database," eurostat (website), European Commission,

accessed August 07, 2018, http://ec.europa.eu/eurostat/web/lfs/data/database?p_p_id=NavTree portletprod_WAR_NavTreeportletprod_INSTANCE_IFjhoVbmPFHt&p_p_lifecycle=0&p_p _state=normal&p_p_mode=view&p_p_col_id=column-2&p_p_col_count=1.

CHAPTER 7: THE REEMERGENCE OF POPULISM
IN THE INDUSTRIAL WEST

1. Joan C. Williams, "What So Many People Don't Get About the U.S. Working Class," *Harvard Business Review,* November 10, 2016, https://hbr.org/2016/11/what-so-many-people-dont-get -about-the-u-s-working-class.

2. Craig J. Calhoun, *Nations Matter: Culture, History, and the Cosmopolitan Dream* (London: Routledge, 2011).

3. See, for instance, Ronald F. Inglehart and Pippa Norris, "Trump, Brexit, and the Rise of Populism: Economic Have-Nots and Cultural Backlash," Harvard Kennedy School, Faculty Research Working Paper Series, August 2016.

4. Yann Algan, Sergei Guriev, Elias Papaioannou, and Evgenia Passari, "The European Trust Crisis and the Rise of Populism," *Brookings* (September 2017), https://www.brookings.edu/wp -content/uploads/2017/09/4_alganetal.pdf.

5. Alexander Hamilton, James Madison, and John Jay, *The Federalist papers* (1788), available at https://www.congress.gov/resources/display/content/The+Federalist+Papers, especially Federalist 10, "The Same Subject Continued: The Union as a Safeguard Against Domestic Faction and Insurrection."

6. Evidence available from the author based on analysis of World Value Surveys.

7. David Brooks, "Bobos in Paradise," in *The Inequality Reader: Contemporary and Foundational Readings in Race, Class, and Gender,* ed. David B. Grusky and Szonja Szelényi (Boulder, CO: Westview Press, 2007).

8. Mitchell Petersen and Raghuram Rajan, "Does Distance Still Matter? The Information Revolution in Small Business Lending," *Journal of Finance* 57, no. 6 (December 2002): 2533–70.

9. Christopher R. Berry and Edward L. Glaeser, "The Divergence of Human Capital Levels Across Cities," *Papers in Regional Science* 84, no. 3 (December 2005): 407–44.

10. Chang-Tai Hsieh and Enrico Moretti, "Housing Constraints and Spatial Misallocation," rev. ed., NBER Working Paper No. 21154, May 2017.

11. Han Kim, Adair Morse, and Luigi Zingales, "Are Elite Universities Losing their Edge," *Journal of Financial Economics* 93 (2009) 353–81.

12. Brooks, "Bobos in Paradise"; Charles Murray, *Coming Apart: The State of White America, 1960– 2010* (New York: Random House Digital, 2013); Ross Douthat and Reihan Salam, *Grand New Party: How Republicans Can Win the Working Class and Save the American Dream* (New York: Doubleday, 2008).

13. See Betty Hart and Todd Risley, *Meaningful Differences in the Everyday Experience of Young American Children* (Baltimore: Brookes Publishing, 1995), cited in Richard Reeves, *Dream Hoarders: How the American Upper Middle Class Is Leaving Everyone Else in the Dust, Why That Is a Problem, and What to Do About It* (Washington, D.C.: Brookings Institution Press, 2017), 42.

14. Walter Mischel, Yuichi Shoda, and Monica I. Rodriguez, "Delay of Gratification in Children," *Science* 244, no. 4907 (1989): 933–38; Walter Mischel, Yuichi Shoda, and Philip K. Peake, "The Nature of Adolescent Competencies Predicted by Preschool Delay of Gratification," *Journal of Personality and Social Psychology* 54, no. 4 (1988): 687–96; Jacoba Urist, "What the Marshmallow Test Really Teaches About Self-Control," *The Atlantic,* September 24, 2014, https://www.theatlantic.com /health/archive/2014/09/what-the-marshmallow-test-really-teaches-about-self-control/380673/.

15. Celeste Kidd, Holly Palmeri, and Richard N. Aslin, "Rational Snacking: Young Children's Decision-making on the Marshmallow Task is Moderated by Beliefs About Environmental Reliability," *Cognition* 126, no. 1 (2013): 109–14.

16. Reeves, *Dream Hoarders.*

17. Elizabeth Dickinson, "Coleman Report Set the Standard for the Study of Public Education," *Johns Hopkins Magazine* 68, no. 4 (Winter 2016).

18. Heather Schwartz, "Housing Policy in School: Economically Integrative Housing Promotes Academic Success in Montgomery County, MD," *The Education Digest* 76, no. 6 (February 2011): 42.

19. Sean Reardon and Kendra Bischoff, "The Continuing Increase in Income Segregation, 2007–2012," Stanford Center for Education Policy Analysis, 2016, http://cepa.stanford.edu/content /continuing-increase-income-segregation-2007-2012.

20. Ann Owens, "Inequality in Children's Contexts: Income Segregation of Households with and without Children," *American Sociological Review* 81, no. 3 (June 2016): 549–74.

21. Brooks, *Bobos in Paradise*; Christopher Lasch, *The Revolt of the Elites and the Betrayal of Democracy* (New York: W.W. Norton & Company, 1996); Edward Luce, *The Retreat of Western Liberalism* (New York: Atlantic Monthly Press, 2017); Murray, *Coming Apart*; Robert Putnam, *Our Kids: The American Dream in Crisis* (New York: Simon & Schuster, 2015).

22. "Grammatical Error," *The Economist*, August 13, 2016, http://www.economist.com/news/britain /21704837-lifting-ban-new-selective-schools-would-damage-social-mobility-grammatical -error?frsc=dg%7Ca.

23. Fred Harris and Alan Curtis, "The Unmet Promise of Equality," *The New York Times*, March 1, 2018, https://www.nytimes.com/interactive/2018/02/28/opinion/the-unmet-promise-of-equality .html?rref=collection/sectioncollection/opinion&action=click&contentCollection=opinion°ion= stream&module=stream_unit&version=latest&contentPlacement=18&pgtype=sectionfront.

24. David Autor, David Dorn, and Gordon Hanson, "When Work Disappears: Manufacturing Decline and the Falling Marriage-Market Value of Young Men," NBER Working Paper No. 23173, January 2018.

25. See Autor et al., "When Work Disappears."

26. Campbell F. Scribner, *The Fight for Local Control: Schools, Suburbs, and American Democracy* (Ithaca, NY: Cornell University Press, 2016), 55.

27. National Commission on Excellence in Education, "A Nation at Risk: The Imperative for Educational Reform," *The Elementary School Journal* 84, no. 2 (1983): 113–30. Also see Scribner, *Fight for Local Control*, 175–76.

28. Joseph Fuller, Manjari Raman et al., "Dismissed by Degrees: How Degree Inflation is Undermining US Competitiveness and Hurting America's Middle Class," published by Accenture, Grads of Life, Harvard Business School, October 2017, https://www.hbs.edu/managing -the-future-of-work/Documents/dismissed-by-degrees.pdf.

29. Zoe Baird and Rework America, *America's Moment: Creating Opportunity in the Connected Age* (New York: Norton, 2015), 192.

30. "PISA 2015, Results in Focus." OECD Programme for International Student Assessment, https:// www.oecd.org/pisa/pisa-2015-results-in-focus.pdf

31. Claire Cain Miller, "Do Preschool Teachers Really Need to Be College Graduates?" *The New York Times*, April 7, 2017, https://www.nytimes.com/2017/04/07/upshot/do-preschool-teachers -really-need-to-be-college-graduates.html.

32. Douthat and Salam, *Grand New Party*.

33. "How Groups Voted," Roper Center, Cornell University, https://ropercenter.cornell.edu/polls /us-elections/how-groups-voted/.

34. Shanto Iyengar, Gaurav Sood, and Yphtach Lelkes, "Affect, Not Ideology: A Social Identity Perspective on Polarization," *Public Opinion Quarterly* 76, no. 3 (January 2012): 405–31.

35. John B. Judis, *The Populist Explosion: How the Great Recession Transformed American and European Politics* (New York: Columbia Global Reports, 2016).

36. Guy Chazan, "Germany's Economic Engine Fails to Power Struggling Rural Regions," *Financial Times*, February 27, 2018, https://www.ft.com/content/c6edf308-1875-11e8-9376-4a6390addb44.

37. "European Populism: Trends, Threats and Future Prospects," Institute for Global Change (website), accessed August 6, 2018, https://institute.global/insight/renewing-centre/european-populism -trends-threats-and-future-prospects.

38. Kerwin Kofi Charles, Erik Hurst, and Matthew J. Notowidigdo, "The Masking of the Decline in Manufacturing Employment by the Housing Bubble," *The Journal of Economic Perspectives* 30, no. 2 (Spring 2016): 179–200.

39. Raghuram G. Rajan, *Fault Lines: How Hidden Fractures Still Threaten the World Economy* (Princeton, NJ: Princeton University Press, 2010).

40. Tito Boeri, Prachi Mishra, Chris Papageorgiou, and Antonio Spilimbergo, "A Dialogue between a Populist and an Economist," CEPR Discussion Paper No. DP12763, Feburary 2018.

41. Arlie Hochschild, *Strangers in Their Own Land: Anger and Mourning on the American Right* (New York: The New Press, 2016).

42. Williams, "What So Many People Don't Get."

43. Alberto Alesina, Armando Miano, and Stefanie Stantcheva, "Immigration and Redistribution," NBER Working Paper No. 24733, June 2018.

44. David Autor, David Dorn, Gordon Hanson, and Kaveh Majlesi, "Importing Political Polarization? The Electoral Consequences of Rising Trade Exposure," rev. ed., MIT Working Paper, December 2017, available at https://economics.mit.edu/files/11499.

CHAPTER 8: THE OTHER HALF OF THE WORLD

1. See the insightful two-volume work by Francis Fukuyama on the difference between China and India: *The Origins of Political Order: From Prehuman Times to the French Revolution* (New York: Farrar, Straus, and Giroux, 2011) and *Political Order and Political Decay* (New York: Farrar, Straus, and Giroux, 2014).

2. Yasheng Huang, *Capitalism with Chinese Characteristics: Entrepreneurship and the State* (Cambridge, UK: Cambridge University Press, 2008).

3. Huang, *Capitalism,* 162–63.

4. See Richard McGregor, *The Party: The Secret World of China's Communist Rulers* (New York: Harper, 2010).

5. Huang, *Capitalism.*

6. Ibid., 162–63.

7. Minxin Pei, *China's Crony Capitalism: The Dynamics of Regime Decay* (Cambridge, MA: Harvard University Press, 2016).

8. Chang-Tai Hsieh and Zheng (Michael) Song, "Grasp the Large, Let Go of the Small: The Transformation of the State Sector in China," *Brookings Papers on Economic Activity,* March 2015, https://www.brookings.edu/wp-content/uploads/2016/07/2015a_hsieh.pdf.

9. Hsieh and Song, "Grasp the Large."

10. See Yuen Yuen Ang, "Autocracy with Chinese Characteristics: Beijing's Behind-the-Scenes Reforms," *Foreign Affairs* 97, no. 3 (May/June 2018), https://www.foreignaffairs.com/articles/asia/2018-04-16/autocracy-chinese-characteristics.

11. Huang, *Capitalism,* 234–35.

12. McGregor, *The Party,* chapter 1.

13. McGregor, *The Party*; Pei, *China's Crony Capitalism.*

14. McGregor, *The Party.*

15. Ibid.

16. Daniel A. Bell, *The China Model: Political Meritocracy and the Limits of Democracy* (Princeton, NJ: Princeton University Press, 2015).

17. Shang-Jin Wei, Zhuan Xie, and Xiaobo Zhang, "From 'Made in China' to 'Innovated in China': Necessity, Prospect, and Challenges," NBER Working Paper No. 22854, http://www.nber.org/papers/w22854.

18. János Kornai, "The Soft Budget Constraint," *Kyklos* 39, no. 1 (February 1986): 3–30, https://doi.org/10.1111/j.1467-6435.1986.tb01252.x.

19. See Ang, "Autocracy with Chinese Characteristics," and Elizabeth C. Economy, "China's New Revolution: The Reign of Xi Jinping," *Foreign Affairs* 97, no. 3 (May/June 2018), https://www.foreignaffairs.com/articles/china/2018-04-17/chinas-new-revolution.

20. See Eswar Prasad, *The Dollar Trap: How the U.S. Dollar Tightened Its Grip on Global Finance* (Princeton, NJ: Princeton University Press, 2014), and Kurt M. Campbell and Ely Ratner, "The China Reckoning: How Beijing Defied American Expectations," *Foreign Affairs 97*, no. 60 (March/April 2018), https://www.foreignaffairs.com/articles/united-states/2018-02-13/china-reckoning.

21. See, for example, the discussion in Eswar Prasad, *Gaining Currency: The Rise of the Renminbi* (New York: Oxford University Press, 2016).

22. Robert Barro and Jong-Wha Lee, "A New Data Set of Educational Attainment in the World, 1950–2010," *Journal of Development Economics* 104 (2013): 184–98, data available at http://www.barrolee.com/data/dataexp.htm.

23. See Dani Rodrik, Arvind Subramanian, and Francesco Trebbi, "Institutions Rule: The Primacy of Institutions over Geography and Integration in Economic Development," *Journal of Economic Growth* 9, no. 2 (June 2004): 131–65.

24. See Kalpana Kochhar, Utsav Kumar, Raghuram Rajan, Arvind Subramanian, and Ioannis Tokatlidis, "India's Pattern of Development: What Happened, What Follows?" *Journal of Monetary Economics* 53, no. 5 (July 2006): 981–1019.

25. Shubham Chaudhuri, "What Differences Does a Constitutional Amendment Make? The 1994 Panchayati Raj Act and the Attempt to Revitalize Rural Local Government in India," in *Decentralization and Local Governance in Developing Countries: A Comparative Experience,* ed. Pranab Bardhan and Dilip Mookherjee (Cambridge, MA: MIT Press, 2006).

26. Petia Topalova, "Trade Liberalization, Poverty, and Inequality Evidence from Indian Districts," in *Globalization and Poverty,* ed. Ann Harrison (Chicago: University of Chicago Press, 2007), 291–336, available at http://www.nber.org/chapters/c0110.pdf; Lakshmi Iyer and Petia Topalova, "Poverty and Crime: Evidence from Rainfall and Trade Shocks in India," Harvard Business School Working Paper No. 14–067, September 2014.

27. Campbell and Ratner, "China Reckoning."

CHAPTER 9: SOCIETY AND INCLUSIVE LOCALISM

1. George Megalogenis, "Powering Australia's Economic Surge," *The New York Times,* November 1, 2016, https://www.nytimes.com/2016/11/02/opinion/powering-australias-economic-surge.html.

2. "Gone in Their Prime: Many Countries Suffer from Shrinking Working-age Populations," *The Economist,* May 5, 2018, https://www.economist.com/international/2018/05/05/many-countries-suffer-from-shrinking-working-age-populations?frsc=dg%7Ce.

3. "Concentrate!: A Small Japanese City Shrinks with Dignity," *The Economist,* January 11, 2018, https://www.economist.com/news/asia/21734405-authorities-are-focusing-keeping-centre-alive-small-japanese-city-shrinks-dignity?frsc=dg%7Ce.

4. "Japan's Foreign Minister Says Country to Open to Foreigners," *The New York Times,* September 13, 2018, https://www.nytimes.com/aponline/2018/09/13/world/asia/ap-as-vietnam-japan-migration.html.

5. "Physicians (per 1,000 People)," World Bank (website), accessed August 7, 2018, https://data.worldbank.org/indicator/SH.MED.PHYS.ZS.

6. Dani Rodrik offers a related set of calculations from the World Value Survey in his book *Straight Talk on Trade: Ideas for a Sane World Economy* (Princeton, NJ: Princeton University Press, 2018).

7. Craig Calhoun, *Nations Matter: Culture, History, and the Cosmopolitan Dream* (New York: Routledge, 2007), 139.

8. Sunil Khilnani, *The Idea of India* (New York: Farrar, Straus and Giroux, 1998).

9. Michael Ignatieff, *The Ordinary Virtues: Moral Order in a Divided World* (Cambridge, MA: Harvard University Press, 2017).

10. Alberto Alesina and Eliana La Ferrara, "Ethnic Diversity and Economic Performance," *Journal of Economic Literature* 43, no. 3 (September 2005): 762–800.

11. J. D. Vance, *Hillbilly Elegy: A Memoir of a Family and Culture in Crisis* (New York: Harper, 2016).

CHAPTER 10: REBALANCING THE STATE AND THE COMMUNITY

1. Bruce Katz and Jeremy Novak, *The New Localism: How Cities Can Thrive in the Age of Populism* (Washington, D.C.: Brookings Institution Press, 2017).
2. Luigi Guiso, Paola Sapienza, and Luigi Zingales, "Long Term Persistence," *Journal of the European Economic Association* 14, no. 6 (December 1, 2016): 1401–36.
3. Alberto Alesina and Eliana La Ferrara, "Ethnic Diversity and Economic Performance," *Journal of Economic Literature* 43, no. 3 (September 2005): 762–800.
4. Henry Grabar, "California Bill Would Allow Unrestricted Housing by Transit, Solve State Housing Crisis," *Slate,* January 05, 2018, https://slate.com/business/2018/01/california-bill-sb827-residential-zoning-transit-awesome.html.
5. "Internet/Broadband Fact Sheet," Pew Research Center (website), accessed August 07, 2018, http://www.pewinternet.org/fact-sheet/internet-broadband.
6. "Archive: Internet Access and Use Statistics—Households and Individuals," eurostat (website), https://ec.europa.eu/eurostat/statistics-explained/index.php?title=Archive:Internet_access _and_use_statistics_-_households_and_individuals. Accessed April 2, 2018.
7. Rework America, *America's Moment: Creating Opportunity in the Connected Age* (New York: W. W. Norton, 2015), 186.
8. "Chicago, IL—Issues," SeeClickFix (website), accessed on August 07, 2018, https://en.seeclickfix .com/chicago.
9. "Across India," I Paid a Bribe (website), accessed on August 08, 2018, http://ipaidabribe .com/#gsc.tab=0.
10. Emily Badger, "Blue Cities want to make their own rules. Red states won't let them," *The New York Times,* July 6, 2017, https://www.nytimes.com/2017/07/06/upshot/blue-cities-want-to -make-their-own-rules-red-states-wont-let-them.html.
11. Garry Kasparov, "The Chess Master and the Computer," *The New York Review of Books,* February 11, 2010, http://www.nybooks.com/articles/2010/02/11/the-chess-master-and-the-computer/; Carl Benedikt Frey and Michael A. Osborne, "The Future of Employment: How Susceptible are Jobs to Computerization?," Oxford Martin School (September 2013), https://www.oxfordmartin .ox.ac.uk/downloads/academic/The_Future_of_Employment.pdf.

CHAPTER 11: REINVIGORATING THE THIRD PILLAR

1. Peter Coy, "Keeping Up With the Joneses: Neighbors of Lottery Winners Are More Likely to Go Bankrupt," *Bloomberg Businessweek,* May 29, 2018, https://www.bloomberg.com/news/ articles/2018-05-29/keeping-up-with-the-joneses-neighbors-of-lottery-winners-are-more -likely-to-go-bankrupt.
2. See, for example, the description in Jeremy Heimans and Henry Timms, *New Power: How Power Works in Our Hyperconnected World—and How to Make It Work for You* (New York: Doubleday, 2018)
3. For the first, see Robert D. Putnam, *Bowling Alone* (New York: Simon & Schuster, 2000); Kraut et al., "Internet Paradox: A Social Technology That Reduces Social Involvement and Psychological Well-Being?," *American Psychologist* 53, no. 9 (1998): 1017–31.
4. Keith Hampton, "Netville: Community On and Offline in a Wired Suburb," in *The Cybercities Reader,* ed. Stephen Graham (London: Routledge, 2004), 256–62.
5. Matthew Gentzkow and Jesse M. Shapiro, "Ideological Segregation Online and Offline," NBER Working Paper No. 15916, April 2010.
6. Mark Aguiar, Mark Bils, Kerwin Kofi Charles, and Erik Hurst, "Leisure Luxuries and the Labor Supply of Young Men," NBER Working Paper No. 23552, June 2017.

7. Daniel T. Rodgers, "Prologue," in *Age of Fracture* (Cambridge, MA: Belknap Press, 2012).

8. This section draws on Rashmi Bansal, "The Curious Case of a Clean Clean Indore," *Business Today,* July 2, 2017, https://www.businesstoday.in/magazine/columns/the-curious-case-of-a-clean-clean-indore/story/254144.html.

9. Bruce Katz and Jeremy Novak, *The New Localism: How Cities Can Thrive in the Age of Populism* (Washington, D.C.: Brookings Institution Press, 2017).

10. See Antoine Van Agtmael and Fred Bakker, *The Smartest Places on Earth: Why Rustbelts Are the Emerging Hotspots of Global Innovation* (New York: Hachette, 2016); James Fallows and Deborah Fallows, *Our Towns: A 100,000-Mile Journey into the Heart of America* (New York: Pantheon Books, 2018).

11. See Katz and Nowak, *New Localism.*

12. See Katz and Nowak, *New Localism.*

13. See Fallows and Fallows, *Our Towns.*

14. See Benjamin A. Austin, Edward L. Glaeser, and Lawrence H. Summers, "Jobs for the Heartland: Place-Based Policies in 21st Century America," NBER Working Paper No. 24548, April 2018; Gilles Duranton and Anthony J. Venables, "Place-Based Policies for Development," NBER Working Paper No. 24562, April 2018.

15. See Austin, Glaeser, and Summers, "Jobs for the Heartland."

16. Ibid.

17. See, for example, Amy Goldstein, *Janesville: An American Story* (New York: Simon and Schuster, 2017).

CHAPTER 12: RESPONSIBLE SOVEREIGNTY

1. Alex Hern, "Fitness Tracking App Strava Gives Away Location of Secret US Army Bases," *The Guardian,* January 28, 2018, https://www.theguardian.com/world/2018/jan/28/fitness-tracking-app-gives-away-location-of-secret-us-army-bases.

2. Raghuram G. Rajan and Luigi Zingales, "The Great Reversals: The Politics of Financial Development in the Twentieth Century," *Journal of Financial Economics* 69 (2003): 5–50, available at http://faculty.chicagobooth.edu/luigi.zingales/papers/research/jfereversal.pdf.

3. Clyde Haberman, "Japanese Are Special Types, They Explain," *The New York Times,* March 3, 1988, accessible at https://www.nytimes.com/1988/03/06/weekinreview/the-world-japanese-are-special-types-they-explain.html.

4. Simon Dawson, "Chlorine-washed Chicken Q&A: Food Safety Expert Explains Why US Poultry Is Banned in the EU," *The Conversation,* August 2, 2017, http://theconversation.com/chlorine-washed-chicken-qanda-food-safety-expert-explains-why-us-poultry-is-banned-in-the-eu-81921.

5. Jon Swaine, "Bent Banana and Curved Cucumber Rules Dropped," *The Telegraph*, July 24, 2008, https://www.telegraph.co.uk/news/worldnews/europe/2453204/Bent-banana-and-curved-cucumber-rules-dropped-by-EU.html.

6. Martin Wolf, "Globalization and Global Economic Governance," *Oxford Review of Economic Policy* 20, no. 1, 2004.

7. See, for example, Ha-Joon Chang, *Bad Samaritans: The Myth of Free Trade and the Secret History of Capitalism* (New York: Bloomsbury Press, 2008).

8. Josh Lerner, "The Empirical Impact of Intellectual Property Rights on Innovation: Puzzles and Clues," *American Economic Review: Papers & Proceedings* 99: 2, 343–48, 2009.

9. See Dani Rodrik, *Straight Talk on Trade: Ideas for a Sane World Economy* (Princeton, NJ: Princeton University Press, 2018).

10. See Douglas A. Irwin, "The False Promise of Protectionism: Why Trump's Trade Policy Could Backfire," *Foreign Affairs* 96 (May/June 2017): 45–56.

11. See Raghuram Rajan and Prachi Mishra, "Rules of the Monetary Game," University of Chicago Working Paper, April 2018, http://faculty.chicagobooth.edu/raghuram.rajan/research/papers/Rules-of-game-mar-21-2016-3.pdf; and John B. Taylor, "Ideas and Institutions in Monetary

Policy Making" (presentation), the Karl Brunner Distinguished Lecture, Swiss National Bank, Zurich, September 21, 2017.

12. See Arvind Subramanian, *Eclipse: Living in the Shadow of China's Economic Dominance* (Washington, D.C.: Peterson Institute for International Economics, 2011).

CHAPTER 13: REFORMING MARKETS

1. This follows from work with Luigi Zingales.

2. Patricia Dermansky, "Should Australia Replace Section 181 of the Corporations Act 2001 (Cth) With Wording Similar to Section 172 of the Companies Act 2006 (UK)?," 4, available at https://law.unimelb.edu.au/__data/assets/pdf_file/0003/1709832/60-Should_Austalia_replace_s181_of_the_Corporations_Act3.pdf.

3. Joseph A. Schumpeter, *Capitalism, Socialism, and Democracy* (New York: Harper, 1950), 84, 85.

4. Luigi Zingales, *A Capitalism for the People* (New York: Basic Books, 2010), and Luigi Zingales, "Towards a Political Theory of the Firm," *Journal of Economic Perspectives* 31, no. 3 (Summer 2017): 113–30, https://doi.org/10.1257/jep.31.3.113.

5. Willard F. Mueller, "The Celler-Kefauver Act: The First 27 Years (A Study Prepared for the Subcommittee on Monopolies and Commercial Law of the Committee on the Judiciary, House of Representatives, 95th Congress, 2nd Session)," (Washington, D.C.: U.S. Government Printing Office, 1978), 17.

6. One of the concerns of the supporters of the Celler-Kefauver Act was that "increasing centralization of the private sector adversely affected small local communities whose business enterprises were controlled by large corporations headquartered in faraway financial centers."

7. Allen N. Berger, Nathan H. Miller, Mitchell A. Petersen, Raghuram G. Rajan, and Jeremy C. Stein, "Does Function Follow Organizational Form? Evidence From the Lending Practices of Large and Small Banks," *Journal of Financial Economics* 76, no. 2 (2005): 237–69.

8. See Jeremy C. Stein, "Information Production and Capital Allocation: Decentralized vs. Hierarchical Firms," *Journal of Finance* 57, no. 5 (2002): 1891–1921.

9. Michele Boldrin and David Levine, "The Case Against Patents," Federal Reserve Bank of St. Louis Working Paper Series 2012–035A, https://s3.amazonaws.com/real.stlouisfed.org/wp/2012/2012-035.pdf; Michele Boldrin and David Levine, *Against Intellectual Monopoly* (Cambridge, UK: Cambridge University Press, 2008).

10. Steve Jobs et al., Portable display device, USD670286S1, priority date June 01, 2010, and granted June 11, 2012.

11. "Can Genes Be Patented?," Genetics Home Reference, U.S. National Library of Medicine (website), accessed August 07, 2018, https://ghr.nlm.nih.gov/primer/testing/genepatents.

12. "Seven Years a 'Cobbler,'" Swiss Federal Institute of Intellectual Property (website), accessed August 07, 2018, https://www.ige.ch/en/about-us/the-history-of-the-ipi/einstein/einstein-at-the-patent-office.html.

13. See, for instance, Jaron Lanier, *Who Owns the Future?* (New York: Simon and Schuster, 2013), and Eric A. Posner and E. Glen Weyl, *Radical Markets: Uprooting Capitalism and Democracy for a Just Society* (Princeton, NJ: Princeton University Press, 2018).

14. See, for example, Luigi Zingales and Guy Rolnick, "A Way to Own Your Social-Media Data," *The New York Times*, June 30, 2017, https://www.nytimes.com/2017/06/30/opinion/social-data-google-facebook-europe.html.

15. See Posner and Weyl, *Radical Markets*, or Lanier, *Who Owns the Future?*, for elaborations of arguments on data ownership.

16. Steve Eder, "When Picking Apples on a Farm With 5,000 Rules, Watch Out for the Ladders," *The New York Times*, December 27, 2017, https://www.nytimes.com/2017/12/27/business/picking-apples-on-a-farm-with-5000-rules-watch-out-for-the-ladders.html?smprod=nytcore-ipad&smid=%E2%80%A6.

17. Michael J. Sandel, *What Money Can't Buy: The Moral Limits of Markets* (New York: Farrar, Straus and Giroux, 2013).

18. See Michael Walzer, *Spheres of Justice: A Defense of Pluralism and Equality* (New York: Basic Books, 1983).

19. "Money in Film: Businessmen Are Always the Villains," *The Economist,* October 16, 2015, https://www.economist.com/blogs/prospero/2015/10/money-film.

EPILOGUE

1. John Maynard Keynes, "Economic Prospects for our Grandchildren" in *Essays in Persuasion,* (New York: W.W. Norton & Co., 1963): 358–73.

INDEX